11th Edition

ENGLISH FORCAREERS

BUSINESS, PROFESSIONAL, AND TECHNICAL

11th Edition

ENGLISH FORCAREERS

BUSINESS, PROFESSIONAL, AND TECHNICAL

Leila R. Smith

Roberta Moore

PEARSON

Boston   Columbus   Indianapolis   New York   San Francisco   Upper Saddle River
Amsterdam   Cape Town   Dubai   London   Madrid   Milan   Munich   Paris   Montreal   Toronto
Delhi   Mexico City   São Paulo   Sydney   Hong Kong   Seoul   Singapore   Taipei   Tokyo

Editor in Chief: Stephanie Wall
Acquisitions Editor: Sarah McCabe
Editorial Project Manager: Karin Williams
Editorial Assistant: Kaylee Rotella
Marketing Manager: Erin Gardner
Inhouse Production Liasion: Alicia Ritchey
Senior Operations Specialist: Pat Tonneman
Art Director: Diane Ernsberger
Cover and Interior Designer: Candace Rowley

Cover Art: top left StockLite/Shutterstock; top right Illustrart/Shutterstock; bottom left Shebeko/Shutterstock; bottom right TFoxFoto/Shutterstock
Lead Media Project Manager: Karen Bretz
Full-Service Project Management: Barbara Hawk
Composition: Element
Printer/Binder: LSC Communications
Cover Printer: LSC Communications
Text Font: Melior LT Std, ITC Stone Sans Std

Credits and acknowledgments borrowed from other sources and reproduced, with permission, in this textbook appear on the appropriate page within text.

Smith, Leila R., author.
  English for Careers : Business, Professional, and Technical / Leila R. Smith, Roberta Moore.—Eleventh Edition.
     pages cm
  Includes index.
  Previously published: 2010, 10th ed., annotated instructor's ed.
  ISBN 978-0-13-261930-1
1. English language—Business English—Problems, exercises, etc. 2. English language—Technical English—Problems, exercises, etc. I. Moore, Roberta, 1947- II. Title.
PE1115.S62 2014
428.2'02465—dc23
                                        2012041152

ISBN 10: 0-13-261930-X
ISBN 13: 978-0-13-261930-1

8 2020

contents

UNIT 1: Mastering the Art of Good Writing

3   Sentence Fundamentals   38

UNIT 2: Knowing Your Subject

4   Nouns: Forming Plurals   68

5   Nouns: Forming Possessives   82

6   Pronouns: Types and Their Uses   96

UNIT 4: Perfecting Sentence Punctuation

12 Punctuation: The Semicolon, Colon, and Other Marks 244

13 Punctuation: The Fine Points 263

UNIT 5: Writing for Career Success

14 Polished Writing Style   290

15 Capitalization, Abbreviations, and Numbers   318

introduction to the student

WELCOME TO *ENGLISH FOR CAREERS*!

You are about to embark on a journey that will end with you feeling more confident in your skills as a writer and communicator. In today's job market, communication skills are essential to success. Employers want to hire and promote people who not only speak and write well but also have the ability to navigate the complex landscape of today's print and electronic forms of communication. This course will help you develop the key skills that will make you a good communicator and a valued member of the workforce: reading and comprehending, building a substantial vocabulary, and speaking and writing the language that is necessary for success in the workplace—grammatically correct Standard English. *English for Careers* will also help you develop the habit of self-directed learning through use of the print and technology-based supplements that align course work with your individual needs.

THE LANGUAGE OF CAREERS

The language we use, both spoken and written, significantly affects our ability to earn a good living, advance in a career, and even enjoy good social contacts. What kind of language does a business, professional, or technical career require? The answer is Standard English—the language of careers. This is the common language used for writing and speaking across all fields of endeavor. The extent to which your use of English is "standard" versus "nonstandard" depends on your cultural and social environment and the English principles you've learned and put into practice.

In our culture, it is common to use several language styles to communicate with different people in various situations. Imagine having fun with a group of adults at a party; now picture yourself teaching a young child how to cross the street safely. Think about how your communication style would differ. In addition to the normal adaptation to individuals and situations, your region of the country, your local community and peer group, and possibly the place where you were born, if not an English-speaking country, will influence your use of English grammar and vocabulary. Perhaps you use slang or a regional or community dialect in everyday conversation with certain friends and family. You might already be accustomed to a different communication style with other acquaintances or in the workplace. We all vary our communication style in different situations, but we all need need to speak Standard English—the universal language of careers in the United States and around the world. *English for Careers* will help you perfect your use of Standard English so that you can communicate comfortably, confidently, and correctly in the world of careers.

THE *ENGLISH FOR CAREERS* LEARNING SYSTEM

This book is different. You don't browse through it. You don't read it like other books. You learn your way through it! In *English for Careers,* you don't just focus on grammar terms and rules. You learn how to apply those rules to communicate successfully and confidently in the workplace. The information you need is presented in an interesting and efficient way that makes learning easier. You will read succinct summaries about language usage and then apply them to test your understanding. You will develop the habit of using reference materials to broaden your vocabulary and practice the writing process that confident writers use to polish their communications. You will leave the course with the ability to apply the Standard English grammar, mechanics, usage, speaking, and writing principles as they are used by well-informed and well-educated people.

Chapter Opening

Objectives
Each of the 15 chapters opens with dynamic graphics and a list of chapter objectives that tells you exactly what skills and knowledge you should acquire by the time you complete the chapter.

Career Connection
At the beginning of each chapter, you will enjoy reading this short essay that provides insight into how the skills you are learning will benefit you in the job market.

Reading, Application, and Self-Evaluation

Pretest
At the start of each chapter, you can test your prior knowledge before you begin reading.

Reading and Chapter Review
As you complete each major section of a chapter, you will be directed to the Chapter Review section to complete a corresponding Worksheet exercise that lets you immediately test yourself on what you have learned. These are self-check exercises. The answers are in Appendix D. Use a blue or black pen to complete the exercises and then make corrections with a different color. When ready to review, you'll know which answers you had wrong. Then you can reread the corresponding text and complete the Appendix C Supplementary Practice exercises.

Checkpoint
This summary of key principles helps you assess your knowledge.

End-of-Chapter and Unit Activities

Communications Connection
This feature provides you with opportunities to learn basic concepts about writing and speaking applications in the real world of business communications.

Writing Practice
You will have the opportunity to apply your skills to writing assignments, such as developing job search documents, writing business communications, conducting interviews, and preparing oral presentations. Your instructor has the answers to the exercises and will evaluate your written work.

Proofreading Practice
At the end of each chapter, you will test your knowledge of grammar rules with challenging and interesting documents and articles that you can edit in the text using proofreading marks or by accessing the eText applications online. Your instructor will provide the answers.

Unit Recap and Writing/Speaking Practice

These activities test your knowledge of the chapters in each unit and provide a chance to apply what you have learned. Your instructor will use these applications to evaluate your progress.

Self-Study Practice and Tutorials

Appendix B: Word Power

These important activities are a fun way to increase your mastery of language used in a broad variety of career fields and across the social spectrum. You can work individually and with a team to broaden your vocabulary and improve spelling.

Appendix C: Supplementary Practice

Each exercise gives you additional opportunities for "drill and practice" across the board, which helps you gain mastery of grammar and writing principles, or you can select the exercises that target your weak areas.

What's in It for You?

A Proven Method That Works

Because you are immediately applying what you learn throughout the course, *English for Careers* enables you to understand grammar and writing better and remember the concepts you have learned. Immediate feedback (with answers in the back of the book) is satisfying and encourages you to continue with enthusiasm. Challenging writing and speaking applications provide you the opportunity to improve your skills and become a more confident communicator.

Incidental Learning

While using *English for Careers*, you also learn more about today's workplace, and you increase or develop a success-oriented attitude. Many of the practice sentences in the exercises, as well as other activities, deal with business practices, workplace cultural diversity, expected behavior in today's international marketplace, workplace etiquette, and helpful attitudes for self-development.

Competence and Confidence

After successfully completing this course, you will be a more competent writer and will enjoy confidence in the correctness and effectiveness of your speech and writing. Good communication skills, more than any other single factor, determine who gets the good job, who keeps it, and who gets the promotion. You'll find that coworkers and even supervisors will come to you for business English help. They will soon sense that you are the company expert in grammar, punctuation, spelling, and communication style.

Enjoyment of Language

Although learning isn't all fun and games, people don't learn very much unless they enjoy the experience at least some of the time. You'll find bits of humor hidden in the various exercises and learn some new things about language that will make you feel more confident and put your mind in a learning mode. Enjoy *English for Careers*. With a positive attitude, you'll find that your command of English will be a lifelong asset to your career and personal life, and you will have some fun along the way!

about the authors

LEILA R. SMITH, Los Angeles Harbor College Professor Emeritus of Office Administration, has a New York University bachelor of science degree in business education and a University of San Francisco master's degree in education. In addition to Harbor College, Professor Smith taught at Bay Path College in Massachusetts, in California's Pierce and Valley Colleges, and in New York City proprietary schools. Among her many professional activities, she has been a Fulbright exchange instructor, teaching English and communication in the business department of City and East London College in London, England, for an academic year.

A federal grant enabled her to study methods of applying brain research to business English instruction. This study also culminated in the writing of the text *RSVP—Relaxation, Spelling, Vocabulary, Pronunciation*. Other publications include the texts *Communication and English for Careers* and *Basic English for Business and Technical Careers*, as well as professional newsletters and articles in professional journals.

She has served as communication editor for the *Business Education Forum*, the journal of the National Business Education Association. Professor Smith, a recipient of the Pimentel Award for Excellence in Education, has conducted workshops and seminars on business English and communication and on teaching and learning methods for educators, corporate groups, and government agencies and has worked in various business capacities.

ROBERTA MOORE is a communications professional, writer, editor, and author residing in New York City. She holds a bachelor of arts degree in English literature from Wayne State University in Detroit, Michigan. Ms. Moore is currently affiliated with the Metropolitan Transportation Authority (MTA) in New York City—the largest mass transit system in North America. She is director of communications for the MTA's Business Service Center, the organization's back office shared services operation that serves more than 100,000 MTA employees, retirees, and vendors, providing human resources, financial, and information technology services. Ms. Moore is the "Communications Department" of the operation, where she develops and oversees all print and electronic communications.

Ms. Moore has held editorial and executive positions with some of the nation's leading publishing houses, specializing in business education, office technology, and business English and communications. In addition to developing hundreds of educational programs, she has traveled throughout the country conducting training workshops for teachers and publishing professionals and speaking at educational conferences and on college campuses. She has also done consulting in the field of corporate communications, specializing in employee diversity training and issues of special interest to the small business community, as well as writing speeches for top executives, newsletters, and a variety of corporate literature.

Ms. Moore is coauthor of the *Pearson Business Reference and Writer's Handbook* and several textbooks: *Career Success: The Attitude Advantage*, *College Success*, *Telecommunications*, *Telephone Communication in the Information Age*, and *Applied Communication Skills Series: Grammar* and *Writing Sentences*.

acknowledgments

The authors and editors of *English for Careers, 11th Edition*, would like to thank Sharon Rinkiewicz, Broward College, Fort Lauderdale, Florida, for her role as consulting editor on this edition.

We would also like to thank the following instructors for their assistance:

Diana Carmel, Golden West College

Daniela Liese, Stevens Henager College

Gregg Nelson, Chippewa Valley TC

Adell Shay, Los Angeles Harbor College

Lorraine Smith, Fresno City College

A finely crafted book can result only with the assistance of a talented and dedicated publishing staff. The authors of *English for Careers, 11th Edition*, wish to thank the following Pearson Education team members for their invaluable contributions to this work: Stephanie Wall, editor in chief; Sarah McCabe, acquisitions editor; Judy Leale, senior managing editor; Karin Williams, editorial project manager; and Kaylee Rotella, editorial assistant.

unit one

Mastering the Art of Good Writing

© Picture-Factory/Fotolia

After completing Chapter 1, you will be able to do the following:

- Acquire the "dictionary habit"—using dictionaries regularly to improve vocabulary, word choices, spelling, and pronunciation.

- Choose a printed dictionary that best meets your needs and use the full range of information it provides.

- Select electronic dictionaries and thesauruses to consult when working at the computer.

- Use a reference manual to expand your use of language, improve your writing style, revise content, and correct errors in your writing.

- Supplement electronic tools to check spelling and grammar errors when editing and proofreading your work.

1

References and Resources

career connection

THE TOP 10 SKILLS EMPLOYERS WANT

What skills are employers looking for? The National Association of Colleges and Employers conducts an annual survey asking employers what they are looking for in college graduates. Here are the top 10 skills:

1. Ability to work in a team structure
2. Ability to verbally communicate (speaking and writing)
3. Ability to make decisions and solve problems
4. Ability to obtain and process information
5. Ability to plan, organize, and prioritize work
6. Ability to analyze quantitative data
7. Technical knowledge related to the job
8. Proficiency with computer software programs
9. Ability to create and/or edit written reports
10. Ability to sell or influence others

This course will help you develop the skills employers value most—ensuring greater success in the workplace, no matter what your chosen career might be.

Source: *Job Outlook 2012*, National Association of Colleges and Employers (www.naceweb.org).

PRETEST

Fill in the blanks to complete these statements about resources and words.

1. A comprehensive dictionary containing at least 250,000 entries is known as an _____ dictionary.

2. A hardcover college dictionary with at least 100,000 entries is known as an _____ dictionary.

3. The pronunciations, spellings, and vocabulary widely used and respected by well-educated people are known as _____.

4. Meanings of words change; old meanings are referred to in dictionaries as _____.

5. The place to find the publication date of a dictionary is on the _____.

6. The people who compile dictionaries are called _____.

7. A _____ is a reference tool that helps you find the best word to express your meaning.

8. The key to correct pronunciation is placing the accent on the right _____.

9. Abbreviations such as *adj.* and *n.* tell you a word's usage according to the _____.

10. Words with similar meanings are _____; words with opposite meanings are _____; words that sound the same but are spelled differently are _____.

CHECK YOUR ANSWERS ON PAGE 432.

Essential Resources for Writers

wordPOWER

Words are more powerful than ever in today's culture where communication is instantaneous and where privacy is fast becoming a thing of the past. We used to hear, "Think before you speak"; today it is equally important to "Think before you write." Improving your vocabulary is one key to ensuring that what you say is what you really mean to convey.

Your English skills will be a big factor in your future success. Doing well academically and in your chosen career—and even enjoying beneficial social contacts—requires full command of **Standard English**—the common language used in the workplace across all fields of endeavor. Your written and spoken use of language speaks volumes about you.

No matter how much you know or how good your other skills may be, good grammar and spelling are essential. Without them, employers will make the mistake of assuming that you are not well educated and will underestimate your intelligence.

This course begins with a review of basic resources that will help you polish your use of Standard English—both spoken and written. The resources that skilled speakers and writers use—a good dictionary, thesaurus, and reference manual—should always be kept nearby to assist you.

Dictionaries

A good dictionary is an essential tool for word usage, spelling, and vocabulary building.

The words you use to communicate tell a listener or reader about you. Words can make you appear to be a foggy or a clear thinker. Words can make you sound well educated and informed, or they can make you sound ignorant. They affect how people react to you or to the organization you represent. Developing a broad vocabulary is a key ingredient to academic and career success.

Confidence comes with being able to call on the "right" words when you need them. You often hear the word *articulate* used to describe a person who is an excellent communicator. Excellent communicators are those who have a broad vocabulary and are able to speak and write clearly. But communication is not only about clarity. It is also about expressing yourself in a way that engages others to listen to or thoroughly read what you have to say. This is what improving your word choice can do for you in the workplace, and it's why you should develop "the dictionary habit."

Dictionaries tell you which pronunciations, spellings, and vocabulary are Standard English and which are non-Standard, informal, slang, or vulgar. When two pronunciations are in common use, the one shown first is the **preferred usage**. Dictionaries also provide guidance on *how to use* the language. They tell you the meanings that are modern and those that are outdated—**archaic** is the word used by many dictionaries for outdated words or definitions.

word**POWER**

Don't pass over unfamiliar words when you're reading. Make a habit of looking up the meaning and thinking about expanding your vocabulary.

SELECTING A GOOD DICTIONARY

Dictionaries are the most comprehensive language resource, and you should always have a good printed edition of a college dictionary close at hand for reference. At work, it is a good idea to have an online dictionary on your computer's toolbar.

If you need to shop for a new printed dictionary, your online bookstore might have a feature that lets you see inside the book, but it's best to go to a bookstore or library to review and compare features. Dictionaries have their own "language" for explanations, formats for entries, and categories of information given about words. They also offer different material in the front matter and back matter. **Front matter** is the explanatory information in the front of the dictionary that includes such items as usage notes, pronunciation keys and symbols, and abbreviations. **Back matter** at the end of the dictionary provides additional information about language and usage.

Printed Dictionaries

A good hardcover or paperback college dictionary is the basic type of dictionary you need at home or to carry with you while in school. They typically have around 100,000 entries and very useful information in the front and back. These are the most popular types of **abridged dictionaries**—they are updated frequently, some as often as annually. They are available in multiple sizes, from large hardcover editions for your bookshelf to pocket size.

Unabridged dictionaries are comprehensive compilations of English language words with typically at least 250,000 entries. Unless you have a professional or a strong personal interest in language, you don't need an unabridged dictionary. When you do need one, visit your local or college library. Because unabridged dictionaries are so comprehensive, they are not updated as often as abridged dictionaries, so be aware of this when you are using one.

When shopping for a dictionary, you'll find that many publishers include "Webster" in their titles because of the fame of lexicographer Noah Webster, who spent 20 years handwriting the first comprehensive American dictionary, *An American Dictionary of the English Language*. This dictionary had 70,000 entries and was the standard for many years. Check out the best-seller listings to see which of the versions that carry the Webster name are the most widely used.

PRINTED DICTIONARIES

To select a printed dictionary, you can review the top-selling printed versions on Amazon.com and BarnesandNoble.com. The following college and pocket dictionaries are good for workplace communication as well as for home and family use. When you select one of these, be sure it is the latest edition.

- *American Heritage Dictionary of the English Language*
- *American Heritage College Dictionary*
- *Merriam-Webster's Collegiate Dictionary*
- *Microsoft Encarta College Dictionary*
- *Random House Webster's College Dictionary*
- *Webster's New World College Dictionary*
- *Oxford American College Dictionary*

word**POWER**

The people who compile dictionaries are called **lexicographers**. They record new words, new meanings, new usage, spellings, and pronunciations of our very complex and ever-changing English language.

Electronic Resources

There are many popular online resources, including most of the top-selling printed dictionaries' online versions. One convenient aspect of these electronic tools is that they combine a dictionary and thesaurus in one place. Many also offer a variety of language skill-building tools that make them fun and interesting to use.

If you tend to do your school or business work on-the-go, you might also want to look into the variety of handheld electronic dictionaries and apps for portable devices. Some electronic devices also include translators for foreign languages. Electronic resources are excellent, but they are very different from what you find in a college dictionary in book form. It is best to use both.

POPULAR ONLINE DICTIONARIES AND THESAURUSES

These online dictionaries offer a wide range of information and links to many language sources. Spend time exploring them and discover the features that you like best. (Keep in mind that Web addresses are fluid and might change subsequent to the printing of this book.)

Merriam-Webster Online—www.merriam-webster.com

yourDictionary.com—www.yourdictionary.com

OneLook.com Online Dictionary—www.onelook.com

Cambridge Dictionaries Online—http://dictionary.cambridge.org

Dictionary.com Online—www.dictionary.com

DICTIONARY ENTRIES

When selecting a printed dictionary, review the various sections to find all the useful information offered. The following sections describe the standard information you will find in the definitions of a good college dictionary.

Guide Words and Entries

Guide words located at the top of each page list the first and last words on the page. Use them to locate entries quickly. This might seem obvious, but because most people have a habit of scanning when looking for something on the printed page, there is a tendency to do the same when using a dictionary. Getting in the habit of using the guide words is a more efficient way to find the word you're looking for.

Entries contain the definitions of the word and much more. They include some or all of the following:

- Syllables
- Pronunciations
- Definitions
- Parts of speech
- Alternative spellings
- Etymology (history of the word)
- Usage label (in what context the word is used)
- Picture of the item
- Synonyms
- Words derived from the entry word, such as *typographical* near the end of the *typography* entry
- Plurals
- Capitalization
- Year the word was first seen in print

Your dictionary will have a complete explanation of how to interpret its code for all this information. The following section provides a review of some of the basics of layout and "code" that you will find in most dictionaries.

Syllables

Syllables help you with spelling, pronunciation, and word division at the end of a line. All dictionaries separate the syllables of each entry with a symbol—usually a centered dot, for example: di·vi·sion in·ter·pret.

When a hyphen separates syllables, you know that the entry is a compound word that requires a hyphen (this is a rule of spelling). Most non-hyphenated compounds are not listed in the dictionary. If you look up a compound word and do not find it spelled with a hyphen or as one word, you can assume that it is spelled as two words.

Pronunciation Key

The syllable of a word that receives the most force or emphasis when spoken is shown with an **accent mark**, also called a **diacritical mark**. The three degrees of emphasis are weak, no accent; strong, primary accent; and medium, secondary accent. To interpret this code, see the pronunciation key in your dictionary. When words have more than one correct pronunciation, the *preferred* one is given first.

Parts of Speech

In Chapter 2, you will learn about how words are used as different parts of speech in sentences. In dictionaries the parts of speech are indicated with an abbreviation, for example, n. = noun, adj. = adjective, conj. = conjunction, and v or vb = verb.

Words that have completely different meanings when used as different parts of speech are sometimes listed in separate entries. For example, *track* means one thing as a verb and another as a noun.

Definitions

One, two, or more definitions may follow the entry word. Each definition is numbered; if a definition has several shades of meaning, these are lettered within the numbered definition.

wordPOWER

Be meticulous about pronunciation. Outside of using poor grammar or the wrong word entirely, mispronouncing words is one error that others use to criticize and possibly draw misperceptions about your level of education and general intelligence.

Usage, Style, and Field Labels

These labels note something special about how the word is used. Examples are *archaic*, *technical*, *informal*, *slang*, *regional*, *non-Standard*, *American*, and *British*. The labels are usually abbreviated; consult your dictionary's front matter for the translation of these codes. Most words in the dictionary are Standard English and don't require identifying labels.

Etymology

Etymology traces the origin or historical development of linguistic forms. Dictionaries provide etymology for some words; for example, English words that originated from other languages. An example is the word *bonhomie*, which originates in French as *bonhomme*, meaning "good-natured man" (*bon* = good; *homme* = man). The English usage means friendliness, as in "He greeted the guests with a display of bonhomie."

GO TO PAGE 14 AND COMPLETE WORKSHEET 1.1.

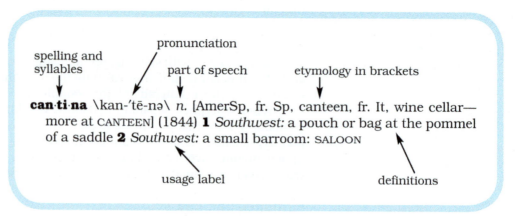

Figure 1.1

NEED A NEW DICTIONARY?

If you already own a dictionary, use this checklist to determine whether you need a new one.

1. I have a hardcover or pocket college dictionary.   _____ Yes   _____ No

2. I own one of the dictionaries recommended here.   _____ Yes   _____ No

3. The copyright date on my dictionary is the newest one
   available for that publication.   _____ Yes   _____ No

If you answered "No" to any of the above, now is the time to buy a new dictionary. We recommend a hardcover college dictionary for use at home and a pocket dictionary if you like to carry one with you.

Thesauruses

Using simple, everyday language is important for clarity in writing and speaking. Other ingredients of clarity include precision in word choice and appropriateness within the context of the communication. In addition to these basic reasons for using a thesaurus, finding just the right word to convey a nuance of meaning or the word that livens up a description for the reader is equally important. A thesaurus helps you avoid clichés and overused words and phrases. Also, do not overlook the importance of a broad vocabulary from your perspective as a listener. Understanding speakers and writers who make use of a broad vocabulary is an advantage in any situation.

Use a thesaurus to look for **synonyms**—words with similar meanings—and **antonyms**—words with opposite meanings—as well as other related words that can enhance your ability to express meaning. In addition to helping you avoid repeating the same word or using clichés or tired expressions, here are some of the things you can achieve in your writing and speaking by using a thesaurus to build your vocabulary:

- Liven up your writing with a more descriptive, interesting, emphatic, or "colorful" word.
- Make your writing clearer or less wordy by substituting a more precise word.
- Avoid harsh or inappropriate words by finding more tactful, less emotional substitutes.
- Find the "right" word when you can't recall it by looking up a similar word.

One advantage of online references is the access to both a dictionary and a thesaurus in one place. You can look up the meaning of a word in the dictionary and then go to the thesaurus to see if there is a better one. The most popular word processing programs, Microsoft Word and WordPerfect, include an online thesaurus. You can find printed combination dictionaries/thesauruses, but the dictionary portion might not be as comprehensive as needed.

Among printed thesauruses, the most famous name is Roget (pronounced *ro·ZHA)*. It is comparable to the name of Webster in dictionaries. Dr. Peter Mark Roget's first edition of *Roget's Thesaurus* was published in

writingTIP

When reading a draft, you might find that you have repeated the same word three times in one paragraph. It might be just the right word, but this kind of repetition jumps out at a reader and makes you sound limited. Use your thesaurus to find a quick solution to avoid sounding repetitious.

writingTIP

Technology provides easy access to vocabulary options and gives us the freedom to feel more comfortable with using a variety of words. It takes no effort when working at the computer to use the thesaurus to liven up your writing and make your language more precise. Technology makes us clearer and more interesting writers—if only we will use it!

1852. Roget's approach was to group words and phrases together based on their association with a single thought or concept. *The Original Roget's International Thesaurus* (latest edition) can be purchased in paperback, and there is also a *New American Roget's College Thesaurus in Dictionary Form* with *A* to *Z* entries. *Merriam-Webster's Collegiate Thesaurus* is also arranged in dictionary format.

You can also access Roget's and Merriam-Webster's online thesauruses. Next time you are online, compare the two; note the differences and see which one you find easier to use.

Reference Manuals

A reference manual is an essential tool for business writing. In addition to being a quick source for ensuring correct grammar and usage in written communications, reference manuals provide the standards for producing business documents. These include formats for letters, reports, charts, tables, and presentation slides.

In addition, a good reference manual helps to eliminate the anxiety that often comes with writing important documents, whether you are preparing a resume and cover letter or a business report or presentation. This kind of writing takes a lot of thought and attention to detail. A good reference manual can make the task much easier.

We recommend the *Pearson Business Reference and Writer's Handbook*, available in print and electronic format. It covers basic rules of grammar, punctuation, spelling, word usage, capitalization, and number usage. You will also find in-depth guidelines for writing and formatting a broad range of business communications, from letters, memos, and reports to resumes, cover letters, and business messages for a variety of situations. In addition to the topics listed above, the handbook includes easy-to-follow steps for achieving the appropriate tone and content to suit the purpose of the message.

A reference manual helps you solve writing problems as they arise so that you don't feel stuck or develop writer's block—the feeling that you are at a loss for words to put on paper. A good reference manual, such as the Pearson handbook, can be used to remind yourself how to get through the basic building blocks of preparing a lengthy communication, such as a report or a proposal or an important letter or email. You can review the process for outlining your ideas, which helps you develop a blueprint to follow before you begin to write. Sections that take you through the entire process of drafting, editing, proofreading, and polishing help you develop a method for approaching any writing task. The handbook also includes styles for writing citations for scholarly writing and provides answers to questions you might have about quoting sources and annotating bibliographies.

writingTIP

Words with similar meanings are included in the definitions of a word. A synonym helps a writer get the exact shade of meaning desired.

You will be able to find an equal amount of useful information in many other reference manuals on the market. Your instructor might have additional recommendations or requirements.

Read, Read, Read

This introductory chapter is intended to provide motivation if you are not already in the habit of using reference sources and to further encourage usage if you are. With these tools as a backup throughout this course, you will become more proficient with language by expanding both your vocabulary and your awareness of how you use language. To supplement your course work and use of reference sources, take time to do as much reading as possible. Read books, printed and online magazines, newspapers, and Internet news sites on a variety of subjects—current events, lifestyle, business, finance, and technology. Read newsletters, websites, and trade magazines related to your chosen career field. Make a special effort to listen to articulate speakers and converse with well-informed, educated people.

Investing time in the goals of improving your language skills and broadening your vocabulary, particularly in the career area that interests you, will give you all kinds of advantages, including the ability to do the following:

- Choose words that allow you to express yourself clearly, tactfully, and interestingly.
- Speak with confidence to colleagues and authority figures in social and professional situations.
- Persuade others to your point of view, both orally and in writing.
- Communicate clearly and correctly when writing job search and workplace communications.

GO TO PAGE 15 AND COMPLETE WORKSHEETS 1.2 AND 1.3.

Checkpoint

After completing this chapter, you have explored the variety of electronic reference tools that are available, and you are familiar with the full range of information to be found in a comprehensive, up-to-date printed college dictionary. Be sure to use the front and back matter for quick access to the assistance and facts they contain. Because a good dictionary is such a versatile reference book, keep a current one on your desk at home as well as at work. Many new words added to the latest editions are workplace-related and useful for your career.

You also appreciate the importance of using a thesaurus to add clarity and precision to your writing and a reference manual to help you improve your writing and ensure that your communications follow current business standards.

communications connection

EDITING AND PROOFREADING YOUR WRITING

In the business world, spelling errors and mistakes in grammar and word usage will hurt your chances for success. An error in a resume, email, or written business document makes the reader cringe, and it says bad things about you. Always take time to edit your writing and use the appropriate reference tools needed to correct your mistakes before anyone sees them.

After writing a draft, you need to read it with your target audience in mind to make sure you have included the necessary information and that the presentation is logical and will be understood by your reader. Begin globally by making sure your message is complete and coherent. Once you are satisfied on that level, then edit and proofread for other mistakes.

Electronic Spelling and Grammar Checker

First, use your word processor's electronic tool to quickly detect and correct mistakes. Here are some cautions to keep in mind when using this tool:

1. **Words may have more than one correct spelling.** When a word has more than one correct spelling, the dictionary entry will show them in order of preference.

   the·ater or the·atre   toward or towards   catalog or catalogue

   What to do: Use your dictionary to ensure correct spelling. You should use the *preferred spelling*. If you happen to use the second spelling, you are not technically making an error, but your reader might not recognize that both spellings are correct. When *also* precedes a second spelling, the second one is less acceptable. Avoid it unless you have a special reason to use it.

2. **Electronic spell-checkers do not detect wrong word usage.** For example, they do not detect the difference between homonyms— words that sound the same but are spelled differently and have different meanings, such as *their* for *there* or *past* for *passed*.

   What to do: Proofread and check for sense as well as spelling.

3. **Electronic grammar checkers are not infallible either.** They sometimes identify items as grammar errors when they are not; they also overlook some types of grammar and writing errors. A frequent electronic grammar check error is to misidentify the subject of a sentence and mistakenly indicate an error in subject-verb agreement. Another is saying that use of passive voice is not correct when, in fact, sometimes it is.

   What to do: Look at each and every error identified and use your own judgment or consult your references to determine if the electronic tool is correct before you hit the "change" button.

Proofreading in Print

When you write short messages such as emails, you will most likely edit and proofread without printing. For longer documents, editing and proofreading from a printout is more foolproof. A good method is to print the document after using the spelling and grammar tool.

Keep in mind that editing and proofreading are more than checking for spelling and typographical errors (typos). Get in the habit of marking your corrections with standard proofreading marks. **Proofreading marks** are a universally used system for marking errors in printed copy and inserting the correction—usually with a red pen or pencil. This is how you will mark errors in the exercises throughout this text (see the inside back cover).

When your corrections are heavy, you should reprint and check each handwritten correction against the new printout. Using this universal method makes it much easier to make the corrections and avoid introducing a new error.

Proofreading Tips

Proofread when you feel alert and are able to focus on the task without distraction:

- Read slowly; concentrate on looking at each word and sentence. Sometimes it helps to read out loud to yourself or someone else.
- Proofread more than once. Your eye will often overlook errors in the first pass.
- Print and proofread more than once when corrections are extensive. Why? Because it is so easy to introduce a new error while you are correcting the current one. A common error is to accidentally delete a word.
- Ask someone else to proofread when you feel uneasy about your final document.

What to look for:

- Typographical or spelling errors
- Omitted words
- Misused words
- Grammar, punctuation, and capitalization errors
- Number style and abbreviation errors
- Errors in standard formatting of business documents

Take time now to review the proofreading marks on the inside back cover of this book. You will find similar charts in your college dictionary, reference manuals, and other communications texts. The marks will be the same—the only thing that might differ is that more or fewer symbols may be shown.

WRITING PRACTICE

Write a brief article describing the kind of writing you currently do and the methods you use to proofread your work. Take into account what you have just read and compare your methods to the recommendations given here. Include a comparison (in chart or narrative form) to analyze where your methods are the same and where they are different.

Date to submit this assignment: _____

PROOFREADING PRACTICE

Who's Smarter—You or the Computer?

The spelling dictionary in a computer can find only three of the spelling errors in the following email. Correct the errors using the proofreading symbols on the back cover and circle the errors that the spell checker *does* find. Also, underline any word groups that your computer incorrectly identifies as having a grammatical error instead of a spelling error.

Deer Cynthia,

Wood you like two go too an food expo next weak? I have a pear of tickets, and eye wood like you to bee my guessed. I here that this show will be won of the seasons' best. If you want too go, I will sin you the information; you can meat me their. Let me no as soon as ewe can, sew I can offer the ticket to sum one eles if you are unable to attends.

Buy the weigh, I called you this passed Monday; you assistant told me you had an cold. I hope you our now on you're weigh back too good health.

Regards,

Paul

chapter review

WORKSHEET 1.1

A. Write **T** (True) or **F** (False) in the blank.

1. _____ Prospective employers tend to assume a poor speller is uneducated or unintelligent.

2. _____ Electronic and printed dictionaries are essentially the same, except that online dictionaries also usually include a thesaurus.

3. _____ In addition to pronunciations, spellings, and vocabulary, dictionaries tell you which words are Standard English or preferred usage and which are non-Standard, informal, slang, or vulgar.

4. _____ If a comma separates two spellings of the same word in the dictionary, it means the first spelling is non-Standard.

5. _____ A diacritical mark is the same as an accent mark.

6. _____ Looking for the Webster brand is the best way to identify a good dictionary.

7. _____ If *or* is between two spellings of the same word in the dictionary, it means either spelling is correct.

8. _____ In a dictionary entry, if a dot or accent mark appears between two syllables, it means you should spell it as two separate words.

9. _____ Some compound words require a hyphen, and others do not.

10. _____ If a compound word is not spelled with a hyphen, you most likely won't find it listed in the dictionary.

B. To answer the following questions, use your own dictionary so that you'll become accustomed to its "code"—that is, the various symbols and abbreviations used.

1. What part of speech is *faux pas,* and what does it mean? _____

_____

2. How many syllables does *quarterback* have? _____

3. Which syllable in *quarterback* has the primary accent: first, second, or third? _____

4. Which syllable in *quarterback* has the secondary accent: first, second, or third? _____

5. Which syllable in *quarterback* has no accent? _____

6. What part of speech is *quarterback* when it means to direct or mislead?
_____

7. Which syllable has the primary accent in the preferred pronunciation of *incomparable:* first, second, third, fourth, or fifth?
_____

8. *Disinterested* and *uninterested* mean the same.
(a) true _____ (b) false _____
(c) maybe _____

9. What words in the pronunciation key of your dictionary illustrate the schwa (ə) sound? _____.

10. According to the preferred pronunciation, which syllable has the primary stress in *affluent* and *affluence?* _____

11. In your dictionary, where is the etymology in relation to the definitions? _____

12. What is the other correct spelling of *catalog?* _____

13. Which does your dictionary show first? _____

14. What two parts of speech are most common for this word?
_____

15. Underline the preferred spelling.

hip hop   Hip Hop   hip-hop   Hip-Hop

CHECK YOUR ANSWERS ON PAGE 432.

WORKSHEET 1.2

A. Answer the following by recalling the information in the chapter and using a dictionary, thesaurus, or reference manual as needed.

1. If you look up a word in a college dictionary and don't find a usage label, what does this mean? _____

_____.

2. The word *also* between two spellings of the same word means
    _____.

3. Show with a dot how to divide *twinkling* between syllables.
    _____

4. The noun *pair* has two correct plural spellings. What are they?
    _____

5. The *i* in the word *juvenile* is pronounced like the alphabet sound of *i*.
    True or False? _____

6. College dictionaries have a pronunciation key _____
    _____ and/or _____.

7. Where in a college or unabridged dictionary do you find detailed
    instructions and explanations of the contents? _____

8. What is the plural of *addendum* and from what language does the
    word originate? _____

9. A word with the same pronunciation as another but with a
    different meaning is a/an (a) homonym (b) synonym (c) antonym.
    _____

10. What is the capital of Spain? _____

B. Use a printed or online dictionary and thesaurus to complete the
    following exercises. Indicate the name of the source(s) used in the blank:

    _____

11. Which is the correct spelling? Use your dictionary if needed.

    a. _____   (a) counter-sign   (b) countersign   (c) counter sign
    b. _____   (a) epilog   (b) epilogue   (c) both a and b
    c. _____   (a) antitrust   (b) anti-trust   (c) anti trust
    d. _____   (a) ocurred   (b) occured   (c) occurred
    e. _____   (a) reccomend   (b) reccommend   (c) recommend

12. Circle the misspelled words: pronounciation, weird, seperate,
    congradulate, persue, villain, persistent, conscience, bachelor

13. Divide these words into syllables with a slash (/) between and circle
    the syllable that has the primary accent:

    a. subtle   _____
    b. rationale   _____
    c. infrastructure   _____

14. Use a printed or online thesaurus to find a synonym (a word with a
    similar meaning) for the following words:

    a. incomparable   _____
    b. incredible   _____
    c. distasteful   _____

15. Write the correct spelling of these frequently misspelled words in the blank. Use your dictionary to check your answers.

    a. accomodations   _____

    b. indispensible   _____

    c. judgement   _____

    d. concensus   _____

    e. acknowledgement   _____

CHECK YOUR ANSWERS ON PAGE 433.

WORKSHEET 1.3

A. Using a thesaurus, replace the italicized words in the following sentences with a word that better expresses the writer's meaning shown in brackets.

Example: The annual profits *rose* quickly above the competition [more precise]. *surged*

1. Our conference center can offer your staff a *very good* working environment. [less clichéd]

    _____

2. Please don't be *hasty* in making your decision [more emphatic].

    _____

3. You lack the *know-how* needed for this position. [less blunt]

    _____

4. I am very *angry* with the way you handled the situation. [softer]

    _____

5. Your behavior at the meeting this morning was *stupid*. [more tactful]

    _____

B. Use a reference manual (or your knowledge) to answer questions 6–10 and make any necessary corrections in sentences 11–15.

6. What are the three styles used to format business letters?

    a. _____

    b. _____

    c. _____

7. The term *memo* is a shortened form of _____.

8. The part of a business letter that contains the message is called the _____.

9. What do the following abbreviations mean?

    a. SEC _____

    b. CEO _____

10. Two types of business reports are _____ and _____.

C. Revise the following sentences where necessary using a reference manual.

11. Almost five thousand people attended the Alliance for Survival Rally.

_____

12. Can you list fifty ways to make five million dollars? _____

_____

13. The Prime Interest Rate went to fifteen percent today._____

_____

14. The Judge said that the U. S. Supreme Court Decision was favorable to my Company. _____

_____

15. The Annual Report listed the Midwest as the most profitable area of the Country. _____

_____

CHECK YOUR ANSWERS ON PAGE 434.

POSTTEST

Use your dictionary when needed to answer the following questions.

1. In the blank, write the correct spelling of the two misspelled words: rediculous, personnel, occurred, ocassion, fulfilled. _____

2. Use a thesaurus (electronic or printed) to find more tactful ways to express the underlined word:

   a. You did a very <u>bad</u> job on this project.

   _____

   b. The decision you made was <u>wrong</u>.

   _____

3. What does NATO stand for? _____

4. Illiterate expressions, vulgarities, and slang are not found in better dictionaries. True or False? _____

5. What does *colloquial* mean? _____

   _____

6. In what year was the Hollywood icon Bette Davis born? _____

7. What was the birth name of Nobel Prize-winning author Toni Morrison?

   _____

8. Give three synonyms for *small.* _____

   _____

9. The word *irrevocable* is pronounced with the accent on the _____ syllable.

10. Which spellings are correct (nation wide, nationwide, nation-wide)? _____ and _____.

CHECK YOUR ANSWERS ON PAGE 434.

Self-Study and Practice Tutorials

wordPOWER

Build your workplace vocabulary and improve spelling skills by completing the exercises in Appendix B on page 349.

Supplementary Practice Exercises

For additional practice, complete the Appendix C exercises for this chapter on page 390.

© George Wada/Fotolia

After completing Chapter 2, you will be able to do the following:

- Define the eight parts of speech and their roles in forming sentences.
- Explain how words are used as different parts of speech in sentences.
- Apply your knowledge of the parts of speech to English principles in your speaking and writing.

2

The Parts of Speech

career connection

WHAT MAKES WRITING SO IMPORTANT?

- Writing is the primary basis on which your work, your learning, and your intellect will be judged—in college, in the workplace, and in the community.
- Writing is portable and permanent. It makes your thinking visible.
- Writing fosters your ability to explain a complex position to readers and to yourself.
- Writing requires that you anticipate your readers' needs. Your ability to do so demonstrates your intellectual flexibility and maturity.
- Writing ideas down preserves them so that you can reflect on them later.
- Writing out your ideas permits you to evaluate the adequacy of your argument.
- Writing stimulates you to extend a line of thought beyond your first impressions or gut responses.
- Writing equips you with the communication and thinking skills you need to participate effectively in democracy.
- Writing is an essential job skill.

Source: Marquette University, *Writing Across the Curriculum* (www.marquette.edu/wac/WhatMakesWritingSoImportant.shtml). Based on brochures from Brown University and the University of Missouri.

PRETEST

Write the name of the part of speech in the blank after its definition.

1. Expresses action or state of being. _____

2. Modifies—tells something about—a noun or pronoun. _____

3. Substitutes for a noun. _____

4. An exclamatory word or phrase that is used to show emotion.

   _____

5. Connects two or more words or parts of sentences. _____

6. Linking words, such as *under*, *with*, and *to*. _____

7. Modifies—tells something about—a verb, an adjective, or an adverb.

   _____

8. Names people, things, abstract concepts, and time and measurements.

   _____

9. Specific nouns that begin with a capital letter. _____

10. Nonspecific nouns that begin with lowercase letters. _____

CHECK YOUR ANSWERS ON PAGE 435.

The Parts of Speech

The **parts of speech** are the grammatical system for organizing words into the following eight categories—*nouns, pronouns, verbs, adjectives, adverbs, prepositions, conjunctions,* and *interjections*—depending on how the words are used in a sentence. Breaking sentences down and analyzing their parts is considered a painful exercise called "learning grammar." Why do you need to do this? Unless you plan to be an English teacher, it actually isn't essential to study grammar in depth. What you *do* need to be able to do is identify, so that you'll correctly use, the basic "tools of the English trade"—and these are the parts of speech.

Whether or not you remember the fundamentals about the parts of speech from past studies, this chapter will help you improve your command of English and be prepared for the material in upcoming chapters. Granted, studying the parts of speech is not what most students consider fun. It's much easier just to try to use the English language properly than to label and categorize words. Although you may dislike the idea of learning grammar or feel you could never master it, try to approach it with an open mind. The *English for Careers* method is different. You'll discover an enjoyable and efficient way to improve your language skills and become a more confident writer. Being able to write fluently and correctly without extensive effort that uses up valuable time is essential to success in any career. This book is designed to help you acquire that skill. As you begin to feel more at ease with the basics of good writing, you will be free to focus on the ideas and content of your message. This is what will boost your success in school and in the workplace.

THE PARTS OF SPEECH

Nouns	Name people, places, things, concepts, activities, and measurements
Pronouns	Substitute for nouns
Verbs	Express action or state of being
Adjectives	Modify nouns and pronouns
Adverbs	Modify verbs, adjectives, and other adverbs
Conjunctions	Join words and groups of words
Prepositions	Link parts of a sentence to show a relationship
Interjections	Express strong emotion

NOUNS

In grammar, **nouns** are defined as words that name people, places, and things. Nouns also name animals, ideas, concepts, qualities, activities and events, as well as measures of time, space, and quantities.

Proper nouns are words that name specific persons, places, and things. They always begin with a capital letter: *White House*, *Professor Alicia Holmes*, *Toronto*, *Secretariat*, *Republican Party*, and *Halloween*. **Common nouns** are nonspecific nouns and begin with lowercase letters: *house*, *instructor*, *city*, *horse*, *organization*, and *holiday*.

You will study the use of nouns in depth in the next unit. For now, the important thing to remember is that nouns are used in sentences as subjects and objects. They tell *who*, *whom*, or *what*.

CATEGORIES OF NOUNS

Persons/Animals	Dr. Davis, accountant, Kathleen, members, brother, Lassie
Places	island, city, Africa, San Francisco, Southern Hemisphere
Things	piano, shirt, *Time*, subway, seat, Eiffel Tower
Concepts	integrity, modesty, beauty, success, democracy
Activities	drinking, running, sleeping, driving, eating, crying
Measurements	week, decade, mile, million, number, yard, month

PRONOUNS

Pronouns are words that take the place of nouns—they are substitutes, such as *he*, *she*, *it*, *them*, *who*, and *everybody*—so that we can avoid repeating the noun when referring back to it.

| Nouns: | Jennifer Louis won the **award**. |
| Pronouns: | **She** was very surprised to learn that **she** would receive **it**. |

A pronoun may also replace a noun that was *not* previously mentioned but is instead understood. For example, "It is hot today" really means "The **air** is hot today." We understand that *it* substitutes for *air*.

Pronouns also play the roles of subjects and objects in sentences. As subjects, they are essential to the creation of a sentence. There is much more to know about pronouns to ensure that you write grammatically correct sentences with ease and use pronouns correctly in speech. We have all hesitated at times before deciding whether to use *she* or *her*, *he* or *him*, and *me* or *I*, for example. There are ways to learn the rules about this usage so that it sticks with you and you don't have to stop and think. You will master these after you study Chapters 6 and 7.

You also probably remember from earlier grammar courses the rules of first, second, and third person. When you review these later in the course, you will appreciate the refresher on pronoun usage and what it contributes to using good grammar with ease.

GO TO PAGE 33 AND COMPLETE WORKSHEET 2.1.

VERBS

Verbs are action, being, or helping words. Every sentence has at least one verb. Action or being verbs are sometimes preceded by one or more **helping verbs**, thus creating a **verb phrase**.

Action verbs tell what the action of the subject is in a sentence. They refer to something you can physically or mentally do: *work, play, invite, write, think, consider, wonder.*

> He **wrote** the application letter and **proofread** it.

> When the manager **received** it, she **read** it thoroughly.

Being verbs—also called **state-of-being verbs** or **linking verbs**—include forms of the verb *to be* (for example: *is, am, are, was, were*), verbs of the senses, and a few other verbs. Being verbs link the subject of the sentence to a word or words that tell something about the subject.

> He **appears** efficient and eager to learn.

> It **seems** as though the meeting will last for at least three hours.

To express time (present, past, and future), possibility (maybe), or emphasis, a **helping verb** may precede the main verb—either action or being. Some being verbs also function as helping verbs. Examples of helping verbs are *have, has, had, should, could, would*. In these verb phrases, the first word is the helping verb.

> Judge Hoover **is** *reading* all of the briefs and **should** *finish* soon.

> He **is** *enjoying* his vacation, although his work **is** *piling* up at home.

RECOGNIZING VERBS AND WORDS THAT LOOK LIKE VERBS BUT ARE NOT

-ing Words

- Most verbs can add *-ing*: *see/seeing, have/having, eat/eating, be/being.* When *-ing* words express action or existence, they are verbs and are always preceded by a helping verb.

   Verb: Recent studies show that honesty **is paying** off in business.

- When an *-ing* word *names* an activity, however, it is a noun. In grammar terms, this is called a **gerund**; a gerund is *not* preceded by a helping verb.

   Noun (Gerund): Paying bills has never been my favorite activity.

   (gerund—*paying*; verb—*has been*)

To + Verb

- When *to* precedes a verb—such as *to eat, to work,* or *to swim*—the result is a noun naming an activity, not a verb. *To* plus a verb is called an **infinitive**. Infinitives are used as **nouns**, as shown in the sentence below: (Infinitives can also function as adjectives and adverbs—more about this in Chapter 8.)

   To achieve it, you have **to believe** it.

   To achieve and *to believe*—*infinitives* name activities; thus, they are nouns, not verbs; the verb is *have*.

GO TO PAGE 33 AND COMPLETE WORKSHEET 2.2.

ADJECTIVES

Modifiers—adjectives and adverbs—are words that describe, limit, or explain. **Adjectives** modify (describe) nouns and pronouns. They add information about *which one*, *what kind*, or *how many*.

Adjectives that describe are useful to readers because they make writing more interesting and specific. When you are specific, your meaning is clearer to your reader. When your writing is interesting, your reader is motivated to continue. To tell what kind of *house*, you might choose *yellow*, *brick*, *contemporary*, *shabby*, *two-story*, or *luxurious*. Carefully select descriptive adjectives to create a picture for the reader or listener.

In the examples below, the adjectives are in bold and the words they modify are underlined.

grammarTIP

The words *a*, *an*, and *the* are known as articles in the world of grammar, but they are also adjectives that tell *which one*. We'll look at these more closely in Chapter 6.

   Respectful <u>employees</u> work well with people from **diverse** <u>backgrounds</u>.

   Upscale gourmet <u>dinners</u> are served in that **elegant** and very **expensive** <u>restaurant</u>.

   A **positive** <u>attitude</u> in our **stressful work** <u>environment</u> requires taking **individual** <u>responsibility</u>.

Adjectives also limit—by telling *how many*. Examples are words such as *more*, *many*, *several*, *few*, and *some* or specific quantities such as *fifty*, *one*, and *2,000*. Use these adjectives carefully in order to make sure your reader gets the message you intend.

I bought **several** <u>reams</u> of paper at Cheapo Depot. OR I bought **20** <u>reams</u> of paper at Cheapo Depot.

In a **few** <u>months</u> we will be moving our offices. OR In **two** <u>months</u> we will be moving our offices.

We have **enough** <u>employees</u> to pack **all** of the <u>boxes</u>. OR We have **five** <u>employees</u> to pack **50** <u>boxes</u>.

ADVERBS

Adverbs describe, limit, or explain verbs, adjectives, or other adverbs. Adverbs add information about *when*, *where*, *how*, or *how much*. Many adverbs—but not all—are formed by adding *-ly* to an adjective, as in these examples.

Adjective	Adverb
peaceful	peacefully
quiet	quietly
exceptional	exceptionally
intelligent	intelligently
attractive	attractively
final	finally
real	really

In the examples below, the adverbs are in bold, and the words they modify are underlined.

Adverbs modifying a verb:

> **Always** <u>prepare</u> invoices **carefully**.

Adverbs modifying adjectives:

> This **extremely** <u>expensive</u> book is required for an **especially** <u>important</u> course.

Adverbs modifying other adverbs:

> Dr. Persley works **so** <u>efficiently</u> that she **almost** <u>never</u> makes a mistake.

CONJUNCTIONS

Conjunctions connect words, phrases, and clauses. The relationship between the words or groups of words is shown by the choice of conjunction. To understand conjuctions, you need to know the different types.

The **coordinating conjunctions** are *and*, *but*, *or*, *nor*, *for*, *yet*, and *so*. These words are used to join parts of speech in a series (nouns, pronouns, adjectives, adverbs, and verbs) and parts of sentences (clauses). They are also used to join two sentences together to make them one sentence when two thoughts are very closely connected.

In the following examples, the conjunctions are in bold, and the words they connect are underlined.

and   Studies show that <u>honesty</u>, <u>ethics</u>, **and** <u>social responsibility</u> pay off in business. [connects a series of nouns]

---

grammar**TIP**

While many adverbs end in *-ly*, some words often used as adverbs don't end in *-ly*. Some examples are *almost*, *even*, *much*, *more*, *very*, *too*, and *well*.

grammar**TIP**

FAN BOYS (*for, and, nor, but, or, yet, so*) is an acronym for memorizing coordinating conjunctions.

but	Raymond said, "It's hard to get a job as a news anchor, **but** the pay is good." [connects two sentences into one]
or	Workplace ethics include not violating civil law **or** company policy. [connects two nouns]
nor	He will neither attend the convention **nor** visit the showroom. [connects two verbs]
for	Samantha decided not to become a doctor, **for** she feared the crushing debt of student loans. [connects two sentences into one]
yet	English is the international language of business, **yet** we should all know how to say "please," "thank you," and "hello" in several languages. [connects two sentences into one]
so	The new manual is very complex, **so** be sure to read every word. [connects two sentences into one]

Dependent conjunctions (also called **subordinate conjunctions),** introduce a dependent clause—a word group that has a subject and verb but does not express a complete thought. The words below are often used as dependent conjunctions. The sentences following the list show the dependent conjunction in bold type; the phrase or clause that it introduces is underlined.

after	so that
although	than
as	unless
because	until
before	when
even though	which
if	while
since	

> Business letters in the United States and Canada are less formal **than** in most other parts of the world.

Than is used as a dependent conjunction to introduce the phrase *in most other parts of the world.*

> The new branch office will be successful **if** Petrina manages it.

If is a dependent conjunction preceding the noun *Petrina* and the verb *manages.*

To change emphasis, the dependent conjunction can be placed at the beginning of the sentence.

> **If** Petrina manages it, the branch office will be successful.

> **Unless** it is repaired this week, we can't use the copier for the report.

PREPOSITIONS

Prepositions link to other words in a sentence to show relationships. These words are often used as prepositions:

about	between	over
above	during	since
across	except	through
after	for*	to
against	from	toward
along	in	under
among	inside	until
around	into	up
at	like	upon
behind	near	with
below	of	within
beneath	off	without
beside	on	

A **prepositional phrase** begins with a preposition and ends with a noun or pronoun, which is called the **object of the preposition**. In these examples, the prepositions are in bold, and the objects are underlined.

> **in** the refrigerator, **at** today's meeting

The preposition and its object *plus any words between* them make up the prepositional phrase.

> Please send the report **to** the entire *committee*.

To is the preposition, *committee* is the object of the preposition, and *to the entire committee* is the prepositional phrase. *The* and *entire* are adjectives describing *committee*. Here are more examples:

> **Under** the antique table is a rug worth millions.

> **Below** the branding signage will be a model **of** the new product design.

> **After** lunch, we need to schedule a lively session that will keep the audience alert.

Remember that a prepositional phrase never has a subject or a verb. If the word group has a verb, it is not a prepositional phrase.

INTERJECTIONS

The eighth part of speech is the **interjection**, an exclamatory word or phrase such as the following: *No way! Congratulations! That's great!* Perhaps you have special ones for certain occasions that fit your way of expressing your emotions or enthusiasm.

There isn't much more you need to know about interjections except this caution: Use them sparingly. The more you exclaim, the more likely your reader will become weary of the excited tone. Emphasis is effective only when it is used sparingly.

GO TO PAGE 34 AND COMPLETE WORKSHEET 2.3.

*For is a conjunction when it means "because"; otherwise, it's a preposition.

writingTIP

In English, we often use a preposition without stating its object, which may be understood, as in the following examples: Please stop **by**. Don't jump **across**. She went **under**. I'll go **up**.

Checkpoint

Parts of speech are versatile tools. Tools are versatile when they do more than one kind of job. So it is with words—most of them can be used as more than one part of speech. The idea is simple: How you use a word in a sentence determines the part of speech.

Consider the word *dancing*. It looks like a verb, doesn't it? After all, it represents *action*. It sounds like a verb too—because it ends in *-ing*. As a matter of fact, it *is* a verb—sometimes. The *-ing* form is a verb only when a helping verb precedes it. Otherwise, the *-ing* word is a noun or an adjective. Compare the following examples:

Verb	He **is dancing** with Fergie. [The complete verb consists of the helping verb *is* and main verb *dancing*.]
Noun	**Dancing** is fun. [*Dancing* is a noun because it names an activity; the verb is *is*.]
Adjective	The child attends a **dancing** class. [*Dancing* is an adjective because it describes the class; *attends* is the verb.]

The word *advocate* can be a noun or a verb:

Noun	The City Council President is a strong **advocate** of bike lanes on city streets.
Verb	Our environmental advocacy organization is promoting a bike marathon to **advocate** for more bike lanes.

Consider the functions of the word *brown* in these sentences:

Verb	Did the chef show you how to **brown** the onions to perfection?
Adjective	We chose **brown** paint for the restaurant interior.
Noun	The decorator said **brown** is the trendy color this year.

When you are editing and proofreading, you need to make sure you have used the correct *form* of a word. For example, beauty (noun), beautiful (adjective), beautifully (adverb). Knowing the part of speech you intended the word to play will help you assess the correctness of your grammar.

communications connection

THE WRITING PROCESS: PLANNING

The writing process is a system used by writers to develop effective communications. The process begins with thinking about your purpose and audience before you begin to write. This course provides opportunities to apply the steps in the writing process to your study of grammar. You have already practiced the editing and proofreading part of the process in Chapter 1. Although these steps are normally done at the end of the process, they were introduced first because this course emphasizes proofreading to eliminate errors in grammar. Now we will look at the steps that have to happen before you begin to write. We will explore all of the steps in the remaining chapters. Refer to Appendix A for an overview.

PLANNING AND ORGANIZING

The writing process begins with planning your message. What is it you want to communicate, and who is your intended audience? Whether you are writing a routine email message or a complex letter or report, planning is essential to clear and concise communication.

Planning involves four key steps:

1. **Define your purpose.** Know what your purpose is and do not stray from it. Use separate communications to deal with different subjects.

2. **Know your reader.** Target your message or the information you include in a longer document to the needs of your reader. The more complex your subject, the more you will need to think about exactly how much detail is needed. Know exactly what you want from the reader and be explicit in your message if a specific action is being requested.

3. **Plan your message.** Make notes or develop an outline to structure your message. Move topics around until you are sure the order is logical and will be clear to your reader.

4. **Gather quality information.** Make sure your content is correct and is adequate to achieve your purpose. Double-check numerical data, calendar dates, dollar amounts, spelling of names, and other such factual information no matter how routine the communication might be.

WRITING PRACTICE

One way to improve your writing is to analyze the good writing of others. If you had to plan a letter of complaint, where would you begin? How would you approach this often sensitive and challenging communication? Your goal is to get the response that will satisfy your needs. Therefore, your choice of words needs to strike a balance. You want to be forceful so that you can convince your reader to do the right thing. You want to prove that your complaint is legitimate. You want to offer a resolution that is precise and clear.

Discuss with your classmates how you and they have handled situations where a complaint was made. Was it done in person? On the phone? By letter or email? What was the outcome? How did the medium affect the outcome? How was the choice of words determined? Was there planning involved or was it spontaneous?

Read the following letter and then answer the questions that follow:

July 29, 20xx

Chrysler Group Customer Care
P.O. Box 21-8004
Auburn Hills, MI 48321-8004

Dear Customer Care Manager:

My husband and I are pleased with the new Jeep Wrangler we purchased on June 25. The dealer, ABC Motors, Inc., provided courteous and prompt service, which we appreciated. We believe this dealer and your organization conduct business fairly and honestly. However, after we had driven the vehicle only 32 miles, we found that the wheels needed balancing. Yesterday we paid $115 (copy of bill enclosed) to have this service performed, although the problem apparently existed when we drove the vehicle out of your showroom.

When we returned the vehicle, we were billed for this adjustment because of the exclusion provisions on page 3 of the warranty. The third paragraph reads, "Normal maintenance services . . . such as . . . wheel balancing . . ." are not covered. However, we believe a condition existing at the time of purchase is not "normal maintenance" and surely should be corrected without charge.

Although we assume a misunderstanding occurred, the dealer would not release our vehicle without payment.

Please contact ABC Motors, Inc. and instruct them to reimburse our payment of $115.

Sincerely,

Leila R. Smith

enclosure

cc: ABC Motors, Inc., 2025 Dealership Lane, Rochester, NY 14614

1. What is the purpose of this message? _____
_____

2. Who is the intended reader? _____
_____

3. Briefly list the order of topics covered. _____
_____
_____

4. What factual details did the writer gather? _____
_____
_____
_____

5. On a scale of 1 to 5, with 1 being poor and 5 being excellent, how would you rate the effectiveness of this letter? Why? _____

Date to submit this assignment: _____

PROOFREADING PRACTICE

Because errors can ruin any message, the rule to remember is this: Don't let others see your mistakes! Instead, *proofread, proofread, proofread.* You began your proofreading practice with Chapter 1, and it will continue throughout the course. Review the proofreading marks on the inside back cover of this book, and then correct the errors in the following article. Your instructor will tell you whether to mark the copy in your textbook or do this activity online.

Developing Good Study Habit

Adults frequently report they have'nt been taught how to study and that they need practical and specific suggestions. Here is a breif list of recomendations that will put in control of your study time:

- Keep in mind that studing is an activity that requires your mine to be engage. It is an active process, not a passive on.

- Organize your books,computer files, and any necesary referance materials befor you begin your study sesion.

- If possible, plan to do studying in one place. We are all creatures of habit. We have places in for sleeping, eating, and batheing; why not hae a specail place for study?

- Begin to study the very minute you sit down at your desk. Do not dealy (go on Facebook, Twitter, send texts), dont assume distractions won't interfere with your productivty.

- Plan a balanced work-study schedule and trying to adhere to it, if you must depart from your schedule at least you will have something definite and planned to which you can return.

- Take a short rest or activity break after 20 to 30 minutes of concentrated study. Short periods of relaxashion or changes in activity able you to renew your study with increased viger.

- See that fiscal factors such as heat, lightnig, and ventilation are satisfactory. to do effective study and reading, you must be comfortable and read for work.

How did you do? Excellent _____ Good _____ Need More Practice _____ (Don't be hard on yourself. This exercise contains some errors you haven't yet studied.)

---

chapter review

WORKSHEET 2.1

A. Circle the 24 nouns in the following sentences. If a noun is made up of two or more words, use one circle.

1. A smile is likely to help even the most challenging situation.

2. Business correspondence in the United States is often less formal than it is in Asia, South America, Europe, and Africa.

3. It is important to your career to accept people of various cultures and to judge them as individuals.

4. Avoid using slang when you speak with coworkers for whom English is a second language.

5. The multicultural neighborhood, classroom, and workplace are typical in the United States, Canada, Great Britain, and many other parts of the world.

B. Insert pronouns in the blanks to replace the words in brackets.

6. [The temperature] _____ is too hot today for running in the park.

7. [This man] _____ will be the next president of the club.

8. [Which person] _____ will be the next governor?

9. [Ashley] _____ talks to [Ashley's] _____ friends on the phone for hours.

10. [These friends] _____ urged [Julie] _____ to contact [George] _____.

CHECK YOUR ANSWERS ON PAGE 435.

WORKSHEET 2.2

A. Circle the nine being verbs and underline the one action verb.

1. She is an assistant.

2. He seems qualified.

3. I am surprised that the tests are not ready.

4. All shipments were on time last week.

5. They think you are the best employee.

6. The music sounds good.

7. Edward appears enthusiastic about being on the program.

B. Circle the complete verbs—helping and main.

8. I do work on the executive floor, but I have not met the president.

9. Judge Hoover has read the lawyer's motion.

10. The jury members are reading the transcripts.

11. He has chosen to take the new job.

12. Professor Dowd will be going to Cairo to teach.

13. In June you will have been working here for five years.

14. He might have noticed the change in tone.

15. Ms. Moultry does sign all the letters herself.

C. Fill in the blanks with verbs that make sense in the sentence. (A helping verb and main verb may be needed.)

16. From time to time most office professionals _____ more computer training, but they may not _____ time for regular college classes.

17. Four out of five companies _____ a great deal of money training their employees.

18. We _____ for your opinion.

19. Workplace etiquette _____ important to employers.

20. Many firms _____ thousands of dollars for etiquette seminars for their employees.

D. Write a preposition in each blank to show a relationship between the verb and the object.

Example: Richard and Marissa walked <u>around</u> the mountain.

21. The movers carried the furniture _____ the new office building.

22. _____ this time, you should know how to find the errors in your writing.

23. _____ all of our setbacks, the team has stuck together.

24. _____ the long haul, you will be rewarded for hard work.

25. The overpass moves cars _____ the highway quickly.

CHECK YOUR ANSWERS ON PAGE 435.

WORKSHEET 2.3

1. Underline the eight nouns in the following sentence:

When interviewers speak with job applicants, they look for competence and skills first, but they also place a great emphasis on enthusiasm, ambition, and flexibility.

2. Circle the eight verbs and underline the ten pronouns:

He wrote the application letter and proofread it. When the manager received it, she looked it over. After she read all the applications, she invited a few applicants for interviews. She has an assistant who helped her.

3. Underline the eight being verbs:

Rebecca Foster is capable, but Keith Jefferson also appears qualified. The job sounds like it is suitable for someone who has a love of sales.

I believe Rebecca showed the most enthusiasm and seems more capable of convincing others. On the other hand, Keith has a lot of sales experience and his track record is impressive.

4. Circle each helping verb and underline each verb phrase.

    a. She does enjoy the work and has stayed late often.

    b. She has met every deadline.

    c. He has left on time every afternoon, but still has completed his work.

    d. This is why I have concluded that Keith is the more efficient of the two.

5. Circle the adjectives in the following sentences and underline the nouns or pronouns they describe.

    a. He has no idea that she ordered new carpeting and a huge new desk.

    b. You seem smart and you know ethics is important.

6. Insert an adverb in the blank to describe, limit, or explain the words in bold.

    a. He **was hired** _____.

    b. The **training** program was delivered _____.

    c. Do you think that I **drive** _____?

    d. You **added** the figures _____.

    e. You **should** _____ **use** good-quality paper for resumes.

7. Write the seven coordinating conjunctions in the spaces below.

    a. _____

    b. _____

    c. _____

    d. _____

    e. _____

    f. _____

    g. _____

8. Write six dependent conjunctions in the spaces below.

    a. _____

    b. _____

    c. _____

    d. _____

    e. _____

    f. _____

9. Circle the prepositions and underline the objects of the preposition.

   a. Alexander will go with you in the corporate jet to a conference for high achievers.

   b. Gregory filed the records under the wrong name in the wrong folder.

   c. They went into the city by bus and then dined at an expensive restaurant.

   d. The staff wanted to attend the meeting and see the fantastic view of the city from the conference room window.

10. Underline the prepositional phrases and circle the prepositions.

   a. Victoria looked at the return address and threw the envelope into the trash.

   b. Courtesy in the workplace means the practice of kindness and consideration toward other employees and customers.

   c. Advertising has a profound influence on the behavior of people and on their lifestyles.

   d. Do you know the difference between a dream and a goal?

   e. Fax the letter from your office to my home.

   f. Radio advertisers are experts at producing spot announcements for their customers.

11. What part of speech is *fish* in each of these sentences?

   a. Let's go to the fish market. _____

   b. We'll fish every day while we're on vacation. _____

   c. We'll have a fish dinner every evening. _____

   d. Dietitians say that fish is a healthful food. _____

12. The word *trade* may be a noun, an adjective, or a verb. What part of speech is *trade* in each of the following sentences?

   a. Would you like a career in international trade? _____

   b. That was not a fair trade. _____

   c. I will not trade that stock. _____

   d. He reads several trade papers. _____

13. Write a sentence using *reading* as the part of speech listed.

   a. verb _____.

   b. noun _____.

   c. adjective _____.

14. Write two sentences using *plant* as the parts of speech listed.

    a. verb _____ .

    b. noun _____ .

15. Change the incorrectly used adjectives to adverbs; write the correct form in the blank.

    a. He is sure going to win the salesperson of the year award again.

    _____

    b. We're real disappointed about losing the Dell account.

    _____

CHECK YOUR ANSWERS ON PAGE 436.

POSTTEST

Fill in the blanks with the name of the part of speech.

1. To name persons, animals, things, ideas, places, times, or activities, use a/an _____ .

2. To show or suggest action or state of being, use a/an _____ .

3. To describe a verb, adjective, or adverb, use a/an _____ .

4. To begin a prepositional phrase, use a/an _____ .

5. To describe a noun or pronoun, use a/an _____ .

6. A prepositional phrase may not include a/an _____ .

7. The coordinating conjunctions are _____ .

8. *Because* is an example of a _____ conjunction.

9. A word that substitutes for a noun is called a/an _____ .

10. *I*, *me*, *my*, *mine*, and *myself* are examples of _____ .

CHECK YOUR ANSWERS ON PAGE 438.

Self-Study and Practice Tutorials

wordPOWER

Build your workplace vocabulary and improve spelling skills by completing the exercises in Appendix B on page 352.

Supplementary Practice Exercises

For additional practice, complete the Appendix C exercises for this chapter on page 393.

© Yuri Arcurs/Fotolia

After completing Chapter 3, you will be able to do the following:

- Identify the elements that make a complete sentence.
- Recognize independent and dependent clauses and essential and nonessential phrases in sentences.
- Recognize and correct sentence fragments, run-ons, and comma splices.
- Use writing techniques for achieving variety and interest in sentence construction.

3

Sentence Fundamentals

career connection

THE IMPORTANCE OF GOOD WRITING

Between emails, texts, and Tweets, our society spends a lot of time communicating via the written word. We spend more time writing in our professional and personal lives than we probably imagined we would back in school. What you may not realize is that these written exchanges can boost your career or hinder it, depending on how you treat them.

Lilia Fallgatter, an author and e-learning consultant, has enough experience as a hiring manager in higher education to know that writing skills affect every career.

"How you write speaks volumes about you," Fallgatter stresses. "Incorrect grammar, spelling, punctuation and usage make a bad impression and can affect your credibility on the job. With the advent of text messaging, instant messaging and social networking sites such as Twitter, more people are abandoning the rules of writing. The use of abbreviations and failing to use capitalization and punctuation are extremely informal and do not translate well to the professional setting."

Fallgatter is quick to point out that, all things being equal, in a showdown between two job applicants, she'll choose the better writer.

Even emails deserve attention. All business communications should be treated with some level of professionalism. Although not every email is a letter to the CEO [Chief Executive Officer], don't forget that these messages can be forwarded to anyone. In a culture where emails are more prevalent than face-to-face conversations, your writing is the face of your professional image.

Source: Excerpted from "The Importance of Good Writing" by Anthony Balderrama, © CareerBuilder.com, 2009. Reprinted with permission.

PRETEST

Fill in the blank to correctly complete the sentence.

1. To be a complete sentence, a group of words must have a
   _____ and a _____, and it must
   _____.

2. The parts of speech that may be the subject of a sentence are
   _____ and _____.

3. The part of speech that acts as the predicate of a sentence is a
   _____.

4. Subjects and verbs must agree in _____ and
   _____.

5. A group of words that has a subject and a verb is a
   _____.

6. A clause that has a subject and a verb and can stand alone as a
   complete thought is _____.

7. A clause that has a subject and a verb but cannot stand alone is
   _____.

8. A word group lacking the basic sentence requirements but capitalized
   and punctuated as a sentence is a _____.

9. Two independent clauses that are not joined with punctuation result in
   a _____.

10. Two independent clauses that are joined by a comma
    without a coordinating conjunction or a semicolon result in a
    _____.

CHECK YOUR ANSWERS ON PAGE 438.

Sentence Basics

Written workplace communications must be clear, correct, logical, concise, and courteous. This sounds like a lot to achieve, but it isn't so hard when you approach it one sentence at a time. From sentences, you build paragraphs, and from paragraphs, you build a message that achieves your goal.

This chapter focuses on how to achieve the basic goal of writing sentences that will make it easy for readers to understand your message. You will learn how to correct some common sentence errors that prevent writers from achieving their objectives and some techniques for making your writing more engaging for your reader.

PROBLEMS YOU WILL AVOID WITH POLISHED WRITING

- Readers are distracted by an error and lose focus on the message's important content.
- Readers must write or phone for clarification, thus wasting their time and yours.
- Readers misunderstand a message, and the result is a failed or an incorrect transaction.
- Readers feel frustrated trying to figure out a poorly written message when other tasks are competing for their attention, creating negative feelings toward you.
- Readers get the impression that the company you work for is not efficient, knowledgeable, or competent.

WRITING COMPLETE SENTENCES

A **sentence** is a group of words that expresses a complete thought. To be complete, a sentence must have the essential elements that make it a sentence: a **subject** and a **verb** (a **predicate**). The subject tells *who* or *what* is doing the action. The predicate is a verb that describes the action or state of being of the subject.

The Subject

The subject may be one word (the **simple subject**)—a noun or pronoun—or a group of words that includes modifiers (the **complete subject**). The following subjects in bold type identify *who* or *what* the sentence is about.

Who	**Mr. Estevez** is our newest call center supervisor.
	He received the promotion after two years as a customer service representative.
	Do **you** want to improve your pronunciation and vocabulary?
What	**Learning** a second language takes time and effort.
	To stop now would be a mistake.
	A very simple solution to the problem is to study harder.
What and Who	**A good textbook** can help you learn a foreign language, but **you** also need to listen to native speakers on the radio, on television, and in films.

All of the above sentences are statements. In a statement that tells someone what to do—called a **command** or **polite request**—*you* is understood as the subject.

(You) Leave the file on my desk.

(You) Let me know when you want to meet.

(You) Send me the report by close of business today.

Often commands are expressed more courteously by adding "please," but the subject is still *you.*

(You) Please show your identification to gain access to the elevators.

writing**TIP**

Keep in mind that the writing process is a series of steps that begins with a draft. Your sentences might not be perfectly constructed at first. Always write the first version with the idea that you will revise, edit, and proofread.

The Verb (Predicate)

A sentence must have at least one **verb** that expresses action (such as *go, walk, provide*) or state of being (such as *is/are/am, was/were, be/been*). A **helping verb** sometimes precedes the main verb that expresses action, having, or being.

> We **opened** the new building on January 6. [action verb]
>
> Ms. Hirsch from Green Investments, Inc. **will be** our financial consultant. [being verb]
>
> The crime **was** embezzlement and the punishment **fits** the crime. [being and action verbs]
>
> They **will** both **speak** at the annual meeting in Omaha. [helping plus action verb]
>
> Most successful companies **operate** with honesty and social responsibility. [action verb]
>
> **Does** he **know** Jonathan Edwards **is** the CEO? [helping plus action and being verb]

Subject-verb agreement is a key element of writing correct sentences. This means that verbs must agree with their subject in person and number. To make sure the verb agrees with the subject in person and number, you have to first be able to correctly identify the subject. Remember what you learned about the parts of speech and the different roles they play in sentences. A word that is a noun or a pronoun *may not* be the subject of the sentence. For example: *The nature of birds is to sing.* In this sentence, *nature* is the subject; *birds* is the object of the preposition *of*; therefore, *is*, not *are*, is the correct verb to use. You will study subject-verb agreement in depth in Chapter 9.

Clauses in Sentences

The difference between a short sentence and a long sentence is the number of clauses and phrases. To correctly write and punctuate sentences, you need to understand these sentence parts.

A **clause** is a group of words in a sentence that has a subject and a verb. A clause may be either dependent or independent. Every sentence must have at least one **independent clause**, a word group that has a subject and verb and can stand alone as a complete thought that makes sense. Otherwise, it is not a sentence. A dependent clause, on the other hand, has a subject and a verb, but it *cannot* stand alone as a complete sentence. It depends on other parts of the sentence to give it meaning and should not be treated as a sentence—beginning with a capital letter and ending with a period or other end-of-sentence punctuation.

In the following example, *Stock prices continue to fall* is an independent clause with a subject (*prices*) and verb (*continue*) that express a complete thought.

> **Stock prices continue to fall**, even though the economic indicators are strong.

The second part of the sentence, *even though economic indicators are strong*, is a dependent clause. It has a subject (*economic indicators*) and a verb (*are*), but without the first part of the sentence, it does not express a complete thought.

Not a sentence   *When* we classify people by the kind of work they do.

This dependent clause has a subject and verb but does not make sense because it is an incomplete thought. When editing your writing, look for dependent clauses masquerading as sentences (word groups that begin with a capital letter and end with a period or other end-of-sentence punctuation). It is easy to catch them if you look for dependent conjunctions. The word *when* is a **dependent conjunction** in the above example. Remember, conjunctions join sentence parts. You need to connect the dependent clause to an independent clause. Another option is to reword the dependent clause to make it a complete thought. Here is an alternative:

> When we classify people by the kind of work they do, we run the risk of misjudging them.

WORDS THAT FUNCTION AS DEPENDENT CONJUNCTIONS

after	before	since	until	whether
although	even though	so that	whatever	while
as	if	though	when	why
as long as	once	unless	where/whereas	
because	provided that	unless as	wherever	

Phrases in Sentences

A **phrase** is a group of words that may contain a subject or a verb *but not both*. Phrases play different roles in sentences. They can function as subjects, verbs, and modifiers. A phrase acting as a subject or a verb is an **essential phrase**—without it, the sentence will not make sense. A phrase functioning as a modifier may be essential, or it may be a **nonessential phrase**.

Essential phrase   **To skip breakfast** is a sure way to feel tired by lunchtime.

To skip breakfast is a phrase functioning as the subject of the sentence; it is essential to the meaning.

Nonessential   **On my way to work** I had an idea for a new way to save the company money.

On my way to work is a nonessential phrase functioning as a modifier of the subject *I*. It is a prepositional phrase that is not essential to the meaning of the sentence.

writing**TIP**

Recognizing phrases in sentences and the roles they play helps you avoid writing incomplete sentences.

GO TO PAGE 51 AND COMPLETE WORKSHEET 3.1.

Types of Sentences

Clauses and phrases add meaning and interest to a sentence by providing **variety** in sentence length and level of complexity. By varying your sentence structure, you make your writing more engaging for the reader. Knowing where to place phrases and clauses puts the emphasis where you need it to make your message clear. For example, dependent conjunctions such as *when, even though, although,* and *until* introduce clauses that add explanation to the main thought of the sentence.

Think about the continuum of writing style from a simple beginning reader for children starting school to a college-level textbook. In children's books, all the sentences are short and easy to understand. At the college level, you sometimes have to read a complex sentence two or more times before you can understand it. Good business writing lies somewhere in between these extremes. You want to be understood easily, but you don't want your writing to sound so simple that your reader is turned off. You want to sound "businesslike" but not too wordy or bureaucratic to be understood.

Think about the following sentence types as you write. These categories are based on how many and what kind of clauses a sentence contains. Being aware of this helps you analyze your writing to achieve a good mix of conciseness, clarity, variety, and interest. This is a skill that good writers have in their bag of tricks. You can acquire this skill by editing your writing. Sometimes it helps to read sentences out loud. Lack of clarity often sounds louder in your ears than it does when reading silently to yourself.

In the following examples of different sentence types, independent clauses are underlined once; dependent clauses are underlined twice.

1. A **simple sentence** has only *one independent clause*. A simple sentence can be long or short.

   I give tours of our facilities.

   I give tours of our packaging and shipping facilities to groups of business owners from our overseas operations.

2. A **compound sentence** has *at least two independent clauses*.

   My job is challenging, but I enjoy every minute of the workday.

Both clauses could stand alone, but they read better when joined. Compare: My job is challenging. I enjoy every minute of the workday.

3. A **complex sentence** has *one independent clause* and *one or more dependent clauses*.

   After I complete my bachelor's degree, I plan to go to graduate school.

   After I complete my bachelor's degree, I plan to go to graduate school, even though it will be expensive.

4. A **compound-complex sentence** has *at least two independent clauses* and *one or more dependent clauses*.

   I can't afford to go to graduate school full time, but my company will pay tuition if I take job-related courses, even though my major is unrelated.

ADDING VARIETY AND INTEREST TO YOUR WRITING

Consider joining independent clauses.

Original   Jane likes to work. She is almost a workaholic.
Revised   Jane likes to work, but she is almost a workaholic.

Consider combining two short simple sentences by making one of the clauses dependent.

Original   Jane likes to work. She needs to get more rest.
Revised   Although Jane likes to work, she needs to get more rest.

Avoid repetitive construction.

Original   Write in code. That is how you convey the information secretly.
Revised   By writing in code, you convey the information secretly.

Original   The dean's office is next to the reception room. It is on the first floor.
Revised   The dean's office is next to the reception room on the first floor.

Original   Measuring industrial output is relatively easy. Measuring an education system's output is difficult.
Revised   While measuring industrial output is relatively easy, measuring an education system's output is difficult.

Original   Some manufacturers engage in wholesale trade. They are not regarded as wholesalers. Their primary function is that of manufacturing.
Revised   Some manufacturers engage in wholesale trade. They are not, however, regarded as wholesalers because their primary function is manufacturing.

Ending Sentence Punctuation

Using the correct punctuation to end sentences might seem obvious because you've been doing it in everything you've written for many years. Nevertheless, a review here will remind you about the rules that can provide that extra touch of confidence in the correctness of your writing.

THE PERIOD

Use a period after a **statement** or **command**:

Statement: We emailed the invoice last week.
Command: Take the guests to the reception area.

Also use a period after a courteous request or indirect question. A **courteous request** means action is desired. It may or may not sound like a question, but in either case, it does not call for a reply. An **indirect question** is a statement that sounds like a question.

Courteous request: Please sign and submit the form within five days.
                          Would you please send me the original document.

Indirect question: I asked whether or not it is true that you are leaving the company.

THE QUESTION MARK

Use a question mark after a direct question. A **direct question** calls for a reply.

Direct question:	Will you pay the bill this week or next?

Capitalize and use a question mark after a shortened form of a question, which in grammar is known as an **elliptical question**. Capitalize each question.

Elliptical question:	Do you intend to return my deposit? If so, when?
	What transportation do you want to take to the airport? The shuttle? A limo? Let me know.

Use a question mark after a sentence that might be considered presumptuous or discourteous if punctuated as a courteous request.

Request:	Would you please approve my request for vacation leave?

In an email to your supervisor, you might want to word the request as a question. If directed to a peer, you can end it with a period.

THE EXCLAMATION POINT

Use an exclamation point at the end of a sentence to express strong feeling. Also use an exclamation point at the end of an interjection.

Oh, no!

Please send your check today!

Congratulations!

Let's get this done today!

Now that's what I call a great presentation!

An exclamation point following a statement, command, or courteous request enables the reader to sense strong emotion or urgency. If the words are spoken instead of written, voice and facial expressions transmit the strong feeling to the listener.

GO TO PAGE 52 AND COMPLETE WORKSHEET 3.2.

writing**TIP**

An exclamation point is often used in advertising and sales writing. It is not used often in other workplace writing. With overuse, such as several sentences in succession, the exclamation point loses effectiveness. Also avoid using an exclamation point to emphasize how wonderful, cute, or funny your words are—they should speak for themselves.

Avoiding Common Sentence Errors

Many people have trouble editing their own writing because they can't recognize their mistakes. This section helps you recognize the common mistake of writing a group of words that looks like a sentence but is not.

SENTENCE FRAGMENTS

A **sentence fragment** is a word group beginning with a capital letter and ending with an end-of-sentence punctuation mark but lacking the key elements—a subject and a verb forming an independent clause that is a complete thought.

writing**TIP**

Fragments are sometimes written intentionally and are acceptable in some forms of writing—short handwritten notes, informal emails, and even formal writing in the fields of creative writing and journalism. In most business writing, fragments are to be avoided.

One type of fragment is a dependent clause capitalized and punctuated as a complete thought. You can correct this error by deleting the dependent conjunction and beginning the next word with a capital letter.

Fragment	When she completes her culinary degree at the end of the month.
Sentence	~~When~~ She completes her culinary degree at the end of the month.

Another way to correct a fragment is to add an independent clause before or after the dependent clause.

Sentence	When she completes her culinary degree at the end of the month, Sherri hopes to get a job in the hotel industry.
OR	Sherri plans to work at a resort hotel when she completes her culinary degree at the end of the month.

The examples below show the different ways you can turn a fragment into a complete sentence and express the thought clearly and interestingly. Dependent clauses are underlined.

grammar**TIP**

Commas will be discussed more in-depth later in the course. For now, though, understand that when a sentence begins with a dependent clause, use a comma after the clause. No comma is needed when the sentence ends with the dependent clause—as in the second and fourth examples.

Since prices will continue to fall, competition will get stronger.

Competition will get stronger since prices will continue to fall.

Although websites are now easier to create, well-trained people still command high salaries.

Well-trained people still command high salaries although websites are now easier to create.

COMMA SPLICES AND RUN-ONS

Now that you understand how to handle sentence fragments, you need to know how to avoid two other common types of sentence errors: the comma splice and the run-on sentence. Run-ons and comma splices occur when you incorrectly join two or more independent clauses.

A **run-on sentence** occurs when independent clauses are not joined by a connecting word (a coordinating conjunction) or punctuation (for example, a semicolon).

A **comma splice** occurs when you join two or more independent clauses with a comma but without a coordinating conjunction.

Run-on	Chad suggested this item we approved it.

Nothing joins the independent clauses.

Comma splice	Chad suggested this item, we approved it.

Only a comma joins the independent clauses.

Correction	Chad suggested this item **and** we approved it.

You can correct a comma splice or run-on by making the two independent clauses separate sentences or by joining them with a coordinating conjunction (*and, but, or, nor, for, so,* or *yet*).

Here are more examples:

Run-on	Use gestures to reinforce your message don't cross your arms.
Comma splice	Use gestures to reinforce your message, don't cross your arms.

Correction	Use gestures to reinforce your message. Don't cross your arms.
	Use gestures to reinforce your message, but don't cross your arms.
Run-on	Pop culture is part of our society there is no escape.
Comma splice	Pop culture is part of our society, there is no escape.
Correction	Pop culture is part of our society. There is no escape.
	Pop culture is part of our society and there is no escape.
Run-on	Arnold said the recession is over employers are stepping up their hiring.
Comma splice	Arnold said the recession is over, employers are stepping up their hiring.
Correction	Arnold said the recession is over because employers are stepping up their hiring.

There are two additional ways to avoid run-ons and comma splices: Insert a semicolon alone or a semicolon followed by a **transitional expression** (for example, *however* or *therefore*) to join independent clauses.

Comma splice	Chad suggested this item, we approved it.
Correction	Chad suggested this item; we approved it.
	Chad suggested this item; *therefore*, we approved it.

Change one of the independent clauses to a dependent clause; then the word group is not a run-on or comma splice.

Correction	Since Chad suggested this item, we approved it.

PUTTING IT ALL TOGETHER

- A **complete sentence** has a subject, a verb, and is an independent clause. A word group—a dependent clause or a phrase—lacking these sentence requirements is a **fragment**.
- Both a **run-on** and a **comma splice** consist of independent clauses joined *without* a coordinating conjunction *or* a semicolon.
- A comma joins the independent clauses of the comma splice—but not the run-on. Other correct commas, however, may be elsewhere in the sentence.
- To avoid a run-on or comma splice, do one of the following:
  - Separate independent clauses with a period followed by a capital letter.
  - Join independent clauses with a comma and coordinating conjunction.
  - Join independent clauses with a semicolon, either with or without a transitional expression following the semicolon.
  - Make one of the independent clauses dependent.

Coordinating conjunctions:	*and, but, or, nor, for, so,* and *yet*
Transitional expressions:	*also, however, therefore, in fact, furthermore, in addition, nevertheless, otherwise, consequently, that is*

GO TO PAGE 52 AND COMPLETE WORKSHEET 3.3.

Checkpoint

You have learned the following concepts that are essential to writing complete sentences. As you apply this knowledge to your writing, you will be able to spot errors more easily and make corrections that improve the quality of your writing.

- A sentence must have a subject and a verb (a predicate) and must be an independent clause.
- A clause is a word group with a subject-verb combination. It may be independent or dependent. A fragment is an incomplete idea masquerading as a sentence since it begins with a capital letter and ends with a period.
- A run-on is two or more independent clauses with neither punctuation nor a coordinating conjunction between the clauses.
- A comma splice has a comma between the independent clauses of a run-on.
- You can add variety and interest to your writing by varying the type and the length of your sentences.

communications connection

THE WRITING PROCESS: DRAFTING

In Chapter 2 you focused on the planning aspect of the writing process. When it's time to begin writing, always start with the idea that you will revise. Even the most experienced writers make changes on their drafts. Your thoughts will flow more smoothly if you write quickly and get all your thoughts down without stopping to make changes or reorganize.

As your sentences flow, develop paragraphs based on the key points you want to cover. Keep in mind that readers don't like to be confronted with long blocks of text. Breaking content into paragraphs provides a structure for the information, and this aids reading and understanding. Each paragraph needs an opening sentence that introduces the main idea, followed by supporting statements that provide details.

As you draft, try to develop an **opening**, a **body** (the main content), and a **closing**. Opening and closing paragraphs are often short—sometimes just one or two sentences is enough. A brief and clear opening tells the reader what the communication is about and is followed by the main message. A closing sentence or short paragraph might briefly summarize key points, express appreciation, or directly state what you want the reader to do.

WRITING PRACTICE

Practice drafting without stopping to make changes or reorganize by writing three or four paragraphs about why you selected the occupation that you are in or are planning to enter. Complete the planning and organizing steps of the process before you begin to write (refer to Appendix A). Approach your subject in any way you wish. Here are some suggestions: You might choose to compare your choice to other options you have considered. Are you sold on the choice you have made, or would you consider making a change to an area where there might be more opportunity? What are the things that you find most attractive about the field you have chosen? What do you think the drawbacks might be?

Date to submit this assignment: _____

PROOFREADING PRACTICE
More Proofreading Tips

1. Use your spell checker, proofread from the screen, and make corrections before printing.
2. Proofread again from printed pages.
3. Proofread for sense, not just for spelling and correctness.
4. Don't rely on anyone else's accuracy or skill when a document is your responsibility. When someone has prepared a document for you, do not approve, submit, or sign the document until you proofread it yourself.
5. Remember, everyone makes errors, but successful people find and correct their own errors before anyone else finds them.

Use proofreading marks or the online text of this article on career preparation to correct spelling and typographical errors, poor sentence construction, and other errors that your spell checker will not find. Change punctuation *only to correct a run-on, comma splice, or fragment.* Keep the wording as is.

Career Planning—Know the Marketplace You Plan to Enter

You should know what's going on in your field of interest start keeping abreast of facts and trends long before you jump into the marketplace. What sourcs should you use? Most fields have professional journals or newsletters in print and online. Which provide "insider" information on what's new and important. Websites of trade organizations and government agencys are also good sources.

Also, your local newspaper's busness section will contain articles on a board range of businesses and their activities. You never know what type of business and industries will be feature, therefore reading the paper daily—in print or online—is a plus. You may find a company profile useful when you're ready for interviewing, another article may forecast job opportunities or salary trends. Other sections of the newspepar might be relevant to your interest as well perhaps you want to work in the sports, entertainment, food, or travel industries. Many newspapers have sections and regular columns devoted to these topics. if yours does not, check the many career websites online they advertise jobs nationwide and many websites also cover the job market trends and opportunities in different states.

Start a career planing file for sources of information about your field or industry now, you'll be glad you did when it comes time to apply for jobs.

How did you do? Excellent _____ Good _____
Need More Practice _____

chapter review

WORKSHEET 3.1

A. Subjects tell who or what the sentence is about. Verbs tell what the subject does, is, or has. Write the subject(s) and the verb(s) in the blanks. One sentence has the "understood subject" *you*. Another has two subjects and two verbs.

	Subjects	Verbs
Example: The new assistant is in the office now.	assistant	is
1. The director could have filmed the scene much faster.	_____	_____
2. You must be computer literate to get a good job.	_____	_____
3. The winner sees an answer for every problem.	_____	_____
4. The loser sees a problem in every answer.	_____	_____
5. The books were put on the shelf.	_____	_____
6. What you earn depends on what you learn.	_____	_____
7. The new members of the team have uniforms.	_____	_____
8. Three visitors arrived yesterday.	_____	_____
9. Please give me the ledger.	_____	_____
10. Professor Friede found five errors.	_____	_____

B. A clause is a word group with a subject and a verb. Each item below is a clause. Six clauses are independent and six are dependent. Follow these instructions: (1) In the blanks, write *I* for **independent** or *D* for **dependent**. (2) Cross out the word that makes the clause dependent and then make the clause independent by adding capitalization and closing punctuation. (3) Change the independent clauses to sentences using the proofreader's mark for capitalization.

Example: D ~~since~~ the new assistant didn't know the meaning of *chronological*.

_____ 11. she couldn't arrange the reports in chronological order.

_____ 12. because many organizations have similar problems with employees.

_____ 13. although an information technology professional needs excellent communication skills.

_____ 14. in the workplace you may converse with many people.

_____ 15. since they have limited English skills.

_____ 16. don't laugh at someone's pronunciation or grammar errors.

_____ 17. when the trucker arrived with the shipment.

_____ 18. it's better than I thought.

_____ 19. although she prefers driving to flying.

_____ 20. after you've learned a few phrases in other languages.

CHECK YOUR ANSWERS ON PAGE 438.

WORKSHEET 3.2

A. Use proofreading marks to revise these sentences by adding a dependent conjunction that makes one clause dependent. Correct punctuation where needed.

Example: A company finds its high stock price is discouraging new investors,ₛₒit might initiate a stock split.

1. The future is that time when you'll wish you had done what you're not doing now you cannot undo the past.

2. He places big orders with us, his sales rep gives him a special discount.

3. The plant was operating on a 24-hour basis, management refused to adopt a three-shift schedule.

4. Professor Bailey explained that studying business communication at Wright Business School is enjoyable, the new student wouldn't believe it.

5. Vanessa said we need the latest dictionary for Chapter 3 language changes constantly.

B. Add periods, question marks, and exclamation points; correct comma splices with periods and capital letters.

6. I wonder whether he uses voice recognition software

7. The report is good, but where is the appendix

8. Would you please send these items by overnight mail to us

9. A winner says he fell, a loser says somebody pushed him

10. Management makes important policies and decisions; we just carry them out

11. Do you know what a subprime mortgage is

12. Would Thursday be more convenient for you

13. Take advantage of this deal today

14. Would you please fax this report before you go to lunch

15. I heard you got a new job that's wonderful

CHECK YOUR ANSWERS ON PAGE 439.

WORKSHEET 3.3

Write **R** for run-on, **CS** for comma splice, or **C** for correct sentence. Underline the dependent conjunctions. Insert corrections as needed.

Example: C When you buy more shares of stock, you increase your voting power at the corporation's annual meeting.

_____ 1. A workaholic is a person who is addicted to work.

_____ 2. He knows the definition of *workaholic*, even though he is not a person who is addicted to work.

_____ 3. The highest achievers are passionately committed to their work they are not workaholics.

_____ 4. Although the highest achievers are passionately committed to their work, they are not workaholics.

_____ 5. The highest achievers are passionately committed to their work, although they are not workaholics.

_____ 6. High achievers take more short vacations than the average person, they often get new ideas for their work during these vacations.

_____ 7. Studies show that taking time off to relax results in a more productive workforce many employers often have to remind their employees to use their earned vacation leave.

_____ 8. Workaholics work long hours because they fear losing the job or not impressing the boss favorably.

_____ 9. Because high achievers feel a strong sense of commitment to their work, they work long hours.

_____ 10. High achievers define skills needed for their career and set out to get them.

_____ 11. Observations about high achievers are from Charles Garfield's book *Peak Performers*, Mr. Garfield studied hundreds of top achievers.

_____ 12. Always leave a job on good terms, for you may need a reference in the future.

_____ 13. During an interview, don't forget to ask *your* questions also remember to thank the interviewer for the appointment.

_____ 14. Listen attentively during an interview make eye contact with the interviewer.

_____ 15. Human Resources directors are skilled at asking questions that cannot be answered by a simple "yes" or "no."

_____ 16. The winters are long and cold in Indianapolis, but this gives IVY Tech students more time to study.

_____ 17. "Love competence in the performance of your tasks begin now."—Lao Tzu

_____ 18. A rolling stone gathers no moss, yet it does get a certain smoothness from its rolling.

_____ 19. "Mix a little foolishness with your serious plans it is lovely to be silly at the right moment."—Horace, Roman Poet and Philosopher (He wrote it correctly.)

_____ 20. Turn left at the corner of Boston Boulevard and Woodward Avenue, which is not a violation of traffic rules during most of the day.

CHECK YOUR ANSWERS ON PAGE 439.

POSTTEST

Write **C** for correct, **R** for run-on, and **CS** for comma splice. Then use proofreading marks to make corrections with a comma and one of the seven coordinating conjunctions (*and, but, or, nor, for, yet, or so*).

Example: ____R____ You can vote in person by attending a corporation's annual meeting‸ you can vote by using an absentee ballot.

(or)

_____ 1. Professor Wayne was able to repair the motor quickly, he has had no formal training in mechanics.

_____ 2. He didn't notice any of the errors, there was no way he could have corrected them.

_____ 3. The Human Resources Department is on the third floor the interviewers are out to lunch now.

_____ 4. The new equipment is being shipped to you at once, you should receive it by the end of the week.

_____ 5. Possibly Joyce can attend the conference maybe Michael can go in her place.

_____ 6. We need to send a gift to the new client, I have no idea what it should be.

_____ 7. Goods are delivered either to the receiving area of a department store or to the central warehouse of a chain.

_____ 8. "Experience is an expensive school, but fools will learn in no other."—Benjamin Franklin

_____ 9. Anthony is the new accountant in our office he is not a CPA.

_____ 10. We often avoid planning, the difference between achieving and not achieving is goal setting.

CHECK YOUR ANSWERS ON PAGE 440.

Self-Study and Practice Tutorials

word**POWER**

Build your workplace vocabulary and improve spelling skills by completing the exercises in Appendix B on page 354.

Supplementary Practice Exercises

For additional practice, complete the Appendix C exercises for this chapter on page 396.

Mastering the Art of Good Writing

recap—chapters 1–3

Test your mastery of Unit 1 by completing these exercises. Your instructor will provide the answer key or have you submit your work for scoring.

A. DICTIONARY SKILLS

Number right: _____ **out of 25**

Fill in the blank with the correct answer.

1. What is the name of your dictionary? _____

2. What does a lexicographer do? _____

3. Dictionaries *describe* how English is used. They don't *prescribe* how to use English. (a) true _____ (b) false _____

4. To interpret the abbreviations used in your dictionary, look in the _____

5. If you're having difficulty thinking of just the right word for something you're writing, look up a related word in a _____

6. If you need help with writing business documents, a business _____ will help you.

7. *Abstract* is used as what parts of speech? _____

8. The treasurer (dispersed/disbursed) all the funds. _____

9. What does the abbreviation ILGWU mean? _____

10. Like *Webster* in dictionaries, the famous name in thesauruses is _____

11. What do you find in a thesaurus? _____

12. Which syllable has the primary accent in the preferred pronunciation of *incomparable*: first, second, third, fourth, fifth? _____

13. Using a college dictionary or a thesaurus, find a synonym (word with a similar meaning) for *incongruous.* _____

14. What was the nationality of the poet and playwright Dante? _____

15. Is a college dictionary abridged or unabridged? _____

16. *Disinterested* and *indifferent* mean the same. (a) true _____ (b) false _____ (c) maybe _____

Referring to your dictionary, divide these words into syllables by rewriting the word and drawing a diagonal (/) at the end of each syllable. For a one-syllable word, draw the diagonal at the end.

17. worked _____

18. getting _____

19. contagion _____

Name: _____ **Date:** _____

20. beetle _____

21. fullness _____

22. Write a brief definition obtained from your dictionary for the following:

    a. prepotent _____

    b. pisciculture _____

    c. effusive _____

    d. primavera _____

23. Correctly pronounce a, b, c, and d above.

24. What does it mean if a word *doesn't* have a usage label? _____
_____

25. What is the definition in your dictionary for *bombed*, and what is the slang or colloquial meaning for *bomb*? _____
_____

B. PARTS OF SPEECH

Number right: _____ **out of 25**

Insert suitable nouns in the blanks.

1. The _____ insisted on giving difficult tests to all the _____.

2. The _____ in Lake _____ is extremely deep.

3. _____ wrote an excellent _____.

4. _____ was a conscientious _____.

5. Our _____ is closed on _____.

Insert suitable pronouns in the blanks.

6. Paralegals _____ are word processing experts get the best jobs.

7. Thank _____ for faxing _____ resume.

8. _____ wrote to us about _____.

9. If _____ goes wrong with _____ plans, we'll blame _____.

10. Give _____ to _____ wants or needs _____.

Insert suitable verbs in the blanks.

11. Many Americans _____ another language in addition to English.

12. Vince _____ the letter and then _____ it.

13. In Sweden don't _____ your beverage until the host _____ "Skoal."

14. Diablo Valley students _____ the float that _____ the prize.

15. The IRS _____ our tax return and _____several errors.

Insert suitable adjectives in the blanks.

16. The _____ photocopier is _____ to use.

17. Please make _____ reservations for a _____ show.

18. Professor Taylor had an _____ plan for teaching the Vietnamese language.

19. The _____ chairs and the _____ desk look _____ in your _____ office.

20. Write a _____ report outlining your _____ plan.

Convert these adjectives to adverbs.

21. happy _____

22. joyful _____

23. real _____

24. busy _____

25. generous _____

Name: _____ **Date:** _____

C. SENTENCE FUNDAMENTALS

Number right: _____ **out of 25**

Fill in the blank with T for True and F for False.

_____ 1. To be a sentence, a group of words needs only a subject and a verb.

_____ 2. The predicate of a sentence and the verb are the same.

_____ 3. An independent clause can stand alone as a complete sentence.

_____ 4. If a dependent clause is joined to an independent clause, the result is a comma splice.

_____ 5. A clause is a word group with a subject and a verb.

_____ 6. A phrase is a word group with a subject and a verb.

Fill in the blanks.

7. A noun or pronoun that tells who or what a sentence is about is called the _____.

8. A word that tells what the subject does, is, or has is what part of speech? _____

9. A word group beginning with a preposition that has no subject or verb is called a _____.

10. A clause beginning with a dependent conjunction is called a _____.

11. A comma between the independent clauses of a run-on creates a _____.

12. Two independent clauses joined with a semicolon can create a _____.

13. A _____ is a group of words that begins with a capital letter and ends with a period, but is not an independent clause.

14. A phrase may be _____ or _____, depending on whether or not the sentence would have the same meaning without it.

Write F for fragment, S for sentence, R for run-on, and CS for comma splice.

_____ 15. Because of the establishment of this law.

_____ 16. The hanging of greens, such as holly and ivy, is a British winter tradition that originated before the Christian era.

_____ 17. We went to Paris for the holidays, the windows of department stores were filled with fabulous displays of animated figures.

_____ 18. In Mexico the home is decorated and ready to receive guests by December 16 that date marks the beginning of the Mexican Christmas celebration, *Las Posadas*.

_____ 19. Japanese businesspeople who understand English say it is often difficult for them when Americans speak too fast.

_____ 20. Thanking you for your attention to this problem.

_____ 21. She is the purchasing manager and he is the assistant manager they run a very efficient operation.

_____ 22. Hoping to hear from you soon.

_____ 23. She is the purchasing manager, he is the assistant manager.

_____ 24. When working at the computer, take frequent breaks before you get too tired.

_____ 25. Do desk work for no more than 30 minutes at a time, then take a mini-holiday of one to two minutes.

Name: _____ **Date:** _____

writing for your career

FOCUS ON THE WRITING PROCESS

In this unit, you have focused on mastering the fundamentals of writing skills for today's marketplace. Written communications, both print and electronic, make the world of business go around. Reports, presentations, blogs, websites, Facebook pages, advertising and promotional materials, white papers, and proposals are all common vehicles for business communications today. This is what places writing among the top skills that employers look for. Employees who are effective communicators are vital to an organization's success and are often rewarded by career advancement.

Activities at the end of each unit in this text will provide you with an opportunity to learn more about writing business documents that are relevant to today's workplace. This unit has focused on the writing process. You have learned that the **writing process** steps are planning, organizing, drafting, revising, editing, and proofreading. You have already begun to use the process; now we will focus on the beginning steps in more depth.

PLANNING

As you learned in Chapter 2, whether you are writing a routine email message or a complex letter or report, planning is essential to clear and concise communication. Planning involves four key steps:

1. **Define Your Purpose**
   - Before you begin writing any communication, know what your precise purpose is and do not stray from it.
   - Use separate communications to deal with different subjects to make it easier for your reader to respond.

2. **Know Your Reader**
   - Target your communication to the needs of your reader.
   - Know exactly what you want from the reader and be explicit in your message if a specific action is being requested.
   - Use language that is familiar to your reader or define terminology if necessary.

3. **Plan Your Message**
   - Make notes or develop an outline to structure the organization of your message.
   - Break content into topics to provide a structure for the information; this aids reading and understanding.
   - Decide exactly how much detail is needed. Should you include factual data to support the information? The more complex your subject, the more you will need to think about and outline the details required.
   - Move topics around until you are sure the order is logical and will be clear to your reader.

4. Gather Quality Information

- Make sure your content is correct and adequate to achieve your purpose.
- Double-check numerical data, calendar dates, dollar amounts, spelling of names, and other such factual information, no matter how routine the communication might be.

DRAFTING

Begin writing with the idea that you will revise. Even the most experienced business writers make changes on their first drafts. Your thoughts will flow more smoothly if you write quickly and get all your thoughts down without stopping to make changes or reorganize. Keep in mind that length does not determine whether or not you need to revise. Sometimes the shortest message requires the most precise language, and this can often take more than one try to achieve. Here are the keys to effective drafting:

1. Develop Paragraphs

- Use your outline or planning document to identify paragraph breaks based on the key points you want to cover.
- Begin each paragraph with a **topic sentence**—an opening sentence, that introduces the main idea—followed by supporting statements that provide details.
- Keep in mind that readers don't like to be confronted with long blocks of text. In the revision stage, review each paragraph and look for places to break up long blocks of text.
- As you draft, formulate your content into three main sections: an opening, a body, and a closing. A brief and clear **opening** tells the reader what the communication is about. The **body** contains the main message. The **closing** can be a sentence or short paragraph that briefly summarizes key points, expresses appreciation, discusses next steps, or directly states what you want the reader to do. Opening and closing paragraphs are often short—sometimes just one or two sentences is enough. An example follows.

Subject:	Shipping Confirmation – January 3 Order
Date:	1/5/20xx 8:52:14 AM Eastern Daylight Time
From:	customercare@goldgems.com
To:	rgoldman@xxx.com

Order Confirmation #57268
Dear Richard Goldman:

> Opening provides a brief introduction stating the reason for writing.

Thank you for shopping with us. The three dozen gold charms you ordered January 3 were shipped overnight today. Your order number is 57268. Your order is on its way and can no longer be changed. If you need to return an item from this shipment or manage other orders, please go to your <u>account</u> on goldcharms.com.

Body is broken into two paragraphs. Each provides details on a different topic.

The closing provides contact information and a courteous closing statement.

The attached order form provides details and the UPS tracking number for the package. This completes your order. We apologize for the delay due to the late arrival of our latest shipment, but we believe you'll be pleased with the rapid turnover of these delicately engraved charms.

We appreciate your business and look forward to continuing the relationship. Kim Silverstein, our sales representative, will be in to see you soon to show you our newest sterling bracelets—designed by Pagliano, the famous Italian silversmith. She will contact you within the next week to make an appointment.

Meanwhile, if you need any assistance regarding this order or another purchase, please contact me. I can be reached by calling toll-free 800-000-000 Monday-Thursday, 8:30 a.m. to 4 p.m., and Friday, 8:30 a.m. to 1 p.m. EST.

It is a pleasure doing business with you.

Sincerely,

Karen Jones
Manager, Customer Care
GoldGems, Inc.
jjones@goldgems.com

There is no "right" or "wrong" way to separate content into paragraphs, only good or poor judgment. The logical organization of your subject will determine the number and length of paragraphs. Avoid a "chopped-up" look of too many short paragraphs one after the other. Long paragraphs, however, look hard to read and discourage busy people from concentrating on the message.

2. Use a Friendly Tone

Compose business communications in a friendly, conversational tone, but use complete, clear sentences and Standard English. Today, business writing style is getting more informal than ever before. Even so, modern business writers may find themselves going out of their way to use bureaucratic language that will make them sound "businesslike." This is exactly the opposite of good workplace writing. These guidelines will help you achieve an appropriate tone for most audiences:

- Avoid words with many syllables. Instead, select words that deliver your message clearly and completely and that help build a good relationship between you (and your company) and the reader.

- Don't attempt to sound impressive by adopting a stiff, formal tone. This just makes writing come across as pretentious, and it detracts from clarity.

- Use straightforward language that says exactly what you mean. This style can boost productivity (you will compose more quickly), improve customer relations, and reduce costs caused by misunderstandings.

- Avoid "antique" jargon: *We/I trust, aforementioned, aforesaid, herein, hereto, herewith, in due course of time, for your perusal … This will acknowledge your request for … I am writing to inform you … This is to advise you …*

- Modern style experts advise taking the "just-say-it" approach: *Attached are … Enclosed is … In response to your request we are … We have reviewed your proposal … Thank you for …We received …*

Here are some additional examples that will give you a feel for avoiding stiff (and wordy) writing and adopting a friendly tone:

Antique	Our organization sincerely regrets any inconvenience caused you by our inadvertent miscalculation of the amounts on our invoice No. 2482.
Modern	We apologize for the error on our Invoice No. 2482.
Antique	This letter is to advise you that the merchandise you ordered is out of stock. We regret to inform you, therefore, that we cannot fulfill your requested order at this time, but it will remain pending until we are able to make shipment on the anticipated date of March 1.
Modern	Thank you for your order for one dozen gold birthday charms. Although we are temporarily out of the charms, we expect them from our factory the first week in March. We'll rush them to you as soon as they arrive.

REVISING

After finishing the draft, read it and make improvements on screen, then print and reread it. At this stage, you might make content changes, such as moving paragraphs or sentences around for a more logical flow. You might decide to add or remove details and check the accuracy of factual information.

Ultimately, you will check for faults based on all of the principles you have learned so far and the ones in the chapters to come. The following are a few more ways to avoid pitfalls that are common to workplace writing. Knowing how to find these faults and correct them will help you polish your writing even further.

3. Use Clear Language

Writing that uses too many words will lose your reader's attention. Wordy writing is similar to bureaucratic writing because it often results when you attempt to "sound official" instead of using simple, everyday language. Many wordy expressions are also commonly used, and we tend to pick them up because we see or hear them frequently.

Always aim for clarity and conciseness by editing wordy phrases. Here are a few examples of expressions to avoid—along with suggestions for writing concisely and clearly without sacrificing courtesy.

AVOID	USE
allow me to introduce myself	I am *or* state business without introduction. The signature of your correspondence (letter or email) should include your name and title. In letters, company information is available in the letterhead; in emails, include your company name.
I am writing to *or* This letter will inform you	Omit this type of introduction and open with the rest of the statement.
In the near future	soon *or* a specific date
At your earliest convenience	Omit, be specific, *or* give approximate time
Don't hesitate to call *or* Please feel free to call	Please call

AVOID	USE
We regret to inform you that	We're sorry that
Allow me to state that	Omit; just make the statement
May I take the liberty of	Omit or just do it
We are in receipt of	We received *or* Thank you for
Attached please find	Here is/are, Enclosed is/are, Attached is/are
reached the conclusion	concluded
for the purpose of	to, for
in a satisfactory manner	satisfactorily
utilize	use
in the event that	if
due to the fact that	because

When planning your communications, consider the amount of time needed to go through the revision process. It takes time and care to cut excess verbiage from business communications and academic writing, such as term papers. Blaise Pascal, an eminent 17th-century French philosopher and mathematician (for whom Pascal computer language was named), ended a letter to a colleague with these words: "I have made this letter so long only because I have not had the time to make it shorter."

4. Use Concise Language

Concise writing means that each word contributes to the purpose of the message. This is the opposite of **redundant writing**, which is the purposeless repetition of words or ideas. Unless repetition is for special effect, express an idea just once. Compare these examples of redundancy and how they were revised:

Original   It is absolutely essential that each and every widget be round in shape.

Revision   Each widget must be round.

Original   The consensus of opinion is that although the object is 4 feet long in size, we can see it visually from a distance of 50 feet.

Revision   We believe that although the object is 4 feet long, we can see it from 50 feet.

Original   We requested final completion of the project by the year 2014.

Revision   We requested completion of the project by 2014.

Change redundant expressions to concise ones:

REDUNDANT	CONCISE
advance planning	planning
all throughout	throughout
cooperate together	cooperate
final outcome	outcome
free gift	gift
my personal opinion is	my opinion is *or* I believe
new innovation	innovation
past history	history

REDUNDANT	CONCISE
repeat again	repeat
return back	return
round in shape	round
true facts	facts
visible to the eye	visible
whole entire	whole *or* entire [never both]
the color yellow	yellow

5. Emphasize the Positive

People respond best to positive ideas. Even if you have something negative to write about, you can often find a positive way to express it. Try to write about what you or your company *can* do, not what you *can't* do.

Negative	We cannot conduct this seminar with fewer than ten students.
Positive	We can conduct this seminar with ten or more students.
Negative	We're sorry we can't extend more than $3,000 credit to you.
Positive	We are pleased to extend to you a $3,000 credit line.
Negative	We do not give refunds without a receipt.
Positive	Merchandise may be returned for a full refund when accompanied by a receipt.

Please refer to these guidelines and Appendix A, Writing, Editing, and Proofreading Guidelines throughout the course as you work on improving your writing.

recap—writing for your career

Write T (true) or F (false) in the blank.   **Number right:** _____ **out of 25**

_____ 1. Good writers follow specific paragraphing rules.

_____ 2. The first and last paragraphs of written communications are often the shortest.

_____ 3. Most communications written in the workplace don't require any planning.

_____ 4. For the sake of time, try to write only one draft whenever possible.

_____ 5. Even routine communications require fact checking.

_____ 6. Long, businesslike words give readers the impression you are well educated.

_____ 7. Conversational-style writing should be avoided in business communications.

_____ 8. In workplace writing, it is more important to get to the point than to spend time worrying about relationships.

_____ 9. Business writing is more informal than it used to be.

_____10. To be sure a message states your policy clearly, stress what your company cannot do.

Rewrite the following sentences to sound to eliminate excess verbiage.

11. I am writing to inform you that I have received the book that you sent me, and I sincerely appreciate your kindness. _____

12. In accordance with your request, we are herewith enclosing the price list. _____
_____

Use a positive tone to rewrite these negatively expressed sentences.

13. We hope you will not be disappointed. _____

14. We are not open after 8 p.m. on weekdays or on weekends after five. _____
_____

15. You can't have a refund. We only give gift cards on returned merchandise. _____
_____

Rewrite these sentences to eliminate the redundancies.

16. We want to suggest to you that first and foremost you pack each and every basic essential. _____
_____

17. Final completion of the research investigation revealed and showed that the UFO is small in size, triangular in shape, and purple in color. _____

Name: _____ **Date:** _____

Improve the following sentences according to the principles you have learned.

18. This letter is to advise you that the parts you ordered were shipped today via overnight air by FedEx. _____

19. We believe you won't have any trouble with our newly designed products. _____
_____

20. We have forwarded the price list to you by fax. If you have any questions about any of the items, please do not hesitate to contact us at your earliest convenience. _____
_____

21. I am of the opinion that the event is well attended whenever it is held during the month of December. _____

22. I would like to request that you please repeat the instructions again. _____

23. Please advise us as to whether or not you can attend by responding to this invitation no later than June 15. _____

24. We are unable to fulfill your order for the Desk Master gift set until you remit payment in full in the amount of $165.08, plus shipping in the amount of $7.95 by check, money order, or credit card as indicated on the attached order form. _____
_____
_____

25. I am writing to let you know that we are in receipt of your letter of application and that we appreciate your interest in working for GreenCities.com. _____
_____

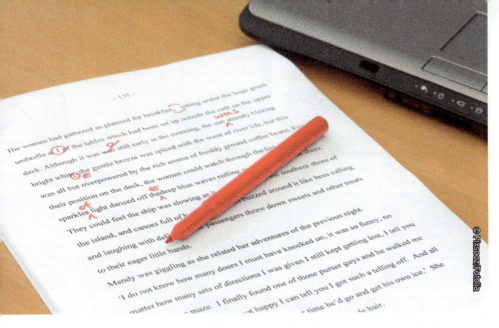

Knowing Your Subject

©FotolEdhar/Fotolia

After completing Chapter 4, you will be able to do the following:

- Follow the basic rules of forming noun plurals in your writing.
- Form plurals of irregular nouns.
- Form plurals of proper names and words adopted from foreign languages.
- Form plurals of compound nouns by using the dictionary when needed.
- Apply your writing skills to a team writing project.

4

Nouns: Forming Plurals

career connection

WHAT DO EMPLOYERS LOOK FOR IN A RESUME?

Beyond the candidate's ability to meet standard criteria—having the "right" major or work experience—employers are most likely to look for evidence that the candidate is able to work in a team. According to the National Association of Colleges and Employers (NACE), nearly 80 percent of employers search for evidence that the potential employee can work in a team, and more than three-quarters indicated they want the resume to show that the candidate has leadership abilities and written communication skills.

This information comes from NACE's *Job Outlook 2012* survey, in which problem-solving skills and a strong work ethic round out the top five "soft skills" that employers look for on resumes. "In fact," says Edwin Koc, NACE director of research, "overall, results show that the ability to work in a team is the number one soft skill employers seek in their new hires." Consequently, job candidates need to showcase that ability in their interactions with employers, not just on the resume, but in the interview as well.

The survey showed that employers look for evidence of the following when screening resumes:

1. Ability to work in a team
2. Leadership skills
3. Written communication skills
4. Problem-solving skills
5. Strong work ethic

NACE offers more resume advice in "Write the Right Resume" at http://bit.ly/NACEResumeHelp.

Source: Job Choices 2012—Business, National Association of Colleges and Employers,© 2011.

PRETEST

Spell the plurals of these nouns. For words with two correct spellings, write both in the blank.

1. cabinet   _____

2. ally   _____

3. injury   _____

4. resource   _____

5. facility   _____

6. tattoo   _____

7. domino   _____

8. accessory   _____

9. alto   _____

10. potato   _____

CHECK YOUR ANSWERS ON PAGE 441.

Basic Rules of Noun Plurals

In Chapters 2 and 3, you learned that nouns function in sentences as the subject: they tell *who* or *what* is doing the action. They also function as objects of the verb; that is, they receive the action of the verb. In addition, nouns act as the object of the preposition in prepositional phrases.

This chapter covers how to form plurals of nouns. Knowing noun plurals will enable you to spell them correctly and use the right form of the noun in writing grammatically correct sentences. These are the basic rules:

- The plural form of nouns is formed in most cases by adding *s* or *es*:

    business/businesses   tax/taxes   check/checks   candle/candles

- Nouns that end in *y* preceded by a consonant change the *y* to *i* and add *es*:

    country/countries   baby/babies   industry/industries

- Some nouns do not have plurals:

    honesty   ethics   helpfulness   work   math

- Some nouns change their spelling to form the plural:

    child/children   loaf/loaves

THREE EXCEPTIONS TO *S* AND *ES*

Every rule has exceptions and these are three important ones:

- Nouns ending in *y*: if a **vowel** (*a, e, i, o,* and *u*) precedes *y*, simply add *s*.

    valley/valleys   attorney/attorneys   turkey/turkeys

If a **consonant** (all letters other than vowels) precedes *y*, change the *y* to *i* and add *es*.

industry/industries   company/companies   hobby/hobbies

- Nouns ending in *o*: if a vowel precedes the *o*, add just an *s*.

studio/studios   rodeo/rodeos   radio/radios

If a noun ends in *o* preceded by a consonant, look it up to find out whether to add *s* or *es*.

memo/memos   domino/dominos/dominoes (both are correct)
tomato/tomatoes   potato/potatoes
banjo/banjos   solo/solos

- Nouns ending in *f*: no useful rules determine how to spell plurals of nouns ending in *f*. When in doubt, check the dictionary because some simply add *s*, and others change the *f* to *v* and add *es*.

rebuff/rebuffs   chief/chiefs   belief/beliefs
wife/wives   knife/knives

Irregular Nouns

Many nouns do not follow the basic rules. They form their plurals in irregular ways. Committing these plural forms to memory is the best way to avoid misspelling. The following are the main categories of irregular noun plurals.

- The spelling changes: some irregular nouns change their spelling to form the plural:

woman/women   mouse/mice   tooth/teeth   foot/feet

- The spelling does not change: some irregular nouns are spelled the same whether they are singular or plural:

aircraft   British   deer   fish
Japanese   series   statistics

The **British are** accustomed to rowdy debates in Parliament.

British is a term used to describe natives of England.

A **series** of lectures **is** being planned for the spring semester.

The network's new TV **series have** received good reviews.

- Spelling can be singular or plural: some nouns ending in *s* are singular or plural, depending on the meaning. Your dictionary shows which meanings are singular and which are plural. If one of these nouns is the subject of a sentence, be sure to choose the correct verb form.

politics   species   economics   mechanics

The **politics have** often outweighed common sense.

Politics is the focus of my World History course.

writing**TIP**

Check your dictionary when you are unsure about spelling a plural. Typically, the plural is not listed for nouns that just add *s* or *es*. When plurals are irregular, you sometimes find two spellings in the dictionary; use the one listed first.

GO TO PAGE 77 AND COMPLETE WORKSHEET 4.1.

writing**TIP**

Check some of these words in your dictionary; notice that the word is repeated following the abbreviation *pl*. This tells you that the plural spelling is the same as the singular. For some irregular nouns, dictionaries show two correct plurals—either without an *s* or with it—like "deer n. pl. deer, *also* deers." Choose the first spelling when you see the word *also*, as you learned in Chapter 1.

grammar**TIP**

Do not add an apostrophe to make nouns or all-capital letter abbreviations plural.

- Some nouns ending in *s* are always singular, while others are always plural:

  Always singular: *news*   *aeronautics*

  Always plural: *scissors*   *proceeds*

The latest **news is** that the statistics are completely bogus.

Scissors are an item that airport security will likely confiscate.

Aeronautics is the principal industry in that town, and the **proceeds** from it **have** doubled.

Proper Nouns

Proper nouns are names of specific people, places, and things. To make a proper noun plural, you can usually just add *s* or *es*, but there are a couple of important "don'ts" to remember:

- Do not add an apostrophe or change the spelling of a name (proper noun) to form a plural even though it may end in *y*, *o*, or *f*. To form the plural of *wolf*, you change the *f* to *v* and add *es* to get *wolves*. But if you mean *Mr. and Ms. Wolf*, you wouldn't say, "The Wolves are coming for dinner," but, rather, "The Wolfs are coming to dinner."
- Never use an apostrophe to form the plural of a proper name.

  Four hundred **Taylors** are listed in the telephone directory.

  The **Lopezes** have a new website for their business.

"Adopted" Nouns

The English language has many words that we have "adopted" from other languages. Some of these words follow the spelling rules of their original language. Sometimes an English plural spelling has been adopted as well; then we have two plurals to choose from. It is helpful to know both forms as they may have different uses. Check your dictionary for pronunciation and usage of foreign plurals.

PLURALS OF WORDS ADOPTED FROM FOREIGN LANGUAGES

Singular	Original Language Plural	Singular Ending	Plural Ending	English Plural
formula	formulae	a	ae	formulas
alumnus	alumni	us	i	alumni
stimulus	stimuli	us	i	stimuli
analysis	analyses	is	es	analyses
diagnosis	diagnoses	is	es	diagnoses
criterion	criteria	on	a	criteria or criterions
phenomenon	phenomena	on	a	phenomena
curriculum	curricula	um	a	curriculums
memorandum	memoranda	um	a	memorandums
addendum	addenda	um	a	addendums

Reading widely gives you more exposure to words like the examples in the preceding chart so that you will more easily remember how to spell them. When in doubt, consult your dictionary. If a word has two plurals that mean the same, use the one appearing first in the dictionary entry.

Here are a few adopted nouns that cause common errors:

- *Formulae* is used in scientific and technical communication, but otherwise use *formulas*.

- *Criteria*, not *criterions*, is the preferred plural in American English usage. One *criterion is*, but two *criteria are*.

- *Data* and *media* are now widely used as both singular and plural forms and are accepted as singular in some newer dictionaries.

GO TO PAGE 78 AND COMPLETE WORKSHEET 4.2.

Compound Nouns

A noun made up of more than one word is a **compound noun**; for example, *high school*. Compound nouns are written as one word, as two or more words with a hyphen, or as separate words: *handbook, tie-in, time clock*. The following guidelines apply:

- To form the plural of compound nouns spelled as one word, usually add *s* or *es* to the end of the word—unless the noun is irregular.

  bookcases   spoonfuls   headlines   businesswomen (irregular)

- To form the plural of compound nouns with a hyphen between the parts, you need to know the correct spelling or consult the dictionary to find out which part to make plural.

  sister**s**-in-law   letter**s** of credit   write-off**s**   trade-in**s**

  If the dictionary shows two ways to form the plural, choose the first.

  notaries public or notary publics

- To form the plural of compound nouns with no hyphen, follow the general rules of forming plurals. Dictionaries generally do not list compounds that are not hyphenated.

DICTIONARY CODE FOR COMPOUND NOUNS

In the dictionary the spelling of compound nouns is indicated as follows:

- A dot or accent mark with no space between the parts means it is written as one word. The dot or accent mark indicates syllables.

- A space between the words or no dictionary entry means they should be written as separate words.

- Use a hyphen only if you see a hyphen between the parts of the dictionary entry.

grammarTIP

Do not confuse compound nouns that are always hyphenated with words that form compound adjectives when modifying a noun. For example, the words *up to date* are not hyphenated unless they modify a noun: *The monthly report is up to date*; but, *The up-to-date monthly report is ready.* You will learn more about hyphenation of adjectives in Chapter 10.

Compound nouns change over time from being separate words to hyphenated words to one word as they become a part of everyday usage. *Basketball*, *handheld*, and *website* were originally separate words. As each became more popular, the spelling changed. Our language is always evolving in spelling and usage. Reading will help you keep up with changes.

GO TO PAGE 79 AND COMPLETE WORKSHEET 4.3.

Checkpoint

You have learned the basic rules of noun plurals. Most nouns form the plural by add *s* or *es*. Nouns that end in *y* change the *y* to *i* and add *es*. Irregular nouns don't follow these basic rules. The spelling may or may not change, and some are always singular or always plural. You've reviewed irregular plural spellings and pronunciations and forming plurals of compound nouns. You have also learned to recognize plurals of words that English has adopted from other languages. The words you've studied in this chapter point out how helpful it is to continue relying on your "dictionary habit" and expanding your reading as a means to developing a broader vocabulary.

communications connection

TEAM WRITING THAT WORKS

In the workplace, a team effort is often required to produce important communications, such as reports, proposals, and presentations. The team effort might be formal, with each team member being assigned a responsibility for certain parts of the finished product. It might also be informal, with the person who is primarily responsible relying on colleagues for facts and figures or to check a draft to ensure quality and accuracy.

Following are key points to think about when working with a team on a writing project:

1. Who is responsible? Will one person take the lead, or will the communication be broken into parts with different writers taking the lead on each part?

2. What is the role of each team member? Is one person assigned the task of drafting with others having input, or will the writing be divided among team members?

3. What information is each person to provide? When?

4. What is the style and format desired for the finished product? If different people contribute, determining a consistent style and format up front makes less revising and editing work in the end. For example, should charts and graphs be used? If one section has charts or graphics to display information clearly, and other sections have only text that might be better presented with graphics, your end result

will confuse your audience. You want your reader or viewer to have a seamless reading or listening experience—not to feel like the pieces of a puzzle have been put together.

5. Who will edit the final draft of the document? At least one team member should be assigned to edit the document for continuity and consistent writing style.

6. How will reviewing be handled? Should all team members review each draft? How much time will be allowed for reviews and revisions? Creating a seamless communication that is free of errors is more likely when you take advantage of having multiple reviewers.

7. What is the deadline? All team members should agree on and be aware of the timeline. Having a timeline does not just mean the due date for the completion of the project. It also means breaking the project into stages and developing due dates for each stage. This will help to ensure that the team functions smoothly from the beginning to the end of the project.

WRITING PRACTICE

Work with a partner or a team of three or four to write a set of instructions on how to do something that requires multiple steps. The audience is a person who does not know how to do the task. The explanation must be clear enough that your reader could perform the task by following your written instructions. Choose something that you and your team members understand or something you are interested in researching, such as how to get a role as an extra in a film, how to paint a mural, how to prepare a complete meal for guests, or how to find a good internship.

Assign roles that fit the team members' individual expertise and interests. Decide on the medium that will work best (oral, written, or a combination), and follow the guidelines above for planning and developing the project. In the drafting and revising stage, be sure to check writing style for complete sentences with smooth transitions and variety in the length and structure of sentences. Also make sure sentences are clear, concise, logical, and grammatically correct.

Date to submit this assignment: _____

PROOFREADING PRACTICE

Any time you write a business letter or email message, absolutely error-free copy is required. Proofreading is challenging because it requires concentration on so much at the same time: errors in spelling, word choice, meaning, noun usage, numbers, capitalization, and consistency (did you treat like things alike?).

If you proofread on your screen, start by running your spell-checker and make needed corrections. Next, either on the screen or in a printout, slowly read each line of type for sense, correctness, and clearness. Looking at each sentence individually focuses your attention.

The following is a sales letter sent as an email. Correct the noun errors, using proofreading marks or online. In addition, be sure that you make corrections in sentence structure based on what you learned in Chapter 3. (See the inside back cover of this book for proofing marks and Appendix A for proofreading guidelines.)

From: **Manny Kahlil**

To: **Carolina Gonzales**

Subject: **Partnering with 21st Century Office Interiors**

Dear Ms. Zonzales:

This is to follow up on our telephone conversation of September 21. Thank you for your interest in 21st Century Office Interiors, I hope you will make a decision to work with us. We can help your sales staff by providing you firm with a new dimension of client service—an inferior design tie in with the sale of office space and studioes, clients looking for new office facilitys often ask about computer desks, book-cases, ergonomincally designed chaires, and durable carpeting. Prices and availability of these items are the criterion on which they base there decision, this is were we come in to help close Gonzaleses sale. At no charge to you, we can furnish a complete office space to fit any type of floor plan you offer, this will be an important sales aid to you that will pay off in faster and increased sales.

We would be happy to met with you or one of your key sales representative's to provide more information and discuss how we might work together. Please give us a call the next time you have a client with an office furnishing need we will prove that a partnership with 21st Century would be mutually beneficial.

Sincerely,
Manny Kahlil
President
21st Century Office Interiors LLC
555-555-5555

How did you do? Excellent _____ Good _____
Need More Practice _____

chapter review

WORKSHEET 4.1

A. Spell the plurals of these nouns. For words with two correct spellings, write both in the blank. Have your dictionary handy.

1. itinerary   _____

2. portfolio   _____

3. ferry   _____

4. money   _____

5. wolf   _____

6. zero   _____

7. piano   _____

8. authority   _____

9. hero   _____

10. melody   _____

11. knife   _____

12. tariff   _____

13. proxy   _____

14. survey   _____

15. plaintiff   _____

16. wife   _____

17. chief   _____

18. cargo   _____

19. attorney   _____

20. memento   _____

B. In the blanks, write plurals of the nouns. See your dictionary if in doubt about common nouns (those beginning with lowercase letters). Some of these plurals are spelled the same as their singular form.

Example: Perkins <u>Perkinses</u>

1. corps   _____

2. economics   _____

3. deer   _____

4. George   _____

5. series   _____

6. Chinese   _____

7. Jones   _____

8. aircraft   _____

9. fish   _____

10. stepchild   _____

C. Write **S** or **P** in the blank to show whether the noun is singular or plural. If a noun may be used either way, write **S/P**. Consult your dictionary as needed.

Example: premises P̲

_____ 11. trousers

_____ 12. corps

_____ 13. mumps

_____ 14. statistics

_____ 15. news

D. Use the dictionary or word clues to decide whether the noun subjects (shown in bold type) require a singular or a plural verb. Then circle the correct verb for that subject.

Singular Verbs	is	was	has
Plural Verbs	are	were	have

Example: The new **pants** (was/were) shortened.

1. The **scissors** (have/has) sharp edges.

2. **Mathematics** (is/are) my favorite course.

3. These **statistics** (is/are) accurate.

4. The **proceeds** (was/were) counted yesterday.

5. All **earnings** from this show (are/is) being given to charity.

6. **Clothes** (is/are) all over the floor.

7. **Genetics** (is/are) an important field in modern science.

8. Each day's **news** (was/were) carefully edited.

9. Do you think **politics** (is/are) a subject to avoid discussing at a party?

10. Several lecture **series** (was/were) offered in anthropology.

CHECK YOUR ANSWERS ON PAGE 441.

WORKSHEET 4.2

A. With the help of your dictionary, spell the plurals of these words. If two plurals are correct, write both of them in the blank.

1. formula   _____

2. alumnus   _____

3. basis   _____

4. census   _____

5. criterion   _____

6. axis   _____

7. parenthesis   _____

8. crocus   _____

9. appendix   _____

10. concerto   _____

11. index   _____

12. analysis   _____

13. medium   _____

14. diagnosis   _____

15. bureau   _____

B. Write **S** or **P** to show whether these nouns are singular or plural. Use your dictionary.

Example: nucleus <u>S</u>

_____ 16. alumna

_____ 17. criteria

_____ 18. alumnus

_____ 19. data

_____ 20. hypotheses

_____ 21. kibbutzim

Circle the correct form.

Example: The (media/medium) is sometimes as important as the message.

22. Television is the preferred (media/medium) for our ad campaign.

23. How many (criterion/criteria/criterias) did they consider?

24. Many people forget to type the closing (parentheses/parenthesis).

25. Several (alumnus/alumni/alumna) attended the opening game.

CHECK YOUR ANSWERS ON PAGE 442.

WORKSHEET 4.3

A. Use your dictionary for help with spelling these compound nouns. All of them are shown here as one word. Show whether the expression is one solid word, a hyphenated word, or two or three separate words. Some dictionaries give more than one spelling for certain plurals; if yours does, include both.

	Singular	**Plural**
Example:		
notary public	notary public	notaries public/notary publics
1. followup	_____	_____
2. textbook	_____	_____
3. tradein	_____	_____
4. editorinchief	_____	_____
5. runnerup	_____	_____
6. spaceflight	_____	_____

7. headhunter   _____   _____

8. minorleague   _____   _____

9. chiefofstaff   _____   _____

10. volleyball   _____   _____

B. Test your spelling and vocabulary by filling in the blank with the noun that is defined. The first letter of each word is given.

Example: My sister's husband: <u>brother-in-law</u>

1. Nongender-specific words for *businessmen*: **b**_____
    b_____

2. One who starts a legal action: **p**_____

3. A compound noun meaning programs for use in a computer:
    s_____

4. The place where you work or live: **p**_____

5. Plural of publishing executive: **e**_____

6. Freight carried by a ship: **c**_____

7. The singular and plural of this military subdivision are spelled the same but pronounced differently: **c**_____

8. Carrying case for holding papers or a list of investments:
    p_____

9. Written authorization to act for another: **p**_____

10. A plural noun that means profits from a commercial or other venture; when the same word is a verb, the accent is on the second syllable: **p**_____

11. A travel plan: transportation, times, dates, hotels: **i**_____

12. An object that is a reminder of the past, such as a souvenir:
    m_____

13. Persons authorized to guarantee signatures on legal documents:
    n_____

14. The plural of chassis: **c**_____

15. Something we want more of at income tax time (compound noun):
    w_____

CHECK YOUR ANSWERS ON PAGE 442.

POSTTEST

Write the letter of the best answer in the blank. It's all right to use your dictionary.

_____   1. Stockholders mail in their (a) proxys (b) proxi (c) proxyes (d) proxies.

_____   2. Aeronautics (a) were (b) was my favorite subject.

_____ 3. They are our (a) alleys (b) allys (c) allies (d) alloys in the controversy.

_____ 4. Her (a) sister-in-laws (b) sisters-in-laws (c) sisters-in-law manage the office.

_____ 5. To import from Thailand, we need two (a) letters-of-credit (b) letters of credit (c) letter of credits (d) letters of credits (e) letter's of credit.

_____ 6. Both (a) secretarys (b) secretaries (c) secretarys' (d) secretary's seemed confident as they interviewed for the data control position.

_____ 7. The inventory indicates we have three (a) celloes (b) cello (c) cellos (d) cello's (e) cellos' in our Music Department.

_____ 8. Although James McCarthy is the president, three other (a) McCarthy's (b) McCarthies (c) McCarthys' (d) McCarthys are on the Board.

_____ 9. The (a) Jones's (b) Jones (c) Joneses (d) Jones' invited us to dinner.

_____ 10. The nouns (a) cargo and embargo (b) vertebra and chassis (c) addenda and appendix (d) tariff and bill of lading have almost the same meaning.

CHECK YOUR ANSWERS ON PAGE 443.

Self-Study and Practice Tutorials

wordPOWER

Build your workplace vocabulary and improve spelling skills by completing the exercises in Appendix B on page 357.

Supplementary Practice Exercises

For additional practice, complete the Appendix C exercises for this chapter on page 400.

© Goodluz/Fotolia

After completing Chapter 5, you will be able to do the following:

- Form possessives of singular and plural nouns.
- Form possessives of compound nouns.
- Correctly place the apostrophe when forming possessives.
- Expand your knowledge and use of business terminology.

5

Nouns: Forming Possessives

career connection

TAILORED RESUMES ARE IN

If you don't remember a time when desktops, laptops, and mobile computing devices didn't exist, ask an older adult to describe preparing a resume in those days. He or she will tell you that retyping a document was a cumbersome chore, and one perfectly prepared resume was used for all job interviews. In contrast, today's job seekers have word processing, which makes it easy to revise or tweak their resume for each new job opportunity. Tailoring your resume to the job, the company, and the industry can make the difference between you and another candidate who doesn't take the time to do so.

Remember the first step of the writing process: know your audience. Various industries have their own language—known as industry jargon—and they respect job candidates who are familiar with it. If you are stepping outside the boundaries of your major or exploring opportunities in multiple industries, make an effort to learn the terminology that companies and recruiters use in their job descriptions. Read industry journals, peruse websites, and talk to people in the field whenever possible. Visiting job expos and attending conferences are also great ways to learn industry language.

Also learn the correct pronunciation of jargon and the meaning of industry acronyms (words formed from abbreviations). Misuse, misspelling, or mispronunciation will negate the effort you have made. And remember, whenever you revise or update your resume, proofread the new version and have at least one other person proofread it as well.

PRETEST

Use proofreading marks to correct words with unneeded apostrophes and insert an apostrophe (') or apostrophe *s* ('s) where needed. Write C if the sentence is already correct.

_____ 1. Many boss's seem oblivious to whats going on with worker's.

_____ 2. A shoe manufacturer recently opened two stores on the citys south side.

_____ 3. His brother-in-laws manager has the training for the job.

4. Mens and boys clothes are on sale.

_____ 5. Mr. James companies boosted wages by 30 percent. (name is James)

_____ 6. The CEOs of 100 companies wrote to Ms. Perkins office. (name is Perkins)

_____ 7. We studied Knoxs proposal to offer perks like medical and life insurance to boost all our sales representatives commissions. (name is Knox)

_____ 8. *Whistlers Mother* hangs in the worlds most famous museum, the Louvre, in Paris.

_____ 9. The students texts were written by some of the worlds leading scholars.

_____ 10. The Onassis name was one of the shipping industry's most famous.

CHECK YOUR ANSWERS ON PAGE 443.

Forming Possessive Nouns

Possessive nouns show the relationship between two nouns. The first shows possession, or ownership, and the second shows who or what is being possessed. To form the possessive, just consider the first—the possessor—and decide whether it is singular or plural. This noun is the one that requires an **apostrophe** to show possession. (It doesn't matter whether the second noun—what is possessed—is singular or plural.) Both singular and plural nouns form the possessive with an apostrophe. This chapter reviews where to place the apostrophe. Here is the general rule to remember: Add an apostrophe before the *s* if the noun is singular; add an apostrophe after the *s* if the noun is plural.

Singular noun   **Springfield's** population is larger than I thought.

Tennessee's weather is a lot warmer than I expected.

The **chairperson's** report is very brief.

A **week's** vacation goes by too fast.

Plural noun	The **representatives'** speeches can be no more than five minutes.
	Soldiers' uniforms from past wars are on exhibit.
	Please deliver the **secretaries'** new desks by Friday.
	The citizens will not tolerate another **two years'** delay.

Keep in mind that when a plural noun ends in *s*, use the apostrophe only when you need to show possession.

Not possessive	The **brothers** are **investors** in private companies.
	Our **auditors** reported that the **accountants** made numerous **errors**.
Possessive	The **brothers'** investment in private **retailers'** parking structures is paying great dividends.
	Our **auditors'** report indicates that the **accountants'** errors were numerous.

PLURAL NOUNS ENDING IN *S*

Add only an apostrophe to make a plural noun that ends in *s* possessive.

The **dentists'** desks are on wheels.

The **witnesses'** statements are false.

Send the **technicians'** report to the lab.

Three **days'** work is needed to complete the job.

The **Hawkeses'** office is in Rock Springs.

PLURAL NOUNS THAT DON'T END IN *S*

If a plural possessive noun does not end in *s*, add *'s* to make it possessive.

Men's suits are very tailored this year.

The trustee controls the **children's** assets.

The **alumni's** contributions to the **Women's** Fund were small.

APOSTROPHE BEFORE OR AFTER?

When forming possessives, the general rule is that the apostrophe is placed before the *s* when the noun is singular and after the *s* when the noun is plural. This came about several hundred years ago when possession was expressed by using the pronoun *his* after the first noun. Instead of saying *the clerk's desk*, they said *the clerk his desk*. If you say this old-fashioned possessive form fast, you hardly hear the first two letters of *his*. Therefore, people began spelling the expression without the *hi*—*the clerk s desk*. Writers began to use the apostrophe to show omission of one or more letters, which is how we ended up with the form *the clerk's desk*.

If more than one clerk shared the desk, the original wording would have been *the clerks their desks*. This, in turn, was shortened to *the clerks' desks*—with the apostrophe after the *s* to show that *their* was left out after the plural word *clerks*.

grammarTIP

In Chapter 4, you added *s* to nouns to make them plural. Because the *s* also makes nouns **possessive**, be careful to avoid confusing plurals with possessives. To form the possessive of nouns, use an apostrophe (') and an *s*. Do not use an apostrophe in plural nouns that are not possessive.

This method still works for determining whether to place the apostrophe before or after the *s*: Once you've decided the noun is possessive, see whether it is singular or plural. If singular, put the apostrophe where *his* would have been in the 1700s. If plural, insert the apostrophe where *their* would have fit. Various singular and plural possessive relationships are shown below.

Singular	**Plural**
the **banker's** salary	**students'** books
Mr. Harris's daughter	the **Joneses'** twins
boy's toys	**women's** hats
Ohio's population	Midwestern **states'** population
Niagara Falls' weather	**tourist destinations'** weather
chair's report	**representatives'** speeches
a day's vacation	**two years'** delay

EXCEPTION TO THE APOSTROPHE RULE

Some proper names that have two or more syllables and end with an *s* sound awkward to pronounce if you add *'s* to show possession. In this case, you can use only the apostrophe. For one-syllable names, add the *'s*.

Mr. Seagrams' executive assistant	*not*	Mr. Seagrams's executive assistant
Joyce Simons' office	*not*	Joyce Simons's office
The Schwartzes' art gallery	*not*	The Schwartzes's art gallery

COMPOUND NOUNS

All words, including compound nouns (nouns made up of two or more words), form possessives at the end, not somewhere in the middle. If a compound singular noun is possessive, add *'s* to the end.

The reporters were amused by the **editor-in-chief's** remarks.

My **brother-in-law's** appetite amazes me.

Remember that some compound words become plural by adding *s* to the first word: *editors-in-chief, brothers-in-law.*

Newspaper reporters listened attentively to five **editors-in-chief's** speeches.

The *s* after *editor* makes the compound noun plural; the *'s* after *chief* makes it possessive.

My **brothers-in-law's** appetites amaze me.

The *s* after *brothers* makes the compound noun plural; the *'s* after *law* makes it possessive.

If a possessive sounds clumsy, reword the sentence to avoid the need for a possessive form.

writing**TIP**

Sometimes an organization's name sounds as though it should have an apostrophe, but some do and some don't. Always check organization names and write them exactly as the organization does.

Vons (a supermarket chain) has no apostrophe.

Macy's (the department store chain) has an apostrophe.

My **brothers-in-law's** huge appetites amaze me. [correct but clumsy]

Rephrase to sound less awkward:

I am amazed that my **brothers-in-law** have such huge appetites. *OR*

I am amazed that my **husband's brothers** have such huge appetites.

GO TO PAGE 91 AND COMPLETE WORKSHEET 5.1.

Possessives and Prepositional Phrases

A possessive noun can replace a prepositional phrase. Prepositional phrases (word groups beginning with a preposition) may convey the same meaning, but possessive nouns are more concise.

the **auditor's** friend	friend **of the auditor**
teachers' salaries	salaries **of the teachers**

When a possessive sounds natural, use it instead of a prepositional phrase. If the result seems awkward or changes the meaning, use a prepositional phrase. For example, *the interior of the house* sounds better than *the house's interior*.

The following examples show how replacing prepositional phrases with possessive nouns can make your writing clearer and more concise.

The records prepared **by the accountants** were taken to the **office of the secretary**.

The accountants' records were taken to **the secretary's office**.

In revising this sentence, the writer assumes that the reader will know the records were *prepared by* the accountant. If that were not the case, the first prepositional phrase should stand.

Is the **population of Nevada** smaller than the **population of Arizona**?

Is **Nevada's population** smaller than **Arizona's**?

In the second example, *population* is understood but not stated after *Arizona's*, thus avoiding needless repetition.

To find out whether to use an apostrophe and *s* (*'s*), reverse the order of the nouns and put *of* between them: **Carol's** brother—brother **of Carol**. If reversing the nouns and inserting *of* delivers the intended meaning, then the first noun needs an apostrophe: **Carol's** brother.

Checkpoint

You have learned a few basic rules that ensure accuracy when forming possessives. When you proofread your writing, keep these principles in mind:

- Use an apostrophe to make both singular and plural nouns possessive. Make a singular noun possessive by adding *'s*; make a plural noun that ends in *s* possessive by adding an apostrophe only; make a plural noun that does *not* end in *s* possessive by adding *'s*.

- Check to make sure the possessive is what you meant to write. To test for possessives, reverse the order of the two nouns and insert **of** between them (*aunt **of** Charlene* is *Charlene's aunt*).

- If a plural noun that ends in *s* is not possessive, do not use an apostrophe.
- If adding *'s* to a name with two or more syllables makes the word hard to pronounce, add an apostrophe only. (*Mr. Watkins' home is near mine* instead of *Watkins's*).

GO TO PAGE 93 AND COMPLETE WORKSHEETS 5.2 AND 5.3.

communications connection

WORKPLACE VOCABULARY POWER

According to the *Microsoft Encarta College Dictionary*, a maven is an "expert or a knowledgeable enthusiast of something." Be a wokplace vocabulary maven by reading the following sentences to increase your familiarity with the meaning, spelling, and pronunciation of these words that cut across industries. Then complete the exercise by writing the letter of the word in bold next to its definition. If you're unsure of a meaning or pronunciation, look it up in your dictionary.

1. Our bank's **(a) FDIC** insured account is ideal as an income **(b) CD**.
2. The **(c) annual report** provides details about our **(d) merger** with the June Company Department Stores.
3. We bought the **(e) stock** because we expect it to **(f) appreciate**, not **(g) depreciate**.
4. We have a **(h) deficit** because of all the **(i) downtime** on the new equipment.
5. The **(j) balance sheet** had already been **(k) audited** before the **(l) liabilities** were discovered.
6. His grandsons are the **(m) beneficiaries** of the **(n) mutual funds**.
7. This **(o) corporation** is very sensitive to its **(p) shareholders**.
8. The **(q) concierge** can provide a guest with an **(r) itinerary**.
9. One of his **(s) fringe benefits** is a **(t) 401k**, and another is a low-interest **(u) mortgage**.
10. **(v) Outplacement** is often helpful when a business is about to be **(w) liquidated**.
11. A **(x) CEO** has to answer to the company's **(y) board of directors**.

Insert the letter of the word that matches the definition.

a)	FDIC	i)	downtime
b)	CD	j)	balance sheet
c)	annual report	k)	audit
d)	merger	l)	liabilities
e)	stock	m)	beneficiary
f)	appreciate	n)	mutual funds
g)	depreciate	o)	corporation
h)	deficit	p)	shareholders

q) concierge
r) itinerary
s) fringe benefits
t) 401k
u) mortgage

v) outplacement
w) liquidate
x) CEO
y) board of directors

1. _____ Annual message to stockholders providing information about the financial status and progress of a corporation.

2. _____ To increase in value.

3. _____ Examination of financial records of a business to determine accuracy and honesty.

4. _____ Statement of assets, liabilities, and net worth as of a certain date.

5. _____ Chief Executive Officer—the head of a company or organization.

6. _____ Paid vacations, insurance coverage, pension plans, part-time college tuition fees, and so on, given to employees in addition to salary or wages.

7. _____ Certificate of Deposit—a written message from a bank to a depositor showing the percentage of interest to be paid during a specified time period.

8. _____ A person employed at a hotel or an apartment building to help the residents in various ways.

9. _____ A body of elected or appointed members who jointly oversee the activities of a company or organization.

10. _____ A body formed to act as a single entity operating under a charter granted by a state and authorized to do business under its own name.

11. _____ Federal Deposit Insurance Corporation—a US government corporation that protects bank deposits that are payable in the United States up to $250,000.

12. _____ Time during which equipment is unable to be used until it has been adjusted or repaired; also used generally to refer to time when one is not busy or not engaged in work.

13. _____ Shortage of money; the opposite of surplus.

14. _____ Joining of two or more businesses into a single body.

15. _____ Investment in a corporation that entitles holders to vote on various corporate matters and to share in the company's profits.

16. _____ Decline in value.

17. _____ The obligations or debts of a business or an individual.

18. _____ Professionally managed collective investments in various stocks and bonds.

19. _____ A detailed written schedule of activities, commonly used for travel and group activities.

20. _____ To close the affairs of a business and sell the assets; to turn assets into cash.

21. _____ A company's assistance in finding jobs for its employees who have been terminated.

22. _____ Owners of stock (or shares) in a corporation.

23. _____ A retirement plan for employees.

24. _____ A person designated to receive benefits from an insurance policy, a will, or a trust fund.

25. _____ Pledge of property (real estate) as security for a loan.

CHECK YOUR ANSWERS ON PAGE 443.

WRITING AND SPEAKING PRACTICE

With the brief assignment that follows, you will improve your business vocabulary, your general knowledge of the workplace, and your ability to speak and listen effectively on business subjects.

Assignment

1. Read a current article related to your field of interest. Select an article from a national newspaper or magazine (print or online), such as *The Wall Street Journal*, the business section of the *New York Times*, *Fortune*, or a specialized publication in your field.

2. Prepare a three-minute presentation to tell your classmates about what you read. For the writing part of this assignment, develop an outline and make notes about what you will say for each topic listed. Rather than writing out your whole speech, try to rely on your notes to deliver your talk in a conversational tone using your own words. If you need to use quotes from the article, make sure you tell your audience when you are quoting directly.

3. Select at least one word or concept from the article that might be unfamiliar to some students. Write the word or phrase on the board and give an easy-to-understand definition.

4. Make sure you know the meaning of all the words in the article and include explanation of any other terms that might not be familiar to your listeners.

5. Listen attentively and courteously to your classmates presentations.

Evaluation

Your classmates may critique your presentation on these criteria: clarity of your message, appropriate volume, eye contact, and overall manner of presentation.

Date to submit this assignment: _____

PROOFREADING PRACTICE

In addition to being up on your business lingo, you also need to have a degree of cultural competence, that is, familiarity with cultural icons associated with the mainstream, including famous works of art. Have fun with this short essay about a famous work of art and where you can go to see it. After completing the exercise, go online to read about these two cultural icons. Add eight apostrophes to this short essay and correct all other errors.

Whistler's Mother

In the worlds most famous museum, the louvre in Paris, hangs a painting by Americas celebrated artist, James McNeill Whistler. This paintings formal title is *An Arrangement in Gray and Black*, but it is better known by the simple name *Whistlers Mother*.

Studies have been made to explain this portraits almost universal appeal, but what criterias can an art critic use to judge a painting? Critics are not like scientists. They cannot set up controlled experiment's in which a number of stimulus are shot into subject's and data collected on the subjects reactions. No, an art critic relys on inner emotions and sensitivity when analyzing a painting. Analyses of a painting is very personal.

When you visit Paris and look at *WhistlersMother*, what will you see? Will you, like most of us, be left wondering about the source of this portraits greatness?

How did you do? Excellent _____ Good _____

Need More Practice _____

chapter review

WORKSHEET 5.1

A. Use proofreading marks to correct the use of the apostrophe and plural forms of nouns.

1. Mr. Smiths and Ms. Perkins assistants will tour New York Citys tallest buildings during a weeks vacation. (Her name is Pat Perkins.)

2. My son-in-laws business is as successful as my sons. (one son)

3. The meeting was held at my brothers office and both of the Martinez attended. (one brother)

4. The old saying, "Womens work is never done," is harmful to womens and mens roles in modern society.

5. His daughter-in-laws is bankrupt.

B. Some nouns in the following sentences are possessive, but the apostrophes are left out. Insert the apostrophe where it belongs and underline the noun that names what is possessed. Write **C** for "correct" if a sentence doesn't require an apostrophe.

Example: The artist's <u>books</u> were left in Mr. Fox's <u>office</u>.

_____ 6. The Byrneses have sent four altos to try out for the operas.

_____ 7. Our editors stories please his readers greatly.

_____ 8. His brothers-in-law manage the offices.

_____ 9. His brother-in-laws manager has been transferred to Guam.

_____ 10. The Schwartzes own property in the swamp lands of Brazil.

_____ 11. The attorneys offices are in new buildings.

_____ 12. South Dakotas resources are listed in the back pages of two almanacs.

_____ 13. Mens and womens clothing are on sale in all our stores today.

_____ 14. Have you shipped Ms. Lopezs orders yet?

_____ 15. One of the film industrys most talented directors, Steven Spielberg, lectures at UCLA.

_____ 16. The crews strength was spent in useless maneuvers. (one crew)

_____ 17. Californias gold mines were less profitable than its orange groves.

_____ 18. These vineyards supply more than 75 percent of this nations wine and raisins.

_____ 19. Mattel and Lego are among the worlds largest toy manufacturers.

_____ 20. The former Claremont Mens College is now simply Claremont College.

_____ 21. Oral communications on the job include making presentations, giving directions, and participating in meetings.

_____ 22. Toms new book was published by a world-renowned university press.

_____ 23. What was supposed to be several hours work took more than three days to do.

_____ 24. Important to James Cash Penneys success was how he treated employees.

_____ 25. Barbies worldwide fame is probably Mattels greatest success.

CHECK YOUR ANSWERS ON PAGE 443.

WORKSHEET 5.2

A. Write the singular possessive, the plural, and the plural possessive.

Singular	Singular Possessive	Plural	Plural Possessive
Example: lawyer	lawyer's	lawyers	lawyers'
1. representative	_____	_____	_____
2. week	_____	_____	_____
3. witness	_____	_____	_____
4. James	_____	_____	_____
5. country	_____	_____	_____
6. man	_____	_____	_____
7. Asian	_____	_____	_____
8. wife	_____	_____	_____
9. father-in-law	_____	_____	_____
10. congresswoman	_____	_____	_____
11. Jones	_____	_____	_____
12. family	_____	_____	_____
13. Webster	_____	_____	_____
14. hour	_____	_____	_____
15. Wolf (name)	_____	_____	_____
16. wolf	_____	_____	_____
17. organization	_____	_____	_____
18. boss	_____	_____	_____
19. woman	_____	_____	_____
20. child	_____	_____	_____

CHECK YOUR ANSWERS ON PAGE 444.

WORKSHEET 5.3

A. Insert an *'s* or just an *s* where needed, or write **C** for "correct." Show clearly whether an apostrophe is before or after the *s*. Make any necessary spelling changes to nouns. Do not change verb forms. Read for sense before correcting.

Example: Mr. Williams' book is the club's choice.

_____ 1. The Columbuses never dreamed Chris would become so famous.

_____ 2. Two years interest is due on the note.

_____ 3. Health is a persons most valuable possession.

_____ 4. Mens fashion change almost as quickly as women.

_____ 5. Be prepared to come at a minute notice.

_____ 6. Mr. Rokers signature was needed two day ago.

_____ 7. The store was having a sale on lady's coats.

_____ 8. The Jones estate in West Palm Beach is being renovated for the holidays.

_____ 9. Brunswick population has increased during the past five year.

_____ 10. Mr. Jenkins cubicle is next to the large conference room on the 10th floor.

_____ 11. Several coaches reports included details about their player health.

_____ 12. We studied Keats poetry in our literature class.

_____ 13. Montreal and Quebec are in Mr. Hendrix territory.

_____ 14. Three Marx brother film were shown on TV.

_____ 15. The hostess needs to stand at the doorway and call all the guest name .

B. Write sentences in which you shorten these phrases by using a possessive noun.

Example: son of Mr. Ames <u>Mr. Ames's son is the auditor.</u>

1. books of George _____.

2. wife of Mr. Adams _____.

3. vacation of a week _____
_____.

4. home of the Adamses/office of Mr. Adams _____
_____.

5. store of my sisters _____.

6. name of the server _____
_____.

7. problems of the members _____.

8. commissions of the salespeople _____
_____.

9. work of two years _____
_____.

10. studio of my mother-in-law _____.

11. words of Moses _____.

12. streets of Dallas _____.

13. report of the auditor _____.

14. notice of ten minutes _____.

15. expense accounts of the supervisors _____
_____.

C. Correct the following sentence and fill in the blank:

Student's who put apostrophe's into plain plural's will receive shock's when they get grade's on the examination's in a few day's. Remove _____ apostrophes from this sentence.

CHECK YOUR ANSWERS ON PAGE 444.

POSTTEST

Insert apostrophes where needed, delete unneeded apostrophes, and fix incorrect plurals. Write **C** for "correct" to the left of sentences needing no change.

_____ 1. The deans view is that your attitude needs drastic changes. [one dean]

_____ 2. Hiring 1,000 employees for the merger will add to the company's 22,000-member workforce.

_____ 3. Many Americans take their mothers out to restaurants on Mothers Day.

_____ 4. Yesterdays job skills cannot succeed in todays marketplace.

_____ 5. Green Interiors, Inc. has two weeks to accept or reject our companys offer.

_____ 6. My sister-in-laws public relations manager completed three years of college. [Two of my brothers' wives are partners and share a public relations manager.]

_____ 7. Yamada and Jones is one of the citys finest law firms.

_____ 8. Emily Jones reputation as a criminal lawyer is excellent.

_____ 9. The Information Technology Divisions ideas have the CEO attention in this company.

_____ 10. Send the proposal to the agencies presidents.

CHECK YOUR ANSWERS ON PAGE 445.

Self-Study and Practice Tutorials

wordPOWER

Build your workplace vocabulary and improve spelling skills by completing the exercises in Appendix B on page 359.

Supplementary Practice Exercises

For additional practice, complete the Appendix C exercises for this chapter on page 403.

© Michaeljung/Fotolia

After completing Chapter 6, you will be able to do the following:

- Use the correct forms of pronouns as subjects and objects in sentences.
- Identify different types of pronouns and correctly use them in sentences.
- Correctly form possessives of pronouns.
- Expand your knowledge and use of business terminology.

Pronouns: Types and Their Uses

career connection

PLAY UP YOUR EDUCATION CREDENTIALS

Kim Isaacs, Monster.com resume expert says you can use your resume's education section to outshine your competition. If you are unsure about the best way to present your education, here are some of Isaac's tips:

- Place experience before education if you have five or more years of experience related to your goal. Hiring managers will be more interested in your job accomplishments than your education.
- Place education before experience if you are a recent graduate or have fewer than five years of work experience. If you are changing careers and have continued your education to support your new goal, education should come first.
- If you are a student or recent graduate, list your grade-point average (GPA) if it is 3.0 or higher. Consider including a lower GPA if you are in a very challenging program. Add your major GPA if it's higher than your overall GPA.
- If you haven't completed your educational program, list the number of credits completed or the type of study undertaken. For example:

  College of Staten Island—Staten Island, New York

  Completed 90 credits toward a BA in political science, 20xx–20xx

Source: Kim Isaacs, Monster resume expert, "Put Your Education to Work on Your Resume," http://www.monster.com, May 2012.

PRETEST

Write the letter of the correct answer in the blank.

1. Please give it to _____.

   A) he and I

   B) him and I

   C) he and me

   D) him and me

   E) a or d

2. _____ students want more homework.

   A) We

   B) Us

3. Please give more assignments to _____ .

   A) us students

   B) we students

4. Is he older than _____?

   A) I

   B) me

5. Only Ms. Englehart and _____ use Excel regularly.

   A) you

   B) yourself

6. They voted _____ a bonus.

   A) theirself

   B) themself

   C) theirselves

   D) themselves

7. _____ on first base?

   A) Who's

   B) Whose

8. He can invite _____ he pleases.

   A) whoever

   B) whomever

9. _____ of you might find a job online today.

   A) Every one

   B) Everyone

10. Fullerton College opens _____ new building today.

   A) it's

   B) its

   C) their

   D) there

CHECK YOUR ANSWERS ON PAGE 445.

Pronoun Usage

Pronouns are so much a part of our everyday language that it hardly seems necessary to study them. The problem, though, is that our common usage has developed many habits of speech that are not Standard English when it comes to using pronouns. We hear them all the time to the point where, in some cases, it is the correct form that now sounds foreign to our ears. For example, is it "Her and I went to the movie" or "she and I"? While loose language is acceptable in many environments, poor usage in the workplace never is—even in "unimportant" messages. This in-depth review of types of pronouns and how to use them will help you clear up any habits of pronoun usage that don't conform to the expectations for workplace writing *and* speaking.

See the box that summarizes pronoun types and their definitions.

TYPES OF PRONOUNS

- **Personal pronouns** refer to people and things: *I, me, he, she, her, him, they, them, we, us, it, one*
- **Possessive pronouns** show possession: *my, mine, his, hers, yours, ours, our.*
- **Indefinite pronouns** refer to unspecified people and things: *all, many, everything, anything, several, many, nobody, few, somebody, everything*
- **Interrogative pronouns** are used to ask a question: *who, whom, what, which, whose*
- **Demonstrative pronouns** point to a noun or pronoun: *this, these, that, those*
- **Reflexive pronouns** refer back to the subject or a clause in a sentence: *myself, themselves, yourself,* and other words with the suffix *-self* or *-selves;* also *each other, one another*
- **Relative pronouns** join nouns (show the relationship) to other parts of the sentence: *that, which, who, whomever*

Personal Pronouns

Personal pronouns refer to people and things, for example, *I, you, me, he, she, it,* and *they.* The forms of these pronouns change, depending on the person or thing that is the reference, as follows:

- **first person**: refers to the person or people speaking or writing
- **second person**: refers to the person or persons spoken or written to
- **third person**: refers to the person(s) or things(s) spoken or written about

The forms of personal pronouns also change according to form of the noun they are referring to as follows:

- **singular**: one
- **plural**: more than one
- **masculine**: male gender
- **feminine**: female gender

PERSONAL PRONOUNS

First-person pronouns refer to the person or persons doing the speaking or writing:

Singular	I	me	my	mine	myself
Plural	we	us	our	ours	ourselves

Second-person pronouns refer to the person or people spoken or written to:

Singular or Plural	you	your	yours
Singular	yourself		
Plural	yourselves		

Third-person pronouns are the person(s), people, or thing(s) spoken or written about:

Singular Masculine	he	him	his	himself
Singular Feminine	she	her	hers	herself
Singular Neutral	it	its	itself	
Plural Neutral	they	them	their	theirs

Recognizing these categories of personal pronouns helps you choose the correct form of the pronoun to use. For example, you would not use a singular pronoun to refer to a group; you would also not use a masculine pronoun to refer to a female or vice versa. This is obvious, but keep in mind that when editing and proofreading your work, you are looking for your mistakes. Leaving the *s* off of a word changes it from plural to singular—something that is easy to overlook and an error that your electronic spell-checker will not detect.

PRONOUN CASE

The second important guideline for choosing the right personal pronoun is recognizing **pronoun case**. This is the grammar term that refers to the role a personal pronoun is performing in the sentence. While pronouns can function as subjects and objects as parts of speech, they do perform a third role, which is to show possession. The terms for these roles are as follows:

- **Subjective case**—a personal pronoun acting as the subject of a sentence (also called **nominative case**)
- **Objective case**—a personal pronoun acting as the object of a verb or preposition
- **Possessive case**—a pronoun that shows possession

Pronoun Case

Personal Pronouns	Singular			Plural		
Person	Subjective*	Objective	Possessive	Subjective	Objective	Possessive
First person	I	me	my, mine	we	us	our, ours
Second person	you	you	your, yours	you	you	your, yours
Third person	he, she, it	him, her, it	his, hers, its	they	them	their, theirs
	who	whom	whose	who, whoever	whom, whomever	whose

*Also called nominative.

Subjective Case

Use the subjective case when a pronoun is the *subject* of a sentence; it tells *who* or *what* a sentence is about.

> **Joan** and **Kemal** attend graduate school in business administration.

Joan and *Kemal* are the subjects that tell who; *attend* is the action verb.

> **He** and **she** are graduate students at the state university.

He and *she* are subject pronouns used to replace *Joan* and *Kemal; are* is the being verb. When you have trouble remembering whether *he and she* or *him and her* is correct, omit one of the pronouns. You easily see that *Him is a graduate student* would be incorrect. You can apply the same test to this sentence:

> **He** and **I** also plan to attend graduate school and study for our MBAs.

He plans to attend or *I plan to attend* would be correct. *Him plans to attend* and *Me plan to attend* are obviously wrong.

Subject Pronouns After *Being* Verbs

A pronoun following a *being* verb must be a subject pronoun. This rule is important in *written* English. In 21st-century *spoken* American English, however, either an object or a subject pronoun is acceptable after a *being* verb.

Being Verbs	*am, is, was, were, been, be*
Subject Pronouns	*I, we, you, he, she, they, it, who*
Object Pronouns	*me, us, you, him, her, them, it, whom*
Writing	It **is he**, not Jerry, who sold it.
	It **was I**, not she, who sent it.
Speech	It **is him**, not Jerry, who sold it.
	It **is them**, not Jerry, who sold it.

Say the following sentences out loud, and you will see the difference in the correct forms needed for written English versus the incorrect forms that are commonly accepted in everyday speech.

Incorrect	The only experts in the group **were her** and **me**.
Correct	The only experts in the group **were she** and **I**.

Incorrect	The winners might **have been him** and Raul.
Correct	The winners might **have been he** and Raul.

To test for correctness, turn the sentence around to make the object the subject—then you will easily hear what is correct. You wouldn't say *Her (or me) is the only expert in the group* or *Him might be the winner.*

Correcting Subjective Pronoun Errors

Most subject pronoun errors occur when two or more pronouns are used together, such as *he and I,* or when a noun is used with a pronoun, such as *Jonathan and I.* Confusion occurs as to whether to use *I, me,* or *myself.* As you saw in the preceding examples, you will usually make the right choice if you imagine one of the pronouns or the noun omitted; then decide whether the sentence "sounds right."

The following examples show how to use this "trick."

Incorrect	Jonathan and **me** went to the concert. OR Jonathan and **myself** went to the concert.
Correct	Jonathan and **I** went to the concert.

Leave *Jonathan* home, and you know that *Me went to the concert* or *Myself went to the concert* are both wrong.

Incorrect	**Him** and **me** attended the concert.
Correct	**He** and **I** attended the concert.

Both pronouns are wrong; you wouldn't say *Him attended the concert* or *Me attended the concert.* Therefore, change objective pronouns—*him/me*—to subjective pronouns *he/I.*

Sometimes the noun and pronoun have no conjunction (*and/or*) between them. This happens when you combine a noun and a pronoun that have the same meaning to show emphasis or to make your meaning clear. Which is right, *we* clerks or *us* clerks? You can tell which to use when you see the rest of the sentence. Imagine omitting the noun, then decide whether the sentence sounds right:

Incorrect	**Us students** need a longer lunch break.
Correct	**We students** need a longer lunch break.

Omit the noun *students: Us need a longer lunch break* is obviously wrong. *We need a longer lunch break* sounds right.

Habits of speech carry over to writing and can cause mistakes in subject pronoun usage. Many people make the mistake of using *me* in this kind of sentence:

Incorrect	**Shirley** and **me** are having lunch together next week.
Correct	**Shirley** and **I** are having lunch together next week.

To avoid this mistake, remember this rule: *A being verb = a subject pronoun.* This will help you avoid making this error. Say it often until *I* begins to sound right.

OBJECTIVE CASE

Review the chart on page 101 showing the objective case of personal pronouns.

Object of a Verb

Use the objective case when the pronoun is the object of a verb.

> Please **call** Janet or **me** with the information.

The objective pronoun *me* is the object of the action verb *call*. In this example, you have a noun and a pronoun as objects. If you think *Please call Janet or I* might be correct, remove *Janet* from the sentence. It sounds natural to say, *Please call me*; it would not sound right to say, *Please call I*.

To find out if a verb has an object, say the subject and verb and then ask *whom?* or *what?* If you get an answer, the answer is the object, as in the following examples:

> Give the extra work to **him** and **me** because we work very quickly.

Ask, *Give the work to whom?* Answer: *him* and *me*. *Him* and *me* are the object of the verb *give*. Use the object pronouns, not the subject pronouns *he* and *I*.

> Nick expects **her** to attend.

Whom does Nick expect? Answer: *her*. Use the object pronoun *her*, not the subject pronoun *she*.

> The company owes **him** money for his expenses.

Him is the object of the verb *owes*.

Object of a Preposition

When the pronoun is the object of a preposition, such as *between*, *among*, *under*, *below*, *over*, *with*, *of*, *to*, *in*, or *into*, also use the objective case. You will recall from Chapter 2 that prepositions begin prepositional phrases. A prepositional phrase ends with an object, which is a noun or an objective case pronoun. If you say the preposition and ask *whom?* or *what?*, the answer is the object. In the following sentences, the prepositions are underlined, and the objects of the prepositions are in bold type.

> Among the five <u>of</u> **us**, two have attended training and three have not.

Us is the object of the preposition *of*.

> Please get the contract ready <u>for</u> **me** as soon as possible.

Me is the object of the preposition *for* (*You* is the understood subject of this sentence).

> Just <u>between</u> **you** and **me**, the meeting was dull.

In this example, you might be tempted to use the pronoun *I* instead of *me*, but the objective case is the right choice.

Correcting Objective Pronoun Errors

The combination of two pronouns is the hardest for many people to get correctly. As with subject pronouns, when no conjunction separates object pronouns from a noun, use the omission test.

Incorrect	Would you consider giving **we salespeople** longer lunch breaks?
Correct	Please give **us salespeople** longer lunch breaks.

Omit the noun *salespeople*, and you immediately know that *Would you consider giving we longer lunch breaks* can't be right.

Incorrect	Please give **we students** a voice in setting campus rules.
Correct	Please give **us students** a voice in setting campus rules.

Omit the noun *students*, object of the action verb *give*, and you know that *Please give we a voice in setting campus rules* can't be right.

Incorrect	Send a car for **Ms. Dahlberg** and **I** immediately.
Correct	Send a car for **Ms. Dahlberg** and **me** immediately.

Omit *Ms. Dahlberg*, object of the preposition *for*, and you immediately know that *Send a car for I immediately* can't be right.

With two pronouns connected with a conjunction—such as *you* and *me* or *you* and *I*—it's harder to tell which is right. As with subject pronouns, you can imagine omitting the object pronouns one at a time to make sure you are using the correct one.

Incorrect	Professor Boone will discuss the problem with **he** and **I**.
Correct	Professor Boone will discuss the problem with **him** and **me**.

Omit *he* or *I*, and you know *Professor Boone will discuss the problem with he* or *with I* is wrong. Change subjective pronouns *he/I* to objective pronouns *him/me*—objects of the preposition *with*.

Incorrect	Give the report to Pat Garner and **I** tomorrow.
Correct	Give the report to Pat Garner and **me** tomorrow.

Omit *Pat*, and you know *Give the report to I tomorrow* can't be right.

SUBJECT/OBJECT CONFUSION

Some subject and object pronouns are often confusing. *Me* and *I* are examples. Is it "John and **me** can work late this evening" or "John and **I** can work late"? Based on the "omit one" test, you now know that *John and I* is the correct way to say it. (Remove *John*, and you know the right pronoun is *I*.) This section covers some other ways to test whether you are using the correct pronoun case.

Comparisons

Pronoun usage gets confusing in sentences that make comparisons when "understood words" are left out to avoid wordiness. The words *than* or *as* usually introduce comparatives in sentences where understood words are omitted. For example:

> Keisha helped sell tickets. Did the other volunteers sell more tickets than (**she/her**)?

In this sentence, the word *sold* or *did* is understood:

> Did the volunteers sell more tickets than *she sold*?

Now it is easy to determine that *her* would be incorrect. *She* is the right pronoun even though it might sound wrong to your ears because you have heard it said incorrectly so often. Nevertheless, always strive to use the correct form in business speaking and writing.

If you're not sure whether to use a subject or object pronoun when understood words are omitted, just complete the expression or imagine it completed. Here are some more examples; the omitted words are in parentheses. When you add the phrase shown in brackets, you know which pronoun is correct.

> No one wants to please you more than the manger and (**me/I**).

Incorrect	No one wants to please you more than the manager and **me** [want to please you].
Correct	No one wants to please you more than the manager and **I** [want to please you].

> Do you like him better than (**I/me**)?

If you add the understood words *like him* or *do* after the questionable pronoun, you easily choose *I*, not *me*.

Incorrect	Do you like him better than **me** (do)?
Correct	Do you like him better than **I** (do)?

More Than One Meaning

In some sentences, either a subject pronoun or an object pronoun is correct. The choice depends on what you want the sentence to mean. Let's take another look at the preceding example:

Correct	Do you like him more than **I** [like him]?

If you add the understood words *you like* before the pronoun in question, the meaning changes—and you need a different pronoun.

Incorrect	Do you like him more than [you like] **I**?
Correct	Do you like him more than [you like] **me**?

To be certain you choose the right pronoun, mentally complete any sentence that omits understood words in a comparison. If more than one meaning is possible, use the words that deliver the meaning you intend.

GO TO PAGE 116 AND COMPLETE WORKSHEET 6.1.

POSSESSIVE CASE PRONOUNS

Review the chart on page 101 listing the possessive form of personal pronouns. Use the possessive case when a pronoun **shows possession** (ownership).

> That iPhone is **mine** and this one is **his**.
>
> Kevin asked that you return **his** equipment by tomorrow.

It is easy to remember the pronouns used to show possession because you use them all the time. The most important thing to remember about possessive pronouns is this: Do not use an apostrophe with any of the personal possessive pronouns. They already show possession in the way they are spelled. *Use an apostrophe only with possessive nouns and contractions.*

Personal Possessive Pronouns

That is **my** idea.	That idea is **mine**.
This is **his** idea.	This idea is **his**.
That is **her** business.	That book is **hers**.
These are **our** jeeps.	Those jeeps are **ours**.
This is **your** dollar.	That money is **yours**.
These are **their** jeans.	Those jeans are **theirs**.
The lizard lost **its** tail.	**Whose** tail is that?

POSSESSIVE PRONOUNS AND CONTRACTIONS

Errors often occur because some *possessive pronouns* and *contractions* sound alike but are spelled differently. Be aware of the differences below and make sure you have used the right word in your writing, depending on the meaning you want. Contractions are covered in detail in Chapter 13.

Possessive Pronouns	Contractions Requiring Apostrophes
your—Your job pays well.	**you're** (you are)—You're a rich man.
its—Its wing was injured.	**it's** (it is)—It's a short distance away.
whose—Whose responsibility is it?	**who's** (who is)—I know who's here.
their—Their problem is serious.	**they're** (they are)—They're in debt.

REFLEXIVE PRONOUNS

Pronouns that end in *self/selves* are called **reflexive pronouns**. You use these pronouns all the time in speaking and writing. The thing to remember is that *they cannot be used as the subject of a sentence.* They are always objective case pronouns. These are the reflexive pronouns:

First person	myself, ourselves
Second person	yourself, yourselves
Third person	himself, herself, itself, oneself, themselves

These pronouns are used to reflect either emphasis or action *back* to the noun or pronoun to which they refer. For example:

> I asked **myself** whether or not I was making the right decision.
>
> If you want a job done well, do it **yourself**.
>
> They treated **themselves** to a big lunch.
>
> I bought **myself** a business class ticket for the long trip to Europe.

When to Use Reflexive Pronouns

Use reflexive pronouns in two situations only:

1. To emphasize the noun (or pronoun) to which the pronoun refers:

   > **I** did that job **myself**.
   >
   > **You yourself** know better than that.
   >
   > **We ourselves** are to blame.
   >
   > Vicki always does the hardest work **herself**.

2. To direct the action back to the subject of the sentence:

   > **They** took care of **themselves**.
   >
   > **He** frequently talks to **himself**.
   >
   > **He** corrected **himself** immediately.
   >
   > **She** does the easy work by **herself**.
   >
   > **She** placed **herself** at great risk.

Correcting Reflexive Pronoun Errors

The most common error writers and speakers make with reflexive pronouns is to use them in place of objective pronouns:

Incorrect	The store gave a discount **to** Ms. Beckham and **myself**.
Correct	The store gave a discount **to** Ms. Beckham and **me**.
Incorrect	The documents must be signed **by** your boss or **yourself**.
Correct	The documents must be signed **by you** or your boss.

Another fairly common error is the use of words that sound like reflexive pronouns but actually do not exist in the English language. These "nonwords" include *hisself*, *theirself*, and *theirselves*.

word**POWER**

The "made-up" reflexive pronouns, such as *hisself* and *theirselves*, are in the Merriam Webster dictionary. They are labeled as "dialect."

Indefinite Pronouns

Indefinite pronouns refer to nonspecific people or things, so they do not have first-, second-, and third-person forms. Indefinite pronouns also do not change form when used as subjects or objects.

Use indefinite pronouns to refer to nonspecific persons or things.

INDEFINITE PRONOUNS

all	each	more	others
any	everybody	most	several
anybody	everyone	no one	some
anyone	everything	nobody	somebody
anything	few	none	someone
both	many	nothing	something

grammarTIP

Do not confuse the possessive form of indefinite pronouns with a **contraction**. In the sentence *Everybody's going to the company picnic*, *everybody's* is a contraction meaning *everybody is*.

INDEFINITE POSSESSIVE PRONOUNS

Indefinite pronouns that have a possessive form show it by adding *'s*.

> **Someone's** jacket was left in the conference room.
> Her decision to leave the firm isn't **anyone's** fault.
> This must be **somebody's** saxophone.
> One should mind **one's** own business.

Indefinite pronouns may also be part of a contraction.

> **Everyone's** going to the office party. [everyone is]
> **Everything's** fine at the regional office. [everything is]
> **Somebody's** already using the conference room. [somebody is]

CORRECTING INDEFINITE PRONOUN ERRORS

Indefinite pronouns can be tricky, so we are going to spend some extra time looking at their usage and some of the things about them that trouble writers. You will notice that many of the indefinite pronouns are compound words that are spelled as one word, except for *no one*. One common error is mistaking other forms of these words for the one-word pronoun. In some sentences, these expressions are not pronouns; the first part is an adjective and the second a noun. In that case, write them as two words. Fortunately, you don't need to analyze the grammar to know whether to use one word or two. Just apply these two tests:

> *Any one* and *every one* are an adjective and a noun when the preposition *of* follows. They should not be joined.

Not a pronoun	**Any one of** you might be asked by the general manager to go to Topeka.
	Every one of you deserves credit for the success of this project.
Pronouns	**Anyone** who has a good reason may go to Houston.
	Everyone might go to San Diego if we win the sales contest.

AVOID VAGUE PRONOUN USAGE

Avoid using *they* or *you* in a vague sense when you mean people in general or those in authority. Use specific nouns instead or rephrase to omit the need for a noun or pronoun.

Original: They won't renew your financial aid if your GPA drops.

Revised: The financial aid office won't renew students' financial aid if their GPA drops.

Original: You're prohibited from purchasing cigarettes if you're under 18.

Revised: State law prohibits merchants from selling cigarettes to people under 18.

GO TO PAGE 118 AND COMPLETE WORKSHEET 6.2.

Other Types of Pronouns

A short look at some of the other types of pronouns is an opportunity to learn some ways to remember correct use for some of the more troublesome ones. The categories that tend to cause confusion are listed below. As you can see, some words belong to more than one category, depending on their use in the sentence.

- **Relative pronouns** refer to nouns that name people and things elsewhere in the sentence to clarify *who*, *whom*, *which*, *that*, *whichever*, *whoever*, or *whatever* is being spoken about.

- **Interrogative pronouns** are used to ask a question. They are *who*, *whom*, *what*, *which*, and *whose*.

- **Demonstrative pronouns** point to and identify a noun or pronoun. They are *this*, *these*, *that*, and *those*. *This* and *these* refer to things or people nearer in distance or time. *That* and *those* refer to people or things farther away in distance and time.

The remainder of this chapter covers the specific words in these categories that give writers the most headaches. Studying this material and doing the exercises will help you develop the habit of using these pronouns correctly. Your reference manual is a good source to use as well whenever you find yourself confused about these pronouns.

WHO AND WHOM

Those who truly care about their English try hard to use *who* and *whom* correctly, yet they often err by using *whom* where *who* belongs. Some people correct themselves like this: "Who ah whom ah who ah is the treasurer of this company?" Then we have who/whom cowards who mumble the mystery word and hope the listener won't notice. Many well-educated people, however, do use *who* and *whom* correctly.

Now here's the good news: Some language experts recommend eliminating *whom* from *speech* to avoid awkward pauses and mumbles. But, for *writing* in the workplace, we recommend taking some care and making sure that you are using *who* and *whom* correctly. It takes just a few

writingTIP

Just remember that categories help us organize our study of pronouns and other parts of grammar, but it is the usage that you need to focus on and practice so that it becomes second nature. Keeping your reference manual handy is the best way to be confident that your usage is correct.

seconds if you know the "trick." In speech, just use *who* unless you're certain about your choice of *whom*.

Imagine *He* or *Him*

Here is the trick to correct usage: Imagine replacing *who* or *whom* with *he* or *him* (disregard whether the person is male or female). If *he* fits, use *who* or *whoever*; if *him* sounds right, use *whom* or *whomever*. Both *him* and *whom* end with *m*, making it a good memory device.

> Mr. Agresta is the man (**who**/whom) gave me the package.

He gave me the package—not *him* gave me the package; therefore, choose *who*.

> Jim Young, (**who**/whom) we understand visited you yesterday, is a database expert.

Jim Young is a database expert; we understand *he* visited your office yesterday—not *him* visited; therefore, choose *who*.

> Dr. Perry, (who/**whom**) Prudential hopes to hire, has the highest qualifications.

Dr. Perry has the highest qualifications; Prudential hopes to hire *him*—not hire *he;* therefore, choose *whom*.

> Assign the report to (whoever/**whomever**) you wish.

Assign the report to *him;* therefore, choose *whomever*. If either *he* or *him* fits in the same place, choose *who* or *whoever*, not *whom* or *whomever*:

> You should go with (**whoever**/whomever) is ready first.

Him fits after *with* (objective case), but *he* fits before *is* (subjective case). Therefore, use *who*. Why? Always allow a subject to have priority over an object.

If the sentence is a question, change it to a statement before imagining the *who/whom* choice as *he/him*.

> (Who/Whom) are you going with?

Change to a statement:

> You are going with **whom**.

Him, not *he*, sounds right after *with*. Another way to look at it is that *You* is the subject of the verb *are going;* therefore, the object pronoun *whom* is needed as the object of the preposition *with*.

WHO AND *THAT*

These two pronouns, used to refer to people and things, often confuse speakers and writers. Here are the rules to follow:

> Use *who* to refer to a specific person:
>
> > John is the person **who** shares his technical knowledge.
>
> Use *that* to refer to groups of people:
>
> > I invited the staff members **that** needed to attend.

Use *that* to refer to general or specific things:

Group of things	Last week we presented the awards **that** recognize five years of service.
Specific things	The Quarterly Sales Report is the one **that** I need by tomorrow.

WHICH AND THAT

grammarTIP

"Nonessential" does not mean that the phrase is not necessary or should be removed. It's purpose is to add information to the sentence, even though it does not change the meaning.

Use *which* and *that* to refer to nouns other than persons. Use *that* to introduce essential phrases; use *which* to introduce nonessential phrases. In the following sentence, the meaning is the same with or without the phrase that begins with *which*.

Nonessential	My new high heels, which cost more than $50, fell apart today when I was at work.

In this sentence, the phrase beginning with *that* is essential to point out the specific magazine that is being targeted.

Essential	The magazine **that** is best known in the industry is the one we need to target.

WHAT AND WHICH

writingTIP

Set off a nonessential phrase with commas if it falls in the middle of the sentence. Do not set off clauses beginning with *that*.

In spoken English, the tendency to use these two pronouns interchangeably is pretty widely accepted. In writing, however, it is still important to distinguish between the two because the error tends to stand out more glaringly than when spoken.

Use *what* when referring to one; use *which* when referring to more than one.

What day of the week are airline ticket prices most likely to drop?

Which days of the week are the best for getting cheap fares?

Incorrect	What one of these books do you recommend?
Correct	Which one of these books is a good vacation read?

THIS/THESE AND THAT/THOSE

These demonstrative pronouns are not as troublesome as the previous ones because most speakers use them correctly. Usage that we usually hear correctly we tend to write correctly. However, here are some bad habits of usage that hurt the ears and are deadly in writing:

Using *them* in place of *those*:

Incorrect	I took **them** books back to the library two weeks ago.
Correct	I took **those** books back to the library two weeks ago.

If *them* is used as a personal pronoun referring to a group, the sentence *I took them to the library two weeks ago* is correct.

Using the expressions *this here* or *that there* (they tend to be regional) or inserting unnecessary words when using demonstrative pronouns are unacceptable in business writing:

Incorrect	**That there** bookcase is heavy—don't lift it!
Correct	**That** bookcase is heavy—don't lift it!
Incorrect	**Those** cars **there** in the parking lot don't belong to us.
Correct	**Those** cars in the parking lot don't belong to us.

GO TO PAGE 119 AND COMPLETE WORKSHEET 6.3.

KEY PRINCIPLES OF PRONOUNS

- Use a subject pronoun as the subject of a verb and an object pronoun as the object of a verb or of a preposition.
- In workplace writing, use subject pronouns after "being" verbs.
- *Who* is acceptable in speech for subjects and objects. However, when writing, use *who* as a subject and *whom* as an object.
- Use a reflexive (self/selves) pronoun only when another pronoun will not make sense in that position in the sentence. Never use *hisself, theirselves, themself,* or *theirself!*
- The pronouns *hers, ours, yours,* and *theirs* never have apostrophes. However, indefinite possessive pronouns (such as someone or everybody) do have apostrophes before the s when used in possessive forms.
- Distinguish between possessive pronouns and contractions that sound alike but are written differently, such as *its/it's* and *your/you're.*
- Except for *no one,* compound indefinite pronouns are written as one word (*someone*)—unless "of" follows or the meaning indicates two words are required.
- Avoid vague use of pronouns, such as *you* and *they,* when referring to people in general or an authority; use specific nouns instead.

Checkpoint

Using pronouns incorrectly is an easy thing to do given the looseness with which we sometimes speak in everyday conversation. When you enter the world of business, you should not have to ponder over whether to use *I* or *me, who* or *whom,* and so on. You should *know* how to decide. When speaking with colleagues or clients, you should not have to be self-conscious about your grammar. You should be *confident* that your grammar is correct.

Whether preparing a report for the president of your company, a letter to an important customer, or an informal email message, mastering pronoun usage is important because it helps make your speech and writing grammatically flawless. Now you can be more conscious of pronoun usage and apply what you have learned to your speaking and writing. You have achieved your goal when the correct usage sounds right to you and you don't have to stop to think about it. Your objective is for others to concentrate on your message and not be distracted by mistakes.

communications connection

WORKPLACE VOCABULARY POWER

Continue the work on your workplace vocabulary from Chapter 5. Read the following sentences to increase your familiarity with the meaning, spelling, and pronunciation of these words that cut across industries. Then complete the exercise by writing the letter of the word in bold next to its definition. If you're unsure of a meaning or pronunciation, look it up in your dictionary.

1. Some **(a) tabloid media** may engage in **(b) slander** and even **(c) libel** from time to time.

2. **(d) Antitrust legislation** prohibits most **(e) monopolies**, but **(f) amalgamation** is often legal.

3. This **(g) start-up** will not be successful because of the rapid **(h) turnover** of employees.

4. Slow **(i) turnaround time** for production caused decreased **(j) revenues** in the third **(k) quarter**.

5. The website crash was caused by **(l) spyware** installed by a dishonest competitor and failure of its **(m) webmaster** to keep the **(n) firewall** security up to date.

6. Pepsi Cola and Nissan Motors, **(o) multinational corporations** doing business within the **(p) European Union**, had to deal with the global economic **(q) recession**.

7. These **(r) conglomerates** are always watchful of the **(s) euro's** **(t) exchange rate**.

8. The **(u) hacker** was showing off by infiltrating a financial planner's **(v) proprietary** records.

9. Because we don't have a **(w) quorum**, the extra chairs we **(x) requisitioned** aren't needed.

10. He listed the value of his home as **(y) collateral** on the loan application.

Insert the letter of the word that matches the definition.

a) tabloid media	n) firewall
b) slander	o) multinational corporation
c) libel	p) European Union
d) antitrust legislation	q) recession
e) monopoly	r) conglomerate
f) amalgamation	s) euro
g) start-up	t) exchange rate
h) turnover	u) hacker
i) turnaround time	v) proprietary
j) revenues	w) quorum
k) quarter	x) requisition
l) spyware	y) collateral
m) webmaster	

1. _____ Exclusive control of the supply of a commodity or service.

2. _____ A company with subsidiaries or branches in many nations.

3. _____ Joining of two or more businesses into a single body; also called a *merger*.

4. _____ Laws against monopoly-type business practices that result in a business making unfair profits.

5. _____ Time elapsed between starting a task and completing it.

6. _____ Part of a computer network built to control incoming and outgoing network traffic in order to prevent damage to the system.

7. _____ Change in employees because of people leaving and being replaced in an organization; also refers to sale of products that are then replaced by additional merchandise.

8. _____ A new company that is just beginning to operate as a business.

9. _____ Software installed on a hard disk without the user's knowledge; it can be used to relay encoded information.

10. _____ The number of members of an organization required to be present to have a formal meeting at which business is transacted.

11. _____ Total income produced.

12. _____ A written request, made within an organization, for supplies or equipment.

13. _____ An untrue written statement, usually published, that injures another's reputation.

14. _____ The currency unit used in many of the European Union countries.

15. _____ Price of one country's money in relation to the price of another's, for example, the rate at which pesos, euros, francs, yen, rupees, and so on can be exchanged for dollars.

16. _____ Borrower's property held by a lender as security for payment of a loan.

17. _____ A person who infiltrates personal or organizational computer systems.

18. _____ News outlets that tend to emphasize sensational topics and celebrity gossip.

19. _____ One who organizes or updates information on a website.

20. _____ An economic and political confederation of member states that are located primarily on the continent of Europe.

21. _____ Untrue *spoken* remarks about someone that harm the person's reputation. (*Libel* refers to untrue *written* remarks.)

22. _____ A division of the calendar year into three-month intervals.

23. _____ A corporation comprised of different business types that provide a variety of goods and/or services.

24. _____ A period of reduced economic activity.

25. _____ Exclusive legal right of ownership of something protected by secrecy, patent, or copyright.

CHECK YOUR ANSWERS ON PAGE 445.

WRITING PRACTICE

Experienced writers avoid using vague pronouns when referring to people in general or those in authority. Using *they* and *you* instead of a specific noun can leave your reader confused or make you sound as though you are making generalizations instead of stating facts. Revise the following sentences by replacing the vague references with specific nouns. Eliminate extra words where you can.

1. *They* give *you* grants or loans if *you* can prove *your* income is at a level that qualifies you to receive financial aid.

   _____

   _____

2. *You're* prohibited from driving in this state if *you've* been drinking.

   _____

3. In this state you can't get your driver's license unless you're 16 or older.

   _____

4. They're looking to interview as many qualified candidates as possible so they can find at least five outstanding new employees.

   _____

   _____

5. They say your chances of success are increased when you pursue work that you enjoy.

   _____

   _____

Date to submit this assignment: _____

PROOFREADING PRACTICE

Correct sentence construction, plurals, possessives, noun and pronoun usage, and typographical errors in the following email message.

Dear Mr. McIntyre:

I am responding to you're advertisement for a customer service associate at the new spa you are opening at Greenville Mall. I am familiar with your companys services and have expereince working the fitness industry that would fit well with the qualification's your requesting.

My last positon was with the health club at the downtown Hyatt Hotel, were my associate and me were responsible for managing the center. Him and me oversaw operations of the facility for six hours daily. This job helped myself develop skills in scheduling customers, overseeing maintenance staff, and maintaining safety rules. I feel comfortable in handling everyone of these areas of responsibility.

Details of my background are listed in the attached resume. I can offer references from prior employers who I have worked for. I would like to request and appointment for a personal interview to discuss how you and me can apply my knowledge of quality spa services to ensure the success of your new business adventure.

Sincerely,

Jared Underwood

How did you do? Excellent _____ Good _____
Need More Practice _____

chapter review

WORKSHEET 6.1

A. Circle the correct pronoun form.

1. If (she and me/her and I/she and I/her and me) study, we'll do better work.

2. Please tell Walter and (I/me) the best way to get to your office.

3. (They/Them) as well as Carla are involved in the Dallas County project.

4. (We/Us) paralegals need more training in the procedures.

5. Julia Garcia and (I /me) used to work together frequently.

6. Joining the union would be good for (we/us) pasta chefs.

7. Deborah, the manager of public relations, phoned Suzy and (I/me) to discuss the project.

8. Gordon Townsend authorized Stephen and (she/her) to go to Fort Lauderdale.

9. Do (we/us) students have a vote on whether to have a final exam?

10. Letoya Denova and (he/him) could travel to the sales meeting together.

11. Is it alright with you if Luanne shows Donald and (I/me) the salary proposals?

12. Christopher asked both you and (I/me) to contact him.

13. This committee needs Terry as well as (they/them).

14. Everyone except Ms. Rosenblatt and (he/him) works in Omaha.

15. (Him and me/He and I) have an advantage in this situation.

16. The presentation should be divided between Allan Parks and (I/me).

17. Jamal Hendricks and (him/he) will share the responsibility.

18. (We/Us) Americans transfer the fork to the right hand after cutting food.

19. The company sent (her/she) and Ariana to London.

20. The director told Ray and (I/me) about downtown Lancaster.

21. Were you and (he/him) preparing a PowerPoint presentation that day?

22. The committee invited you, not (he/him), to speak at the luncheon.

23. Professor Newsom wants Lee and (I/me) to work on the project.

24. You and (them/they) should devise a new production schedule.

25. Let's keep the surprise ending to the program just between you and (I/me).

B. Using the chart on page 103 as needed, circle the correct pronoun in each of the following sentences and write in the blank whether it is in the subjective or the objective case.

1. Marie, Larry, and (me, I, myself) lost all our quarters at the casino. _____ case

2. Please give the instructions to (he, him, himself) and the assistant. _____ case

3. Bob and (me, I, myself) went to the concert. _____ case

4. When you hear the test results for (she, her, herself) and Kirby, you'll be very surprised. _____ case

5. (Who/Whom) is the best person to talk to about the position? _____ case.

C. Write a subject pronoun in the subject blank of each sentence and an object pronoun in the object blank. If in doubt, see the chart at the beginning of this chapter.

Subject	Object of Verb	Subject	Object of Preposition
1. _____ believe	_____.	5. _____ am staying with	_____.
2. _____ admires	_____.	6. _____ are starting with	_____.
3. _____ respects	_____.	7. _____ is leaving with	_____.
4. _____ knows	_____?	8. _____ are going with	_____?

D. Fill in the parentheses with the understood completion word or words.

1. He loves the job more than she (_____).

2. He loves his job more than (_____) her.

3. I know the vice president better than he (_____).

4. I know the vice president better than (_____) him.

5. Ms. Guthrie can operate the device as well as he (_____).

CHECK YOUR ANSWERS ON PAGE 446.

WORKSHEET 6.2

A. Draw a line through the pronoun and contraction errors and write the correct word in the blank. Write **C** beside the only correct sentence.

1. _____   Reserve the apostrophe for it's proper use, and omit it when its not needed.

2. _____   Its color has faded.

3. _____   Yours' is the room with the green door.

4. _____   Your to use your own books today.

5. _____   If your running behind schedule, let you're sister help.

B. Draw a line through the incorrect pronouns, and write the correct pronoun in the blank. Write **C** in the blank if the sentence is already correct.

_____ 1. The president himself will attend the meeting.

_____ 2. The question was whether the speakers had contradicted theirselves in the course of the debate.

_____ 3. She can do the work faster than him.

_____ 4. Neither his assistant nor himself is willing to pick up the package today.

_____ 5. Always give copies of reports to Joyce Moore and myself.

_____ 6. Victoria usually leaves earlier than Ramon and I.

_____ 7. The others usually leave right after Ms. Nixon and me.

_____ 8. Wallace runs just as fast as he.

_____ 9. Rhoda and Isabelle often ask themself that question.

_____ 10. Only Joe Englehart and yourself know how to fix the equipment.

_____ 11. Deborah and myself listened to them with great interest.

_____ 12. I may find myself looking for a new manager.

_____ 13. We ourselves are excluded from the contract.

_____ 14. They felt like themselves again after the crisis had passed.

_____ 15. She injured herself while they were in Oshkosh.

_____ 16. The Indiana team members voted theirself a pay increase.

_____ 17. Good table manners require that you spoon soup away from yourself.

_____ 18. He gave hisself a raise.

_____ 19. I intend to put me on the program as the last speaker.

_____ 20. Gomez himself should have known better than to buy 100 shares of GYPCO in a bear market; don't blame yourself.

C. Make the corrections needed for written English. Use the proofreading mark for insert space and use the close space symbol where no space is needed. Write C at the end of the sentence if it is correct.

1. Noone from this office responded.

2. Everyone of the books was sold yesterday.

3. Everyone has to have an access code in order to enter the office on weekends.

4. In American business situations, keeping some one waiting is considered rude.

5. The designer is willing to use anyone of the three colors.

D. Use a reflexive pronoun or an indefinite pronoun that makes sense in each of the following sentences.

1. My group had _____ to represent us at the meeting because _____ was busy.

2. The receptionist needs _____ to replace him while he goes to lunch.

3. The manager _____ gave me permission to use a company car.

4. If there is _____ that can be done to help meet the deadline, _____ should volunteer to do it.

5. I threw a big party for _____ to celebrate my promotion.

CHECK YOUR ANSWERS ON PAGE 446.

WORKSHEET 6.3

B. Circle the correct pronoun. Apply the tricks you learned.

Example: We referred a programmer to you (who/(whom)) we believe you will like.

1. You should go with (whoever/whomever) is leaving first.

2. The company wishes to purchase cars (which/that) require the least upkeep.

3. The the task force is looking for someone (who/that) wishes to lead the group.

4. Mohammed is the one (who/whom) should do the work.

5. (Who/Whom) will Professor Serrano select for the job?

6. (What/Which) one of the new employees would you like to mentor?

7. (Who/Whom) will you support for the board position?

8. (Who/Whom) should we ask to investigate the suspected fraud?

9. The employees (who/that) joined the company recently are learning quickly.

10. (Whoever/whomever) is willing to work hard will be given the responsibility.

11. The losing candidate will support (whoever/whomever) the convention chooses.

12. New competitors are the ones (who/that) we feared the most in this economy.

13. The type of clothing (which/that) is considered acceptable as "business casual" is described in the office handbook.

14. We think he is the professor (who/whom) you will want at Carl Sandburg College.

15. Jorge Santiago is a person (who/that) will enjoy working in this environment.

16. Give the scholarship to the one (who/whom) needs it most.

17. (What/Which) restaurant is your first choice for the retirement luncheon?

18. Please bring the documents (which/that) may or may not be needed.

19. She is the administrative assistant (who/whom) I recommended for the position.

20. You are the court reporter (who/whom) I requested for the deposition.

21. Professor Costner is the instructor (who/whom) I believe could help you.

22. These types of problems, (which/that) are hard to solve, provide good experience.

23. Letoya Ferguson is the one (who/whom) helped me most in Seattle.

24. The board will approve (whoever/whomever) we select for vice president.

25. It is these kinds of questions (which/that) we must prepare for in advance.

CHECK YOUR ANSWERS ON PAGE 447.

POSTTEST

Circle the correct pronoun or word group for written English.

1. Carla's high grades on the exam made her mother and (I/me/myself) very proud.
2. They make you stand in the registration line for hours. The applicants must stand in line for hours.
3. (No one/Noone) regrets this incident more than (I/me/myself).
4. Is Mike Terry better qualified than (her/she)?
5. Yoshi has a better background in Hebrew than (they/them).
6. Mine is faster than (your's/yours'/yours) and (her's/hers).
7. (Who/Whom) did you say will handle the new account?
8. Lee became acquainted with the planner (who/whom) was in charge of the convention.
9. (Him/He) and (me/I/myself) will report it to (whoever/whomever) is in charge.
10. If (it's/its/its') too late, give the information to (whoever/whomever) needs it.

CHECK YOUR ANSWERS ON PAGE 447.

Self-Study and Practice Tutorials

wordPOWER

Build your workplace vocabulary and improve spelling skills by completing the exercises in Appendix B on page 362.

Supplementary Practice Exercises

For additional practice, complete the Appendix C exercises for this chapter on page 404.

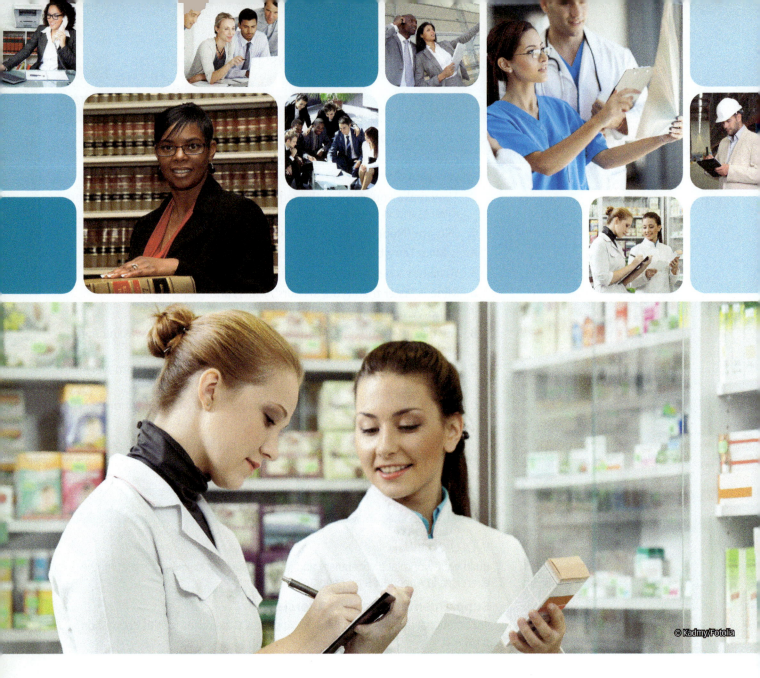

© Kadmy/Fotolia

After completing Chapter 7, you will be able to do the following:

- Use clear pronoun references to ensure that meaning is understood.
- Choose pronouns that agree with their antecedents in number and gender.
- Use correct pronouns when referring to collective nouns and indefinite pronouns.
- Use pronouns to make your writing free of gender bias and vague references.

7

Pronouns: Agreement and Writing Principles

career connection

THE ONLINE APPLICATION

Asking job applicants to submit job applications online is the norm today with most large companies. Printed and written applications on paper have become a thing of the past. Here are some guidelines to be aware of when completing an online application.

- The online application might have fields that are required and some that are optional. Pay close attention to what is required and make sure you enter the requested information in the corresponding field.
- Read the job advertisement carefully and make notes on how your skills match the qualifications. When describing your experience, wherever possible, use the same language that the company uses in describing the job duties and qualifications required. Many employers screen applications according to keywords in the job description, so this will increase your chances of being selected for further consideration.
- Be prepared to provide your resume while you are in the process of completing the online application. You may be prompted to upload your resume, which means you can attach the document from your computer file, or the application will allow you to cut and paste the text into the online template.

- Make sure the resume you plan to submit online does not contain a lot of formatting, such as boldface, underlining, bullets, and various type fonts. These do not translate well from one system to another. (You can prepare a version with formatting that looks good in print to take with you on job interviews.) Consult your reference manual for guidelines on formatting.

- Before hitting the "submit" button on the online application, go back and proofread each field you filled in to make sure your spelling, punctuation, and sentence structure are correct. It's okay to use fragments in a resume, of course. Again, your reference manual can guide you.

PRETEST

Circle the correct pronoun.

1. No company wants to see (their/its) stock price fall due to bad publicity.

2. Each of the supervisors assigns (his or her, their) staff members' goals for the quarter.

3. Everyone in the training session gave (his, their, his or her) best effort.

4. Someone must claim (his or her, their) lost laptop, or it will be donated to charity.

5. Ask Ms. Norman or Mr. Jankowski for (his or her/their) key to the conference room.

6. The team agreed that (its/their) uniforms needed to be replaced.

7. Every student in the class needs (his/his or her/their) own computer.

8. Government regulations require state employees to report (their/his or her) outside earnings.

9. Each delegate at the convention (cast his vote/voted) electronically.

10. Either the builder or the contractors will do (its/their) best to resolve the dispute with the City Planning Office.

CHECK YOUR ANSWERS ON PAGE 448.

Clear Pronoun References

You know that pronouns substitute for nouns—a simple concept to keep in mind, but one that needs to be taken a step further. When you use a pronoun to substitute, you need to be certain that your reader or listener clearly understands the **pronoun reference**. When the noun or pronoun you are referring to is unclear, your listener or reader will be confused.

The noun or pronoun that you are referring to is called the **antecedent**. These grammar terms are useful in understanding how to make pronouns agree with the noun or pronoun for which they are a substitute. Consider this scenario: You look over at a group of colleagues and say, "I admire him because he is willing to share his knowledge with others." Your listener will likely ask, "Who do you mean?" or "Who are you referring to?" (Or he or she might say, "To whom are you referring?") Without a clear reference for the pronoun *he*, the meaning of your statement needs clarification.

If you had said, "I really admire John because he is willing to share his knowledge with others," your meaning would be crystal clear. *John* is the antecedent of the pronouns *he* and *his*.

When writing simple sentences that have a simple subject, the pronoun reference is usually quite clear and easy to follow. When writing longer sentences that have compound subjects or when nouns become separated from the pronoun that refers back to them, it is especially important to provide the reader with clear references to the antecedent.

Each pronoun should mean to the reader precisely what you want it to mean.

Original	**Kathy Mayo** hired a new **manager**, and **she** intends to expand the department.
Revised	Kathy Mayo hired a new **manager** who will be responsible for expanding the department.

The original sentence is not clear. Who will expand the department, Kathy Mayo or the new manager? In the revised sentence, the pronoun *whose* clearly refers to its antecedent, *manager*.

In some instances, when the pronoun reference isn't clear, you need to rephrase the sentence or replace a vague noun or pronoun with a specific one.

In the following sentence, which should be cut back—the musical number or the speech?

Original	The **musical number** and the **speech** are both too long. Try to cut **it** back to no more than ten minutes.
Revised	The **musical number** and the **speech** are both too long. Try to cut **them** down to five minutes each.

In the next example, the pronoun has no antecedent. This makes the use of *they* meaningless—the reader or listener doesn't know who *they* are. The best way to avoid this is to rewrite.

Original	**They** keep the streets clean in Auburn Hills.
Revised	The streets are clean in Auburn Hills. The sanitation department keeps Auburn Hills' streets clean.

The most important thing about pronoun references and antecedents is that their forms must be in agreement to be grammatically correct—or you could just say in order to make sense. Agreement must be in number—they must both be singular or both plural—and in gender. If the antecedent is masculine, feminine, or gender-neutral (neither masculine nor feminine), the pronoun must be the same.

Number Agreement

A pronoun and its antecedent must both be singular or must both be plural.

Singular	**Jennifer**, the club president, paid **her** dues in September.

The singular possessive pronoun *her* refers to the singular subject *Jennifer*.

Plural   The **club members** must pay **their** dues semiannually.

The plural possessive pronoun *their* refers to the plural subject *club members*. If there are two or more antecedents joined by *and*, use a plural pronoun.

> **Dr. Lawrence Cannaday** and **his wife Mary** gave a reception at **their** home.
>
> **Bill, Jonathan, and I** are running late, and **we** hope you won't start without **us**.
>
> **Rebecca and I** are planning **our** presentation for next week's conference.

When the conjunction is *or* or *nor*, the above rule does not apply. While *and* joins antecedents, making them plural, the conjunctions *or* and *nor* split the antecedents into two single entities. In this case, the pronoun reference should agree with the nearer antecedent in number.

In some cases, you can make the pronoun reference agree with the antecedent that is closest to the pronoun.

> Neither **Jeff nor** his **associates** use **their** full lunch hour these days.

In other cases it is best to revise.

Original	Either **Ethan or Jennifer** left **her** briefcase in the meeting room.
Revised	Either **Ethan or Jennifer** left **a** briefcase in the meeting room.

grammarTIP

The grammar rule says if *nor* or *or* joins the parts of the antecedent, the pronoun should agree in number with the antecedent that follows *or* or *nor*. But this rule doesn't always lead to clear pronoun reference. Use it and then ask, Is the meaning clear? If not, revise.

Gender Agreement

Gender agreement means that male, female, or gender-neutral antecedents must have male, female, or gender-neutral pronoun references.

Female	**Maribell Rivera** brings **her** children to the office day care center.
Male	**Franklin** plans **his** day by setting priorities each morning when **he** arrives.
Neutral	Any size **company** needs policies that are clear to **its** employees.

When you use a gender-neutral noun or pronoun, compose the sentence so that the reference is also gender-neutral. Always avoid the shortcut of using only male gender—*his, he,* or *him*—to refer to both males and females or people in general. This outdated practice is referred to as **gender bias** because it excludes females. Instead, use either *he or she* or *his or her*; reword the sentence to use the plural forms *they* or *their*; or find some other way to say it.

Original	**Every salesperson** was asked to personally contact **his** top five clients at least once a month.
Revised	**Every salesperson** was asked to personally contact **his or her** top five clients at least once a month.
Revised	**All** of the **salespeople** were asked to contact **their** top five clients at least once a month.

Some writers don't like the "his or her" usage, and all writers should avoid repeating it numerous times in the same document. Rewording is usually not very difficult if you are willing to take the time.

writingTIP

Another technique writers use to avoid repeating *his or her* is to alternate use of *his* and *her*. This works when you are writing something like a list of instructions or examples where repeated references occur.

Original	An **employee** has to meet **his** quota no matter how tight the market is.
Revised	An **employee** has to meet **his or her** quota no matter how tight the market is.
Revised	**Employees have** to meet **their** quota no matter how tight the market is.

GO TO PAGE 133 AND COMPLETE WORKSHEET 7.1.

Agreement with Collective Nouns

Pronoun-antecedent agreement can be challenging when a pronoun is used to refer to a collective noun. **Collective nouns** name groups of people, animals, or things. Examples: *audience, committee, crowd, group, staff, class, jury, squad, team.*

A couple of grammar rules will help you clear up confusion about the usage.

1. If the members of the group act as one (a single unit), use a singular pronoun—*it*, *its*, or *itself*—to substitute for a collective noun.
2. If the members of the group act separately or disagree, use a plural pronoun—*they*, *them*, *their/s*, or *themselves*—to substitute for a collective noun.

An example of a collective noun is *jury*; when a jury announces a verdict, it acts as a single unit.

writingTIP

Some writers make the mistake of assigning a gender to collective nouns. For example, they write, "The family decorated his or her lawn for Halloween." Since groups may have members of both genders, keep in mind that collective nouns that name groups are always gender-neutral.

Original	The **jury** announced **their** verdict.
Revised	The **jury** announced **its** verdict.

The plural pronoun *their* is incorrect because members of a jury act as one when they give a verdict. The singular pronoun *its* refers to *jury* acting as a unit. Another option is to eliminate the pronoun.

Revised	The **jury** announced the verdict.

A jury acts as a single unit when arriving at a verdict, but the members act as separate individuals when putting on coats.

Original	The **jury** put on **its** coats as it prepared to leave.
Revised	The **jury** put on **their** coats as they prepared to leave.

The revised sentence is technically correct but awkward. The following is better:

Revised	The **jury members** put on **their** coats as they prepared to leave.

In the following example, the meaning is that the committee as a whole disagreed with some other group or person about the issue.

Original   The **committee** disagreed about whether **it** should take strong action.

If you meant to say the committee members acted separately in disagreement with each other, the sentence would have to be revised:

Revised   The **committee members** disagreed about whether **they** should take strong action.

By using *committee* as an adjective instead of a noun, and inserting the word *members* as the antecedent, the meaning is clear. This is how your knowledge about the parts of speech is put into practical use.

NAMES OF ORGANIZATIONS

Use a singular pronoun to substitute for names of organizations, for example, *companies*, *unions*, *stores*, *schools*, *governments*, or *government agencies*. Though the college named below has many students and employees, use a singular pronoun because it is *one* organization.

Original   Davenport College opens **their** offices at 8 a.m.
Revised   Davenport College opens **its** offices at 8 a.m.
Revised   Davenport College offices open at 8 a.m.

The second revised sentence is better. The same idea is expressed smoothly and with fewer words. Rephrasing to omit the pronoun usually improves the wording. In the following example, IRS is a collective noun requiring a singular pronoun, *its*.

Original   The Internal Revenue Service (IRS) revised **their** 1099 form.
Revised   The Internal Revenue Service revised **its** 1099 form.
Revised   The Internal Revenue Service revised the 1099 form.

grammarTIP
When it comes to nouns, you can have one boy or you can have several boys. However, with collective nouns, such as family, even though the word itself is singular, it is also understood that there is more than one person in a family.

Do not confuse collective nouns with the plural form of the nouns, for example, *juries, companies, colleges, classes, teams*. Use a plural pronoun to substitute for a plural noun.

The **companies** announced **their** merger simultaneously in New York and in Chicago.

By recognizing collective nouns, you can avoid choosing incorrect pronouns to substitute for them. Your understanding of collective nouns will also help with subject-verb agreement (covered in Chapter 9).

GO TO PAGE 136 AND COMPLETE WORKSHEET 7.2.

Agreement with Indefinite Pronouns

Indefinite pronouns refer to a nonspecific person or thing or more than one person or thing. They can be challenging when it comes to pronoun-antecedent agreement because some indefinite pronouns are always singular, some are always plural, and some are singular or plural depending on their use in the sentence. See the list of indefinite pronouns that follows.

INDEFINITE PRONOUNS

Always singular		Always plural	Singular or plural
another	much	both	all
anyone	neither	few	any
anybody	nobody	many	more
anything	no one	others	most
each	nothing	several	none
every	one		some
everybody	somebody		
everyone	someone		
everything	something		

With pronouns that are always singular, remember to use singular pronoun references such as *his*, *her*, or *its*—not the plural *their*. In informal speech, this rule is frequently ignored, but it is still important in workplace writing.

Spoken	**No one** is consulting **their** lawyer about it.
Written	**Everyone is** consulting **his or her** lawyer about it.
Spoken	Is **anyone** willing to drop off a package on **their** way home?
Written	Is **anyone** willing to drop off a package on **his or her** way home?

Note that when pronouns that are always singular precede a noun, they become adjectives, as in the following examples:

Every student in physical education needs **his or her** own locker.

Every student in men's physical education needs **his** own locker.

Each building has **its** own heating unit.

GO TO PAGE 137 AND COMPLETE WORKSHEET 7.3.

For pronouns that can be singular or plural, the context of the sentence determines whether to use a singular or plural pronoun.

Some of the milk spilled out of its container.

Some of the children lost their mittens.

The prepositional phrases *of the milk* and *of the children* are modifiers of *Some*, providing the context for choosing the correct pronoun reference.

writing**TIP**

When referring to collective nouns, rephrasing to omit the pronoun usually improves the wording.

Checkpoint

You have learned that pronoun references must agree with their antecedents in number (singular or plural) and in gender (masculine, feminine, or neutral). Reword sentences to avoid use of the dated masculine to refer to males and females or people in general. This usage is known as gender bias.

Don't be bound by rules so much as by sense and clarity. Using the writing process gives you the freedom to draft and make mistakes. Review and revise as much as time allows to make sure your meaning is clear. For example, the conjunctions *or* and *nor* don't always neatly follow the grammar rule of agreement with the one closest to the antecedent. Clarity often requires revising, and various types of pronouns present challenges in pronoun agreement.

References to indefinite pronouns and collective pronouns require careful review for meaning. Keep in mind that except for *no one*, compound indefinite pronouns are written as one word (someone), *unless* "of" follows or the meaning indicates that two words are required. If the members act separately or disagree, use a plural pronoun. Names of organizations are always considered singular.

communications connection

AVOIDING GENDER BIAS

When communicating in the workplace, choose language that is without gender identification unless it is relevant. Many terms that include the word *man* can be expressed in neutral gender without sounding clumsy. If an expression sounds awkward, rephrase it. Following is a list of terms that were once commonly used and are now considered biased, along with their modern substitutes. It is more important to be aware of avoiding gender bias and being able to recognize it in your drafts than it is to remember all of the various gender-neutral terminology. Remember, you always have your dictionary, thesaurus, and reference manual to rely on.

AVOIDING GENDER BIAS IN YOUR WRITING

Avoid	Use
mankind	human beings, society, humankind, humanity
man-made	synthetic, artificial, constructed, factory-made
manpower	workers, employees, crew, laborers, staff, workforce
workmen	workers
businessmen	business workers, businesspersons or businesspeople, professionals, executives, managers
cameraman	photographer, cinematographer
chairman	chairperson, chair, leader, moderator, coordinator, facilitator
clergyman	member of the clergy, minister (or term specific to the religion; rabbi, priest, imam, reverend, and so on)
congressmen	congressmen and congresswomen, congressperson/s, representatives, legislators
husband/wife	spouse
fireman	firefighter
girls (when referring to adults)	women
insurance man	insurance agent
mailman	mailperson, letter carrier, postal worker
male nurse	nurse
male secretary	secretary
policeman	police officer

Avoid attaching *ess* or *ette* to a noun to create a feminine word for historically masculine roles:

actress [still often appropriate]	actor [preferred by some females]
poetess, authoress	poet, author
proprietress	proprietor
waitress/waiter	waiter/server

WRITING PRACTICE

A. Use proofreading marks to eliminate gender-biased terms in these sentences. Your instructor will provide the answers.

1. Mankind can rejoice when people find a way to settle conflicts without wars.

2. The waiters and waitresses will need training on service for the big reception.

3. Ask the men from our office if they wish to play golf during the convention.

4. The chairman needs a good understanding of parliamentary procedure.

5. The president invited the managers and their wives to a formal dinner.

6. The common man wants his piece of the American dream.

7. Several female policemen are being honored at the ceremony.

8. Please ask the actress to autograph the programs.

9. Consider becoming a cameraman; they are in great demand in the film industry.

10. The girls in my office go to lunch at noon.

11. Wednesday is Administrative Assistants' Day so invite all the girls for lunch.

12. She plays golf as well as her male colleagues.

13. Her brother is a male nurse.

14. We prefer garments made of natural rather than manmade fabrics.

15. Can you recommend a good insurance man?

PROOFREADING PRACTICE

Proofread the following article to correct errors in pronoun usage as well as any other errors you find.

Character Counts

Employer's place a great deal of importance on honesty and integrity. Those two trait are not easy to spot on a job candidates resume or in the course of a job interview. So how can you portray these characteristics for potential employees that might be looking for it. Each organization has his own set of standards, and individual managers have his or her personal standard as well. Neither you nor me can guess what each one is using as their criterion.

Here are some ideas to consider. Use it to present yourself in a way that conveys your awareness of ethics in the workplace:

1. Research the organization and, when possible, the person with who you will interview. Websites and social networking sites are resources that provide clues as to what ethical issues are important to a potential employer. Do workers handle confidential information? Are employees responsible for handling money or other aspects of finance that involve trust? Does the company

---

have a lot riding on keeping their ideas hidden from competitors? See how you can describe your skills and experience in ways that relate to these interests.

2. Think of experiences you have had that show your sense of honesty and integrity. Include mentions of that into your resume. When you go for an interview, plan to mention examples of these experiences to your interviewer. If they don't ask directly about ethics, don't be afraid to bring them up if you can work them into the conversation.

3. Try to make contact with people whom are knowlegeable about the business or industry. Talk to him or her about the personal qualities that employers require.

4. Request references from you're previous employers, instructors, and others whom are familiar with your character. Ask he or she to comment on your character traits and work ethic.

As a job applicant, you are selling yourself and must anticipate what the buyer is looking for. Never forget that character is part of the equasion.

How did you do? Excellent _____ Good _____

Need More Practice _____

chapter review

WORKSHEET 7.1

A. In the blank below "Best," write the letter of the best form for written workplace communication. In the next blank, write the letter of the only *incorrect* form.

Best   **Incorrect**

_____ _____   1. a. A person can usually improve if he really tries.

b. A person can usually improve if they really try.

c. People can usually improve if they really try.

d. A person can usually improve if he or she really tries.

_____ _____   2. a. When customers express their
dissatisfaction, listen courteously.

   b. When a customer expresses his
dissatisfaction, listen courteously.

   c. When a customer expresses his or her
dissatisfaction, listen courteously.

   d. When a customer expresses their
dissatisfaction, listen courteously.

_____ _____   3. a. Every one of the contractors submitted
his or her bid today.

   b. Every one of the contractors submitted
bids today.

   c. Each contractor submitted his bid today.

   d. Every contractor submitted their bid today.

_____ _____   4. a. Did anyone here lose his notebook?

   b. Did anyone here lose a notebook?

   c. Did anyone here lose their notebook?

_____ _____   5. a. Everyone should write his name on the
form.

   b. Everyone should write their name on the
form.

   c. Everyone should write his or her name
on the form.

   d. You should each write your name on the
form.

_____ _____   6. a. The teacher gave the student 20 minutes
to finish her test.

   b. The teacher, Mr. Evans, gave Barbara
Westmaas 20 minutes to finish her test.

   c. The teacher gave Barbara Westmaas
20 minutes to finish the test.

   d. The teacher gave Barbara Westmass
20 minutes to finish his test.

_____ _____   7. a. The CEO of the company and the staff
moved to its new location.

   b. The CEO of the company and the staff
moved to their new location.

   c. They moved to their new location.

   d. Generation X Advertising Agency moved
to its new location.

_____ _____ 8. a. Each applicant and resume will be evaluated on their first impression.

b. Each applicant and resume will be evaluated on its impression.

c. Applicants and resumes will be evaluated on their first impression.

d. Each applicant and resume will be evaluated on the first impression.

_____ _____ 9. a. My colleagues, Ellington and Savanna, are taking their seminar on the road.

b. My colleagues, Ellington and Savanna, are taking the seminar on the road.

c. My colleagues, Ellington and Savanna, are taking a seminar on the road.

d. My colleagues, Ellington and Savanna, are taking his or her seminar on the road.

_____ _____ 10. a. A charitable organization is exempt from taxation as long as it follows IRS regulations.

b. A charitable organization is exempt from taxation as long as they follow IRS regulations.

c. Any charitable organization is exempt from taxation as long as it follow IRS regulations.

d. Charitable organizations are exempt from taxation as long as they follow IRS regulations.

B. Revise the following sentences by replacing the vague references with specific nouns and pronouns or completely rewording. Eliminate extra words where you can.

1. The company encourages you to use direct deposit for your paycheck.

_____

_____

2. Edward took his car to the mechanic and he said he thought it needed a tune-up.

_____

_____

3. They open some of the department stores at midnight on Black Friday.

_____

4. *They're* looking to interview as many qualified candidates as possible so *they* can find at least five outstanding new employees.

_____

_____

5. As teachers and students prepared for the standardized tests, they reassured them and tried to calm their nerves.

_____

_____

CHECK YOUR ANSWERS ON PAGE 448.

WORKSHEET 7.2

A. List collective nouns in the six blanks below. See how many you can think of without referring to the preceding pages.

1. _____

2. _____

3. _____

4. _____

5. _____

6. _____

B. Circle the correct answer within the parentheses.

1. When the members of a group named by a collective noun, such as *team*, act separately or disagree, the pronoun is (singular/plural).

2. When a group named by a collective noun acts as one, a pronoun substituting for it is (singular/plural).

3. Aerojet Corp. has (its/their) offices in Escanaba, Michigan.

4. The sales office is on the third floor; (they are/it is) open until five.

5. Segal Institute always pays (its/their) bills promptly.

6. Metro College revised (its/their) application form.

7. Her family is planning (its/their) vacation for August this year.

8. The Board of Directors will hold (its/it's/their) next meeting at Mount Hood.

9. The city should regulate (its/it's/their) hiring policies more carefully.

10. The committee will review the new data at (its/it's/their) next meeting.

11. Why can't (they/the janitorial service) keep this place clean?

12. We all know (you shouldn't throw trash/trash shouldn't be thrown) from a car window.

13. When good ideas are suggested by staff members, (they/the ideas) should be given consideration.

14. Environmental concerns were raised by the City Council and every member had (his or her/a) unique perspective.

15. Every employee hopes to be recognized for (their/his or her) best efforts on a project.

CHECK YOUR ANSWERS ON PAGE 448.

WORKSHEET 7.3

A. Underline the pronoun that correctly completes the sentence.

1. The Navy recalled (its/their) ships from dry dock.

2. (Every one/Everyone) must make (his or her/their) own decision.

3. Nordstrom's will open (their/its) doors early for the sale.

4. Each building has (its/their) own security guard.

5. (No one/Noone) regrets this incident more than (I/me/myself).

6. Each candidate for office must spend millions of (his or her/their) own money.

7. Either Jeff or his wife Mary will take (her/their) daughter to school.

8. Neither Michael nor his classmates were ready for (his/their) exam.

9. Committees often make (its/their) decisions too slowly.

10. The manager and her assistant are decorating (her/the manager's) office.

11. Senators must use (his or her/their) own funds for this project.

12. The corporation publishes (its/their) annual report in the first quarter.

13. A few mechanics completed (his or her/their) work by 4 p.m.

14. Everyone on the team must pull (his or her/their) own weight.

15. The committee members must submit (its/their) budget by August 1.

B. Rewrite the following sentences to correct agreement errors.

16. Everyone in this department should be sure their nouns and pronouns agree in number in their written communications. [When correcting this sentence, note that *Everyone* is a singular pronoun but that *their* is plural.] _____

_____

_____

17. Every mechanic finished their work quickly. _____

_____

18. Every boy and girl in the class needs (his or her/their) own book.

_____

_____

19. Each applicant should write their name in the blank. _____

_____

_____

20. No one was willing to take responsibility for their part in the disaster.

_____

CHECK YOUR ANSWERS ON PAGE 449.

POSTTEST

Use proofreader's marks to correct the pronoun agreement errors in the following sentences. Write C after the sentences that are already correct.

1. The chairperson asked the board members to cast his or her vote on the proposal.

2. Each staff member must make his or her own travel plans.

3. Every speaker is expected to create his own presentation for the meeting.

4. Every person in the group needs their own laptop.

5. Each participant should sign their name on the attendance sheet.

6. Every department must develop their budget based on historical spending.

7. The manager and the staff took great pride in their achievements.

8. The company moved their new operation to a downtown location.

9. Every member of the jury has cast their vote on the verdict.

10. The top ten salespeople will be able to take his or her chosen guest on an all expenses paid vacation.

CHECK YOUR ANSWERS ON PAGE 449.

Self-Study and Practice Tutorials

wordPOWER

Build your workplace vocabulary and improve spelling skills by completing the exercises in Appendix B on page 364.

Supplementary Practice Exercises

For additional practice, complete the Appendix C exercises for this chapter on page 407.

Knowing Your Subject

recap—chapters 4–7

Test your mastery of Unit 2 by completing these exercises. Your instructor will provide the answer key or have you submit your work for scoring. If you need additional practice, complete the Supplementary Practice Exercises in Appendix C.

NOUNS: PLURALS AND POSSESSIVES

Number right: _____ **out of 25**

A. Use proofreading symbols to correct the compound noun errors in the following paragraph.

1. My brother in law asked me to design a letterhead for his stockcar company, which accepts tradeins.

2. Because his cars have high pricetags, he wants the letter head to be classy.

3. Business-casual attire may be worn in the office as long as meetings are not being conducted with outside business-people.

4. The stock holders meetings will be held on Friday at 10 a.m. All South-West regional managers are expected to attend.

5. Do not be persuaded to down size your department because preestablished sales quotas are not met every quarter.

B. Circle the correct form of the words in the blanks. When needed, use your dictionary to check on both singular and plural spellings, definitions, and pronunciation.

6. My allies/allys found the cargo/cargoe mentioned in both memoranda/memorandum.

7. Please put the bills of lading/bills-of-lading/bill of ladings in the portfolio/portfolioe, as they will be a good tie-in/tie in with the data/datum.

8. The alumni/alumnus were given copies/copys of the itinerarys/itineraries as mementos/mementoes.

9. The notaries public/notary publics/notaries-public gave the affadavits/affadavits' to the editors in chief/ editor in chiefs/editors-in-chief.

10. An importer must know the criteria/criterion for determining the amount of the tariff as well as how to get the letters of credit/letters-of-credit.

11. An addendum/addenda to the contract states that the attorneys/attorney's distribute the proceeds from the sale according to the stated criteria/criterion.

12. The technicians in our laboratorys/laboratories do not understand the various phenomenon/phenomena that affected the experiment.

13. The altos/altoes sang solos/soles for the company choirs/choir's annual concert.

14. The author of the textbook about college curriculums/curricula distributed an up to date/up-to-date syllabus/syllabi.

15. According to the media/medium, proxys/proxies from 1,000 stockholders were received at these facilties/facilities'.

Name: _____ **Date:** _____

C. Underline the noun that is the possessor of the other noun in the following word groups and place the missing apostrophe either before or after the *s*.

16. a very angry customers complaints

17. an honorable judges decisions

18. a hazy afternoons shower

19. the two factories contracts

20. the chic womans fashion sense

21. a months interest

22. a sale on childrens clothes

23. Virginias improving economy

24. the happy employees pay raise

25. the Europeans accent

PRONOUNS: TYPES, USAGE, AND AGREEMENT

Number right: _____ **out of 25**

1. Is Mike Terry better qualified than (her/she)?

2. They completed more of the programming curriculum than (I/me).

3. The two who will join the department are Jill Edelson and (he/him).

4. The Rock Springs plant is owned by Martinez and (me/I/myself).

5. Neither Ms.Yamomoto nor (I/me/myself) will visit the Maryland plant.

6. (Some one/Someone) left (his or her/their) keys at the reception desk.

7. My racing car is faster than (your's/yours'/yours) and (her's/hers).

8. (Everybody's/Everybodys/Every body's) getting a raise.

9. (Who's/Whose/Whos) laptop computer is missing?

10. (Who/Whom) did you say will handle the new account?

11. The host seated (hisself/himself) between Artie and (me/I/myself).

12. Lee became acquainted with the planner (who/whom) was in charge of the convention.

13. (Him/He) and (me/I/myself) will report it to (whoever/whomever) is in charge.

14. If (anyone/any one) of the men would like a ticket, (he/they) may have one.

15. If (it's/its/its') not too late, give the information to (whoever/whomever) needs it.

16. We sent emails to all (who/whom) we thought might visit our showroom.

17. Each officer was issued (his/their/a) new uniform yesterday.

18. The guests of honor were Nancy Burnett and (I/me/myself).

19. Her family members are taking (it/it's/their) vacations at different times this year.

20. The Internal Revenue Service revised (its/it's/their) forms again this year.

21. The Maintenance Department is on the third floor; (it's/they are) open every day.

22. (It's/Its) (I/me) who should take the risk.

23. Give the heaviest workload to (he/him) and (I/me).

24. It was not (me/I/myself) who made the suggestion.

25. He wants (we technicians/us technicians) to take responsibility for the project.

Name: _____   **Date:** _____

writing for your career

DEVELOPING A WINNING RESUME

Do you already have an up-to-date, polished resume? If so, this unit activity can be used to critique it and determine whether it could use improvement. If you do not have an up-to-date, polished resume, use this time to plan your approach and write your draft.

Your resume represents you to an employer and, in most cases, stands between you and further consideration for a job. It can either screen you in or screen you out. In today's Internet-based approach to the job search, applicants worry that they are competing against unknown (but huge) quantities of competitors whose resumes might be superior. In addition, studies show that the people who screen resumes don't spend a fraction of the time reading them that the writer takes to put together what he or she hopes is a "winning" resume. When you take into account the automated screening technique of scanning resumes for keywords, you could end up feeling discouraged. Like any challenging task, the best way to handle it is to start with a plan and take it step by step. Use the writing process to plan, draft, revise, edit, and proofread. In this case, formatting is a big part of the drafting and revising process.

A resume is a summary of your employment background and experience, highlighting personal facts that relate to the position you are seeking. Many excellent books and websites are available to guide you in preparing a resume that will give you the confidence you need when pursuing a job search. Review resume samples from many sources and make note of the sections included and the formatting ideas that fit your situation. When developing the format, keep in mind the advice you read in this chapter's "Career Connection" about formatting in a resume you will present or send in print versus one you will download or cut and paste into an online job application.

In addition, you will need to find out all you can about the job for which you are applying. Armed with this information, you can focus on those aspects of your background, education, experience, personality, and interests that will get you past the applicant screener on the other end of the electronic applications system.

PARTS TO INCLUDE IN A RESUME

- **Contact Information**—Placed at the top of the resume, this includes your name and contact information. Include your mailing address, telephone number(s), and email address. An important caution: If your current email address is a nickname, something funny or cute, or refers to something personal about you known among friends, change it. A professional, straightforward email address using your name is mandatory on a resume. If you have a website or Facebook page that is related to the job application, list it below the email address. Do not list a Facebook page that contains personal photos and information not relevant to your career.

  Example: JENNIFER J. RODRIGUEZ
  1000 Light Street
  Baltimore, Md 21230
  Phone: 410-000-0000
  Fax: 410-000-0001
  jjrodriguez@xxx.com

- **Summary or Professional Profile**—This section is optional, so think about whether you have a key selling point related to your skills and experience that can be summarized in a statement or short paragraph. When you apply for different jobs, you can tailor this section to emphasize education, work experience, personal qualities, and/or skills that are relevant to each potential employer's needs.

Example: College graduate with Marketing degree and work experience as public relations intern for an international financial firm. Excellent written and oral communication skills; able to create strong graphics and text for a variety of promotional materials.

- **Objective**—Many employers expect to see an objective at the top of the resume, although it also is not mandatory. If included, make it a short statement describing the type of position you are looking for. Decide how tightly you want to focus your career search. If you have been trained for a specific type of work and feel comfortable focusing on a particular type of position, then be explicit. If not, a more general statement can be used.

Example: Specific: A lighting technician position that provides the opportunity to apply my education and skills as a Certified Apprentice Lighting Technician.

General: An entry-level position in live theater, concert, or special event lighting.

- **Employment History and Work Experience**—This section is required. It provides a list of your current and previous employers. Include company names and addresses, dates of employment, and positions held. This information can be combined with a list of items describing your most important job functions and achievements, or it can be listed separately. The two most widely used ways of organizing work experience are chronological and functional. A third method combines the two. These styles are described on page 144.

To the extent possible, describe your background using the language that the potential employer uses to describe the job requirements. Of course, this can be done only if such a match exists. Where there is no match, look at the more general qualities mentioned and focus on what you have to offer in those areas.

Develop the list of duties you performed using language that tells the employer what you accomplished or the special skills you used. Use action words that capture the application of a duty or skill. In the "Career Connection" section of Chapter 8, you will find a list of action words to help you get started. Where possible, include facts and/or statistics that support your achievement claims. For example, if you cite customer service experience, how many customers did you assist weekly? Did you propose or help implement solutions to customer issues? Be as specific as possible, but remember to make the description concise. Save long examples for the interview.

Example: Job duty description: Greeted customers, checked reservations, assigned tables.

Achievement description: Contributed to the restaurant's reputation for outstanding service by efficiently and courteously handling check-in and seating of customers.

- **Education**—List all education-related information, whether or not you received a degree in every instance. Start with the highest level of education achieved. List schools attended, date of graduation, majors and degrees, or number of hours earned toward a degree. If you have little work experience, you might opt to list your educational background before work experience.

Example: EDUCATION
- Associate's Degree, Accounting, Cuyahoga Community College, Cuyahoga County, Ohio, 20xx
- Currently have 30 credits toward Bachelor's Degree, Business Administration, Ohio State University
- "Best Accounting Practices" Seminar sponsored by National Association of Certified Public Accountants, 20xx

- **Special Skills and Achievements**—If you have any special training, technical skills, involvement in professional or civic organizations, volunteer activities, awards, or other achievements—professional or personal—relevant to your job search, list them at the end of the resume. This should not be an effort to "pad" your resume. Decide whether it will be persuasive and make it brief.

- **References**—Use this heading if you intend to list the contact information on the resume. Most employers do not require references until a job offer is being made. Make sure that you have people lined up to provide your references so that you will be prepared.

Options for Resume Style

Resume styles are based on the order in which the information is presented. Your goal is to create a presentation that best points out to potential employers your skills and qualifications for the job. Choose one of the following standard formats, which employers are accustomed to seeing.

- **Chronological** This style lists employers and work experience from the most recent to the earliest. It works well if you have had a series of jobs that provided experience that is closely or at least somewhat related to the position you are seeking. If the jobs aren't closely related, try to word your list of responsibilities, achievements, and skills to show the employer how the experience will transfer. If you have worked in several unrelated fields or if you don't have much work experience, this style might not present you in the best light. You might want to try developing a functional resume.

- **Functional** This style lists your qualifications without tagging them to specific employers. It summarizes work experience, skills, and achievements that match the requirements of the type of position being sought. In this format, you can elect to place the emphasis on your education if you don't have work experience. Use headings such as "Technology Courses," "Technical Proficiency," "Business Courses," and "Communication Skills" if you are placing more emphasis on your education. If you are placing emphasis on work-related skills, use functional headings, such as "Management," "Leadership," "Sales," or "Child Care," followed by a list of achievements and responsibilities that emphasize your strengths.

  In the section following the list of functions, provide the data about your employment history (company names and addresses, job titles, and dates of employment). List organization names, addresses, and years with each employer, beginning with the most recent.

- **Combination** This style merges the chronological and functional styles. It lists important skills, educational background, and/or achievements first (functional) and then specific employment data and brief descriptions of responsibilities and achievements with each employer (chronological).

writing for your career recap

PLANNING

Use the information provided here as well as your reference manual and information on the Internet to plan the content and style of your resume. Here are some recommended websites for sample resumes—the resources are endless on the Web: US Department of Labor: Careeronestop.org; National Association of Colleges and Employers: http://bit.ly/NACEResumeHelp.; CareerBuilder.com; America Online (AOL): http://jobs.aol.com

You might decide to try out different styles or create more than one version for different types of employers or career areas that you intend to explore. Plan which of the following parts you will include and the style you will use: headings, employers, job responsibilities, skills and experience, achievements and action words to use as descriptors, education, references' names and contact information, special skills and achievements.

DRAFTING

Develop a draft of your resume or polish your current one. Use the chronological template provided here or one of the other styles. Include the optional sections only if you feel they will enhance your completed product.

Sample Resume Template: Chronological Style

First and Last Name
Address
City, State Zip Code
000-000-0000
name@email.com

SUMMARY

OBJECTIVE

WORK EXPERIENCE

Dates
Job Title
Employer, City, State
- Responsibilities, achievements, and skills

Dates
Job Title
Employer, City, State
- Responsibilities, achievements, and skills

Dates
Job Title
Employer, City, State
- Responsibilities, achievements, and skills

EDUCATION

SPECIAL SKILLS AND ACHIEVEMENTS

Sample Resume Template: Functional Style

First and Last Name
Address
000-000-0000
name@email.com

OBJECTIVE

SUMMARY

PROFESSIONAL ACHIEVEMENTS

Management
- Skills and achievements
- Skills and achievements
- Skills and achievements

Customer Service
- Skills and achievements
- Skills and achievements
- Skills and achievements

Sales
- Skills and achievements
- Skills and achievements

WORK HISTORY
- Date, Job Title, Employer name and address
- Date, Job Title, Employer name and address
- Date, Job Title, Employer name and address

EDUCATION

SPECIALIZED TRAINING

Revise, Edit, and Proofread

Work with your classmates or find others who are willing to read and critique your draft or the resume you are currently using. Use the writing process to revise, edit, and proofread the finished document.

©Andres Rodriguez/Fotolia

Mastering Verbs and Modifiers

© Endostock/Fotolia

After completing Chapter 8, you will be able to do the following:

- Use verb tenses correctly to express the time of action and state of being.
- Distinguish between regular and irregular verbs in forming tenses.
- Correctly form tenses of irregular verbs or use the dictionary to find their correct forms.
- Define forms of words that are called gerunds, infinitives, and verbals and explain their use in sentences.

8

Verbs: Types, Tenses, and Forms

career connection

KEYWORDS AND ACTION VERBS

When scanning or reading resumes, employers look for keywords that match job skills. **Keywords** can be phrases, technology terms, industry jargon, names of computer software applications, and other specific skills required in a particular field. In your resume and cover letter, you can incorporate these words into your descriptions of your experience. Use terms that are up to date in your field and use concrete action words to describe your achievements.

Following is a list of action words that can replace language which simply describes a job duty. These words say, "I can produce results." They are a precise and engaging way to communicate what you can offer to the employer.

accomplished	conducted	developed	headed	launched	originated	publicized
achieved	contracted	directed	identified	maintained	oversaw	reviewed
arranged	contributed	eliminated	implemented	managed	performed	revitalized
assisted	coordinated	established	improved	marketed	planned	solved
attained	created	evaluated	increased	monitored	prepared	streamlined
chaired	decreased	expedited	initiated	motivated	presented	supervised
collected	demonstrated	facilitated	introduced	operated	processed	trained
compiled	designed	formulated	instituted	organized	produced	wrote

PRETEST

Circle any incorrect verbs and write the correct verb form in the blank.
If the verb is already correct, write C.

_____   1. Georgette and Samuel talks on the phone every morning.

_____   2. She told him that Anchorage was larger than Boise.

_____   3. Demand for workers keep increasing, causing wages to rise.

_____   4. He been watching TV all day.

_____   5. When the West was young, capital punishment meant
being hung.

_____   6. Waiting for the arrival of the senator, he stood at the
window all afternoon.

_____   7. They had all ran for public office in the past.

_____   8. If the group of volunteers arrives by noon, please give me
a call.

_____   9. A box of our most expensive tools is on the table.

_____ 10. If I was you, I would look at Internet sites for a job.

CHECK YOUR ANSWERS ON PAGE 450.

Verb Tenses

In Chapter 2, you learned that verbs are where the action is. In this chapter, you will learn about the different forms of verbs and how to correctly use them in your writing. See "Some Basics About Verbs" on page 151 for a reminder of what you have already studied.

Verbs express the action or being in a sentence. *Action* or *being* occurs in three principal time periods: **past**, **present**, and **future**. The term **tense** is used for *time*. Some actions or states of being occur over a period of time; for example, something may start in the past and continue into the present or start in the present and continue into the future. Here are some ways we express time:

It is being done at the present time:

I **am working** on the project.

It started in the past and is continuing in the present:

I **have been working** on this project for days.

It was done in the past:

I **worked** on the project earlier today.

It will be done in the future.

I **will work** on this for days if necessary.

It is being done in the present and will continue in the future.

I **will be working** on this until at least 7 p.m. tonight.

FORMING TENSES OF REGULAR VERBS

Verbs are classified as regular or irregular, based on how the basic word changes to form the tenses that show the time of the action or state of being. **Regular verbs** form tenses by adding s, ed, or ing to the basic form.

walk	walks	walked	walking
call	calls	called	calling

Some dictionaries provide forms of verbs. Look up the verb *walk* in your dictionary. (Be sure to look at the verb *walk*, not the noun.) In some dictionaries, *walks*, *walked*, *walking* are next to the entry word. This means that all forms of regular verbs are included in that dictionary. Note that some dictionaries do not show the forms of regular verbs because it is assumed that you will know how to add *s*, *ed*, or *ing* to indicate verb tense.

SOME BASICS ABOUT VERBS

1. **Every sentence has at least one verb.** The verb tells what the subject *does* (action verbs) or what the subject *is* (being verbs).

   Some verbs consist of one word:

   Action   The bank manager **interviewed** two loan applicants.

   Our systems analyst **purchased** a new firewall program.

   Being   The sales director **was** in the office.

   Other verbs consist of two or more words: one or more **helping (linking) verbs** and a main verb.

   The human resources director **has been interviewing** those applicants all day.

   Has and *been* are helping verbs; *interviewing*, an action verb, is the main verb.

   The software engineer **should have been** here today.

   Should and *have* are helping verbs; *been*, a being verb, is the main verb.

2. **Infinitives are the basic forms of verbs preceded by to.** Examples are *to cook, to dance, to have, to be, to love, to work,* and *to send*. Do not confuse an infinitive with the action or being verb in a sentence. An infinitive is not used as a verb; the verb is elsewhere in the sentence. In the following sentences, the infinitive is in bold.

   The manager wants **to hire** a new assistant.

   The subject is *manager*; the verb is *wants*.

   The applicant seems **to want** the job.

   The subject is *applicant*; the verb is *seems*.

3. **Choosing a verb form depends on tense (time), number, and person.** Number and person agreement will be covered in Chapter 9.

   Tense   When does the action or being take place—past, present, or future?

   Number   Does the verb have a singular or plural subject?

   Person   Is the subject of the verb in first person, second person, or third person?

Simple Present

If the subject is a singular noun or pronoun other than *you* or *I*, form the present tense by adding *s* to the basic verb form.

Singular noun	In Spain a **visitor** to a home often **receives** a gift from the host.
Singular pronoun	**It appears** to be a mistake.

If the subject is a plural noun or pronoun or *you* or *I*, the present tense is the basic verb form without *s*.

Plural noun subject	**Evelyn** and **Jermaine take** the train to the office.
Plural pronoun subject	**They seem** experienced enough for the work.
Subject is *I*	**I walk** home from work every day.
Understood subject *you*	Please **mail** the checks.

Present Participle

The *ing* form of the verb is called the **present participle**. Use it to indicate that an action or state of being is in progress. The present participle requires a helping verb.

> If you **are planning** a party, be sure to include all of the volunteer staff members.

> We **are considering** both Elliot and Robert for the new supervisor position.

> They **will be working** on the new design every day from now on.

The present participle always ends with *ing* and is usually formed by simply adding *ing* to the unchanged basic form: *see*, *seeing*. Be aware, however, of other spelling variations:

- Sometimes a final *e* is omitted before adding *ing*—*love*, *loving*
- Sometimes a final letter is doubled before adding *ing*—*win*, *winning*

writing**TIP**

Most of the non-Standard English verb forms brought to your attention in this chapter are noticeable in business or professional environments. For that reason, it is important that you acquire this information about verbs and develop the habit of using Standard English.

Past and Past Participle

For regular verbs, the simple past and the past participle are the same: Add *ed* or *d* to the basic verb form to indicate that the action or being was in the past—as in *earned* and *died*. Use this form of any regular verb either with or without a helping verb. Both *I earned* and *I have earned* are correct, depending on the idea you wish to express.

> The contractor **finished** the construction.

> The contractor **has finished** every project on schedule.

> The Department of Transportation can tell you how many people **died** in car crashes last year.

> According to the Department of Transportation report, more people **have died** in car crashes since texting has become a hazard on the road.

wordPOWER

If English is your second language, be especially alert to adding *ed* to regular verbs if the past tense is required—*call, called*—or if *have, has,* or *had* precedes the verb—*have called, has called, had called*.

Simple Future

Future tenses always use helping verbs because English (unlike other languages) has no principal verb form to express the future. The helping verbs *will* and *shall* before the basic verb form show action or being that will take place in the future. In the case where either *shall* or *will* is correct, *will* is standard usage. The example below is one of the few common uses of the word *shall* in modern English.

> He **will call** the office tomorrow.
>
> **Shall** I drop you off on my way to the meeting?

Not only in American but also in Canadian and British English, the distinctions between *shall/will* and *should/would* are mostly ignored except in legal documents. In most of the English-speaking world, however, *will* and *would* predominate. The principles for traditional or formal use of *shall/will* and *should/would* are shown below in case you require this information.

- Use *shall* or *should* with first-person singular or plural pronoun subjects. Use *will* or *would* with all other subjects.

  > I **shall** prepare a report for you. [first-person singular]
  >
  > We **should** like to help you. [first-person plural]
  >
  > You **would** be arriving about 7 a.m. [second person]
  >
  > Auditors **will** examine the records. [third person]

- For questions about the future, use *shall* or *should* with a first-person pronoun. For statements about the future, use *would* or *will* (or contractions such as *I'll*) with any noun or pronoun.

  > **Shall** (or **Should**) we send this to your advertising department?
  >
  > **Shall** (or **Should**) we fly to Charlotte with you tomorrow?
  >
  > I **will** send the questionnaire to our Marketing Department.
  >
  > **We'll** obtain the information.
  >
  > You **will** go to the training course on Thursday and Friday.
  >
  > We **would** like to have Abigail meet the new client.

- Use *should* with any subject to mean "ought to."

  > She **should** go to work properly dressed.
  >
  > I **should** eat the fruit, not the chocolate.

- Use *would* with any subject to mean something that habitually occurs.

  > We **would** always eat the chocolate instead of the fruit.

SENTENCES WITH TWO OR MORE VERBS

When a sentence has two or more verbs, generally express them in the same tense.

Present tense	She **thinks** I **am** a millionaire.
Past tense	Mr. Meek **wrote** me a note in which he **said** I **passed** the accounting final.

For a general truth or something still going on, use the present tense, even if a verb elsewhere in the sentence is past tense.

No   Mr. Chung **told** us that Tokyo **was** larger than New York City.

Yes   Mr. Chung **told** us that Tokyo **is** larger than New York City.

Even though he told us in the past, Tokyo *is* still larger.

No   Joan **demonstrated** in Binghamton that our printer **performed** better than any other.

Yes   Joan **demonstrated** in Binghamton that our printer **performs** better than any other.

Since our printer still performs better *now—performed* (past tense) is wrong.

No   What **were** the titles of the books you **borrowed** from the library?

Yes   What **are** the titles of the books you **borrowed** from the library?

Although you borrowed the books in the past, the titles are still the same.

GO TO PAGE 164 AND COMPLETE WORKSHEET 8.1.

word**POWER**

The word *tense* is used in grammar to mean *time*—indicating *when*. Look up the word *tense* in your dictionary to see how it is defined as a term of grammar and its other definitions.

Forming Tenses of Irregular Verbs

Irregular verbs are verbs that do not follow a set pattern when changing tense. Some irregular verbs change spelling for past, present, and future; some change spelling only for one tense. The verb *begin* is an example of a common irregular verb.

Present	Please **begin** the presentation. [The singular pronoun subject *You* is understood.]
Present	Ms. Gina Hecht **begins** a new assignment today. [The singular proper noun subject requires adding *s*.]
Present Participle (in progress)	I **am beginning** to understand the new regulations. [Double the final letter before adding *ing*; needs a helping verb.]
Past Tense	The band **began** to play the national anthem. [Change the *i* to *a* instead of adding *ed*; no helping verb.]
Past Participle	By the time we arrived the meeting **had begun.** [Change the *i* to *u* instead of using the basic form with a helping verb; this form also needs a helping verb.]

RECOGNIZING IRREGULAR VERBS

Mastering verbs forms requires the ability to recognize verbs that might be irregular. Refer to "Common Irregular Verbs" on page 155, and look them up in the dictionary to be sure of form or spelling.

The words in column 1A are the basic forms. Use them alone with *you*, *I*, or a plural subject. Also use them with the helping verbs *will*, *shall*, *would*, *should*, *do*, *did*, *does*, *might*, *may*, *can*, and *could* to form past and future tenses, no matter what the subject is.

No Helping Verbs

You drink smoothies too fast. [subject is *you*]

I choose the beach for today's trip. [subject is *I*]

They break easily. [plural pronoun subject]

These **surfers wear** identical clothing. [plural noun subject]

With Helping Verb

He **would drink** smoothies all day if he could.

He **did choose** me for the competition.

I **should take** the best one.

Ms. Flood **does run** the business.

The forms in column 1B are the present tense forms ending with *s*. Use them with any singular subject except *I* or *you*.

Singular pronoun subject   Everybody **goes** to lunch at the same time.

Singular noun subject   Professor Seilo **understands** the problem.

Common Irregular Verbs

Column 1A	Column 1B	Column 2	Column 3
		Simple Past (no helping verb)	Past Participle (use helping verb)
Present	Present		
begin	begins	began	begun
break	breaks	broke	broken
bring	brought	brought	brought
choose	chooses	chose	chosen
do	does	did	done
drink	drinks	drank	drunk
give	gives	gave	given
go	goes	went	gone
hang (suspend)	hangs	hung	hung*
lay	laid	laid	laid
lie	lay	lain	lain
ring	rings	rang	rung
rise	rises	rose	risen
see	sees	saw	seen
sink	sank	sunk	sunk
speak	speaks	spoke	spoken
stand	stands	stood	stood
swing	swings	swung	swung
take	takes	took	taken
wear	wears	wore	worn

Hang meaning a method of putting to death is regular: *hang, hangs, hanged.*

Simple Past

Column 2 verbs are the simple past forms. Use them with any subject. Do not use a helping verb. (For some verbs, columns 2 and 3 forms are the same.)

> She **ran** away.   The glass **broke**.   The bells **rang**.

writingTIP

Although the irregular verbs in the preceding chart are among the most commonly misused verbs, they aren't the only ones. To avoid incorrect use of irregular verbs, careful writers refer to the dictionary when in doubt.

Past Participle

Column 3 forms are the past participles. Use them with a helping verb, such as *have*, *has*, *had*, *been*, *was*, or *were* and with any subject.

Singular   She **has** run away.

The **glass had broken**.

Plural   They **have** run away.

The **glasses had broken**.

The Perfect and Progressive Tenses

There is far more to know about verbs than you probably ever hoped to learn. A few more fine points about verbs will contribute to your ease as a writer.

PERFECT TENSES

You have learned that tense tells the time of the verb, that is, when the action or state of being takes place. The simple tenses are past, present, and future. The **perfect tenses** are past perfect, present perfect, and future perfect; perfect tenses are formed by combining *have*, *has*, or *had* with a past participle.

The **past perfect** tense indicates that one past action occurred before another past action; use the past perfect to show the more distant past.

had + **past participle**

> I **had planned** to visit the Ford plant while I was in Detroit.

The **present perfect** tense indicates an action that began in the past but still continues today. It also indicates a past action at an unspecified past time.

writingTIP

If you have trouble understanding the concept of beginning in the past but continuing today, think of your long-time friends. You met them in the past, but you still know them today.

has or *have* + **past participle**

> I **have seen** *Harry Potter and the Goblet of Fire* five times. [At some point I saw the movie, but we don't know when].

The **future perfect** tense shows that action will have been completed before a specific future time.

will have or *shall have* + **past participle**

> On our anniversary, we **will have been** business partners for five years.

PROGRESSIVE TENSES

The **progressive tenses** combine a form of *to be* with the present participle of a verb to show that action is or was in progress. When editing your writing refer to the chart below to make sure you have used the correct helping verb to express the precise meaning you want to convey.

USING THE PROGRESSIVE TENSES

Present progressive	Is happening now or temporarily	Dan is working today.
Past progressive	Was in progress during a specific past time	He was working all day.
Future progressive	Will be in progress in the future	They will be working next week.
Present perfect progressive	Has been in progress continually	He has been working all day.
Past perfect progressive	Had happened continuously at an unknown past time	The students had been texting the answers prior to the exam.
Future perfect progressive	A continuous action that will be completed at some time in the future	By the holiday, they will have been working for a week.

writing**TIP**

We'd, *I'd*, *you'd*, and so on are appropriate in conversation, in personal letters, and in informal messages—but not in business letters, reports, or other more formal communications.

EMPHATIC FORMS

Emphatic forms are used to add special emphasis to the verb. The emphatic form combines *do*, *does*, *did*, or *will* or *shall* with the verb's basic form.

- **Past Emphatic:** *did* + basic form

  Despite the problems, we **did leave** on time.

- **Present Emphatic:** *do* or *does* + basic form

  He **does work** in Arlington, but he lives in the District of Columbia.

- **Future Emphatic:** *will* + basic form

  I **will** finish college no matter what happens. [first person]

  The enemy **shall** not succeed. [third person]

GO TO PAGE 166 AND COMPLETE WORKSHEET 8.2.

Verb Mood

Another to way to think about selecting the right verb form to communicate what you intend is called **verb mood**. The mood conveys the manner in which you want the action in a sentence to be interpreted by the reader. The three verb moods are indicative, imperative, and subjunctive.

- **Indicative Mood:** used to make a statement or ask a question.

  Alonzo Williams **is** the assigned project manager.

  Is he **allowed** to make decisions about expenses?

- **Imperative Mood:** used to make a polite request or command.

  Deliver the contracts to the CEO in person.

  Please **take** me with you to the luncheon.

- **Subjunctive Mood:** expresses doubt, a wish, or a condition contrary to fact.

  I **might get** a lower grade than I expected.

  We **ask** that the work **be** done by noon.

  If I **were** you, I **would have asked** for a higher salary.

Verbals

Verbals are forms of verbs that are functioning as nouns, adjectives, or adverbs. The three kinds of verbals are gerunds (also called verbal nouns), participles (also called verbal adjectives), and infinitives, which may be nouns, adjectives, or adverbs.

GERUNDS (VERBAL NOUNS)

As the alternate name implies, a gerund is a word that looks like a verb and may even have an object—but it always functions as a noun. **Gerunds** always end in *ing*. You can distinguish them from true verbs because a verb ending in *ing* is always preceded by an auxiliary (helping) verb.

He is majoring in **marketing**.

Is majoring is the verb; *marketing*, a gerund, is the object of the preposition *in*.

Marketing a new iPhone app isn't as easy as you might think.

Marketing is the subject of the verb *is*.

PARTICIPLES (VERBAL ADJECTIVES)

A **participle** sometimes looks like a verb, has tenses, and may have an object, but it functions as a **verbal adjective**.

Verbals functioning as adjectives are readily distinguished from verbs because verbs ending in *ing* are always preceded by helping verbs.

Verb	The woman who ran from the reporter **is wearing** a red dress.
Verbal	The woman **wearing** the red dress ran from the reporter.

Wearing is a participle introducing the participial phrase *wearing the red dress*. This phrase modifies the noun *woman*; the verb is *ran*.

Verbals ending in *ed* may act as modifiers, not verbs.

Verb	The merchandise I **ordered** last month has just arrived.
Verbal	Merchandise **ordered** last month has just arrived.

The verbal *ordered* modifies the noun *merchandise*, which is the subject of the verb *has arrived*.

Verbal	**Ground** up, the meat tastes much like beef hamburger.

---

grammarTIP

When trying to distinguish between the participle and a verb, remember that the participle may look like a verb but acts as an adjective; in other words, it describes a noun or pronoun.

Example: I fried some chicken for dinner last night.

I ate fried chicken for dinner last night. (Is anyone frying anything in this sentence? No, this sentence is simply telling you what kind of chicken I ate.)

The verbal *Ground* is modifying the noun *meat*, which is the subject of the verb *tastes*.

Perfect participle verbs show action occurring in the past, but they have helping verbs.

> **Having ordered** the software last week, we were pleased to receive it so soon.

Having ordered is a perfect participle modifying the pronoun *we*; *software* is the object of the perfect participle *having ordered*. *We* is the subject, and *were pleased* is the verb.

INFINITIVES

Infinitives are verbals that function as adjectives, adverbs, or nouns; they consist of *to* plus the basic verb form or participle. Sometimes *to* is omitted from an infinitive but understood. The **present infinitive** uses *to* plus the basic verb form.

> We plan **to take** the deposition now.

The **perfect infinitive** is for action that took place before the action of the verb; it uses *to* plus a helping verb plus a participle form.

> We expected **to have finished** the report yesterday.

In the two example sentences above, the infinitives are nouns because they are the objects of the verbs *plan* and *expected*. *Deposition* and *report* are objects of the infinitives. The following example has two "perfect" infinitives and a third one (*lost*) in which *to have* is understood.

> "'Tis better **to have loved** and **lost**/Than never **to have loved** at all."
> (Alfred, Lord Tennyson)

SPLIT INFINITIVES

Split infinitives are "split" by inserting an adverb between *to* and the verb, as in *to finally succeed*. Grammar traditionalists recommend that infinitives not be split. Modernists, however, suggest that the "don't split infinitives" rule sometimes results in awkward writing. When that is the case, we recommend that you split the infinitive.

Awkward   He wants **to quickly do** the work.

The infinitive is split, and the sentence is awkward, so revise.

Revised   He wants **to do** the work **quickly**.

Awkward   He hopes **to finish finally** this project.

The infinitive is not split, but the sentence sounds awkward. Revise and use the split infinitive to improve the sentence.

Revised   He hopes **to finally finish** this project.

GO TO PAGE 167 AND COMPLETE WORKSHEET 8.3.

Checkpoint

Bad habits of speech have a way of finding their way into our writing. You are fortunate if you live, go to school, and work around a population of people who speak perfect English because only that will "sound right" to you. In reality, though, we hear some incorrect usage so often, that when we hear something that is correct, it sounds wrong. It is the intent of this chapter and the next one to heighten your awareness of correct usage. Once you develop the habit of using the writing process to edit and revise your work—checking for grammatical correctness and recalling what you have learned in this course—correct usage will sound right most of the time.

While studying this chapter you might have recognized a particular usage you've been careless about following. To rid yourself of this bad habit of speech, repeat the correct form out loud until it sounds natural to your ears. Three of the most common serious verb errors follow. If you make errors like these, hurry to acquire the habit of using Standard English verbs.

1. Using *was* when *were* is required:

    If I *was* you, I wouldn't stay up so late.

    We *was* there for half an hour.

    In both cases the verb should be *were*. Practice saying (to yourself), "If I *were* you" several times a day. Then try saying (to yourself), "If I *was* you," and you'll find it no longer sounds correct.

2. Using the simple past with a helping verb:

    He had *wore* that same shirt yesterday.

    The verb should be *worn* (*or* He wore that same shirt yesterday).

3. Using the past participle without a helping verb:

    I know he *done* a good job because I *seen* it.

    Use *did* and *saw*, or use helping verbs before *done* and *seen*.

communications connection

LETTER STYLES AND FORMATS

Business letters follow a format that is standard throughout the business world. This format is easy to follow once you have an understanding of the essential parts. In this section you will learn how to format the parts of a personal business letter—the style you would use for a cover letter to a potential employer.

Standard Letter Parts

The standard parts of business letters from the top of the page to the bottom are listed below. See how these parts are formatted in the illustration on page 217 at the end of this unit.

Letterhead

This is preprinted paper that has the sender's name and contact information. *Letterhead* is the business term for *stationery*. In a business setting, the company name are always at the top. The address, phone number, and so on may be at the top or bottom.

When writing a personal business letter, such as a cover letter, create personal stationery by typing your name and contact information in a letterhead style at the top of the page. You can use a word processing or desktop publishing template or create your own design. If you use a word processing template, be sure to select one that is appropriate for business. This means less is more—a simple, uncluttered design is most appropriate. Also avoid using colorful templates so that any black-and-white prints or photocopies will be readable and attractive.

If you are sending a letter as an attachment to an email, paper is not an issue. If you are printing it, use good quality 8½- by-11-inch paper. White or off-white paper is standard.

Date

This is the day that you are sending the letter. To ensure accuracy for the recipient, make sure you don't use the date on which you started drafting if it is earlier than the date sent.

Type the date two or three lines below the printed letterhead. Always spell out the complete word for the month; do not use *nd*, *th*, *rd*, or *st* after the figure for the day.

June 2, 2013

Note that in some settings, you will see the date expressed in the international and military style with the date preceding the month and year:

2 June 2013 [no comma]

Inside Address

This contains the name and address of the person and/or company to receive the letter (also typed on the outside of the envelope). Type the inside address single-spaced; begin the first line two to four lines below the date. If your letter is very short, you can space down as many as ten lines to help balance the letter in the center of the page.

Maria C. Hernandez

---

99 W. 70th Street   **000-000-0000**
New York, NY 10023   **mchernandez@xxx.com**

January 3, 20xx

Professor Mary Rowe
Human Resources Department
Miami Dade Community College
11380 NW 27 Avenue
Miami, FL 33179

Dear Professor Rowe:

- Spell out personal titles (e.g., Professor, Reverend) except *Ms., Mr.,* and *Dr.* In workplace correspondence indicating a woman's marital status (Mrs. or Miss) is unnecessary and out of date.
- Write the organization name exactly as it is written by the company. If you don't know, look it up in a directory or consult the organization's letterhead or website. Spell out street names and designations such as *Avenue, Street,* and *Court.*
- Spell out state names or use the two-letter postal abbreviations (see your reference manual).

Salutation

This is a formal greeting that always begins with "Dear." Begin typing two line spaces after the inside address. Precede the name with a professional title, such as *Dr., Captain, Father, Rabbi, Senator, Professor,* or with a personal title, such as *Mr.* or *Ms.,* unless you are on a first-name bases with the recipient. Punctuate the salutation with a colon.

> Dear Professor Rowe:
>
> Dear Ms. O'Rourke:
>
> Dear Bob:

If no professional title is known and you don't know whether you're addressing a man or a woman, use the complete name in the salutation.

> Dear Chris O'Brien:

Body

This is the message. Begin it two line spaces below the salutation. Single-space the body but double-space between paragraphs.

Leaving a blank line between paragraphs eliminates the need to indent the first line. While it isn't wrong to indent paragraphs, this style is infrequently used today (it was useful when correspondence was handwritten.) See the illustration on page 218.

Complimentary Closing

This is the last line of the letter before the signature and signals the end of the message. Type the closing two line spaces below the last line of the body and capitalize only the first word.

Complimentary closings used frequently today include the following:

> Sincerely,
>
> Sincerely yours,
>
> Regards,
>
> Best regards,
>
> Cordially,

Respectfully is inappropriate for ordinary business letters but may close a letter to a judge or high-ranking government, school, or church official. Closings such as *Very truly yours* and *Yours truly* are considered outdated.

Signature

This is the writer's name. Type it four line spaces below the closing to allow space for the writer's handwritten signature. In a business setting, the name is followed by the sender's job title and department name. If the job title fits on the same line as the name or department, it is optional to type it this way, separated with a comma.

Sincerely,

Larry Lutsky

Larry Lutsky

Vice President

Real Estate Holdings

Regards,

JoAnn R. Michels

JoAnn R. Michels

Manager

Accounts Payable

Sign letters using blue or black ink. Do not use a title (Mr., Mrs., Ms.) with your signature in business letters.

WRITING PRACTICE

Using a word processing template or your own design, create a personal letterhead that you can use for writing a cover letter to an employer. Refer to the information you have just learned to develop a template on the letterhead for the letter parts that need to be included.

Date to submit this assignment: _____

PROOFREADING PRACTICE

Use proofreading marks or go online to correct errors in the following message.

Dear Colleagues:

As we approach the holiday season, I wanted to remind you about our companys policy regarding to give or to receive gifts form person's and business entities with which your department did business over the pass year. It is important to be remembering that our code of ethics required "zero tolerance" of violation of this policy If you have had any questions about what constitute a business relationship or how the terms "gift" are defined, please reads the Code of Ethics Policy on our company website.

Our CEO Jeremy Soledad remind us, "We represent an organization that must maintain the publics' trust and, therefore, we must be operating under the highest ethical standards. During the holidays, please be especialy vigilant about not nly gifts, but also holiday parties, industry-sponsored ceremonys, and other events."

What would you do if you receive an invitation to a holiday party from a business college, receive a gift, or are in doubt about whether something you receive was a gift? You can refer to the Code of Ethics Polcy or contact my office for more guidance.

Thank you for your corporation. Happy Holidays!

Jeannette Douglas

Senior Employee Relations Manager

How did you do? Excellent _____ Good _____
Need More Practice _____

chapter review

WORKSHEET 8.1

A. In the blank, write the correct form of the verb in parentheses based on the *tense* indicated in parentheses at the end of the sentence. Add a helping verb if necessary.

Example: They (talk) <u>talked</u> every day on the telephone last week. (past)

1. He (work) _____ very accurately. (present)

2. The president (need) _____ your decision now. (present)

3. Ms. DeVries (move) _____ to Lakeport. (past)

4. They (sail) _____ to Catalina this week. (*ing* form)

5. The floor is slippery because the custodian (wax) _____ it. (past)

6. Good manners in the workplace (be) _____ essential to success. (present)

7. The world (look) _____ brighter from behind a smile. (present)

8. Dr. Perry (climb) _____ up the ladder to reach the carton. (past)

9. Left of the plate, you (find) _____ an entrée fork and a salad fork. (future)

10. They (want) _____ something they cannot have. (present)

11. She (want) _____ something she cannot have. (present)

12. He (want) _____ something he could not have. (past)

13. She (want) _____ something she cannot have. (future)

14. An employee's appearance (influence) _____ the way he or she is treated. (present)

15. He believes Ms. Yu (select) _____ a business career. (past)

16. Michael (consider) _____ that problem tomorrow. (future)

17. Dennis (consider) _____ that problem now. (*ing* form)

18. I (stay) _____ at that hotel on every business trip. (present)

19. We (watch) _____ the stock market reports all day. (past)

20. Marketing people (discuss) _____ international sales. (past)

B. Each of the following sentences has a verb error. Cross out the incorrect verb and write the correct form in the blank.

   Example: has We knew that Orlando ~~had~~ a parade every Wednesday year-round.

   _____ 1. The officer said that obeying traffic laws was necessary for accident prevention.

   _____ 2. Seth asked if New York was the biggest city in the USA.

   _____ 3. I brought the data with me that you said you needed.

   _____ 4. Who were the authors of the books on yesterday's best-seller list? (Hint: Authors haven't changed since yesterday.)

   _____ 5. Gary said the old HP 150 color printer was now in Lois's office.

   _____ 6. The people meeting in the conference room were former employees of General Motors. (Hint: They haven't died.)

   _____ 7. He taught us that rivers flowed into oceans. (They still do.)

   _____ 8. We learned that no scientist knew with certainty how the universe originated.

   _____ 9. The Chicago police have not discovered where the $5 million was.

   _____ 10. The CEO praised the office staff for having been so efficient. (Hint: The office personnel are still efficient.)

   CHECK YOUR ANSWERS ON PAGE 450.

WORKSHEET 8.2

A. Cross out the incorrect irregular verb and write the correct form in the blank.

Example: <u>hung</u> I hanged up all my clothes.

_____ 1. I thought it was broke, but it had just wore out.

_____ 2. He begun to work when the bell rung.

_____ 3. He choose the best one for himself.

_____ 4. He had chose the best one for himself yesterday.

_____ 5. She do all the complaining, and he just stand around. (present)

_____ 6. He had drunk all the tea before the sun had rose.

_____ 7. The children have ate all the fresh strawberries.

_____ 8. We seen that Smith done a good job on the pricing.

_____ 9. They had flew to Taiwan last year.

_____ 10. They went to the convention before she quitted her job.

_____ 11. The child had ran away after he had broke the window.

_____ 12. She had wore the new suit yesterday.

_____ 13. He had gave me a ticket to the luncheon.

_____ 14. I seen him before he had spoke.

_____ 15. I had took it with me before you went away.

_____ 16. They always wears suits to the office.

_____ 17. She seen that file before.

_____ 18. "If a man don't know what port he's steering for, no wind is favorable," said the Roman philosopher Seneca.

_____ 19. David swinged his tennis racket and then flung it down on the ground.

_____ 20. Last week the manager give Carlos three days to write the report.

B. Fill in the blanks with the "principal parts" of these irregular verbs. Consult your dictionary if you're unsure of the correct form.

BASIC VERB	PRESENT PARTICIPLE (*ing* ending)	SIMPLE PAST (no helping verb)	PAST PARTICIPLE (requires helping verb)
Example: beat	beating	beat	beaten or beat
1. be*	_____	_____	_____
2. bite	_____	_____	_____
3. blow	_____	_____	_____
4. come	_____	_____	_____
5. cost	_____	_____	_____
6. fall	_____	_____	_____
7. forget	_____	_____	_____
8. freeze	_____	_____	_____
9. hide	_____	_____	_____
10. lead	_____	_____	_____
11. pay	_____	_____	_____
12. shake	_____	_____	_____
13. sink	_____	_____	_____
14. sing	_____	_____	_____
15. throw	_____	_____	_____

*Other "parts": *am, are, is.*

Each sentence below has one or more incorrectly used irregular verbs. Use proofreading marks to make the corrections. When in doubt, consult your dictionary for spelling.

16. Ms. Bogue has beat all records and is wining.

17. Sean payed the bill because the job was done right.

18. Ed has broke two rules and has hid the evidence.

19. Ms. Farrell hanged the picture but had forgot about it.

20. Mr. James could have stayed another day if he had wrote to me.

CHECK YOUR ANSWERS ON PAGE 450.

WORKSHEET 8.3

Write sentences with a singular subject except *you* or *I*. Use the present tense form of the verb.

Example: beat She regularly **beats** her husband at tennis.

1. begin _____

2. give _____

3. approve _____

Write sentences using the following verbs in the present progressive tense.

Example: gather The volunteers are **gathering** signatures for the petition.

4. run _____
5. rise _____
6. fix _____

Write sentences using the following verbs to show past tense without a helping verb.

Example: talk He **talked** on the phone for an hour.

7. win _____
8. sing _____
9. quit _____

Write sentences using these verbs in the past perfect tense.

Example: drink We **had drunk** the punch before the party ended.

10. hide _____
11. pay _____
12. be _____

Write sentences using these verbs in the present perfect tense.

Example: give **They give** shoe polish with all shoe purchases.

13. cost _____
14. ship _____
15. produce _____

CHECK YOUR ANSWERS ON PAGE 451.

POSTTEST

Circle the correct answer. Refer to your dictionary when in doubt.

1. Ms. Nixon explained that many more people (live/lived) in Torrance now.
2. If I (was/were) not certain how to get there, I wouldn't give you directions.
3. Mr. Sedirko has (chose/chosen) three people to take deposition notes.
4. The film industry (employ/employs) many extras for walk-on parts.
5. If I (were/was) you, I would take advantage of this opportunity.
6. Ms. Timm told me that I (did/done) the right thing in Monterey.
7. I wish that the new plans for San Antonio College (was/were) ready.
8. You have (broke/broken) one of the rules.
9. She is the only one of the attorneys who (do/does) the research.
10. They (sunk/sank) the ship.

CHECK YOUR ANSWERS ON PAGE 452.

Self-Study and Practice Tutorials

wordPOWER

Build your workplace vocabulary and improve spelling skills by completing the exercises in Appendix B on page 367.

Supplementary Practice Exercises

For additional practice, complete the Appendix C exercises for this chapter on page 408.

© Goodluz/Fotolia

After completing Chapter 9, you will be able to do the following:

- Apply rules of subject-verb agreement with singular and plural subjects.
- Identify subjects and verbs in various types of sentences and apply rules of subject-verb agreement.
- Apply rules of subject-verb agreement in sentences with personal pronouns, compound subjects, and collective nouns as subjects.

9

Subject-Verb Agreement

career connection

THE INSIDE SCOOP ON POTENTIAL EMPLOYERS

You work long and hard to perfect your resume (several versions) and cover letter (tailored to each application). Wouldn't you like to know what happens when they reach the employer's hands? The Internet is a great source of information about how employers think about and behave toward job applicants. Following are a few interesting facts from a survey conducted by the Society for Human Resource Management, which surveyed members of the Employment Management Association and received more than 500 responses from human resource professionals.

Here is some of the data and what it means for you when writing a cover letter:

- **Always include a cover letter**—28% said they will not consider a resume if it is not accompanied by a cover letter.
- **Keep it brief**—23% of respondents said they do not consider applicants if their cover letter is longer than one page.
- **Engage the reader's interest**—83% of respondents said they spend only an average of one minute or less reading a cover letter.
- **Personalize when possible**—69% view personalized cover letters positively and approximately 29% view them neutrally.
- **Edit and proofread thoroughly**—78% said they would remove an applicant from consideration if the cover letter has typos.

PRETEST

Underline the verb that is correct in the following sentences.

1. Kelly (writes, write) an entry in her diary every night.

2. All the students (want, wants) a good grade on the exam.

3. The executive and his two assistants (arrives, arrive) at the airport at noon.

4. Neither of us (is, are) going to the concert.

5. There (was, were) a house for sale on Birch Street.

6. The supervisor, as well as all the executives, (does, do) the job evaluations.

7. Each of the members (is, are) writing a set of bylaws.

8. The baby (cries, cry) whenever she is hungry.

9. The new answering machine (records, record) all of our messages.

10. The three pathologists (speaks, speak) to the medical classes each quarter.

CHECK YOUR ANSWERS ON PAGE 452.

A Review of Sentence Basics

This chapter is about making sure subjects and verbs agree in number and person to avoid errors that are very distracting to readers who know their grammar. Along with spelling errors and typos, these are the most common types of errors that leave a poor impression in business writing.

A quick review of sentence structure principles that you learned in Chapter 3 will serve as a foundation for the rest of the chapter. The examples in this section do not show subjects and verbs in bold type. From your study of previous chapters, you should be able to identify the different types of sentences, sentence parts, and parts of speech. See if you can identify them before reading the explanatory text that follows each example.

IDENTIFYING SUBJECTS AND VERBS

- Every sentence has at least one independent clause, that is, a group of words that includes a subject and a verb and communicates a complete thought. The verb is the *action* or *being* word; the subject is the *noun* or *pronoun* that tells who or what is doing or being.

- A sentence always begins with a capital letter and ends with closing punctuation, such as a period or question mark.

  The manual is short. Have you read it yet?

- To find a subject, first find the verb. Then ask *who?* or *what?* before the verb. The answer is the subject.

  The engineers study mathematics.

The verb is *study.* Who studies? The subject is *engineers.*

- If a sentence has more than one independent clause, each clause has its own subject-verb combination.

  Some students study and others daydream.

  Who studies? Students. Who daydreams? Others. The subjects are *students* and *others*; the verbs are *study* and *daydream*.

- Although the subject is usually in front of the verb, sometimes the order is reversed. The order is almost always reversed in questions.

  Will after 9 a.m. be a good time to call you?

  The verb is *will be*; the subject is *time*; *after 9 a.m.* and *to call you* are prepositional phrases.

  Are six laptops enough?

  The verb is *are*; the subject is *laptops*.

- Questions are usually worded in either of two ways: (1) The subject comes between the helping verb and the main verb. (2) If a helping verb isn't needed, the verb simply precedes the subject.

  Do the girls study?

  Do is the helping verb; *study* is the main verb; *girls* is the subject. You can test this by turning the question into a statement: *The girls do study.*

  Are the girls smart?

  Are is the verb; *girls* is the subject; *smart* is an adjective.

- A subject is always a noun or a pronoun; however, it may look like a verb when it names an activity.

  Studying is my favorite activity.

  Studying (a gerund) looks like a verb, but in this sentence it is a noun (naming an activity) and is the subject of the sentence.

  To run would be foolish.

  To run (an infinitive) looks like a verb, but it is a noun (naming an activity); the verb is *would be*.

- The understood *you* may be the subject of a sentence that gives a command or makes a polite request.

  Put a new cartridge in the printer.

  The subject *you* is understood; the verb is *put*.

  Please call before Friday.

  The subject *you* is understood; the verb is *call*.

- Introductory or describing words (phrases) may precede the subject. A related word group within a sentence that does not have both a subject and a verb may be a phrase or a clause.

  This morning, the receptionist will open the office.

The verb is *will open*. Who will open? The subject is *receptionist*. *This morning* is a phrase.

> In Schenectady, students study history.

The subject is *students*; the verb is *study*.

> Ambitious and diligent students study every day.

The subject is *students*; the verb is *study*; *ambitious* and *diligent* are adjectives.

- Sometimes a prepositional phrase separates the subject from the verb. The subject is never within a prepositional phrase.

> The *seminar in Washington, DC*, begins promptly at nine in the morning.

The verb is *begins*. Who or what *begins*? The subject is *seminar*. The prepositional phrase *in Washington, DC*, is not part of the subject.

- Sometimes one clause "interrupts" another clause; that is, a clause may separate the subject and verb of another clause.

> Alice, who has many skills and talents, is an RN.

The independent clause is *Alice is an RN*; the dependent interrupting clause is *who has many skills and talents*.

- A compound subject has two or more nouns or pronouns.

> Laziness and irresponsibility impede success.

The compound subject is *laziness* and *irresponsibility*.

- A compound verb has two or more main verbs.

> Robin works and goes to school at night.

The compound verb is *works* and *goes*.

GO TO PAGE 183 AND COMPLETE WORKSHEET 9.1.

Subject-Verb Agreement

The basic rule is simple: A subject and its verb must agree in number and person. If the subject is singular, use a singular verb; if the subject is plural, use the plural verb form. To apply this rule correctly, you need to remember how to form the appropriate verb tense and how to determine whether the subject requires a singular or a plural form.

Most agreement errors occur when a verb form is used that ends with *s* (singular) when it shouldn't or that does not end with *s* (plural) when it should. With noun subjects that are clearly singular and plural, mistakes are less likely, but always proofread your draft carefully and beware of relying on the electronic grammar checker, which may not detect all subject-verb agreement errors.

SINGULAR SUBJECT

Most singular nouns do not end in *s*; singular verbs do end in *s*. Plural nouns end in *s*; plural verbs do not end in *s*.

Singular noun subject	The **honor means** so much to me.
Plural noun subject	The **awards mean** so much to me.

Subjective case pronouns are either singular or plural: *I, he, she, it, you, we, they, who*. *He, she, it*, and *who* always require a singular verb: *He runs, she runs, it runs*. *I, you*, and *they* always require the plural form: *I run, you run, they run*.

Singular pronoun subject	**He runs** five miles every day.
	She was running away.
	Who is running?
Subjects *you, I*	**You are** the winner.
	I work across the street.
Plural pronoun subject	**We ship** widgets everywhere on earth.
	They are the best suppliers of widgets.

COMPOUND SUBJECT

A **compound subject** is made up of two or more nouns and/or pronouns joined by a conjunction (*and, or, nor*). Different rules apply depending on which conjunction is connecting the compound subject.

Joined by *and*

A compound subject joined with *and* is plural and, therefore, requires the plural verb form.

> A **report** and a **letter provide** the information.
>
> **Victoria** and **he are** guarding the secrets.

Joined by *or/nor* or *not only . . . but also*

If the words in a compound subject are joined by *or* or *nor*, make the verb agree with the noun or pronoun following the *or* or *nor*.

> **Martha Jagel** or **Petrina Noor has** the key.
>
> Neither **Mary** nor **they do** the work.

Both nouns are singular. The singular verbs *has* and *do* agree with the second noun. The same rule applies with *not only . . . but also*:

> Not only the **students** but also the **teacher is** stressed during exam time.

The noun *students* is plural; the noun *teacher* is singular; the singular verb *is* agrees with the second noun.

> Not only **Christine** but also the **clerks** usually sort the mail.

The noun *Christine* is singular; the noun *clerks* is plural. The plural verb *sort* agrees with the noun following *but also*.

INDEFINITE PRONOUNS

Indefinite pronouns refer to nonspecific people or things. As you learned in Chapter 7, the following indefinite pronouns are always singular.

anyone	each	somebody
anybody	every	someone
anything	everyone	nobody
either	everybody	no one
neither	everything	one

> **Neither** of them **is** especially appealing to me.
>
> **No one wants** to participate in gossip that is harmful.
>
> **Somebody needs** to step up and take responsibility.

Other indefinite pronouns are always plural: *both*, *few*, *many*, *several*.

> **Several have** been chosen.
>
> **Few take** advantage of the opportunity.

Some indefinite pronouns may be singular or plural depending on the noun or pronoun they refer to in the sentence: *all, any, most, more, some, none*. In the following examples, the pronoun reference is in italics, and the pronoun subject and verb are in bold.

> He did it *all*, but in this case **all is** not good enough.
>
> I contacted the entire *staff*, and **all are** going to attend the game.
>
> We examined the *samples* and **none are** acceptable.
>
> **Some** of the *children* **are** old enough to see the film.
>
> **Some** *type* of mold **is** growing in the walls of the warehouse.

A good way to remember agreement with indefinite pronouns is the following: If *each, every, many, a, an, one, either, neither, another*, or a pronoun ending with *one, body*, or *thing* precedes a subject, the subject is singular and requires the singular verb form.

> **Each man and woman needs** an application form.
>
> **Many an applicant fails** the test because of a spelling error.
>
> **Everyone dines** after 9 p.m. in Spain.

WORDS SEPARATING SUBJECTS AND VERBS

grammarTIP

To ensure that you "ignore" prepositional phrases that separate subjects and verbs, one trick is to place parentheses around all prepositional phrases before you choose the verb. Example: A box (of crackers) is (in the cabinet).

Here is the general rule that makes it easy: When choosing a verb form, ignore words, phrases, or clauses separating a subject from its verb.

No	The **box** of tools **are** on the table.
Yes	The **box** of tools **is** on the table.

The subject is the singular noun *box*. Therefore, use the singular verb form *is*. Ignore the prepositional phrase *of tools* when choosing the verb.

No	The **supervisors**, as well as the CEO, **is** here today.
Yes	The **supervisors**, as well as the CEO, **are** here today.

Ignore the prepositional phrase *as well as the CEO* when deciding on the verb.

writing**TIP**

Although correct, *there* as an opener weakens a sentence. *There (**is/are**) a sandwich and an apple in my lunch box.*

The tendency is to say "There is," but the correct form in writing is *There are a sandwich and an apple in my lunch box.* It would be better to revise the sentence: *A sandwich and an apple are in my lunch box.*

INTRODUCTORY WORDS: *HERE, THERE, WHERE*

In a sentence introduced by *here*, *there*, or *where*, the subject usually follows the verb.

No   There **was** several **boxes** of tools on the table.

Yes   There **were** several **boxes** of tools on the table.

Since the subject is the plural noun *boxes*, use the plural verb form *were*. If you say it out loud, *boxes were*, not *boxes was*, sounds correct.

No   Here comes my sisters.

Yes   Here come my sisters.

The plural subject *sisters* requires the plural verb *come*.

No   **Where's** your sisters?

Yes   Where **are** your **sisters**?

Sisters are sounds correct and must be used in business writing. The use of *where's* is a common usage in everyday speech, but it is grammatically incorrect.

THE PRONOUNS *WHO, WHICH,* AND *THAT*

If *who*, *which*, or *that* is a subject, the verb must agree in number (singular or plural) with the pronoun reference.

No   This is the **man who talk** with you on the phone every day.

Yes   This is the **man who talks** with you on the phone every day.

The pronoun *who* is substituting for the singular noun *man*. Therefore, the singular verb *talks* ends with *s* to agree with *man* is correct. When the plural noun *men* is used, the opposite is true. The plural verb form is required although the same pronoun, *who*, is used

Yes   These are the **men who talk** with you on the phone every day.

THE WORD *NUMBER*

The word *number* is a singular subject if *the* precedes it. If *a* precedes *number*, it is a plural subject.

No   **The number** of restaurants in this neighborhood **are** growing.

Yes   **The number** of restaurants in this neighborhood **is** growing.

No   **A number** of books **has** been written on that subject.

Yes   **A number** of books **have** been written on that subject.

NUMERICAL AMOUNTS

Subjects referring to "parts"—the words *all*, *none*, *any*, *more*, *most*, *some*, and a fraction or a percentage—may be singular *or* plural depending on whether they refer to a plural or singular word.

Singular   **All** of **it is** lost.

Use the singular verb *is* because *it* is singular.

   Plural   **All** of **them are** happy.

Use the plural verb *are* because *them* is plural.

Here's a helpful trick to determine whether "part" subjects are singular or plural: If the item referred to can be counted, it's plural; otherwise, it's singular.

Singular   At least **10 percent** of the **applesauce has** been eaten.

Applesauce can't be counted.

   Plural   **Half** the **apples are** in the refrigerator.

Apples can be counted.

CONTRACTIONS IN WORKPLACE WRITING

Contractions of subject/verb create one word. These are so common in speech that you needn't think twice about agreement. What about contractions in workplace writing? Are they acceptable?

No   Avoid contractions in legal and other formal documents, such as important business letters. Also, do not use *would* or *should* contractions (such as *I'd* for *I would* or *I should*) in workplace writing, although these contractions are fine in speech.

We'd be pleased if **you'd** join us. [okay for conversation or informal email]

We would be pleased if you would join us. [preferred in more formal workplace writing]

Yes   Use contractions in informal workplace writing; they sound concise and friendly. For that reason, this includes some business letters.

I'm going to send you the information right away.

We're always here to help you.

He's an auditor.

You'll always be welcome here.

We've shipped the widgets.

It's a good buy.

Here's the document you requested.

GO TO PAGE 184 AND COMPLETE WORKSHEET 9.2.

IF I WERE . . .

The verb *were* is used to express ideas that are contrary to reality. Use this special form principally when the subject follows *if* or *wish*. Use *were* regardless of what the subject is if the statement is contrary to reality. Use *was* or *is* if the statement is true or *might* be true (except, of course, with *you* or *I*).

True or Might Be True	Contrary to Reality
I was not at home Monday.	If *I were* you, I would stay at home on Mondays. [I can't be you.]
Everyone is going to the meeting.	If *everyone were* to go to the meeting, who would mind the store? [Everyone *won't* go.]
He was aiming for the top, but he lacked the education and experience.	Peter wishes that *he were* a CEO. [He just started as a trainee.]
I was a millionaire last year.	If *I were* a millionaire, I would invest in cutting edge ideas. [Guess what? I am not a millionaire.]

Agreement with Collective Nouns

Collective nouns are words like *club*, *staff*, *management*, *family*, *class*, *faculty*, *company*, *committee*, *crowd*, *jury*, and *names of organizations*. A collective noun is like a single package containing several items. When you refer to the entire "package," the collective noun is thought of as a single unit. If the package is broken up into its parts, you consider the items separately—resulting in ordinary plural nouns.

If a collective noun acting as a single unit is a subject, use a singular verb—the one ending with *s*—for the present tense or for a helping verb.

No	The **faculty are** meeting in Room 406.
Yes	The **faculty is** meeting in Room 406.

Faculty is a collective noun acting as a unit and, therefore, singular.

Yes	The **members** of the faculty *are* meeting in Room 406.
	The **teachers are** meeting in Room 406.

A plural verb is correct with the plural subject *members*; *of the faculty* is a prepositional phrase and cannot include a subject. In the second example, *teachers* is a plural subject.

No	**Macy's have** many employees.
Yes	Macy's has **many employees**.

Organizations are always singular.

No	The **faculty disagrees** about the new grading policy.
Yes	The **faculty disagree** about the new grading policy.

If members disagree, they are not acting as a unit. If the members of a collective noun act as separate individuals or disagree, use a plural verb.

Sometimes the grammatically correct way just doesn't sound right. In that case, change the wording of the sentence so that it is both grammatically correct *and* sounds right.

writing**TIP**

Collective noun principles are more important in business and professional writing than in speech. If in doubt about whether a collective noun is singular or plural, just rephrase the sentence. *Note:* If you are a native speaker of British English, you'll find that collective noun principles of British English differ from those of American English.

No	The **jury goes** home every evening after deliberating.
Yes	The **jury go** home every evening after deliberating.

The jury members go off in different directions to different homes, thus requiring the plural verb *go*. However, the sentence just sounds wrong; in this case, change the wording.

Yes	The **jurors go** home every evening after deliberating.

The subject is now *jurors*, a plural noun requiring the plural verb form *go*, and it sounds right. Another way to say it is:

The **jury members go** home every evening after deliberating.

GO TO PAGE 186 AND COMPLETE WORKSHEET 9.3.

communications connection

ADDITIONAL LETTER PARTS

This section continues the discussion of writing business letters. Refer back to the "Communications Connection" in Chapter 8 to review the letter parts that are required in business correspondence. All business letters have these same parts and additional parts that must be included when you are writing as a representative of an organization. This section covers those additional letter parts.

The following parts may be included in business letters after the closing and signature. These parts are optional; their inclusion depends on the situation.

Identification Initials—The initials of the preparer of the letter are included when a letter is prepared by someone other than the person signing the letter, such as an administrative assistant preparing a letter for an executive. Identification initials provide a record of who prepared the letter.

The initials are typed two spaces after the title/department in the signature block as shown below. Use lowercase letters.

Regards,

Betty Van Meter

Betty Van Meter
Manager
Business Skills Center

lrs

Enclosure: Fall Catalog

Enclosure Notation—Include an enclosure notation when you send something with a letter. This notation tells the reader to look for an enclosure and serves to remind the writer to include it. Type "Enclosure" (singular or plural) or "Enc." at the left margin two lines below the last line of the signature or the typist's initials, followed by a colon and a brief description of the item. The description does not have to be included when the item is described in the body of the letter.

Enc.: Check No. 268

Copy Notation—A copy notation lets the recipient know that others are receiving copies of the letter. It is not optional when others are being copied. Type the notation c: or cc: (they both mean copy; cc is a holdover from the days of carbon copies) at the left margin two lines below the last line of the signature.

cc: Professor Nina Nixon

If you don't want the addressee to know you've sent copies, type *bc* (for blind copy) only on the copy or copies being sent to others (and your file copy)—not the original—followed by the name/s of the recipients/s.

bc: Professor Foster

WRITING PRACTICE

Read a variety of job advertisements in your field of interest and select one that interests you. Prepare a draft of the cover letter you would send to apply for the job. Research the company and the type of position you are aiming for to get a feel for the match between you and the position. Remember to pick up on the language of the industry and the job in describing why you would be a good fit for the company and the position.

Follow the writing process to create a final draft of your letter.

Date to submit this assignment: _____

PROOFREADING PRACTICE

Use proofreading marks or go online to correct spelling, pronoun usage, sentence construction, verb, and subject-verb agreement errors in this article. Do not make changes other than correcting specific errors just mentioned. Never let written material leave your desk without careful proofreading.

A Financial Health Care Plan

Maintaining financial solvency doesn't just happen; it takes careful planning. Here is tip's to help you stay financially healthy:

- Practice delayed gratification—put off buying today what you can do without until you has more money.

- Save and planning for your purchased instead of using credit or going over budget.

- When you have to by be a bargain hunter and a comparison shopper.

- If you shop to fill the time or use it as a relaxing leisure activity, change your habits, get involved in a hobby, do volunteer work, or made up a list of free activities (such as taking a walk, exercising, playing games, fixing things, cooking) that you can do instead.

- Don't make money a source of worry and irritation focus on what you have, not what you don't have. A positive attitude toward money free your mind to handle it constructively and create opportunities for financial improvement.

- Learn about investment assume that this information would be be a necessity in your financial future.

- Healthy finances means have financial goals. Don't assume that you will automatically get better jobss and higher salaries or that you will "grow into" the habit of saving. Financial goals helps you identify and stay focused on what you needs to do to achieve it

How did you do? Excellent _____ Good _____

Need More Practice _____

chapter review

WORKSHEET 9.1

A. Circle the subjects and underline the verbs in these sentences.

1. When you finish the soup, leave the spoon in the plate.

2. Everyone except your brothers was discharged.

3. Lewis and Martin told jokes and sang.

4. Should we tell him the truth?

Circle the subject and underline the correct verb in these sentences.

5. The reason for his difficulties (seem/seems) clear.

6. Nobody (like/likes) this background music.

7. The book and the DVD (fit/fits) in the same package.

8. Something (has arrived/have arrived) from the printer.

9. The phenomenon that caused the explosion (wasn't detected/ weren't detected) immediately.

10. All of the managers at the convention (was taken/were taken) on a tour of the new plant.

B. Underline each verb and circle the subject. Remember that a sentence may have more than one subject-verb combination or may have a compound subject or verb.

Example: A company may issue preferred stock only after common stock has been issued.

1. Do you enjoy the sunset?

2. The financial analysts are doing their jobs well.

3. Will she get a salary increase?

4. Clothing for the workplace should be appropriate.

5. Ask yourself if your appearance sends a message that will benefit your career.

6. For a professional look, women should limit jewelry to a watch, necklace, earrings, and no more than two rings.

7. According to American-style table manners, the diner puts the knife back on the plate, not the table, after he or she cuts a piece of food.

8. However, the knife remains in the diner's right hand in most parts of Europe.

9. Career advancement is more likely for employees who get along well with coworkers, supervisors, and clients or customers.

10. Hard, steady work turns daydreaming into reality.

11. Playing Monopoly is fun.

12. During the past year, our sales have risen dramatically.

13. In 1905 former president of the United States Grover Cleveland said, "Sensible and responsible women do not want to vote."

14. Everyone in the shop is working on the blueprints.

15. Google made its name as an Internet search engine.

16. My assistant, who is very efficient, will gladly help you.

17. Would you like my assistant's help next week?

18. Considerable turnover of personnel is prevalent in the fast-food business.

19. Both poverty and riches are a state of mind as well as of the pocketbook.

20. Good grammar and correct spelling are important in workplace communications.

CHECK YOUR ANSWERS ON PAGE 452.

WORKSHEET 9.2

Decide whether the subjects and verbs agree in the following sentences. Draw a line through incorrect verbs and write the correct form in the blank. If the verb agrees with the subject, write **C** for *correct* in the blank.

_____ 1. Every one of the passengers were waiting in line quietly.

_____ 2. Neither of your responses seem satisfactory.

_____ 3. The report and the letter was on my desk.

_____ 4. Either the report or the letter was on my desk.

_____ 5. Neither the report nor the letter were on my desk.

_____ 6. Not only Richard's story but also Alicia's reasons seem valid.

_____ 7. Not only the assigned books but also the professor's personality is challenging in that course.

_____ 8. Every battery, radio, and antenna are missing.

_____ 9. Everything that was in the garages are gone.

_____ 10. Many a quotation have been memorized and then forgotten.

_____ 11. About half the papers is gone from the file.

_____ 12. All employees except the manager rides the elevator.

_____ 13. Any one of us is willing to help with the report.

_____ 14. A number of members are able to contribute to the fund.

_____ 15. Some friends of mine and their daughter visit me during the holidays.

_____ 16. Only one of the books have been translated into French.

_____ 17. Half the peach pies has been eaten.

_____ 18. The number of books translated into French are small.

_____ 19. She don't want to go to the workshop.

_____ 20. There was several people waiting for the tickets.

_____ 21. The latest figures on yesterday's sale is available.

_____ 22. Each report and letter are on my desk.

_____ 23. A report on the accounts have been completed.

_____ 24. Close friends often greets each other with a hug.

_____ 25. Each of the countries have distinct cultural characteristics.

_____ 26. Neither he nor his assistant pack the items carefully.

_____ 27. Here's the software you ordered.

_____ 28. Every one of my good ideas come to me when I'm relaxing.

_____ 29. Michelle and her aide, who drive in from Kenansville, leaves early.

_____ 30. He usually do his work carefully.

_____ 31. The new copier don't work well.

_____ 32. My cousin, as well as a number of my aunts and uncles, work here.

_____ 33. Neither the attorney nor the paralegal are able to be here.

_____ 34. There goes the new models down the runway.

_____ 35. Another batch of envelopes have arrived incorrectly addressed.

CHECK YOUR ANSWERS ON PAGE 453.

WORKSHEET 9.3

Draw a line through incorrect verbs and any other incorrect words. Write the correct form in the blank. If the sentence is already correct, write **C** in the blank.

_____ 1. If you was ready to take the final, you would not need a tutor.

_____ 2. If it were not for the close friendship of my colleagues, I would have quit long ago.

_____ 3. If he was a better writer, we would offer him the job.

_____ 4. Because she was ill so often last year, she couldn't complete her work.

_____ 5. I wish I was able to help you get the job.

_____ 6. He was a millionaire who spent his money to help the poor.

_____ 7. I wish I was a millionaire.

_____ 8. When I were your assistant, your office weren't in this building.

_____ 9. The nurse wishes that she was a doctor.

_____ 10. We wish the prices was lower, but it never will be.

_____ 11. The members of my staff takes rotating lunch hours every day.

_____ 12. At noon today my colleagues file into the conference room to hear the news.

_____ 13. Wong & Lopez, Inc., have their offices at 10 Park Avenue.

_____ 14. Hiteki Corp. also need new headquarters.

_____ 15. Several groups was invited to the meeting.

_____ 16. For years J. C. Penney stores was called The Golden Rule Stores.

_____ 17. The Senate favor new tax laws.

_____ 18. The company was warned by the fire chief to clear the aisles.

_____ 19. The Social Services Department are submitting their applications.

_____ 20. This class work quietly.

CHECK YOUR ANSWERS ON PAGE 454.

POSTTEST

1. Robert Ball, as well as all his aides, (deserve/deserves) a raise.

2. Neither the engineer nor the designer (is/are) here.

3. The costs of salaries and travel expenses (have/has) been determined.

4. Each girl and boy (is/are/be) doing well.

5. One-third of the pies (have/has) been sold.

6. Accuracy in figures (mark/marks) the expert accountant.

7. She is the only one of the attorneys who (do/does) the research.

8. Rosenberg & McNeil, Inc., (insist/insists) on prompt shipments.

9. The Hartford City Council (were/was) disappointed in the results.

10. The committee (have/has) been unable to agree on the agenda.

CHECK YOUR ANSWERS ON PAGE 454.

Self-Study and Practice Tutorials

wordPOWER

Build your workplace vocabulary and improve spelling skills by completing the exercises in Appendix B on page 369.

Supplementary Practice Exercises

For additional practice, complete the Appendix C exercises for this chapter on page 410.

© Stephen Coburn/Fotolia

After completing Chapter 10, you will be able to do the following:

- Explain the difference between adjectives and adverbs.
- Use adjectives and adverbs correctly as modifiers.
- Identify different types of adjectives and use them correctly.
- Use the correct forms of adjectives and adverbs to express comparisons.

10

Adjectives and Adverbs

career connection

FEATURES OF A QUALITY COVER LETTER

A cover letter introduces you and your resume; it explains your reasons for applying—why you are interested in the company and the position you are applying for. Always try to address a cover letter to a specific person. Here is some advice on what you might include:

- Explain why you are writing and give the source of information about the position (such as advertisement, recommendation of colleague, or interest in the company).
- Highlight key qualifications/achievements related to the position. Emphasize strengths but avoid overkill and exaggeration.
- Keep your description of yourself brief and refer to your attached resume.
- Explain why you are interested in the company and the position.
- Keep it short (no more than a page), write in a professional and courteous tone, format carefully, and make sure the letter is error-free.
- Close courteously and request an interview; indicate how you intend to follow up.
- Print and sign the letter if sent by regular mail; if sent by email, include a complimentary close and type your name and contact information at the bottom.

PRETEST

Circle any incorrect adjectives and adverbs and write the correct form in the blank.

_____ 1. I don't think those type of organizations can profit from such an activity.

_____ 2. An unknown admirer sent me a $11 gift for a NAACP official.

_____ 3. He won't go nowhere with me on a sunny day.

_____ 4. Who do you think is more intelligent—Jamie, Annie, or Josie?

_____ 5. After using product X and product Y, which do you think is best?

_____ 6. This car runs quieter than any other car I have had.

_____ 7. She feels badly about making such a serious mistake.

_____ 8. He knows how to play the drums good.

_____ 9. She is real smart and speaks French very well.

_____ 10. Of our six stores, this one is managed the poorest.

CHECK YOUR ANSWERS ON PAGE 454.

Basics About the Modifiers

You studied adjectives and adverbs—the modifiers—in Chapter 2. A quick review here will set the stage for the rest of this chapter where you will learn more about how to use modifiers to make your writing more effective. Adjectives and adverbs add clarity and deeper meaning to your writing. Use them to explain, describe, tell how many, or add special meaning to the words and ideas they modify.

Adjectives and adverbs are more fun than pronouns and verbs. They add precision, character, liveliness, and color to our language. Imagine how dull our language would be without words like *generous, happily, stingy, cheerfully, prudish, confidently, weaker, meaner, strictest, domineering, shabby, purple*, and *most comfortable*. Now imagine how vague our language would be without adjectives like *several, those, fifth, often, sometimes*, or even the little word *the*.

Communication is difficult at best; we often misunderstand one another. Skillful communicators draw from a wealth of adjectives and adverbs, using those that most effectively communicate the shade of meaning desired. **Adjectives** tell something about—or *modify*—nouns and pronouns. The four kinds of adjectives are articles, pointing adjectives, descriptive adjectives, and limiting adjectives. **Adverbs** tell something about—or *modify*—verbs, adjectives, and other adverbs. Many adverbs are formed by adding *ly* to adjectives; for example, *peaceful* is an adjective, and *peacefully* is an adverb. Other adverbs are totally different from adjectives—words such as *well, often*, or *sometimes*.

THE ARTICLES—*THE, A*, AND *AN*

The **articles** *a, an*, and *the* are adjectives that tell *which one. The* is a *definite article* because it makes the noun following it *definite*—that is, *specific. A* and *an* are *indefinite articles*. Notice the difference in meaning between "the book" and "a book" or between "the apple" and "an apple."

Fine Points of *the*

Using the word *the* is something we take for granted, but even this little word can be an issue, especially for those who speak English as their second language. Look at these two sentences:

We are going to school today.

We are going to *the* office today.

Why don't we use *the* before *school* in the first sentence? Why do we use *the* before *office* in the second sentence? These choices "sound right" to a native of an English-speaking country, but no simple rule governs them. Differences even occur between British English and American English:

British	She is in hospital.
American	She is in *the* hospital.

Managing *a* and *an*

The two little words *a* and *an* can be a problem for almost anyone. Some people use *a* almost exclusively and rarely use *an* when it's needed. However, non-Standard English use of *a* and *an* is noticeable in workplace communication.

   The rules that determine the use of *a* or *an* are quite simple. Not everyone needs to study them because many people automatically use these words correctly. To determine whether you need to study all, some, or none of the rules discussed here, take the following "*A/An* Pretest." If your answers are correct, go directly to the next section. If some of your answers are incorrect, continue studying this section and refer to the information as a reference when you're writing.

word**POWER**

If your first language isn't English, one way to make the different usage second nature is to read a great deal, listen to the radio, watch television and films, and ask coworkers, teachers, and friends to correct you. Your sense of what "sounds right" will develop much more quickly.

A/AN PRETEST

Write *a* or *an* in the blank before each word. Choose what comes to you immediately. Don't stop to think about it.

Example: _____a_____ $10 bill

1. _____ addition
2. _____ carrot
3. _____ egg
4. _____ apple
5. _____ giant
6. _____ honor
7. _____ heater
8. _____ even number
9. _____ hand
10. _____ one-day sale
11. _____ manager
12. _____ onion
13. _____ owl
14. _____ uncle
15. _____ Englishman
16. _____ heir
17. _____ island
18. _____ European
19. _____ IBM office
20. _____ CIA report
21. _____ UN member
22. _____ 2 percent tax
23. _____ X-ray
24. _____ unknown admirer

Check your answers on page 454.

Use of *a* or *an* depends on the *sound* of the word that follows, not necessarily the written letter with which the word begins. If a word following *a* or *an* begins with a vowel sound (the sound of *a, e, i, o,* or *u*), use *an*. Otherwise, use *a*.

an apple   **an e**gg roll   **an i**llness   **an o**wner   **an u**ncle   **an h**onor
a 10 percent raise   **a h**ot rod   **a b**ookkeeper   **a p**uzzle   **a u**niform

Some words begin with a vowel but have a consonant (all letters other than *a, e, i, o,* and *u*) *sound*; they require *a*, not *an*. For example, the *u* in *union* sounds like the consonant *y* in *you*: **a u**nion, **a u**niform, **a eu**logy, and so on. Also, the *o* in *one* sounds just like the consonant *w* in *winner*: **a o**ne-cent stamp.

The letter *h* beginning a word is sometimes silent. For such words, use *an*. The first sound of *honor* is *o*, a vowel sound: **an** honor, **an** honest person, **an** herb (pronounced "urb") garden. (In British English, the *h* in *herb* is pronounced, so **a** *herb* would be correct.)

When using a letter of the alphabet alone or as part of an abbreviation, the letter is preceded by *a* or *an*, depending on the *sound*.

He needs **an FBI** report for **a CIA** officer.

Write **a T** or **an F** in each blank.

Abbreviations pronounced as words instead of individual letters are called *acronyms*, such as NASA,* pronounced *nas'uh*.

He was **a NASA** employee and **an NAACP** member.

POINTING ADJECTIVES

Pointing adjectives tell *which one*. Like articles, they are easy to memorize because there are only four: *this, that, these,* and *those*.

this book	**these** books
that jacket	**those** jackets

You may remember from Chapter 2 that the words *this, that, these,* and *those* are pronouns. Can they be both pronouns and adjectives? Yes! *This, that, these,* and *those* are adjectives when they modify a noun; they are pronouns when used *instead* of a noun:

Adjective   **This book** is the one I want to read.

This points at *book*.

  Pronoun   **These** are the ones I want to read.

These replaces the noun *books*, which is understood.

Adjective   **Those labels** don't match what is in the box.

Those points at labels.

  Pronoun   **This** belongs on **that box**.

This replaces label; *that* points at box.

Here are the only pointers—or tips—you need for *pointing* adjectives:

Use *this* and *that* to point to singular nouns.

This soup is mine. [*This* is a pointing adjective; *soup* is a noun.]
This kind of spice is too hot for **that type** of soup.

---

*If you're unsure of what any of the abbreviations and the acronym (NASA) mean, look them up in your dictionary now.

Use *these* and *those* to point to plural nouns.

No	**Those kind** of spices are hot.
Yes	**Those kinds** of spices are hot.
No	Will **these type** of homes sell in those neighborhoods?
Yes	Will **these types** of homes sell in those neighborhoods?

Revise when the correct usage sounds awkward:

Correct but awkward	Those kinds of roofs are fireproof.
Improved	That kind of roof is fireproof. *OR* Those roofs are fireproof.

When you use the phrase *this kind of*, avoid an unnecessary *a* or *an* after *kind of* (or *type of/sort of*).

No	This kind of a house . . .
Yes	This kind of house . . .

Never use *them* as a pointing adjective; it is a pronoun only.

No	I plan to give them boys a free meal.
Yes	I plan to give those (or these) boys a free meal. *OR*
	I plan to give them a free meal. [*Them* is correct as a pronoun.]

LIMITING ADJECTIVES

Words that "limit" nouns in the sense of quantity are also adjectives. They tell "how many." Limiting adjectives are words such as these:

more	all	50 or fifty
enough	each	no
most	any	every
several	many	numerous
few	some	

We purchased **several** <u>cans</u> of coffee for the office.

I will call you in a **few** <u>days</u>.

Do you have **enough** <u>time</u> to complete the problems in **50** <u>minutes</u>?

DOUBLE NEGATIVES—A BIG NO-NO

When two negative words are used to express one negative idea, the result is a **double negative**. Limiting adjectives such as *no, any,* and *none* are of great use in the English language, but they also are the cause of the double negative, one of the most serious and embarrassing errors in the English language.

While using two negative words to express a single negative idea does not really affect your listener's or reader's ability to understand, it does affect the reaction you get. Using double negatives usually prevents applicants from being hired for better jobs. It isn't important to identify which negative words are adverbs and which are adjectives. Just remember that two negatives shouldn't be combined to express one negative idea.

Here are examples of negative words that should not be combined:

no	none	doesn't	aren't	never	shouldn't
not	nowhere	won't	wouldn't	scarcely	neither
nobody	can't	couldn't	don't	haven't	hardly

Some common double negatives that creep into speech are these:

No   He don't go nowhere without his iPad in tow.

Yes   He doesn't go anywhere without his iPad in tow.

No   Nobody can't say they weren't warned about the deadline.

Yes   Everyone was warned about the deadline.

No   They shouldn't have taken the bus, but they shouldn't have taken the train neither. Both were late.

Yes   They should not have taken the bus or the train; both were late.

Here is an example of what can happen when double negatives get in the way of communication: A student showed his teacher a punctuation quiz before turning it in. "I didn't put no comma there," he said, pointing to one of the sentences. Trying to save him from the horrors of a life of double negatives, the teacher said, "I didn't put *any* comma there, Joe." He replied, "Oh, good, you did<u>n't</u> put <u>none</u> there <u>neither</u>," thus increasing his original double negative to a triple.

If you suspect that you use double (or even triple) negatives, kick the habit by asking an instructor or a friend to tell you privately when you say or write them.

GO TO PAGE 205 AND COMPLETE WORKSHEET 10.1.

Three Degrees of Comparison

Descriptive adjectives change form to show comparison. In grammar, these forms are called **degrees of comparison:** positive, comparative, and superlative.

Using the correct comparative form for most adjectives comes naturally as we speak Standard English the way we hear it spoken. However, certain adjective and adverb comparative forms cause even Standard English speakers some problems.

The positive form of descriptive adjectives does not change; the comparative and superlative degrees are used for comparisons by adding *er/est, more/most,* or *less/least.*

He is **strong**. [positive]

He is the **stronger** of the two. [comparative]

He is the **strongest** of them all. [superlative]

POSITIVE DEGREE—FOR ONE

Positive degree adjectives describe, or modify, a noun or pronoun *without making a comparison.*

old   young   happy   valuable   modern   affluent

The queen's jewels are **old**. [*old* modifies the noun *jewels*]

They are **valuable**. [*valuable* modifies the pronoun *they*]

COMPARATIVE DEGREE—FOR TWO

Comparative degree adjectives compare two nouns or pronouns. To make an adjective comparative, add either *er* to the end of the word or use *more* or *less* before the adjective.

> older
>
> younger
>
> happier
>
> more valuable
>
> less modern
>
> more affluent
>
> Jean is the **younger** of the two sisters, but Marian's life is **happier**.

Two sisters are compared.

> That building is **older** than the one on Vine Street, but the plumbing is **more modern**.

Two buildings and the plumbing in the two buildings are compared.

SUPERLATIVE DEGREE—FOR THREE OR MORE

Superlative degree adjectives compare three or more nouns or pronouns. To make an adjective superlative, add *est* to the end of the word or use *most* or *least* before the adjective.

> oldest
>
> youngest
>
> happiest
>
> smartest
>
> most valuable
>
> least modern
>
> most affluent
>
> most careful
>
> Melvin is the **youngest** of the three sons, and he is also the **most affluent**.
>
> It was the **happiest** day of my life when you gave me your **most valuable** diamond.

You had three or more diamonds.

HOW MANY SYLLABLES?

When forming comparatives, you can distinguish between words that add *er/est* and those that require *more/most* or *less/least* by focusing on how many syllables are in the word.

- One-syllable words:

  Add *er* or *est:* big, bigger, biggest; smart, smarter, smartest

- Two-syllable words ending with *y*:

  Change the *y* to *i* and add *er* or *est*: easier, easiest; heavier, heaviest.
- Two- or more-syllable words not ending with *y*:

  Use *more/most* or *less/least*: more or most careful, less or least beautiful, more/most or less/least important.

Double Comparatives and Superlatives

Never use *more, most, less,* or *least* before a modifier that ends with *er* or *est*. This forms a double comparative or superlative and is as bad as using a double negative.

No	The problem was **more easy** to solve than I expected. [bad comparative]
Yes	That problem was **easier** to solve than I expected.
No	He is the **most laziest** employee I've ever seen. [bad double superlative]
Yes	He is the **laziest** employee I've ever seen.
No	I am **more carefuler** than anyone else. [bad double comparative]
Yes	I am **more careful** than anyone else.

Irregular Adjectives

Irregular adjectives have comparative and superlative forms that differ from those just reviewed. In the dictionary, the entry word for an adjective is usually in the positive degree. For irregular adjectives, you will usually find the comparative forms listed next to it. For example, if you look up the adjective *bad*, instead of *badder* and *baddest*, you find *worse*, which is the comparative form, and then the superlative, *worst*, in that order.* Some other irregular adjectives are *good, better, best* and *many, more, most.*

No	Mine is **more better** than hers. [bad comparative]
Yes	Mine is **better** than hers.
No	I did **worser** on this test than on the last one.
Yes	I did **worse** on this than on the last one. [comparative]
Yes	This is the **worst** grade I've received all semester. [superlative]

GO TO PAGE 207 AND COMPLETE WORKSHEET 10.2.

An Adjective or an Adverb?

Words change from adjective to adverb, depending on what they modify. We add *ly* to many adjectives to form adverbs. For example, adding *ly* to the adjective *occasional* results in the adverb *occasionally*. The information that follows enables you to avoid some common adverb and adjective errors.

- Most (but not all) words ending in *ly* are adverbs.

Adverbs	happily	busily	attractively	cheaply	carefully
Adjectives	happy	busy	attractive	cheap	careful

---

*In newer college dictionaries, *badder* and *baddest* are somewhere in the *bad* entry with the usage label *slang* along with the definition.

---

writingTIP

Avoid the comparative *more* or the superlative *most* before words like *unique* or *perfect*. These are examples of **absolute adjectives**—there are no degrees of comparison. *Unique* means *one of a kind*; therefore, it isn't logical to say that something is *more* unique or *the most* unique. In the same way, *perfect* means "no imperfections"; therefore, *more perfect* or *the most perfect* do not make sense.

wordPOWER

Instead of writing *less* or *least* before an adverb or adjective, you can sometimes choose an antonym (a word that means the opposite of the adverb or adjective). For example, you could replace *less easily, less easy,* or *least easy* with *harder* or *hardest* or *more/most difficult*. Choosing an antonym can liven up your writing and make it more precise.

Some adverbs do not end with *ly*, such as *always, never, often, seldom,* and *very*. Some adjectives do end in *ly*; don't mistake them for adverbs. If the *ly* word describes a noun or pronoun—*curly* hair, *friendly* man—you know it's an adjective.

Sometimes the same word is either an adjective or an adverb.

> He is a **fast** worker.

Fast is an adjective describing the noun *worker*.

> He works **fast**.

Fast is an adverb describing the verb *works*.
Use adverbs (not adjectives) to modify verbs, adjectives, or other adverbs.

No   He arrived on time and **worked quiet**.

The adjective *quiet* is incorrect because an adjective cannot describe a verb—*worked*.

Yes   He arrived on time and **worked quietly**.

The adverb *quietly* tells how he *worked*.

wordPOWER

Spelling tip: The *ily* ending always has one *l*—as in the adverbs *easily, busily,* and *happily*. The *ally* ending always has two *l*'s—as in the adverbs *accidentally, occasionally,* and *officially*.

ADJECTIVE-TO-ADVERB COMPARISONS

To make *ly* adverbs comparative (for two) or superlative (for three or more), use *more/less* or *most/least* before them.

Adjective	Adverb	COMPARATIVE Adverb	SUPERLATIVE Adverb
efficient	efficiently	more/less efficiently	most/least efficiently
beautiful	beautifully	more/less beautifully	most/least beautifully
polite	politely	more/less politely	most/least politely

No   Of all the custodians, the new man works the **most efficient**.
Most efficient is an adjective and is not to be used to describe a verb: *works*.

Yes   Of all the custodians, the new man works the **most efficiently**.
Most efficiently is an adverb correctly modifying a verb: *works*.

No   We obtain parking permits **easier** than the other stores.
Easier is an adjective incorrectly modifying a verb: *obtain*.

Yes   We obtain parking permits **more easily** than the other stores.
The adverb *more easily* correctly modifies the verb *obtain*.

OTHER ADJECTIVE AND ADVERB DIFFERENCES

A modifier placed *after a being verb* must be an adjective modifying the subject. The most common being verbs are forms of *be*, such as *is, am, are, was, were,* and *been*.

> She **is** intelligent.

The adjective *intelligent* modifies *she*, the subject of the being verb *is*.

In addition to forms of *be*, verbs of the senses are often (but not always) being verbs. Typical verbs of the senses are *appear, become, seem, look, taste, sound, smell,* and *feel.* To determine whether a verb of the senses is a being or an action verb, decide whether it refers to action or state of being in that sentence.

> She **looks** carefully for the best bargain.

Looks is an action verb referring to the action of using her eyes to look.

> She **looks** intelligent.

Looks is a being verb because she is not doing the action of looking; *looks* refers to her appearance the adjective *intelligent* modifies *she.*

> I **tasted** the potatoes.

Tasted is an action verb because tasting is action.

> The potatoes **tasted** delicious.

Tasted is a being verb referring to the sense of taste; the adjective *delicious* modifies *potatoes.*

No   I feel **badly** today.

Use of the adverb *badly* here changes *feel* to an action verb. The sentence then means "I do a bad job of feeling" as an action; for example, "I can't feel the difference between hot and cold because my hand is numb."

Yes   I feel **bad** today.

Bad describes how the subject (which is *I*) feels.

Yes   Susan Chin felt **bad** about her hair being **curly**.

Bad describes how susan felt; *curly* describes her hair.

Good/Well and Bad/Badly

The irregular adjectives *good* and *bad* and the irregular adverbs *well* and *badly* frequently create confusion when used to make comparisons:

	Positive	Comparative (two)	Superlative (three or more)
Adjective	good	better	best
	bad	worse	worst
Adverb	well	better	best
	badly	worse	worst

To choose between *good* and *well*, decide whether you need an adjective or an adverb. If an adjective is required, choose *good*. If an adverb is required, choose *well*.

Yes   Professor Stagnaro wrote a **good** report.

The adjective *good* describes the noun *report.*

Yes   It looks **good**.

Good describes the pronoun subject *it; looks* is a being verb.

No   He plays the drums **good**.

Good, an adjective, incorrectly describes *plays*, which is an action verb; do not use an adjective to describe an action verb.

Yes   He plays the drums **well**.

The adverb *well* correctly describes the action verb *plays*.

Yes   The drums sound **good**.

Sound is a being verb; *good* is an adjective correctly describing the noun subject *drums*.

No   She knows English **good**.

Do not use an adjective to describe a verb; therefore, *good* is incorrect.

Yes   She knows English **well**.

The adverb *well* tells **how** she **knows**.
    When referring to health or state of being when speaking, either *good* or *well* is acceptable with the being verb *feel*.

Yes   He feels **good**. *or* He feels **well**.

In writing use *well* when referring to health.

Yes   This morning the patient felt **well** enough to take a walk down the hall.

When being verbs other than *feel* refer to health, use *well*, which becomes an adjective on the subject of health.

Yes   They are all **well**. He is not **well**. She seems **well**.

Good would refer to their behavior.

If health is not the subject, use an adjective after a being verb.

Yes   The sauce smells **good**.

Smells, a being verb, requires an adjective—in this case, *good*—to modify the subject *sauce.*
    Comparative and superlative forms are easy for *good* or *well*: The comparative is *better*, and the superlative is *best*. Both of the following sentences are correct.

Yes   Our products are **better** than theirs.

The comparative **adjective** *better* modifies the noun *products*.

Yes   Our products are designed **better** than theirs.

The comparative **adverb** *better** modifies the verb *are designed.*

Real and Sure

Real and *sure* are adjectives; do not use them to describe *other* adjectives. Remember, adjectives can describe nouns or pronouns only. Only adverbs can describe adjectives.

Better is both an adjective and an adverb—the comparative form of *good* and *well*; see dictionary.

writing**TIP**

Description is good, but excessive use of descriptive words interferes with the effectiveness of your writing. When you revise your draft, decide whether to include or eliminate the *really, surely, extremely, especially, very*, or other "intensifying" word. Particularly avoid overuse of *very*. A sentence such as "The presentation is good" sometimes carries more "punch" than "The presentation is really (or very or extraordinarily) good."

Instead of incorrectly using *real* as an adverb, use a true adverb such as *really, very, extremely, exceptionally*, or *truly*:

No	I'm **real** sorry about being late.
Yes	I'm **really** sorry about being late.
No	He's **real** good at that.
Yes	He's **exceptionally** good at that.

Use *real* as an adjective meaning "genuine."

That is a **real** diamond, not a cubic zirconium.

Here's a quick test for the adjectives *real* and *sure*: If you can substitute *very*, you need an adverb.

No	She is **real [or very] smart**.
Yes	She is **really** smart.

The adjective *real* cannot correctly modify the adjective *smart*; switch to an adverb, such as *really* or *extremely*.

No	That report is **sure good**.
Yes	That report is **especially** good.

The adjective *sure* cannot correctly describe the adjective *good*; replace it with an adverb, such as *especially, certainly*, or *exceptionally*.

GO TO PAGE 210 AND COMPLETE WORKSHEET 10.3.

KEY POINTS ABOUT ADJECTIVES AND ADVERBS

- An adjective modifies a noun or pronoun, and an adverb modifies a verb, an adverb, or an adjective.
- Use *a* before a word or letter beginning with a consonant sound and *an* before a word beginning with a vowel sound.
- Many adverbs (but not all) are adjectives to which *ly* has been added: *accidentally, happily*, and *cheerfully*; not all adverbs end with *ly*—for example, *well, often*, and *always*.
- The positive degree modifies without making a comparison. The comparative degree ends in *er* or is preceded by *more* or *less*. Use the comparative degree to compare two only. The superlative degree ends in *est* or is preceded by *most* or *least*. Use the superlative degree to compare three or more.
- Negative words are either adjectives or adverbs, but it isn't important to identify them as such. Just be sure to use only one negative word to express one negative idea.
- Use *good* as an adjective and *well* as an adverb. The comparative for *good* or *well* is *better*. The superlative for *good* or *well* is *best*.
- *Sure* and *real* are adjectives; don't use them to modify other adjectives. Instead, use the adverbs *surely* or *really* or some other adverb—or omit them altogether, which is often the best choice.

Checkpoint

Everyday usage of adjectives and adverbs is taken for granted, and errors made in speaking are frequently overlooked. Before studying this chapter, you might not have been aware of some bad habits of usage. Remember the rules about adjectives and adverbs as you revise drafts of your written communications—errors will stand out to readers. Also, practice them in your speech. Faulty use of pointing adjectives, comparatives, and double negatives is especially grating to careful users of Standard English in the workplace. Review the troublesome adjective/adverb pairs when you revise your work to double-check that you have used them correctly.

communications connection

OPTIONAL BUSINESS LETTER PARTS

In Chapter 8, you studied the standard parts that are included in all business letters. This section will complete the discussion of optional business letter parts begun in Chapter 9, with descriptions of parts that are used only when the situation calls for it.

Special Notations

These are used to indicate something specific about the message. Examples of special notations are CONFIDENTIAL, BY MESSENGER, CERTIFIED, ATTENTION: _____.

Type special notations in all capital letters a double space below the date.

January 2, 20xx
CONFIDENTIAL
Name Address Address

Subject or Reference Line

This is a notation used to state the letter's main topic and serves as a heading for the message. Type it between the salutation and the body, using either the style shown below or on the next page.

Dear Mr. Wallace:
JOB PLACEMENT OF GRADUATES
The five graduates listed below had high scores on our employment test and . . .

> Dear Ms. Hakim:
>
> Re: Retroactive Wage Increase
>
> I am pleased to inform you that our payroll department has reconciled the discrepancy . . .

Some letters require a name or transaction number. Place this type of reference above the inside address.

> May 10, 20xx
>
> Reference: Policy No. 26382
>
> Name
> Address
> Address

Company Name (at End of Letter)

The name of the organization sending the letter is sometimes typed in all capital letters a double space below the complimentary close, such as when the company name is used in place of an individual's name.

> If you would like to schedule a personal consultation, please call the number above to arrange an appointment.
>
> Sincerely,
>
> SNYDER COMMUNICATIONS, INC.

Postscript (PS)

This item was used frequently before word processing made it easy to go back and insert text within the body of a letter. Today, it is most often used for emphasis (particularly in sales letters), occasionally for a personal message, or for information on a topic different from the rest of the letter.

When a postscript is included, it is the final item on the page. The abbreviation *PS* is correct but not required before the message. Avoid using a postscript for something you forgot to include in the letter. Instead, insert the information where it belongs within the letter.

> PS Please fill out the enclosed reply card and return it today.
> [for emphasis in a sales letter]
>
> PS Have a great time on your Trinidad trip. [personal message added to a letter to a client]

WRITING PRACTICE

Write a short description (about a half page) comparing two coworkers or two other people you know who differ from each other in some way. Choose a specific difference to write about—such as appearance, personality, interests, skills, or talent. Introduce both people and your subject in the opening sentence. Use precise and correct comparative forms.

Opening Sentences

Start immediately with a **topic sentence** to get the reader's interest. A topic sentence gives the main idea (the topic) of the paragraph. These are ineffective openings:

> I am going to write about . . . [We know you're going to write; just get started.]

> This is a comparison of two people I know who differ from each other. [Tell me who they are and what they do. Be specific.]

These are effective openings:

> Amy Lopez and Josh Stern are successful department managers at Magnasoft, Inc.; however, their leadership styles differ considerably.

> Although Professor X and Professor Y are both excellent instructors, their teaching styles are quite different.

> Latisha is a perfect example of how a supervisor should dress for the office, while Carmen is just the opposite.

Body

Continue with sentences supporting your opening statement—or topic sentence. Describe the people with interesting, accurate, and precise words. Anything that doesn't support the topic sentence does not belong in the piece. If you have more than one paragraph, each one should have a new topic sentence. Make sure your ideas flow smoothly from one sentence to the next and from one paragraph to the next.

Conclusion

Conclude with a summarizing sentence. Avoid introducing new information in the closing.

Date to submit this assignment: _____

PROOFREADING PRACTICE

Find and correct spelling, capitalization, grammar errors, and typographical errors. The punctuation is already correct. Correct the printed copy using proofreading marks or go online to correct the document electronically.

What Employers Want

When employer's fill positions, they are looking for more than competence in the basic skills or even real specific technical skills. They also place a higher value on personal qualities such as integrity, self-discipline, ethics, honesty, promptness, and reliability. Be sure that you conduct yourself according in your college courses and work situations so that these qualitys will be noticed by professors and supervisors whom can provide you with job references. Extra responsibilities that you take on, such as tutoring, working with the more elderly, or organizing a food drive build

---

character and show employers what is better about you, your work habits, and your value system.

Here are some expectations common mentioned by employers:

1. Take responsibility for yourself, your work performnce, and your career success.

2. Present yourself positive on time every day.

3. Get along good with others and know how to perform as a member of in a team.

4. Communicate well and ask intelligently questions.

5. Have a stronger work ethic: follow up, follow through, and get things done.

6. Be a problem solver and decision makers; don't wait to be lead by others.

7. Accept feedback and criticism positively the interest of continuously improvement.

8. Know businesses etiquette and exhibit behavior appropriately to the workplace.

Evaluate your work. Excellent _____ Good _____
Need more practice _____

chapter review

WORKSHEET 10.1

A. Write *a* or *an* in each blank.

Example: ___A___ pessimist sees the difficulty in ___an___ opportunity. ___An___ optimist sees the opportunity in ___a___ difficulty.

1. Jan Hinkle was given _____ one-day unpaid leave of absence and _____ eight-day paid vacation.

2. _____ union member took _____ overnight flight to attend _____ important meeting.

3. It is _____ unusual combination to be _____ PhD and _____ MD.

4. They left for _____ meeting in Pasadena about _____ hour ago.

5. _____ thesaurus is _____ invaluable tool for writers.

6. _____ X-ray was needed to determine whether there was _____ injury.

7. _____ UNICEF* representative and _____ NATO* representative were seated next to each other at _____ UN* meeting.

8. _____ *yes* or a *no* in Japanese doesn't always mean what _____ American thinks it means—because of aspects of Japanese culture that differ from American culture.

9. Each time he receives _____ unusual number of orders, the controller requests _____ audit.

10. He walked down _____ hall to get _____ history book for _____ honor student.

11. _____ heir expected to inherit _____ one-acre lot.

12. His sister, _____ heiress, was not _____ honorable woman.

13. _____ uncle of mine planted _____ herb garden.

14. After receiving _____ AA degree, he earned _____ BA in sociology.

15. _____ European executive was _____ CEO in _____ American firm.

B. Use proofreading marks to correct the following sentences.

Example: These kind͡s of dogs can be vicious.

1. Professor Stagnaro wanted those kind of wall-to-wall bookcase.

2. Them books should be returned to the library.

3. If you are not careful, these type of errors will occur frequently.

4. Those sort of ideas are extremely interesting.

5. The CEO will not approve this type of a policy.

6. He wants to buy this here shipment at a discounted price.

7. Please send a shipment of those new kind of air filters to Michelle Miller of Milwaukee.

8. Ask them people to do the work themselves.

9. These kind of mistakes in our accounting cannot be tolerated.

10. That kind of an advertisement doesn't attract our customers.

---

*Consult your dictionary if you need help with the pronunciation of these acronyms (also if you need the definition of *acronym*).

C. Correct these sentences so that they conform to Standard English. Cross out the incorrect double negatives and write the correct words in the blank. Write **C** next to the two sentences that are already correct.

_____ 1. I hardly never do that.

_____ 2. I never said nothing about it.

_____ 3. Don't put none over there as it might spill.

_____ 4. He won't eat no more pizza if he goes to Afghanistan.

_____ 5. If you have a negative attitude, you won't succeed.

_____ 6. He doesn't know nothing about chemistry.

_____ 7. Taylor won't go nowhere with me on Saturday.

_____ 8. When nothing can't be done, don't waste time regretting a mistake.

_____ 9. She hasn't gone anywhere yet.

_____ 10. You couldn't hardly expect Mr. Blank to join that organization.

CHECK YOUR ANSWERS ON PAGE 455.

WORKSHEET 10.2

A. Underline the correct answer.

1. Who is (wisest/wiser), the judge, the minister, or the professor?

2. Who is (wisest/wiser), the judge or the minister?

3. Do you think David or Mario is (best/better) equipped to deliver the presentation?

4. Actually, I would ask Brenda—she is the (best/better) of the three associates.

5. If you take the Belt Parkway to the meeting, you will be going the (longer/longest) possible route.

B. Cross out the incorrect adjective and write the correction in the blank where necessary. In some cases you need only delete a word. Write **C** beside the only correct sentence.

Example: <u>more</u> This lot is the ~~most~~ valuable of the two we saw today.

_____ 6. The most safest neighborhoods are more expensive.

_____ 7. Of the two reports, his is the worst.

_____ 8. He is the younger of the two brothers.

_____ 9. He is the older of the three brothers.

_____ 10. When the figures of the two accountants were compared, the controller found Mr. Higgins' work to be best.

_____ 11. This new alloy is more heavy than any other metal.

_____ 12. This file contains recenter information than that one.

_____ 13. If you use our detergent and brand X, which one will give you the brightest wash?

_____ 14. He's more friendlier than the other sales manager.

_____ 15. When the two images are examined closely, it becomes apparent that the one on the right is biggest.

C. Fill in the blank with the comparative and superlative forms of the irregular adjectives listed. Use your dictionary if necessary. You'll find the comparative and superlative forms next to the positive, which is the entry word.

Example: <u>more</u> many <u>most</u>

	Comparative	Superlative
16. many	_____	_____
17. bad	_____	_____
18. little	_____	_____
19. much	_____	_____
20. good	_____	_____

D. Circle the correct choice.

21. This engine runs (smooth/smoothly) and has great gas mileage.

22. The interior design sketches look (beautiful, beautifully), but they will be hard to pull off.

23. I feel (awful/awfully) sorry about leaving, but it's time to move on.

24. Our bid was submitted (quick/quickly), but we still lost the contract.

25. He spoke (loud/loudly) enough, but a microphone would have been preferable.

Draw a line through the adjective and adverb errors in these sentences and write the correction in the blank or a **C** beside the three correct sentences.

Example: <u>quickly</u> She works ~~quick~~.

_____ 1. The fumes from the refinery smell badly today.

_____   2. Businesspeople should write clear and correct.

_____   3. His sister feels sadly about her loss.

_____   4. Be sure to do the problems careful.

_____   5. The doctor wrote legible.

_____   6. The pie is excellent today.

_____   7. The manager should think deep about that subject.

_____   8. I hope you will treat him fair.

_____   9. This one works as efficient as the new one.

_____   10. Ms. Teller dances the most graceful of all the dancers.

_____   11. Our assistant feels badly about the mistake.

_____   12. The vegetables taste more delicious than ever.

_____   13. "That which we call a rose, By any other name would smell as sweetly."—William Shakespeare

_____   14. They work more quiet today than usual.

_____   15. Some days they work quieter than other days.

_____   16. The Lexus runs smoother than the other cars.

_____   17. You did satsifactory on all the tests.

_____   18. She appears more calmly than her sister.

_____   19. Of the two Las Vegas hotels, the Luxor has the higher rating.

_____   20. The music on this boat sounds more louder today.

_____   21. He feels worser today than he did yesterday.

_____   22. The engine in the truck runs quieter than the one in the car.

_____   23. She appears the most capablest of all the candidates.

_____   24. Compared with Mr. Beligusi, Mr. Rosenberg presented his case more concise.

_____   25. Bernard is the oldest of my two children.

CHECK YOUR ANSWERS ON PAGE 455.

WORKSHEET 10.3

A. Circle the correct choice.

1. Greta writes (good/well/either good or well).

2. Do you get along (good/well/either good or well) with people?

3. I hope he feels (good/well/either good or well) today.

4. He spoke (good/well/either good or well) of Ms. Sorenson.

5. Professor Stanfield feels (bad/badly) about crashing her motorcycle.

B. The following paragraph is from a sales letter meant to bring business to a resort hotel. In the blanks, write the adjectives that modify the 10 nouns in bold type.

Surveys show successful **individuals** like you would be interested in a special **offer** to visit an exclusive resort **hotel** on the beautiful **Pacific,** where the crystal blue **waters** meet the white sand **beaches.** You will enjoy exquisite guest **villas** with Mediterranean **decor** and luxurious **jacuzzis.** You will want to stay in this **paradise** forever.

1. _____ individuals

2. _____ offer

3. _____ hotel

4. _____ Pacific

5. _____ waters

6. _____ beaches

7. _____ villas

8. _____ decor

9. _____ jacuzzis

10. _____ paradise

C. In each blank, insert a one-word adverb to describe or explain the word in bold type. The adverb you select will tell when, why, where, how, or how much.

Example: Dolores Denova **speaks** _____clearly_____.

1. When you **go** _____, you will need a car to drive.

2. A new computer **would cost** _____ than upgrading the old one.

3. Although Dan is on the team, he _____ **plays** in important games.

4. We didn't believe Anne when she said she **had** _____ **cut** her own hair.

5. This _____ **designed** home was featured in *Architectural Digest*.

6. Those are _____ **expensive** restaurants.

7. Nutrition is one of the _____ **important** aspects of health.

8. Good, inexpensive food is _____ **hard** to find.

9. Employees who ignore etiquette while at work **are** _____ **disliked**.

10. I think Billie Horton is _____ **more suitable** for the job than Harvey Lewis.

CHECK YOUR ANSWERS ON PAGE 456.

POSTTEST

Underline the correct answer. Use the dictionary when in doubt.

1. Since both brands are good, order the (less, least) expensive one.

2. Which is (easier, easyer, easiest, easiest) for you to do, a graph or a chart?

3. I (can't, can) hardly believe what I saw.

4. Although Mr. Shue and Ms. Farr are both skilled at typing, Mr. Shue is (more faster, most faster, faster, fastest).

5. The class was asked to sit (quiet, quietly) and read.

6. I hope you (won't do no more, won't do any more) work on that project.

7. This is the (newer, newest, most new) of the six computers in our office.

8. The sewage treatment plants don't smell as (bad, badly) today.

9. When we evaluated our three facilities, we found this one is run (most poorly, most poorest, more poorly).

10. I went to (the, a, an) emergency room when I didn't feel (good, well).

CHECK YOUR ANSWERS ON PAGE 457.

Self-Study and Practice Tutorials

wordPOWER

Build your workplace vocabulary and improve spelling skills by completing the exercises in Appendix B on page 371.

Supplementary Practice Exercises

For additional practice, complete the Appendix C exercises for this chapter on page 411.

recap—chapters 8–10

Test your mastery of Unit 3 by completing these exercises. Your instructor will provide the answer key or have you submit your work for scoring.

A. VERBS

Number right: _____ **out of 25**

Underline the correct verb in the following sentences. The Vietnam Memorial (stands, stood) as a tribute to all who served in the war.

1. The judge has (spoke, spoken) to our law class twice.

2. We (will see, will have seen) the view from the top of the Empire State Building by the time we leave New York.

3. The group of people (is trying, are trying) to gather signatures on the petition.

4. Either the artists or the gallery (was, were) responsible for securing the paintings.

5. The telephone (had rang, had rung) several times before anyone answered.

6. The team (has went, has gone) to the playoffs each year.

7. The manager of the two teams (give, gives) each one a pep talk every morning.

8. Our supervisor (flys, flies) to the corporate headquarters in California.

9. That employee has (broke, broken) every rule in the book.

10. The passengers on the bus were (shook, shaken) by the near accident.

11. (I'd, I would) like to speak to Mr. Bryant about a salary increase.

12. The regional managers had (came, come) to Washington for their annual meeting.

13. The author has (wrote, written) several articles against child abuse.

14. The price of new homes (has fallen, have fallen) ten percent in the last year.

15. The coins (sank, sunk) to the bottom of the pond.

16. The modular workstations (had been, were) ordered last week.

17. The employees of the new tenant (has been, have been) moving into the building for three days.

18. General Electric Corporation (is, are) opening an airplane engine manufacturing plant near my home.

19. The strong wind (blew, had blew) the roof off the building yesterday.

20. The stock prices had (fell, fallen) by the end of the trading season.

Name: _____ **Date:** _____

21. The visitors (were, was) greeted upon their arrival.

22. I (had planned, have planned, planned) on going to Radio City Music Hall when I visited New York.

23. Either Marlin or his friends (is, are) planning to attend the public speaking course.

24. The cast of each new play (tries, try) to memorize the lines before the first rehearsal.

25. Hartman Industries (has, have) a good profit sharing plan for the employees.

Name: _____ **Date:** _____

B. ADJECTIVES AND ADVERBS

1. These (kind, kinds) of rumors cause marriages to break up.

2. Margaret wanted to buy (this, those) kind of candy.

3. The camp counselor wanted (them, those) boys to lead the group.

4. (Them, These) are my parents.

5. (That, Those) woman is my supervisor.

6. (Them, Those) actors are performing in the program tonight.

7. These (type, types) of situations are awkward for us.

8. (These, Them) textbooks are needed in class today.

9. Unfortunately, I make this (types, type) of error often.

10. (That, Those) sort of clothing should not be worn in the office.

11. Susan has (a, an) yellow raincoat that you can borrow.

12. I left (a, an) umbrella in the conference room.

13. A nurse should be proficient with the use of (a, an) hypodermic needle.

14. Craig is (a, an) honorable gentleman.

15. When I forgot to file my return last year, (a, an) IRS agent called me.

16. There was (a, an) 18 percent increase in the rent this year.

17. The firm hired (a, an) FBI agent.

18. There was (a, an) unified agreement between me and the corporation regarding my services.

19. You will have to turn down (a, an) one-way street in order to get to the beach.

20. Which is the (better, best) medication for these patients, Serine or Berine?

21. Here is the (more recent, most recent) of the two photos.

22. That statue is the (less valuable, least valuable) of any in his huge collection.

23. The appetizers recommended by the caterer tasted (delicious, deliciously).

24. If you do (good, well) on the test, you'll be accepted at the college of your choice.

25. The band played so (loud, loudly) that we couldn't hear the sirens.

Name: _____ **Date:** _____

writing for your career

Throughout this unit, you have studied the basic parts of business letters and how to format them. To put it all together, you need to understand how to place all of the parts on the letterhead to make your letter conform to a standard **business letter style**. Style, also called **format**, refers to the layout of the entire document on the page. The features to consider when formatting include the following:

- Alignment of text at the margins
- Width of margins (top, bottom, left, and right)
- Line spacing between the letter parts
- Line spacing between paragraphs
- Size and style of type font used (e.g., Arial, Times Roman, or Calibri)
- Number of pages

A typical business letter does not include graphics other than the letterhead design. In the case of a letter used for advertising, solicitation of contributions, or other "creative" endeavors where graphics might be desired, refer to your reference manual for advice on document design.

LETTER STYLES

Type business letters on quality 8½-by-11-inch letterhead stationery and mail them in matching envelopes (where available). White or off-white paper is most appropriate.

Block Letter Style

In this style, all of the parts are aligned at the left margin. This style, shown on page 217, is used in most organizations today.

CJT Financial Consulting
4825 Lakeville Court
Seattle, WA 98103
206-555-5555
cjthomas@cjtfc.xxx
www.cjtfinancialconsulting.xxx

(1) September 18, 20xx

(2) Professor Adell Shay
Los Angeles Harbor College
1111 Figueroa Place
Wilmington, CA 90744

(3) Dear Professor Shay:

(4) Joe Santona gave us your name as someone who likes to see profit, good business
practices, protection of the environment, and social responsibility all working
hand in hand.

Joe thinks you'll be interested in learning more about how you can have a healthy
profit, growth, and safety while investing wisely in activities you believe in. Few
had even heard of socially responsible investing (SRI) in 1986 when we began to
develop SRI programs. Our decades-long track record has earned us the
confidence ofindividuals like you, small businesses, and large pension funds that
have benefitted from our experience in the social investment field.

We invite you to a complimentary initial consultation, during which we'll discuss
your present needs and financial goals. We'll determine whether we can help you
meet your objectives for short-term profit, long-term growth, and safety through
socially responsible solutions. A brochure is enclosed that shows how we help our
clients achieve peace ofmind while their money works for them.

To arrange a no-obligation appointment, please fill out the enclosed card and
return it to us.

(5) Sincerely,

Clarence J. Thomas

(6) Clarence Joseph Thomas
(7) Certified Financial Planner

(8) kt

(9) Enclosure

(10) c: Joseph Santona

`Serving Investors Since 1971`

1. Date	**6.** Writer's name
2. Inside Address	**7.** Writer's title
3. Salutation	**8.** Typist's initials
4. Body	**9.** Enclosure notation
5. Complimentary close	**10.** Copy notation

Modified Block Letter Style

In the following letter, modified block layout is used. This format is explained in the letter.

Business Training Solutions, LLC

209 W. 66th Street
New York, NY 10023
www.bts.xxx

Phone: 212.555.0125
Fax: 212.555.0145
Email: sbourne@bts.xxx

March 10, 20xx

Keisha Marie Washington
Executive Assistant
The White House
1600 Pennsylvania Avenue
Washington, DC 20500

Dear Ms. Washington:

In the modified-block letter, the date and closing begin at about the horizontal center of the line. The first word of each paragraph may begin at the left margin as in this letter, or it may be indented five spaces for a more conservative look. We recommend using block paragraphs for the more current look shown here. Please note that all other spacing and placement of elements are the same as the more widely used block letter style.

Some people prefer modified-block format because it is more conservative and traditional than the block style. Therefore, modified-block may suggest a more appropriate image for correspondence with financial institutions or political officials.

Congratulations on being named executive assistant in the White House Correspondence Office. I hope this information helps you respond to the many letters your office receives from the people of America. If I can be of further assistance, please don't hesitate to contact me.

Sincerely yours,

Savannah G. Bournce

Savannah G. Bourne
President

Summary of Letter Formatting

- Use a standard font for business letters; 12-point Times New Roman is recommended.
- Use margins of about 1 inch to 1¼ inches left and right. Avoid right-margin justification.
- Leave a bottom margin of at least 1 inch.
- Type the date two or three spaces below the letterhead.
- Spell out the month in the date.
- You can improve the appearance of especially short letters by adding an extra blank line or two before and/or after the date and by enlarging the margins.
  - To fit long letters on one page, decrease the left and right margins to about ¾ of an inch (0.75).
  - To center short or long letters, reduce or enlarge the font size and/or change the font style to one providing either more or fewer characters per line.
  - Print two-page letters double-sided. You needn't number the pages unless the letter has more than two pages. In that case, type a header with the recipient's name, page number, and date on page 2 and succeeding pages:

    Ms. Betty G. Dillard
    page 2
    January 4, 20xx
  - Print additional pages on plain paper (without letterhead) matching the quality and color of the letterhead stationery.

Addressing Envelopes

- Most business letters are mailed in business envelopes known as No. 9 or No. 10.
- Most organizations use envelopes with a printed return address. If you do not have preprinted envelopes, single-space the sender's name and address to print in the upper left corner of the envelope.
- Single-space the recipient's address; use either the envelope default placement or begin at about the center of the envelope.

Folding Letters

- When folding a letter to place in an envelope, you want the top to open first. To achieve this, fold the 8½-by-11-inch sheet in thirds as follows:
  - Bring the bottom third of the letter up and make a crease.
  - Fold the top of the letter down but stop a fraction of an inch before the crease you already made.
  - Make the second crease.
  - Holding the second crease, insert the letter into the envelope.

Take a moment now to fold a sheet of 8½-by-11-inch paper.

Writing for your career recap

The questions below pertain to key points you have learned about letter formatting and styles in Chapters 8 to 10.

Write T (true) or F (false) in each blank.

_____ 1. Spell out the word *copy* in the copy notation of a letter.

_____ 2. It is courteous to let the recipient(s) know who is being copied on correspondence.

_____ 3. The typist's initials should be in capital letters.

_____ 4. The modified-block letter format is considered more conservative than the block format.

_____ 5. A personal title should be used before the letter writer's name.

_____ 6. A *bc* notation should not appear on the original of a letter.

_____ 7. One correct way to type the date in a business letter is 6 June 2009.

_____ 8. The letters *PS* are not required before a sentence that is a postscript.

_____ 9. If a subject line is used in a letter, type it two line spaces below the salutation.

_____ 10. The company name is not required as part of the closing information.

_____ 11. When typing the number for the day in the date of a letter, always include *st, nd, rd*, and *th*.

_____ 12. Today's knowledgeable business letter writers always include a subject line.

_____ 13. If the inside address begins *Mr. Peter Settle*, use *Dear Sir* as the salutation.

_____ 14. The purpose of a postscript (PS) is to add information you forgot to put in the body of a letter.

_____ 15. When writing a personal business letter, create personal letterhead from a word processing template or from your own design.

Name: _____ **Date:** _____

unit four

Perfecting Sentence Punctuation

© Kurhan/Fotolia

© Auremar/Fotolia

After completing Chapter 11, you will be able to do the following:

- Use commas correctly to separate a series of items or adjectives in sentences.
- Use commas correctly to join parts of sentences.
- Properly place commas in sentences and information that contain names of locations and people, dates, and quotations.

11

Punctuation: The Comma

career connection

GROWING INDUSTRIES AND OCCUPATIONS

How well do your career goals and aspirations fit the current and future job market? Today's job seekers must weigh the pursuit of their dream job and career versus the realities of where the opportunities are and will be. The US Department of Labor's Bureau of Labor Statistics (http://www.bls.gov/emp) produces the *Occupational Outlook Handbook*, a thorough source of information about the labor market. It provides detailed descriptions of education, training, and related work experience typically needed for occupations as well as data on salary levels.

The current edition projects that careers related to health care, personal care and social assistance, and construction will have the fastest job growth between 2010 and 2020 (although construction is not expected to regain all the jobs lost in the 2007–2009 recession). Total employment is projected to grow by 14.3 percent over the decade, resulting in 20.5 million new jobs. In occupations in which a master's degree is typically needed for entry, employment is expected to grow by 21.7 percent, faster than the growth rate for any other education category. In occupations in which apprenticeship is the typical on-the-job training, employment is expected to grow by 22.5 percent, faster than for any other on-the-job training category lost during the 2007–2009 recession.

The following chart shows occupational categories that are projected to grow over the next decade.

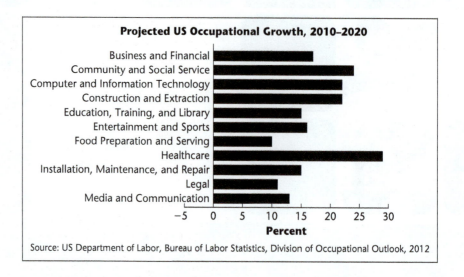

Projected US Occupational Growth, 2010–2020

Source: US Department of Labor, Bureau of Labor Statistics, Division of Occupational Outlook, 2012

PRETEST

Use proofreading marks to insert commas where needed. If no comma is needed, write **C** in the blank.

_____ 1. The majority of management positions today require computer proficiency and organizations must be prepared to provide the necessary training.

_____ 2. The gap between workplace demands and the skills workers have as they enter the labor market provides many opportunities for specialists who can teach professional and technical skills.

_____ 3. Traditionally concentrated in small firms copyright and patent lawyers are now in demand by major corporations.

_____ 4. The increase in temporary employment which continues to grow rapidly in many industries has created a huge demand for temporary employment agencies.

_____ 5. "Healthcare, community and social service and computer and information technology professionals are especially in demand" according to the US Department of Labor.

_____ 6. In fact construction is a growth industry even though its recovery since the recession has been extremely slow.

_____ 7. Did the new technician quit because he received a better offer from a Las Vegas Nevada company?

_____ 8. Either he moves to Puerto Rico within the next month or he doesn't get the job.

_____ 9. Although job growth is expected to be modest over the next few years we do anticipate an upturn in the employee recruitment business.

_____ 10. If you anticipate a need for our services, we will send you a packet of information and follow up with a visit from one of our managers.

CHECK YOUR ANSWERS ON PAGE 457.

Comma Basics

When you speak, pauses in your flow of words help your listener's understanding. When you don't pause at the expected places, your words seem to be out of order, and your listener might stop you and ask for clarification. When you write, punctuation marks replace the pauses, and they are crucial to your reader's understanding.

The comma is the mark that gives writers the most trouble. Commas are one of the "pesky" aspects of grammatically correct writing. Writers have trouble with them usually because they use too many or leave them out. If commas have caused you problems in the past, now is the time to conquer them forever. Once you learn to apply the basic rules for comma use, you will no longer rely on guesswork. These logical rules will help make your writing precise and clear.

When you do the exercises in this chapter, insert a comma only when the rule applies. If you don't think of the rule first, you'll continue to make whatever errors you made in the past. You will have the opportunity to practice applying the rules as you complete the exercises for each section.

ITEMS IN A SERIES

Use commas to separate items in a series of three or more words, phrases, or clauses. Notice the commas between the items in the series below—as well as before the words *and* or *or* that precede the **last word, phrase,** or **clause.** Business communications experts use that final comma because it helps to ensure clarity of business information; academic and literary writers, bloggers, and journalists often omit it.

Word series	Do you prefer **Catalina, Hawaii,** or **Bermuda** for your honeymoon?
	Please order **soft drinks, sparkling water, coffee,** and **tea** for the afternoon break.
Phrase series	Joe believes in government **of the people, for the people,** and **by the people.**
Clause series	**Amish men wear black felt hats all the time, Sikh men always wear turbans,** and **Orthodox Jewish men usually wear skullcaps.** [three independent clauses]
	We believe **that your idea was good, that you planned carefully,** and **that you had a good product.** [one independent clause, *We believe*, followed by three dependent clauses]

If a conjunction precedes each item in the series, omit the commas.

No commas   Engineers **and** physicists **and** chemists are working on the project.

While the preceding example is correct, good writing requires that you omit extra words; therefore, edit this sentence to omit the first *and*. Use the serial comma instead.

Revised   Engineers, physicists, and chemists are working on the project.

When listing items in a series, keep in mind that three or four items is about the maximum number that is comfortable for readers to absorb. If your list is longer, find a way to break your ideas into two or more sentences. Another option is to list the items using numbers or bullets. This will greatly aid your reader's understanding and memory.

Listed items   If you wish to take advantage of the guided mountain hike, make sure you have the proper attire. Suggested clothing and items:

- Hiking boots or other shoes with grip sole
- Loose-fitting clothing
- Backpack
- Bottled water
- Sunscreen

TWO OR MORE ADJECTIVES TOGETHER

Use a comma between *two or more* adjectives that describe the same noun. First you need to determine whether this is the case; if it is not the case, no comma is needed. The following tests will help you make the decision:

Test by Inserting *and*

Whenever you have consecutive adjectives, try inserting the word *and* between them. If the sentence still makes sense, use a comma between the adjectives.

Yes   The seeds were dormant during the **long, severe** winter.
Yes   The seeds were dormant during the **long and severe** winter.

And makes sense between the adjectives *long* and *severe* because both adjectives describe *winter*. Therefore, use a comma instead of *and*. If *and* doesn't make sense between the adjectives, do not insert a comma between them.

Yes   The seeds woke up in the **early spring** thaw.
No   The seeds woke up in the **early and spring** thaw.

And does not make sense between *early* and *spring*. The word *early* modifies *spring*, not *thaw*; therefore, do not use a comma.

Test by Reversing the Adjectives

Another clue that helps you decide whether to use a comma between consecutive adjectives is to reverse their order. If they make sense either way, you need a comma. If the adjectives don't make sense reversed, don't use a comma between them.

Yes   She is a **loyal, intelligent** employee.

Yes   She is an **intelligent, loyal** employee.

Since the sentence makes sense either way, use a comma between the adjectives.

Yes   **Many young** children are being educated at home by their parents.

No   **Young many** children are being educated at home by their parents.

Reversing the adjectives—*young many children*—doesn't make sense, indicating that a comma is not needed between the adjectives.

Joining Independent Clauses

Use a comma before a coordinating conjunction that joins independent clauses. Remember that an independent clause must have a subject and a verb, *and* it must be able to stand alone as a complete thought. Coordinating conjunctions are *and, but, or, nor, for, so,* and sometimes *yet.* (See Chapter 2 if you need a refresher.)

> Joe faxed printouts of the email messages, **but** he forgot to send the invoices.

Two independent clauses are joined by a comma and the coordinating conjunction *but.*

> Joe faxed printouts of the email messages but forgot to send the invoices.

This sentence has only one independent clause; the subject is *Joe;* there are two verbs—*faxed* and *forgot*—and a prepositional phrase, *to send the invoices.* No comma is needed.

RECOGNIZING INDEPENDENT CLAUSES

In the preceding examples it was easy to recognize the independent clauses, but clauses that use *either/or, neither/nor,* and *not only/but also* don't *sound* independent. They *are* independent, however, if each word group has a subject and verb.

> **Either** he lives in Savannah, **or** he lives in a South Carolina suburb.

Two independent clauses are joined by the coordinating conjunction *or* and a comma. *He* is the subject and *lives* is the verb in both clauses.

> **Either** he lives in Savannah **or** in some other Georgia city.

This sentence has only one independent clause with a subject and verb (*he lives*). *Or* connects a prepositional phrase; no comma is needed. Here are some more examples:

> **Not only** is she the best candidate for the job, **but she also** knows the territory.

Two independent clauses; comma is needed.

> Clarissa is **not only** very kind **but also** extremely generous.

One independent clause; no comma is needed.

> **Neither** one of us can go to the luncheon, **nor** do we want to.

Two independent clauses; comma is needed.

> **Neither** the marketing plan **nor** the launch party made an impact on product recognition.

One independent clause; no comma is needed.

Exceptions and Other Comma Rules

The basic rules that you have just studied can be committed to memory fairly easily. But like all rules, there are exceptions and circumstances when they don't apply. Remember, comma use is all about making your meaning clear. Keeping that in mind will help you remember this next set of rules.

EXCEPTION FOR INDEPENDENT CLAUSES

In a short sentence (no more than about 10 words), it is acceptable to omit the comma when *and* or *or* joins an independent clause. If *but*, *nor*, *for*, *so*, or *yet* joins the independent clauses, however, do use a comma before it regardless of sentence length.

> He won **and** I lost.   Either he built it **or** she did.
>
> He won, **but** I lost.   He actually won, **yet** I still can't believe it.

SETTING OFF CONTRASTING EXPRESSIONS

Use a comma to separate two sharply contrasting or opposite ideas. In this case you are inserting a comma for clarity of meaning. Such expressions are generally introduced by *not*, *never*, *seldom*, *but*, or *yet*.

> He often thinks about leaving his job, **but** never his profession.
>
> She loves the movies, **yet** seldom goes to the theater.
>
> Take a bus home from the office party, **not** the subway.

OMITTING A VERB

Fewer words make for concise and clear writing, and varying your sentence structure makes for more interesting reading. At times you can express a thought by omitting a verb that is easily understood from the wording of the rest of the sentence. A comma replaces the omitted verb.

A used photocopier costs $1,245, a new one, $2,300.

Shirley is now in Ohio in a new career and George, still in Alaska.

GO TO PAGE 238 AND COMPLETE WORKSHEET 11.1.

Commas and Introductory Words

Introductory words that explain something about the main idea of the sentence—the independent clause—sometimes, but not always, should be set off with a comma. Following are the rules for introductory expressions:

Use a comma after one-word or very short introductory expressions:

Yes, we'll be glad to introduce you to our purchasing director.

No, I don't believe we will be able to schedule a full-day workshop.

To summarize, we will not be responsible for personal belongings left in unlocked offices.

Use a comma after an introductory "direct address" of the person you're writing to.

Mr. Gregory, are you available for lunch on Friday, June 29, at noon?

A comma is not required after short "place" and "time" introductory phrases unless needed for clarity or emphasis.

Within a year we will know the results of making this investment.

In 2012 our main offices moved from downtown to the suburbs.

In 2012, 25 percent of our sales were in the youth market.

COMMA RULES

- Use commas between items in a series as well as before the conjunction preceding the last item. If conjunctions are used before each item, do not add commas.
- Use a comma between consecutive adjectives if you can insert *and* between them or reverse their order and still make sense.
- Use a comma before *and, but, nor, for, so,* and *yet* when one of these conjunctions joins independent clauses.
- Use a comma to replace omitted verbs that are understood.
- Use a comma before sharply contrasting or opposing expressions. These often begin with a word such as *but, seldom, never,* or *not.*
- Use a comma after an introductory expression—
  - that has a verb
  - that has five or more words
  - when necessary for clearness
  - that is one word: *yes, no, well,* or *oh*
  - that addresses a person by name or title

Use a comma after an introductory expression that includes a verb, even when it is short.

> **I'm not sure,** but I believe tomorrow is the deadline for registration.
>
> **If you can,** please complete the first draft by Monday.

Use a comma after an introductory expression of fewer than five words and no verb form when it is needed for clarity or if it is a transitional expression.

> **Once inside,** the man requested food. [clarity]
>
> **In addition,** a few of our suppliers make special deals. [transitional expression]

Use a comma after an introductory expression of five or more words whether it has a verb form or not.

> **Because of the severe weather forecast,** we are closing the office for the rest of the day.
>
> **Under the sponsorship of the university medical school,** a conference on early childhood nutrition will be held on July 2.

Setting Off Words, Phrases, and Clauses

You will recall from Chapter 3 that varying the length and structure of sentences is important to good writing. Variation contributes to clarity and interest for your reader. Longer sentences will have words and phrases that might need to be set off with commas. To decide whether commas are required to separate parts of sentences, you need to consider whether a word or group of words is necessary to the meaning of the sentence or not. In grammar, these word groups are called nonessential expressions and essential expressions.

NONESSENTIAL EXPRESSIONS

Put commas around words, phrases, and clauses that are not essential to the meaning of the sentence. To decide whether words or phrases are not essential, consider whether the addition aids understanding or adds additional information but does not change the main idea. This type of expression is usually nonessential. It may be a word, a phrase, or a clause. Remember that a phrase does not have a subject and a verb. A clause is a word group that has a subject and a verb; it may be dependent or independent.

In the following sentences the nonessential words are shown in bold print. If you were to remove them, the rest of the sentence would retain its original meaning.

> Any new activity, **little or big**, becomes an adventure when shared with someone special.
>
> The 4D film we saw, **one of the first of its kind**, was followed by a discussion with the filmmaker.
>
> Professor Ingram-Cotton is, **of course**, an expert in this field.

Saying that a word or phrase is nonessential because it doesn't change meaning is not the same as saying it is *not necessary* to meaning or clarity. The test is whether your reader would still be able to understand your meaning without it. Any unnecessary words should be omitted from the sentence. In the following sentences commas are needed to enclose an intervening phrase that adds clarity.

> In 2008, **after a huge fire in the building,** our main offices moved from downtown to the suburbs.

> On the higher floors, **due to building regulations,** the windows do not open.

In the following examples, a nonessential clause is set off from the sentence because the main idea could stand on its own, even though the clause aids understanding.

> Ms. Elaine Esperanza, **who is a nutritionist,** will chair the panel on obesity.

The fact that Ms. Esperanza is a nutritionist tells the reader she is qualified. This is good information to include but is not essential to the main idea that she is going to chair the panel.

> This business plan, **which we have studied carefully,** is unsatisfactory and needs to be rewritten.

The clause tells the reader you have given your opinion serious thought. Depending on who your reader is, this could be important information to include. Nevertheless, your opinion stands without this clarification.

> We'll meet you at 5 p.m., **although we cannot stay long**.

The nonessential clause prepares the reader for your early exit, but the essential information of when you will meet could stand alone.

ESSENTIAL EXPRESSIONS

Do not enclose essential expressions—a word or group of words that is necessary to convey the main idea of a sentence—in commas. To decide whether a word or word group is essential, imagine the words omitted. If the meaning of the rest of the sentence changes, the expression is essential. Try this with the following sentences.

> A training DVD **"Banking for Tweens and Teens"** is one of our bestsellers.

Without the name of the DVD, the reader is left with no information.

> A person **who is a nutritionist** should lead the discussion.

Compare this with the sentence about Ms. Elaine Esperanza in the previous section on nonessential clauses. Here, the same clause is essential.

> Someone **like you** should lead the discussion.

> Bring your resume with you **when you apply for a job**.

> A national organization **that has a research bureau** stands behind our product.

> A city **that can qualify as a disaster area** is eligible to receive federal aid.

Set off a name with commas when the name is not essential to the reader's understanding, and omit the comma when it is.

> My sister-in-law **Pat** lives in Detroit, Michigan.

As I have two sisters-in-law, her name is essential: therefore, it should not be set off within commas.

COMMAS WITH *WHICH* AND *THAT*

The words *which* and *that* are useful for introducing essential and nonessential expressions. Use *which* to begin nonessential expressions and *that* to begin essential expressions.

Essential phrase	Homes **that are beautifully decorated** sell faster.
	A refund policy **that does not have a time limit** is harder to find these days.
Nonessential phrase	Mr. Rich's new office, **which has been beautifully decorated**, is on the third floor.
	Our refund policy, **which requires that merchandise be returned within 30 days**, is very liberal compared to most.

GO TO PAGE 239 AND COMPLETE WORKSHEET 11.2.

COMMA DON'TS

Most prepositional phrases are essential and should not be enclosed in commas. In addition, do not use a comma to separate a subject from its verb.

No   We saw your sales representative, **at the conference**, on May 2.

Yes   We saw your sales representative **at the conference** on May 2.

No   The Board of Directors, **is considering Internet sales**, to increase income.

Yes   The Board of Directors **is considering Internet sales** to increase income.

Four Easy Commas

The remainder of this chapter covers comma use with names of locations and addresses, names of people, dates, and quotations. You probably will find the rules for these four categories much easier to remember than the rules for punctuating parts of sentences.

LOCATIONS AND ADDRESSES

In a sentence, put a comma between the city and state, province, or country. Also place a comma after the state, province, or country when other words follow.

Did you visit **Paris, France,** or **Paris, Kentucky?**

I lived in **Springfield, Massachusetts,** and taught business classes at Bay Path College in Longmeadow.

When address parts are in sentence form, separate the parts with commas; however, never use a comma between the state and the ZIP code.

Please return the software to Computer Learning Center, 3600 Market Street, Philadelphia, PA 19104, before June 8.

The art director lives at 35 Wynford Heights, Don Mills, Ontario M3C 1k9, Canada.

In an address on a letter or envelope, place a comma between the street address and location, such as apartment or suite number, when they are typed on the same line.

> Mr. Nitesh Vora
> 312 Sycamore Lane, Suite 200
> Detroit, MI 48234

DATES

When a date has the month, day, and year, separate the year from the day with a comma. Do not, however, put a comma between the month and the day.

> December 12, 2014

In the middle of a sentence, enclose the year in commas.

> The stadium groundbreaking ceremony will be held on **May 5, 2014,** at the site of the new Dawson College Stadium.

Expressing dates in order of month/day/year is the **American date style**. Do not use commas with the **international or military date style**, which is written in order of day/month/year.

> The international conference will be held in Amsterdam, Holland, on **31 July 2014**.

In a date that has only the month and year, do not use a comma.

> The next convention will take place in **April 2015** in Frederick, Maryland, at the new convention center.

If the year isn't included in a date, use no commas.

> The **March 6** conference was held at Abbie Business Institute.

Place commas around elements of a date or time that explain a preceding date or time in the same sentence.

> At 9 a.m., **Wednesday, January 3,** the sale on women's shoes begins.

MORE COMMA RULES

- Enclose in commas nonessential expressions that interrupt the main idea.
- When choosing between *which* and *that* to begin a clause, use *which* with commas for "nonessential" words and *that* with no commas for "essential words."
- Use commas to enclose a state, province, or country following a city in a sentence.
- Use commas between parts of an address when written within a sentence.
- Use a comma to separate the parts of an address and the city and state on an envelope or inside address of a letter.
- Use a comma before and after dates or times that explain preceding dates or times.
- Use commas to enclose direct quotations that don't end the sentence.
- Do not use a comma before a quotation that blends in with the rest of the sentence.

writingTIP

Skilled communicators tend to use direct address because it is courteous and builds rapport with the reader. *Thank you, Ms. Leslie, for showing me around Grossmont last Tuesday.* Overuse of the technique, however, appears insincere.

NAMES

Direct address is when you use the name of the person to whom you are writing. Use commas to set off the name. Direct address can be used to sound positive and friendly or in a way that sends a more pointed message, as shown in these examples.

> Because of your expertise, Joanne, we're inviting you to lead the discussion.

> The following will explain, Dr. Spellman, just how important this research is.

> Please be advised, Mr. Bergen, that in the future Building Management will insist upon advance notice of large deliveries.

> This is to remind you, Danielle, that your expense reports must be supported by receipts.

QUOTATION MARKS

Use commas to separate a **direct quotation** (the exact words of a person) from the rest of the sentence.

> George said, "Isn't that Stella Glitter signing autographs in the lobby?"

Place a comma or period *before* the closing quotation mark, never after—no exceptions.

End of sentence	Years later, my former boss admitted, "I should have done more to convince you to stay with the company."
Beginning of sentence	"Money is *not* the root of all evil," he said.
Middle of sentence	Jesse whispered, "Don't reveal our plans," but I didn't hear him.
Quote interrupted	"Money," Alicia replied, "*is* the root of all evil."

Do not add a comma when a quotation ends with a question mark or an exclamation mark.

> "Did you ever tell a lie?" asked Ms. Ripley.

> "No, I never did and never would!" exclaimed Mr. Ripley.

A comma is unnecessary before a word or words in a quotation that is "woven" into the rest of the sentence.

> We all sang "Happy Birthday" when Georgette entered the office.

> Jesse answered the big question with a simple "no."

GO TO PAGE 241 AND COMPLETE WORKSHEET 11.3.

Checkpoint

Commas are written signals that can be as effective as a speaker's pauses and voice inflections. Using commas correctly is important in every sentence you write. Misplaced or omitted commas can make a sentence difficult or impossible to understand or can totally change its meaning. Review the boxes that summarize the comma rules throughout the chapter and highlight the ones that you need to go back and review.

communications connection

BUSINESS EMAIL: THE TEMPLATE

In today's workplace, email is the primary means of communication. Even when printed letters and memos are required, they are often sent as an attachment to an email. For the vast amount of everyday communication, however, email has replaced printed letters and memos.

A first consideration in effective email communication is filling in the standard parts of the **email template**. The template has several windows at the top; these vary somewhat, depending on the system you are using, but a typical email template contains the standard parts shown in the figure below. Following are guidelines that will help you follow business standards for emails.

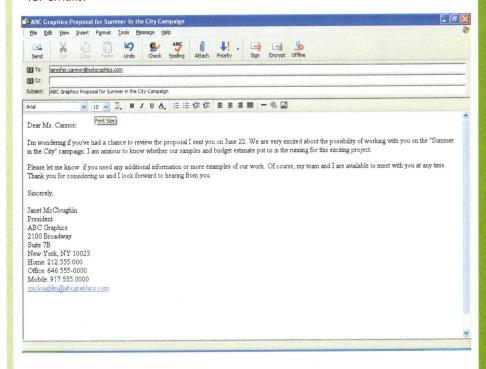

The "To" Window

- Include only the primary recipients—those from whom a response might be expected.
- Use a semicolon (;) or a comma (,) to separate recipients' names/addresses if your system doesn't do this automatically.
- When names/addresses are automatically inserted from an address book, double-check to make the sure the correct ones are showing in the window.

The "Copy" Window

- Include secondary recipients—they are not expected to respond.
- Separate names/addresses with a semicolon.
- Keep in mind that the recipient of a copy might reply to or forward the email to others.

The "Blind Copy" Window

Use blind copies sparingly. Normally, it is courteous to let the recipient know who is being copied, but blind copies are appropriate in the following instances:

- For a mass mailing outside the organization. Placing all addresses in the blind copy window protects the privacy of the recipients.
- When there is a good reason not to let the recipient know who is being copied.
- When the primary recipient has no knowledge of the person being copied.
- Keep in mind that the recipient of a blind copy might reply to or forward the email to others.

The "Subject" Window

Limit the subject of each email to one topic. There are several reasons for this:

- Related emails are easier to organize and track.
- Limiting the topic means the email can be shorter, making it easier to write and more likely to be read thoroughly.
- It will be easier for the recipient to decide if a response is needed and to respond quickly.

A clear specific subject line helps the recipient see immediately what your message is about and prioritize it. Avoid using general terms that need interpretation. Use only a few words that explicitly describe the subject:

Agenda for May 1 Planning Meeting

Request for Budget Information

Are you free for lunch?

Your Monthly Report Is Past Due

WRITING PRACTICE

Write subject lines for emails covering the following topics:

1. You need sales data from several colleagues for a monthly report that is due next Friday, February 16. _____
2. It is the first week of May and you want permission from your supervisor to take a week off in July. _____
3. You and your team need a new printer; the one you have keeps breaking down. _____
4. You need a chart that a colleague used in a presentation at Monday's staff meeting. _____
5. You are organizing a staff luncheon for your administrative assistant to reward her on Administrative Assistants Day. _____
_____

Date to submit this assignment: _____

PROOFREADING PRACTICE

Insert or delete commas and correct any other errors in the following article. Use proofreading marks or go online to correct the document electronically.

Financial Aid—Read the Fine Print

Make sure, that you understand the terms of any contract or financial agreement you enter into with a bank, creditor or any other lending institution. Take the time to read the agreement careful, and make sure you understand everything in it. Remember, asking after you sign is to late! Seek the advice of an expert, if you are unsure about what any of the terms mean.

Before borrowing from a public, financial institution however it is a good idea to consider financial aid, provided by the US government. Federal loans which generally offers borrowers' lower interest rates have more flexible, repayment options.

Keep in mind, that educational loans are treated just like any other creditor arrangement that means that failure to pay, or late payments will be noted on your credit record. Having a clear understanding of the loan terms a commitment to your educational goals and a focus on gainful employment are key elements for future financial solvency. Your future earning potential which depends on having a college degree is worth the sacrifice of paying off a loan.

How did you do? Excellent _____ Good _____

Need More Practice _____

chapter review

WORKSHEET 11.1

Insert commas where needed and write **C** in the blank next to the sentences that are already correct.

_____ 1. The loud electronic music is irritating the customers.

_____ 2. They are about to begin a unique exciting adventure.

_____ 3. Not only does Professor Carroll like sports but she also enjoys music and art.

_____ 4. He asked why you came what you wanted and what you expect to do.

_____ 5. The annual financial report was prepared by a highly paid famous accountant.

_____ 6. Everyone in the office is extremely pleased with Pam's work and we especially appreciate her proofreading ability.

_____ 7. Our showroom is in a small elegant building in a new part of Milwaukee.

_____ 8. He is a bright enthusiastic student.

_____ 9. Carla will call on accounts in Fort Worth Dallas and Austin.

_____ 10. Gabby Douglas is not only an Olympic champion, but she is also an author and speaker.

_____ 11. The executive's marketing expertise in a profitable highly competitive industry was what the record label needed.

_____ 12. The CEO was offered a million-dollar bonus a million-dollar salary and stock options.

_____ 13. Our new advertising booklet was completed last week.

_____ 14. The company is opening a new office in Boston and the telemarketing operation will be moved there in the fall.

_____ 15. I am pleased with Rosalyn's work and I really appreciate her positive attitude.

_____ 16. International students bring not only a wide variety of cultures but also a wide range of learning experiences to the classroom.

_____ 17. Not only will students be better prepared for today's international workplace but they will also be better citizens by learning about other countries and cultures.

_____ 18. Ms. Mack is a member of the prestigious Theta Alpha Delta honorary business education sorority and she will join us at the state convention.

_____ 19. He works out at the gym every morning but he never goes in the afternoon.

_____ 20. In September we hired an administrative assistant; in October a data entry clerk; and in November a website manager.

_____ 21. He arrived at 10 p.m., not 10 a.m.

_____ 22. Either make a down payment or pay the total now.

_____ 23. At the end of the year prices will go down and even more people will be able to afford a new car.

_____ 24. Be sure to send for his brother not his sister.

_____ 25. The last and most successful promotional event was in 2010.

CHECK YOUR ANSWERS ON PAGE 457.

WORKSHEET 11.2

A. Insert commas where needed and write **C** in the blank next to the sentences that are already correct.

_____ 1. Since the board meets only once a month at the next meeting we need to have the members approve the blueprints for the new wing and plans for the fall gala.

_____ 2. Before leaving for the airport, please sign the expense vouchers.

_____ 3. If you take the train you will arrive at 8:45 a.m.

_____ 4. Being in a hurry to end the meeting he skipped the first two items on the agenda.

_____ 5. He didn't make it on time because he drove too fast and rear-ended a police car.

_____ 6. Had he read the directions he would have taken the proper exit and arrived on time.

_____ 7. Hank please let us know if you need our help.

_____ 8. Although their supervisor didn't know it Eddie and Helen worked late to finish the project.

_____ 9. When we walked through the doors of the exclusive Flintridge Inn we knew this was a special celebration.

_____ 10. In Chicago people sunbathe downtown on a Lake Michigan beach.

_____ 11. In this attractive modern dining room which seats 250 you always find a courteous staff at your service.

_____ 12. As we all know real merit is hard to conceal.

_____ 13. Examples of English words taken from American Indian languages are *igloo kayak moccasin skunk* and *persimmon*.

_____ 14. You'll receive the engraved mugs for the holiday party if you order now.

_____ 15. By discreetly motioning to the speaker indicate when five minutes of her time remains.

_____ 16. In 1969 the world's first Internet message was transmitted at UCLA.

_____ 17. Being an alert salesperson he noticed the prospect's gesture of annoyance.

_____ 18. No he hasn't called on us either this month or last month.

_____ 19. Please email the dinner chairperson explaining why we can't attend.

_____ 20. No one in the world has more willpower than the person who stops after eating one peanut.

B. Insert commas to enclose nonessential expressions. No other corrections are required. Write **C** in the blank next to the sentences that are correct.

_____ 1. A closed corporation limits the number of stockholders often members of the same family and conducts business less formally than publicly held corporations.

_____ 2. Sales representatives who increase sales by 50 percent will win a Caribbean cruise for two.

_____ 3. Avoid introducing subjects not on the agenda when you attend a business meeting.

_____ 4. People rarely succeed at anything unless they have fun doing it.

_____ 5. We faxed your January 6 memo to the IRS auditor but have not yet had a reply.

_____ 6. Managers need to know how to realign workers quickly to meet performance goals and staff availability.

_____ 7. Professor Kleinrock of UCLA developed the prototype for the Internet the system of computer-to-computer communications that has resulted in today's cyber culture.

_____ 8. I will of course be busy working on the project all weekend.

_____ 9. The operating costs as you probably know are too high for us to show much of a profit.

_____ 10. A preschool administrator Gloria Rojas telephoned me.

_____ 11. My office which is in Room 103 is in the new building.

_____ 12. The Financial Aid Office which is on the third floor is open daily.

_____ 13. Martin Simon the auditor found a $100,000 error.

_____ 14. The system that was devised by Technocraft Inc. is easy to learn.

_____ 15. The coach gave the book titled *The Inner Game of Tennis* to all of the team members.

_____ 16. Coaches who don't inspire their players should be replaced.

_____ 17. Openness fosters growth and establishes an important feeling of worth which motivates everyone to do the best possible job.

_____ 18. Harold Simon is the attorney who will try the civil case next month.

_____ 19. You can buy the new instruction booklet which gives complete information for only $23.95.

_____ 20. Sandi uses English effectively and correctly and also speaks French fluently.

_____ 21. A great idea it has been said comes into the world as gently as a dove.

_____ 22. The workshop I'm attending "Career Networking in Cyberspace" begins at 2:30 this afternoon.

_____ 23. The exchange student who just arrived from Beijing will help the Lopez family to improve their Chinese.

_____ 24. My Internet service which was working fine yesterday suddenly went down again this afternoon.

_____ 25. The Number 64 bus, which is usually on time, was delayed for over an hour.

CHECK YOUR ANSWERS ON PAGE 458.

WORKSHEET 11.3

A. Insert commas where required. Write **C** in the blank next to the sentences that are already correct.

_____ 1. On March 2 2014 we shipped you five HP LaserJet printers.

_____ 2. In April 2010 Professor Van Vooren became the vice president of the college.

_____ 3. One of Billy Crystal's first "gigs" was in a Long Beach New York nightclub.

_____ 4. The deposition was taken on Friday January 4 at 8:30 a.m. in my office.

_____ 5. Irish Linens Ltd. opened a new shop and Ms. O'Callahan is the general manager.

_____ 6. Little Rock Arkansas was the scene of tragedy and strife in the 1960s.

_____ 7. Goldfinger's Variety Stores Inc. closed the Albuquerque New Mexico store in 2007.

_____ 8. We will be in Edinburgh Scotland on 3 May and London on 6 May 2014.

_____ 9. I hope to interview two members of the British Parliament on 7 May 2014.

_____ 10. Marietta Georgia is the home of Chattahoochee Technical College.

B. The best way to remember the rules for punctuating quotes is to compose sentences that apply them.

11. Compose a sentence that includes a quotation at the end. _____

_____

_____

12. Compose a sentence with a quotation at the beginning. _____

_____

13. Compose a sentence with a quotation in the middle. _____

_____

_____

14. Compose a sentence with an interrupted quotation. _____

_____

15. Write a sentence beginning with a quotation that is a question or an exclamation. _____

_____

CHECK YOUR ANSWERS ON PAGE 459.

POSTTEST

If the commas in the following sentences are correct, write **C** in the blank. Otherwise, make the corrections. Capitalize the first word of new sentences you create.

_____ 1. On Monday March 6 I expect to meet Mr. Lombard president of Lake County Industries, Inc.

_____ 2. When you attend a business lunch do you put your phone on silent?

_____ 3. In a business communication class you can learn oral written and nonverbal strategies for success in a career.

_____ 4. At business meetings wear your name tag high on the right side of your chest for maximum visibility.

_____ 5. An advertising agency acts as an intermediary between a company that wants to advertise and the various media that sell space and time.

_____ 6. Charles Darwin said a man who dares to waste one hour of his life has not discovered the value of life.

_____ 7. My supervisor asked whether I would be willing to work over the weekend again.

_____ 8. Although the new office furniture arrived telephone service was not immediately available.

_____ 9. A factory closing means the community loses jobs tax revenues and consumer buying power.

_____ 10. In Dayton Ohio we have two factories that are about to close the manager said glumly.

CHECK YOUR ANSWERS ON PAGE 459.

Self-Study and Practice Tutorials

wordPOWER

Build your workplace vocabulary and improve spelling skills by completing the exercises in Appendix B on page 373.

Supplementary Practice Exercises

For additional practice, complete the Appendix C exercises for this chapter on page 414.

© Jenner/Fotolia

After completing Chapter 12, you will be able to do the following:

- Use the semicolon and colon correctly to separate parts of sentences.
- Use dashes and parentheses to set off parts of sentences for emphasis and de-emphasis.
- Use brackets to set off words and groups of words in sentences.

12

Punctuation: The Semicolon, Colon, and Other Marks

career connection

NETWORKING YOUR WAY TO SUCCESS

The use of social media and networking to connect with career opportunities is growing. Recruiters, employers, and job applicants are placing LinkedIn, Facebook, and Twitter at the top of their list of social networking tools. The advice of experts can be summarized as follows:

1. LinkedIn is most popular among recruiters. It is used by 95 percent, and has the most advantages for job seekers because it is tailor made for professional networking. You can set up a profile listing your work experience, ask your references to provide recommendations, and join groups related to your career interests.

2. Facebook is used by close to 60 percent of recruiters. When you are job hunting, it is extremely important not to blur the line between social and professional information about yourself. You can use it to reach out to friends who might help you find career opportunities and post content related to your career goals.

3. Twitter is used by over 40 percent of recruiters who use social networking as a source for finding job applicants. Whether you tweet or follow others in your field, you can pick up valuable insights and information.

4. When you create professional profiles, don't forget about the importance of keywords. Keep up with the language of your field and describe your goals and experiences in those terms.

5. Don't let the electronic world define your social network. Joining organizations and attending meetings and functions, asking for informational interviews, and selling yourself in person are equally useful and important.

PRETEST

Use proofreading marks to insert semicolons, colons, commas, brackets, parentheses, and em-dashes where needed.

1. Harold was hurt in an accident therefore he missed three weeks of work.

2. Please send the following by UPS 100 reams of copy paper and 25 printer cartridges.

3. He won money a great deal of money by playing the lottery each week.

4. The young couple saved every penny they could nevertheless it took them 10 years to save for a home.

5. I worked hard believe me to complete this assignment.

6. Mr. Leslie has worked for our company for 30 years therefore he is eligible for retirement.

7. "We will go not now *sic* to whatever is necessary to get the votes," said the senator.

8. Each set of silverware includes 12 each of these utensils salad forks, dinner forks, spoons, and knives.

9. Bring the following supplies with you to class plain white paper, a manila folder, and a good dictionary.

10. The bank's Saturday hours from 9 to noon will soon be changed.

CHECK YOUR ANSWERS ON PAGE 460.

The Semicolon (;)

One of the best-known examples of double meaning caused by the absence of a semicolon is the prophets' written reply to Roman soldiers. The soldiers asked whether they would return from the war. Since death was often the punishment for an inaccurate prediction, the Roman soothsayers took great care with their words: *ibis redibis non morieris in bello*, which means *you will go and return not die in war.* However, as punctuation had not yet been invented, the reader could interpret the prediction either way—that is, with either a pause *before* or a pause *after* "not." Say the sentence both ways, and you will see how the absence of a semicolon enabled the soothsayers to keep their heads no matter how the war turned out.

JOINING INDEPENDENT CLAUSES

The **semicolon** is a halfway mark because it is midway in "pausing value" between a comma and a period. That's why it consists of one of each. Use a semicolon between *closely related independent* clauses that are not joined by a coordinating conjunction—*and, but, or, nor, for, so,* and *yet.**

> Success is getting what you want; happiness is wanting what you get.
>
> Please take this to the messenger center; it closes at 4:30.

*When *yet* joins independent clauses, it may be preceded by a comma, a semicolon, or a period.

Why would you choose to omit the coordinating conjunction? Because the sentence reads better without it, and your writing is more concise without it. As you learned in Chapter 3, you could also separate the two independent clauses into two sentences. To do so, however, would make the rhythm "choppy." While it might be easier to avoid thinking about semicolons by inserting a coordinating conjunction or writing two sentences, your style suffers. Quality writing is what you are aiming for, and the semicolon helps you achieve it.

WITH TRANSITIONAL EXPRESSIONS

Transitional words and expressions, such as *also, however, therefore, in fact, furthermore, in addition, as a result, nevertheless, otherwise,* and *consequently*, are used to show the connection from one idea to another. Transitional expressions are essential for clear writing; they act as signposts to guide your reader from one idea to another. They may be used to begin a sentence or to join two independent clauses (with a semicolon). However, they can also act as interrupters in the middle of a sentence. In this case, place commas around them.

> November and December are our high volume months; **therefore**, I am requesting approval of three new sales positions.
>
> **In addition**, we may need to increase the hours of some of our current staff.
>
> Our budget is**, in fact**, already stretched to the limit for the fourth quarter. **Consequently**, I cannot approve your request.

Use a semicolon before a transitional expression joining independent clauses.

> When you travel in other countries, your name might sound foreign; **therefore**, have a supply of your business cards ready to exchange with people you meet.

Use a comma *after* a transitional expression of two or more syllables:

> We are fully booked on December 24; **consequently,** we cannot accept your request to reserve the Round Room for your dinner party.

Omit the comma after short transitions—*then, thus, hence, still, yet,* and *also*.

> The early 2000s were tough years; **thus** many new technology companies didn't survive.
>
> Please make sure the hotel reservations are confirmed; **also** talk to the caterer personally.

The preceding sentences would also be correct if written as two separate sentences. To separate two independent clauses, simply use a *period* after the first clause and a capital letter to begin a new sentence. *You* decide whether joining or separating will read more smoothly.

Use a semicolon after an independent clause that precedes the transitional expressions *for example, for instance, namely,* or *that is*—if one of these transitions adds an explanation that is also an independent clause.

> When invited to dinner in Egypt, bring a gift; for example, you can bring fruit, pastries, or cookies.
>
> Be prepared to discuss appropriate topics; for instance, some topics may include Egypt's ancient civilizations, Egyptian achievements, and the quality of Egyptian cotton.

WITH COORDINATING CONJUNCTIONS

Place a semicolon before a coordinating conjunction that joins independent clauses—*if* the sentence already has two or more commas.

> Professor Dennison, who works in Huntington, will present the slideshow; but we expect others to participate also.
>
> Through the ages languages have gathered new words; but popular use, as Betty explained, often becomes proper use.

WITH ITEMS IN A SERIES

If there are commas *within* the items of the series, use semicolons *between* the items.

No   AMTRAK stops at Schenectady, New York, West Burlington, Iowa, and Pasadena, California.

It seems as though AMTRAK makes five or six stops.

Yes   AMTRAK stops at Schenectady, New York; West Burlington, Iowa; and Pasadena, California.

The reader easily sees just three stops will be made.

GO TO PAGE 257 AND COMPLETE WORKSHEET 12.1.

The Colon (:)

The **colon** is a stronger pause than a semicolon; use it to introduce and emphasize. Like the semicolon, the colon is used after an independent clause in the middle of a sentence. It signals to the reader: pay attention to what is coming. It may or may not be followed by another independent clause. A few simple rules will help you remember when to use the colon.

WITH WORDS, CLAUSES, AND PHRASES

Use a colon after an independent clause if a clause, a phrase, or even a single word *explains* or *supplements* the main idea expressed. D*o not* capitalize words or phrases introduced by a colon.

> Just one word describes him: competent.
>
> The ethics rule could not be clearer: do not accept gifts from vendors.

When a complete sentence follows a colon, capitalize the first word when you want to emphasize the second senence or when it is a quotation. In this case, a capital letter is needed.

> He added this statement to the contract: "The total fee of $10,000 will be paid in four installments of $2,500 each."

If the sentence is worded so that a dependent clause introduces the quote, follow the rule that an introductory phrase requires a comma.

> Since the contract states, "The total fee of $10,000 will be paid in four installments of $2,500 each," and we didn't do so, please make out a check for $5,000 to cover two installments.

In the following sentence, a capital letter is used for emphasis, but a lower-case letter on the word *we* would also be correct.

> Our mission is clear: We will not be outsold by the competition this year.
>
> Our mission was spelled out in the memo: we will not be outsold by anyone.

WITH ITEMS IN A SERIES OR LIST

Use a colon after an independent clause (a complete sentence) when it introduces items in a series.

> Our goals were clear: growth, recognition, and brand loyalty.
>
> These traits are required of his employees: initiative, loyalty, honesty, and dependability.

Notice how the use of the colon places more emphasis on the items listed. You could also write these sentences as follows:

> Our goals were growth, recognition, and brand loyalty.
>
> The personality traits required of his employees are initiative, loyalty, honesty, and dependability.

If items are listed vertically, use the colon whether or not the introduction is a sentence.

> The qualities he's looking for:
>
> - initiative
> - loyalty
> - honesty
> - dependability
>
> The qualities he's looking for are these:
>
> - initiative
> - loyalty
> - honesty
> - dependability

Do not use a colon before a list if another sentence follows the introductory sentence.

> Please send the following people to my office. I need to see them immediately.
>
> Shuzu Itakara
>
> Frank Chang
>
> Sherrill Frank

IN PARTS OF LETTERS AND EMAILS

Standard punctuation style for business letters and emails that take the place of printed letters requires a colon after the salutation and a comma after the complimentary close.

Salutation	Dear Mr. Archer:
Complimentary Close	Sincerely yours,

In everyday email correspondence, it is standard to use a comma after the salutation.

GO TO PAGE 258 AND COMPLETE WORKSHEET 12.2.

RULES FOR THE SEMICOLON AND COLON

Use a semicolon to join:

- independent clauses that are not joined by a coordinating conjunction
- independent clauses joined by a coordinating conjunction if they have two or more commas
- two independent clauses with transitions
- items in a series when the items have commas within

Use a colon after:

- an independent clause when (1) words that explain the clause follow it, (2) a series or list follows it, or (3) a quotation follows it
- the salutation of a business letter, between the hour and minutes, and in ratios (or proportions)

Dashes, Parentheses, and Brackets

A business writer with good precision understands even the less frequently used marks of punctuation—the dash, parentheses, and brackets. This section reviews the use of these marks so that you will be comfortable that you're using them correctly.

DASHES AND PARENTHESES

Use either the dash or parentheses to set off nonessential expressions in cases where using commas would disrupt the flow and possibly make the sentence harder to understand. Use a **dash** when you want to emphasize nonessential expressions that you would ordinarily enclose with commas. Use **parentheses** when you want to de-emphasize such expressions.

To emphasize	My plan saved the company thousands of dollars last year—actually, it was closer to tens of thousands.
	Creativity—which some consider a skill and not a trait—should be encouraged in the workplace.

To de-emphasize   Mr. Simon (director of the Denver, Scottsdale, and Sacramento offices) said abuses have been common in ads for many weight-loss products.

We spent $10,000 (a relatively small amount) on the spring advertising campaign.

Notice how each mark of punctuation changes where the emphasis is placed in this sentence:

Ordinary   The president of this company, a man who once earned $50 a week as a janitor, is one of the richest men in the country.

Emphasize   The president of this company—a man who once earned $50 a week as a janitor—is one of the richest men in the country.

De-emphasize   The president of this company (a man who once earned $50 a week as a janitor) is one of the richest men in the country.

Of the preceding sentences, a good writer would probably choose dashes to emphasize an interesting—but nonessential—point. However, the commas and parentheses are also correct. In the next example you can emphasize the main idea of the sentence by choosing parentheses to de-emphasize the nonessential information.

De-emphasize   Our supervisor (a new employee) is a holography expert.

However, if you wish to emphasize that the supervisor is new on the job, choose dashes for the nonessential expression. Commas would also be correct.

Emphasize   Our supervisor—a new employee—is a holography expert.

You can also use a dash for emphasis after a word or word group to connect an independent clause.

Dependability, a good attitude, and efficiency—those are qualities required in our employees.

You could also use a colon for emphasis or write the sentence without setting off the clause.

These are the qualities required in our employees: dependability, good attitude, and efficiency.

The qualities required in our employees are dependability, good attitude, and efficiency.

writing**TIP**

As you develop the habit of revising your sentences for clarity, variety, and interest, take the time to use punctuation in the way that most precisely expresses your meaning.

HOW TO TYPE DASHES

There are two types of dashes:

- The **em dash** (—): Make this dash by typing two hyphens between words without inserting any spaces. Use the em dash to set off parts of sentences.

- The **en dash** (–): Make this dash by hitting the space bar after the first word, typing a hyphen, and hitting the space bar again before typing the second word. Another way is to hold down the Ctrl key and hit the "minus" key on your number keypad. Use the en dash to show ranges such as Monday–Friday and 10–15.

OTHER RULES FOR PARENTHESES

Use parentheses to enclose information that is added to a sentence for reference or clarification:

References and dates

> The profits (see chart, page 7) were the highest in the history of the company (1999–present).

Numbers or letters of listed items

> Please send the following as soon as possible: (a) three copies of the project specifications; (b) a schedule outlining dates for completion of each part; (c) your availability dates between now and June 1.

Abbreviations

> Eligibility for membership in the American Association of Retired Persons (AARP) begins at age 50.

Capitalization and Punctuation

When you enclose a complete sentence in parentheses, begin it with a capital letter and end it with a period or other appropriate end-of-sentence punctuation.

> The date of the conference has been postponed because of the budgetary restrictions. (Please keep this information confidential for now.)

When the words in parentheses are not a separate sentence, place the punctuation outside of the end parenthesis.

> We will have to relocate to temporary quarters while the building is renovated (for at least six months).

RULES FOR DASHES, PARENTHESES, AND BRACKETS

- Use dashes to set off an important but nonessential expression. Use an em dash (—) to set off parts of sentences; use an en dash (–) to join numbers. Spaces are not required unless they are a matter of company style.

- Use parentheses to enclose a word or words to be de-emphasized or words that are important but supplementary information.

- Use brackets to insert your own words into quotations and to insert words inside a parenthetical expression.

BRACKETS

Brackets are a stronger way to separate words from the surrounding sentence. They are used mainly to insert your own words into quotations and to insert words inside a parenthetical expression.

In Quotations

To show that you have inserted words to add clarity or information within a quotation, enclose the words in brackets.

> The report stated that, "First-quarter sales [January–March] are 0.05 percent below last year in the same time period."

Sometimes you need to quote words that contain an error. To indicate that the error is from the original source, insert *sic* (which means "it is thus in the original") in brackets. The word *sic* should be italicized.

> The agreement states that "both party [*sic*] must agree and sign off on any amendments."

The agreement has a mistake: The word *party* should have been *parties*.

Expressions Within Parentheses

If you need to insert a point of clarification within a parenthetical expression, use brackets instead of a second set of parentheses.

> To understand the history of the company, I suggest you read the book written by its founder, Jeremy Andrews, *Braking New Ground in the Auto Industry*. (I believe it was published [by a vanity press] in the early 90s, but check Amazon.com.)

GO TO PAGE 259 AND COMPLETE WORKSHEET 12.3.

Checkpoint

Punctuation is a major contributor to easy reading. With punctuation, writers imitate spoken language on paper. Punctuation helps you communicate with precision and without risk of criticism or, worse, dire consequences caused by misunderstanding. Punctuation affects meaning, clarity, ease of reading, and the reader's emotions and mood as well as how important or unimportant an idea seems to the reader.

Punctuation expertise adds professional polish to your business writing. Now you have mastered not only the use of the comma but also the more sophisticated techniques of refining your sentence structure with the use of the semicolon, colon, brackets, parentheses, and dashes.

communications connection

BUSINESS EMAIL: COMPOSING

As you learned in Chapter 11, business emails may have multiple recipients, including the person or person that the message is written "To"; the person or persons copied, and, less frequently, the person or persons being blind copied. Recalling the first step in the writing process—planning your message based on your audience—you will define your subject, limiting it to one topic, and then begin composing the message. This section covers the main message (the body) and the other parts of the message that you may decide to include. For an example of the parts described here, refer to the illustration on page 235 in Chapter 11.

Salutation

As you learned in composing letters, business messages usually begin with a salutation. When writing routine business emails, the salutation is optional. Whether to include one depends on the level of formality and the purpose of the message.

A salutation is essential when writing to someone you don't know well. Unless you are already on a first-name basis with the recipient, use your judgment as to how the person should be addressed. The world of electronic communication is a lot less formal than traditional correspondence, and people often address complete strangers informally.

A formal salutation ends with a colon; an informal salutation ends with a comma.

Informal	Hi Doreen,	Doreen,
Formal	Dear Ms. Lieberman:	Dear Joseph:

If, for example, the writer is applying for a job, a formal salutation is essential if no prior relationship exists. Always consider your reader and how he or she would expect to be addressed. Err on the side of formality.

Body

Follow exactly the same rules of Standard English usage and writing style recommended in this book for all other forms of workplace writing. Stick to the main subject of the email and structure your message so that the main ideas can be broken into paragraphs for ease of reading, comprehension, and future reference.

Closing

A courtesy closing is warranted in any type of email, but when you are using electronic communication in place of a traditional printed letter, always use an appropriate closing followed by a comma, such as "Sincerely," "Sincerely yours," "Cordially," or "Regards." When you know the person well, an informal closing of your choosing is appropriate, or the closing may be

writing**TIP**

Although email is used for informal as well as formal communications at work, accurate punctuation is required in both. Inaccurate email punctuation leads to misunderstandings and conveys an impression of carelessness. Punctuate as carefully and skillfully in a business email as you would in preparing a business communication on paper.

omitted. In place of a closing, many businesspeople end their emails with "Thanks" or "Thank you" as a courtesy, written on the last line of the email and followed by a period.

Signature

Sign off with your first name only or first and last name, depending on your relationship with the recipient. Include a signature block with your full name, business title, company name, and contact information: address, telephone number(s), and email address. Include the email address because many email systems display the sender's full name, not the address.

Email Do's and Don'ts

Do

- Provide a meaningful subject line for your reader.
- Use standard spelling, capitalization, punctuation, and business abbreviations only.
- Double-check your message for grammar and spelling accuracy.
- Prepare email messages that make you appear efficient and courteous.
- Use the blind copy window for large mailings to protect the privacy of recipients' email addresses.
- Respond to emails as quickly as possible or let the recipient know you will need more time.

Don't

- Write emails with all capital letters.
- Write emails in anger.
- Use email and instant message shorthand in business emails.
- Send confidential messages via email.
- Send or forward personal messages, jokes, chain letters, or solicitations.
- Write anything you wouldn't want made public or forwarded to others.
- Respond in anger to an email. Wait until you are calm enough to respond in a professional manner.
- Use your organization's email system to send and receive personal messages.

WRITING PRACTICE

Select ten punctuation principles from Chapters 11 and 12. (See the boxes in each chapter that summarize punctuation rules.) Type the principles concisely but completely. Then compose a sentence to apply each rule. By applying more than one principle within the same sentence, you may write fewer sentences.

EXAMPLE   **Principle 1:** Use a semicolon before a transitional expression that joins two independent clauses.

Principle 2: Use a comma after a transitional expression except for the very short ones.

Sentence for 1 and 2: An executive needs to make decisions quickly; in fact, decisions are often necessary before all the data are available.

Date to submit this assignment: _____

PROOFREADING PRACTICE

Proofread and correct this company policy statement. Correct the printed copy using proofreading symbols or go online to correct the document electronically.

Smoke-Free Workplace:
The Best Company Policy

This policy establishes that the The Best Company, Inc. "TBC" provides a smoke-free enviroment. TBC seeks to provide a healthy workplace eliminate involuntary exposure to secondhand tobacco smoke and contribute to sustainability.

This police applies to office common common space of all buildings owned or leased by TBC both indoor and outdoor space and to all employes consultants temporary workers and visitors'.

All TBC work areas are smoke-free without exception. Smoking is prohibited in all facilities including but not limited to the following locations TBC Board Room private offices conference rooms break rooms elevators halways stairwells storage area and restrooms. Smoking is prohibited in all TBC-owned and leased vehicles however rented vehicles used for company business are excluded from this policy.

Compliance with the Smoke-Free Workplace Policy is mandatory for all workers in the categorys previously stated, and visitors to TBC facilities. This policy is set forth under state, and city regulations consequently anyone who violates this policy may be subject to discplinary action, including but not limited to termination of employment.

This policy must be prominently posted at all facilities department heads supervisors and their designees are responsible for communicating implementing and administering this policy. The Human Resources Department shall attempt too resolve disputes among employees regarding the interpretation and enforcement of this policy.

What kinds of errors, if any, did you miss in completing this proofreading practice—spelling, punctuation, typos? How do you evaluate your English and proofreading skills?

Excellent _____ Good _____ Fair _____

Needs Improvement _____ Other _____

chapter review

WORKSHEET 12.1

A. Insert semicolons and commas where needed. Write **C** before three sentences that are already correct.

_____ 1. Job security hardly exists any more now there is only skill security.

_____ 2. When unemployment is high your skills will enable you to compete.

_____ 3. Stocks can be a surefire way to double your money they are however always a risk.

_____ 4. Our company was one of the first to eliminate ID cards and replace them with an iris-reader in high security areas.

_____ 5. Dominic Anton the transportation chief was upset by the criticism thus he refused to discuss the issue of future fare increases.

_____ 6. Banks he explained pay depositors interest on their savings accounts but borrowers must pay interest to the banks.

_____ 7. The store promised its employees a raise that is each person would receive a five percent increase.

_____ 8. Look at the left side of the top row of letter keys on your keyboard if you don't know what a "qwerty" keyboard is.

_____ 9. The motion was passed by the City Council the vote was 6 to 3.

_____ 10. When speaking with clients whose English is limited keep in mind that their nods and smiles do not necessarily mean they understand and agree with you.

_____ 11. Mr. Johnson completed a speech course nevertheless he was still nervous when he stood in front of the audience.

_____ 12. Angela works two different jobs also she volunteers for the literacy council.

_____ 13. Our records from June through December show that we filled six orders for you every one of them was delivered promptly.

_____ 14. The public relations firm will handle the event that is they will arrange for the location the food and the entertainment.

_____ 15. The new officers are Louise Fuller president Sandra Hall vice president and Gina Hecht treasurer.

_____ 16. The owners sold a large amount of stock therefore they could afford the new office space.

_____ 17. Mark Knowlton has many assets that people don't know about for example he has a law degree.

_____ 18. A president of a big corporation usually earns a higher salary than the president of the United States.

_____ 19. Our business is highly complex and may be difficult to understand it is divided into many departments in which people perform specialized functions.

_____ 20. Like several other applicants his computer skills are good however we selected him because of his excellent writing and oral communications abilities.

CHECK YOUR ANSWERS ON PAGE 460.

WORKSHEET 12.2

Insert a colon where needed and make any other necessary corrections. Write **C** beside correctly punctuated sentences.

1. Please ship the following quantities of desk chairs two dozen Style No. 308 and three dozen Style No. 402.

2. A nutritionist advised that we eliminate eating the following foods for two weeks candy ice cream and snack foods.

3. He has just one goal in life getting rich.

4. "In three words I can sum up everything I've learned about life it goes on."—Robert Frost

5. We plan to visit these cities Winston-Salem Atlanta Newark and Pittsburgh.

6. Two important things can be done to prevent shoplifting place mirrors in strategic locations and post special warning signs.

7. The advertising circular featured several protein specials ground beef whole chickens and sirloin steak.

8. The exhibit hours have been established booths open at 9 a.m. and close at 3 p.m.

9. Here is something worth thinking about a small idea that produces something is worth more than a big idea that produces nothing.

10. Judges have a double duty protecting the innocent and punishing the guilty.

CHECK YOUR ANSWERS ON PAGE 461.

WORKSHEET 12.3

Insert dashes, parentheses, or brackets. The commas are already correct. If a sentence may be correctly punctuated in more than one way, use your judgment. Write **C** beside the correct sentence.

_____ 1. The new board members Dr. Duzeck and Ms. Swenson will meet with the press this afternoon.

_____ 2. Charmaine Dillard a scholarship recipient has agreed to join our mentoring program.

_____ 3. The officers of this corporation the president, the vice president, the treasurer, and the secretary are all graduates of the same university.

_____ 4. The decimal equivalents see Figure 4, page 80 will help you with the percentages.

_____ 5. Harbor Office Supply Company I'll check the address has ordered three photocopiers.

_____ 6. *Roget's Thesaurus* treasury of synonyms, antonyms, parallel words and related words was first published in 1852 by Peter Mark Roget look up the pronunciation of Roget.

_____ 7. The 7-11 chain which featured spoon straws for Slurpees, plastic straws for sodas, and reusable straws for car cups added straws that change color as a drink changes temperature.

_____ 8. Experience, intelligence, and personal skills are required on the job if only more job candidates had them all.

_____ 9. The pop star has money, beauty, intelligence, and charm.

_____ 10. She has all the attributes strong sales good contacts product knowledge of a top performer but no interest in getting promoted.

_____ 11. We must see him at once not tomorrow.

_____ 12. Your bonus payment of $2500 minus tax deductions will be deposited directly to your account.

_____ 13. Roosevelt Island was described as "New York City's ideal place to live a crime-free, auto-free, dog-free new *sic* island in the East River."

_____ 14. The report states that "the majority of new jobs created in America today the second decade of the 21st Century are in small companies" with fewer than one hundred employees.

_____ 15. The three branches of the United States government the executive, the legislative, and the judicial derive their authority from the Constitution.

CHECK YOUR ANSWERS ON PAGE 461.

POSTTEST

Insert the correct punctuation where needed.

1. Some ancient superstitions to ward off evil are very common today though we don't realize it for example saying "Bless you" whenever someone sneezes was once believed to safeguard the sneezer's soul.

2. We were cold freezing is more accurate when we walked on the glacier. (emphasis)

3. New equipment could save the company thousands of dollars for example the old cooling unit is far less efficient than today's models.

4. You can find information about our wedding photo albums on our website PictureYou www.pictureyou.com/weddings.

5. His itinerary includes sales calls in Springfield Massachusetts Urbana Illinois and Galveston Texas.

6. Forget the advertiser's promise that "you'll drop from a size 14 to an 8 with three minutes a day on the ab *sic* machine" it will take a lot more than that.

7. He had allowed the usual discount 8 percent off for cash payment.

8. Keep a space for study on a table or desk also set aside a time for studying each day.

9. Please note each member is responsible for keeping the locker room tidy.

10. In the American system only one person the president can be commander in chief of the armed forces.

CHECK YOUR ANSWERS ON PAGE 462.

Self-Study and Practice Tutorials

wordPOWER

Build your workplace vocabulary and improve spelling skills by completing the exercises in Appendix B on page 376.

Supplementary Practice Exercises

For additional practice, complete the Appendix C exercises for this chapter on page 419.

© Minerva Studio/Fotolia

After completing Chapter 13, you will be able to do the following:

- Use quotation marks correctly when quoting the words of others.
- Use quotation marks and italics to denote various types of word usage and expressions.
- Apply the various uses of the hyphen, including forming compounds and dividing words.
- Use the apostrophe to show possession and to form contractions.

13

Punctuation:
The Fine Points

career connection

GET IN THE DOOR WITH AN INTERNSHIP

How do you get work experience in your chosen field before landing that first great job? You can get advice and timely information about internship opportunities by researching on the Internet. Websites such as thestreet.com and money. usnews.com offer useful information. Here is an overview of some of the tips they provide and a list of helpful websites.

1. **Use the sources on your college campus.** Your instructors and advisors might be able to help you with making contacts in your chosen field. In addition, your school's career center will have information, and many career centers hold job fairs with employers.

2. **Take advantage of Social Networking.** Let your social network (personal, professional, Facebook, LinkedIn, Twitter) know that you are interested in an internship. Follow career information sources on Twitter. You can find a recommended list on the website thestreet.com: "The Best Twitter Feeds for Career Advice," by Seth Figerman (February 16, 2012).

3. **Contact companies directly.** Research information about internships and contacts on company websites. Make contact through the human resources department or directly to principals listed on the website.

4. **Keep your resume updated.** Be ready when an opportunity presents itself. Have a well-written resume and tailor it to the specific internship opportunity you are going after.

5. **Have a list of potential references ready.** Although an internship is not the same as full employment, be prepared with a typed list of references and their contact information, in case they are requested.

    Check out the following websites for information and advice on internships:

    - thestreet.com
    - money.usnews.com
    - internships.com
    - internshipprograms.com
    - summerinternships.com
    - college.monster.com/education
    - forbes.com
    - internqueen.com

PRETEST

Use proofreading marks to correct these sentences by inserting or deleting quotation marks, hyphens, and apostrophes; mark italics by underlining.

1. His boss shouted, Your fired!

2. Mens roles have changed, and its not unusual for successful, hardworking men to also be the primary caretakers of their children.

3. Did you mean ineligible or illegible?

4. During the 1990's I bought technology related stocks that made me rich.

5. Professor Lorraine Ray of Ohio University assigned The Stubborn Little Mark, a funny article about the comma published in last week's San Francisco Chronicle.

6. Elizabeth, who is a good listener, once interrupted me while I read what must have seemed to be a never ending story.

7. Show us someone who habitually oversleeps, and well show you cause for alarm.

8. Shakespeares King Richard III—its opening tomorrow—is my choice for entertaining our clients.

9. Your going to hire that mechanic, arent you?

10. Lets have our book club read the biography of Zelda Fitzgerald, wife of the great 20th century writer F. Scott Fitzgerald.

CHECK YOUR ANSWERS ON PAGE 462.

Quotation Marks with Quotes

You learned some of the basics of setting off quotations with commas in Chapter 11. This section will review these and add some additional points.

Use quotation marks when you are quoting exact spoken or written words of others. This is a **direct quotation**. When you express someone's stated or written ideas in your own words, do not use quotation marks. This is called **paraphrasing**. When you are using the ideas and words of others, you are free to decide whether or not to quote directly or paraphrase. In the following examples, you can see that direct quotations tend to read with greater emphasis on the quote. Either way, you should always give credit to the original source.

Quotation	The hiring manager said, "The applicant should be proficient in using Microsoft Office."
Paraphrase	The hiring manager said the applicant should be able to use Microsoft Office.
Quotation	"A business," Elwood Chapman writes, "is an organization that brings capital and labor together in the hope of making a profit for its owners."
Paraphrase	The principal aim of a business, according to Elwood Chapman, is to bring together capital and labor to make a profit for its owners.
Quotation	President Barack Obama said, "Focusing your life on making a buck shows a certain poverty of ambition."
Paraphrase	President Barack Obama said that focusing your life only on making money shows a certain lack of ambition.

writing**TIP**

Be sure to include the name or a specific reference to the original speaker or writer whether you quote or paraphrase. A good technique is to start with the quoted words and then find a suitable place to insert the source of the statement, as the Elwood Chapman quotation demonstrates.

PUNCTUATION WITH QUOTATION MARKS

Place the opening quotation mark at the beginning of the quote and place commas or sentence-ending punctuation inside the closing quotation mark. Be sure to enclose the entire quote. Check this carefully, particularly when explanatory words interrupt the quote.

"Failure to provide adequate funding," according to the *Washington Post*, "will doom the new legislation from the start."

"Some publishers are born great, some have greatness thrust upon them, and others merely survive television," said John H. Johnson, founder of *Ebony* magazine.

Mr. Johnson received the Magazine Publishers Association award for "Publisher of the Year."

Placement of the quotation mark before or after other marks of punctuation differs from the comma and period as follows:

If a colon or a semicolon is needed with a closing quotation mark, place the quotation mark *before* the colon or the semicolon—no exceptions. This applies to direct quotations of the words of others as well as to use of quotation marks with titles, which is covered in the next section.

The scientists were quoted in the article entitled "Rediscovering the Mind": Carl Sagan, Georgi Lozanov, and Jean Houston.

The accountant explained, "The check was accidentally postdated"; however, we still have not received a correctly dated check from the company.

If a question mark or exclamation mark is required with a closing quotation mark, placement depends on the sentence. When the question mark or exclamation mark applies only to the quotation, it is placed inside the quotation mark.

> Jesse said, "Do you really care?"
>
> "You've got to be kidding me!" she stated vehemently.

When the punctuation mark applies to the whole sentence, it should be placed outside the quotation mark.

> Did you know the memo said merit increases "have been cut"?
>
> You left out the most important word—"immediately"!

Quotation Marks and Italics for Special Usage

Quotation marks and italics are used to indicate special usage of words, expressions, and titles. While these marks can be applied interchangeably to some extent, always use one style within each piece of writing. Consistency makes writing clear for the reader.

WORDS AND EXPRESSIONS

Correct punctuation requires either quotation marks or italics to show that a word or phrase is unusual—for example, a foreign word or a word that might seem out of place to the reader. Here is the way to differentiate use of the two:

- Use italics for foreign words and expressions and to show emphasis.
- Use quotation marks to denote unusual or intentionally incorrect usage, such as slang or very informal language.

grammarTIP

Insert the word *[sic]* into a quote to indicate that a mistake appears in the original source. Refer to the discussion of brackets on page 253.

Foreign words	*E pluribus unum* is a motto found on the Great Seal of the United States.
Slang	Yesterday, the boss told Gerald to "hit the road"—in other words, he was fired.
	No matter what happens, I "ain't gonna" quit this job!
Unusual	Too many "don'ts" in your life can lead to frustration.
Emphasis	The company policy is very clear: smoking is not allowed *anywhere* on the premises—indoors or outdoors.

WORDS REFERRED TO AS WORDS

No doubt you have noticed the use of italics frequently in this book to denote words referred to as words. This is an instance where you can use either italics or quotation marks. Most writers use italics because it takes fewer keystrokes when typing. As mentioned above, use a consistent style in each piece of writing.

writingTIP

In handwritten copy, use quotation marks or underlining.

Do you know how to distinguish between *effect* and *affect*?

The memo looks fine, but please change the word "deadline" to "target date" in the last paragraph.

TITLES OF ARTISTIC AND LITERARY WORKS

Quotation marks and italics are both used to indicate titles of literary and artistic works. You will find extensive coverage of the rules governing punctuation for titles of all types of works—poems, songs, articles, books, paintings, and so on—in your reference manual. Here we will discuss only the basic rules for published works.

Use italics for full-length published books, magazines, newspapers, films, and plays. If italics are not available (when handwriting), underline instead.

David Allen wrote the best-selling book *Getting Things Done*.

According to the *New York Times* review, the film version of *Sex and the City* was a disappointment; but, still, it was a blockbuster at the box office.

Use quotation marks for titles of *parts* of published works, such as articles in magazines or chapters of books.

You can find the article, "Twenty-First Century Career Advancement Strategies," on the *Bloomberg Businessweek* website.

Also use quotation marks for names of short works, such as poems, songs, lectures, and other creative or literary works.

The song "New York, New York" is played every year at the Belmont Stakes, which takes place in Long Island, New York.

People often misquote Robert Frost's poem "The Road Not Taken," but they are usually correct in interpreting the message.

RULES FOR QUOTATION MARKS

- Enclose a speaker's or writer's exact words in quotation marks. Do not use quotation marks when paraphrasing.
- Place commas or periods inside of closing quotation marks.
- Place a colon or a semicolon outside the quotation mark.
- If a question mark or exclamation point is required with a closing quotation mark, placement before or after the punctuation depends on the sentence.
- Use quotation marks or italics (or underline in handwriting) to show that usage of a word or phrase is unusual or to indicate words used as words.
- Use quotation marks for titles of *subdivisions* of published works and short works.

GO TO PAGE 279 AND COMPLETE WORKSHEET 13.1.

The Hyphen

The **hyphen** is a useful mark of punctuation that serves many purposes. The first thing to remember is that it should not be confused with the dash. On the keyboard you can use two hyphens (--) to make a dash, but the hyphen and the dash are two completely different punctuation marks. A hyphen is smaller than an *en dash*, which is smaller than an *em dash*. These were covered in Chapter 12.

Correct hyphen use in compound words is covered here and builds on what you learned about compound nouns in Chapter 4. You will recall that a **compound word** means two or more words expressing one concept. These words may be one connected word, two words with a space, or two or more words connected with a hyphen, such as *nationwide, chocolate chip,* and *hand-me-down.*

COMPOUND NOUNS

Some compound nouns are spelled with a hyphen; this is known as a **hyphenated word**. The spelling is dictated by "common usage" at a given point in time. When a new word or new usage begins, the hyphen is used to show the relationship, and this usually lasts long enough to be documented in dictionaries and reference manuals. Over time, as the word is used in mass media, the usage is widely adopted, and the hyphen may be dropped. An example of a compound noun whose spelling is still evolving is the word *email* or *e-mail*—short for *electronic mail*. The trend is to eliminate the hyphen, but many publications still use it.

In the following sentences, the boldface words are functioning as a single unit to form a noun and are spelled with a hyphen:

> Our designers can help you design a **sofa-bed** that fits the decor of your studio apartment.

> Our latest promotion is designed to get the attention of the average **passer-by** at the mall.

PREFIXES

A **prefix** is an addition to the beginning of a word to denote a particular meaning. For example, adding *non* to a word denotes the absence of something as in *nonfat.* Some words with prefixes are hyphenated, and others are not. When in doubt, consult your dictionary. Generally, short prefixes, such as *non, over, under, semi,* and *sub,* do not require a hyphen.

nonevent   overpayment   underexposed   semisweet   subhuman

Use a hyphen after the prefix *self* when it is joined to a complete word and after *ex* when it means former. The only exception is *selfsame.*

self-control   self-respect   ex-president   ex-husband

If a prefix ending with *e*—such as *re, de,* or *pre*—begins a word that might confuse the reader, use a hyphen.

re-cover   to cover again

recover   to get better from illness or to get something back that had been lost

---

writing**TIP**

When you are unsure of a compound noun spelling, consult your dictionary. If the word is not listed, then it is spelled as two words with a space. Otherwise, your dictionary will show it as either one word or a hyphenated word.

Most *re, pre,* and *de* words do not require hyphens; however, some are optional if the main part of the word begins with *e.*

reheat, deplane, predict   reelect or re-elect   preexist or pre-exist

Use a hyphen after a prefix preceding a capitalized word.

mid-July   un-American

NUMBERS

The numbers from 21 to 99 are spelled with a hyphen when they are not written in figures.

twenty-one   fifty-six   forty-two   ninety-nine

The numbers *one hundred, five million,* and the like are not hyphenated.

COMPOUND ADJECTIVES

The hyphen is also used to join the elements of a **compound adjective**. An adjective combining two or more words is compound and needs a hyphen if it *precedes* the noun being modified. When the compound adjective follows the noun it modifies, the part of speech often changes; it is no longer a compound adjective, and a hyphen is not needed.

> These are **up-to-date** statistics.
> These statistics are **up to date**.
> The manual provides **on-the-job** training.
> You will receive your training **on the job**.

Some adjectives are **permanent compounds**; these will be listed in the dictionary.

> We are expected to give a **first-rate** presentation for the final exam.
> My presentation for the final exam is going to be **first-rate**.
> They are looking for a **high-end** venue suitable for a fancy reception.
> The venue they chose for the reception is **high-end**.

Remember to hyphenate when the modifier comes *before* the noun or if the expression *is spelled with a hyphen in the dictionary.*

To recognize a compound adjective, omit one of the words. Does the phrase still make sense? Does the remaining word keep its meaning? In the following example the meaning is changed completely if you refer to a **first report** or a **four house**. Since *first class* and *four family* cannot be separated, they are compound adjectives. Join them with a hyphen when they precede the noun being described.

> You gave a **first-class** report about life in a **four-family** house.

When the same words follow the nouns *report* and *house*, they are not hyphenated because they are not permanent compounds.

> You gave a report that was **first class** about life in a house with **four families**.

Adverb-Adjective Combinations

Remember that modifiers improve your writing. They provide precision and details that give your words more clarity and make your writing more interesting to your reader. When you use a modifier that combines an adjective and an adverb, you need to decide whether or not a hyphen is needed. Although it might not seem important, use of correct grammar requires it.

Remember from your study of adjectives and adverbs that adverbs can modify adjectives and other adverbs. When you use a compound expression, consider whether the first word is an adverb or an adjective. If the first word of the compound expression is an *ly* adverb, the hyphen is *not* required. If, however, the *ly* word is an adjective, a hyphen *is* needed.

The **fashionably dressed** executive carried an **Italian leather** bag.

No hyphens are required because *fashionably* is an adverb modifying the adjective *dressed*; *Italian* and *leather* are both adjectives but not compound because *leather* can be used without *Italian*, applying the test you learned earlier in this chapter.

My employer is a **friendly-looking** man.

In this case, *friendly* is an adjective; therefore, use the hyphen to create the compound adjective modifying *man*.

Compound Adjectives with Interrupting Words

Sometimes an adjective consists of more than one modifier with an interrupting word (or words) in between. In this case, place a hyphen and space after the first adjective to show that both modifiers are part of the same compound.

The financial adviser said, "Both **long-** and **short-term** gains must be considered."

I ordered **silver-** and **gold-embossed** nameplates for the junior and senior executives, respectively.

RULES FOR THE HYPHEN

- Hyphenate the words for numbers twenty-one through ninety-nine.
- Some words with prefixes are hyphenated, and others are not. When in doubt, check your dictionary.
- A compound adjective requires a hyphen if it precedes the noun being modified. If it is a permanent compound, it will be shown in the dictionary.
- Do not hyphenate common compound expressions that represent a single idea.
- If you need to divide a word at the end of a line, divide only between syllables.

WORD DIVISION

Another use of the hyphen is dividing words at the end of a line of text. Note that you can turn this function on and off in your word processing system. In typed documents, this is the common practice. In printed documents, particularly text that is formatted in columns and justified

---

wordPOWER

Many common compound expressions that express a single idea do not require a hyphen, as in the following examples: A **high school** student found a **Social Security** check in a **mobile home** park. You will remember this because of your habits of checking details in your writing and reading extensively.

writing**TIP**

In general, avoid hyphenated words by turning off your word processor's automatic hyphenation. If you use automated hyphenation, you will need to undo the following automatic word divisions: (1) proper nouns, (2) hyphens on more than two consecutive lines, or (3) hyphens on the last line of a page.

(aligned) at the right column, words are often divided at the end of lines to ensure better spacing between words.

Here is the most important principle of word division: If you need to divide a word at the end of a line, divide only between syllables. If a word is divided at a place other than between syllables (*fl-ower*), the effect of the entire document is destroyed, as the reader wonders, "*Where* did that writer go to school?" or "*Did* that writer go to school?"

Word processing dictionaries hyphenate at the end of almost any syllable, which is fine for newspapers and certain other written materials. For professional-looking documents, however, hyphenate words in the following ways:

- Between syllables. When consulting the dictionary, refer to syllables in the entry word, not in the pronunciation. Dots, spaces, or accent marks—depending on the dictionary—show syllables.

  fol.low.ing [may be divided between the *l*'s or after the *w*]

  stopped [may not be divided because it is a one-syllable word]

- When at least two letters—preferably three—can be typed on the line before the hyphen.

Yes	rec-ognition (three letters)
Yes	re-veal (two letters)
No	a-gainst (one letter)

- When at least three letters can be typed on the next line.

Yes	compil-ing
No	compa-ny

If syllables don't permit the minimum number of letters before or after the hyphen, do not divide the word.

grammar**TIP**

Consult your reference manual for additional guidelines on word division.

GO TO PAGE 279 AND COMPLETE WORKSHEET 13.2.

RULES OF WORD DIVISION

Do not divide

- the last word on a page
- a word containing an apostrophe
- a number expressed in figures
- an abbreviation
- on more than two consecutive lines
- a word with fewer than five letters
- a word of only one syllable
- a proper noun
- between the number and *a.m., p.m., noon, midnight,* or *percent*
- unless at least three letters can be carried to the next line

The Apostrophe (')—Possessive Nouns

Study of the fine points of punctuation could not be complete without a reminder on using the apostrophe. We'll begin with a quick review of possessive nouns covered in Chapter 5. Here are the rules you learned:

- Possessive nouns show the relationship between one noun and another noun. The first noun shows *who* or *what possesses*; the second shows *who* or *what is possessed*. The relationship is made clear by the use of an *s* and an apostrophe in the first noun. A possessive noun always ends with *'s* or *s'*.

- A possessive noun shows such relationships as ownership, authorship, place of origin, type of use to which something is put, and time periods.

SINGULAR AND PLURAL POSSESSIVES

To make a singular noun possessive, add *'s*.

the boss's office	Franklin's *From Slavery to Freedom*
Ms. Jones's secretary	a semester's work

To form the possessive of a singular proper noun with two or more syllables that ends in an *s* sound, you could omit the added *s* to avoid a hard-to-pronounce word.

Socrates' disciples   Ms. Perkins' report   Dr. Adams' prescription

To form the possessive of a plural noun, first look at the last letter of the noun. If the last letter is *s*, add only an apostrophe; if the last letter is not *s*, add *'s*.

Last letter of plural is *s*	Adamses	The Adamses' factory is closed.
	weeks	Three weeks' work was wasted.
	ladies	He designs ladies' clothes.
Last letter of plural is not *s*	alumnae	Who collected the alumnae's contributions?
	men	The men's fortunes were lost at the gaming tables.
	children	Our children's room is neat and clean.

POSSESSIVES VERSUS PLURALS

Make sure that a plural is actually a possessive before you add an apostrophe. Do not add an apostrophe to a nonpossessive plural.

The Joneses own factories all over the world.

Joneses is the plural subject of the sentence; *own* is the verb; no possessive relationship is shown.

BUT

> The Joneses' factories are all over the world.

Factories is the plural subject of the sentence; *Joneses'* tells whose factories and is therefore possessive.

JOINT OR SEPARATE OWNERSHIP

When two (or more) nouns are used together to show something is possessed jointly, add the apostrophe to the second noun.

> Rozini and Marino's factories [jointly owned]

To show separate ownership, add the apostrophe to both (all) owners.

> Rozini's and Marino's factories [individually owned]

The Apostrophe (')—Contractions and Other Uses

The apostrophe has several other functions in addition to showing possession. Some of them, such as contractions, are easy because you use them all the time. Others, such as making abbreviations possessive, are a bit more difficult. This section reviews various uses of the apostrophe.

CONTRACTIONS

Successful written communications for the workplace have a natural and conversational style. One technique to achieve naturalness is using contractions. **Contractions** are shortened forms of words formed by removing one or more letters and replacing them with an apostrophe: *can't, won't, couldn't,* or *it's.* Some contractions, however, are fine for conversation but should not be used in business writing: One example is *would,* as in *I'd, we'd,* or *they'd.* Consider your reader and the situation when deciding how conversational the style of a workplace communication should be. In legal or other formal documents, avoid contractions.

POSSESSIVES AND CONTRACTIONS

Sometimes writers confuse possessives and contractions. A few pronouns that contain the words *one* and *body* often end with *'s* and may be used as either possessives or contractions, depending on the meaning desired.

anyone's	someone's	no one's	everyone's
anybody's	somebody's	nobody's	everybody's

The apostrophe represents the missing *i* in the word *is.*

> *Everyone's* going to that party.
> *No one's* at home.
> *Someone's* on duty at all times.

CONTRACTIONS ACCEPTABLE IN BUSINESS

are not/aren't	I will/I'll	we will/we'll
cannot/can't	is not/isn't	were not/weren't
could not/couldn't	it is/it's	what is/what's
do not/don't	she is/she's	who is/who's
does not/doesn't	should not/shouldn't	will not/won't
has not/hasn't	that is/that's	would not/wouldn't
have not/haven't	they are/they're	you are/you're
he is/he's	was not/wasn't	you have/you've
I am/I'm	we are/we're	you will/you'll
I have/I've	we have/we've	

Now the apostrophe makes the same words possessive.

> *Everybody's* coats are in the closet.

> *No one's* home is available for the party.

> *Someone's* hours are from two to four.

The preceding contractions are correct and appropriate in conversation and in informal business writing.

PLURAL ABBREVIATIONS

An apostrophe is unnecessary to form the plural of all-capital letter abbreviations. Note also that these abbreviations are written without periods. This is the style for most abbreviations today; consult your reference manual to be sure.

> All CEOs on our mailing list should receive a copy.

> There are two YWCAs in Toledo.

Add *'s* to make lowercase abbreviations plural if they might be misread without an apostrophe.

No   Please be sure to "dot your is and cross your ts."

Yes   Please be sure to "dot your i's and cross your t's."

No   The department has sold out of the Mickey Mouse pjs.

Yes   The department has sold out of the Mickey Mouse pj's.

No   Too many *etc.s* usually mean the writer isn't sure of the facts.

Yes   Too many *etc.'s* usually mean the writer isn't sure of the facts.

Plural abbreviations are suitable for documents listing specifications or in invoices and tables. These abbreviations do not require an apostrophe or a period at the end.

5 yds   6 gals   7 lbs

Generally, in correspondence or reports, spell out "quantity words," unless the document contains heavy usage of such data.

> Thank you for shipping five gallons of Chocolate Syrup in seven cartons.
>
> We'll use it to make 250 quarts of chocolate egg cream drinks for the party.

RULES FOR THE APOSTROPHE

- To make a singular noun possessive, add *'s*; to make a plural noun that ends in *s* possessive, add an apostrophe after the *s*. Do not use an apostrophe for a nonpossessive plural.
- When two (or more) nouns are used together to show that something is possessed jointly, add the apostrophe to the second noun. To show separate ownership, add the apostrophe to both (all) owners.
- The apostrophe is also used to form contractions, to make abbreviations plural, as a symbol for "feet" and "minutes," and to indicate a quote within a quote (a single quotation mark).

PLURAL NUMBERS AND WORDS

Do not add an apostrophe to form the plural of numbers or words.

> The temperature in New Brunswick is in the 70s.
>
> She graduated from college some time in the late 1990s.
>
> The young child wrote threes backwards.
>
> Please omit all *therefores*.

POSSESSIVE ABBREVIATIONS

Use an apostrophe in possessive abbreviations, just as with any other noun.

> The AMA's position is clear. [singular possessive]
>
> Our RNs' uniforms are yellow. [plural possessive]

Make *RN* plural by adding *s*; then make it possessive by adding an apostrophe.

MISCELLANEOUS APOSTROPHE USES

As a symbol, the apostrophe has several meanings. The number *4'* means either 4 feet or 4 minutes, depending on the context.

Although *'06* means 2006, avoid this style in business writing, except when referring to a year of graduation, such as "the class of '06," or when referring to decades.

> The Class of '95 will hold its next reunion at the Ritz Carlton.
>
> In the 20th century more cultural changes occurred during the '60s than in any other decade.

Ordinarily use the full number for the century.

> In 2010 our company will celebrate 25 years in business.

Use an apostrophe to represent a single quotation mark when you are placing a quotation or title within a quotation.

> The candidate said, "It was Abraham Lincoln who spoke of 'government of the people, by the people, and for the people'; and that is also my credo."

GO TO PAGE 281 AND COMPLETE WORKSHEET 13.3.

Checkpoint

You have now mastered the art of punctuation! When revising and proofreading drafts, refer back to the rules you have learned in this unit. Now that you understand all of the options, you can choose the marks that get your ideas across most clearly. When you feel unsure, review the summary boxes and refer to your reference manual for more information.

communications connection

SENDING AND REPLYING TO EMAIL

When you have finished writing an email message (see the Communications Connection in Chapter 12), always proofread it before hitting the "Send" button. Check the names of the recipients to make sure you have included everyone you intended and that the names are correct (for example, your address book might have picked up the wrong Michael Smith).

If you are sending attachments, make sure you have attached the correct files and that any documents you are sending are the most recent version. Frequently, documents go through several revisions, so it is important to make sure you have the latest one. Make sure also that you have mentioned the attachment in the email and explained why you are sending it if there is any chance the recipients will not immediately understand.

Sending large files, such as images, or files created in specialized software programs might require checking with the recipient to make sure they can be opened. Converting word processing documents to **PDF** (portable document format) files makes them universally compatible. PDF files will not change format in the transmission process, and the text cannot be manipulated by the recipient.

When replying to email messages, do the following:

- Businesspeople expect a quick response to their messages. Judge by what is the norm in your workplace. Whenever you need more than a day or two to respond, it is courteous to send a brief message letting the person know that his or her message was received and when you anticipate sending a full response.

- When you are going to be away from your email for a day or more, set up an automatic reply message indicating when you will return. If possible, provide a backup person to contact in case an urgent response is needed.

- If the sender of an email has copied others, it is usually courteous to copy them on the reply. However, don't clog people's emails with "Thank you" and "You're welcome" messages.
- As when you send an email, limit your reply to the original topic. If you have other matters to bring up with the sender, send a new message on that topic.
- Know when to end an email "conversation."

Know your organization's email policies:

- Most companies monitor use of their email system, but even if yours doesn't, always apply common sense to communications with people inside and outside your organization.
- Remember that email belongs to the organization and is usually saved on the company's backup system or on the email provider's servers.
- Do not send confidential information or make statements or commitments in emails that you would not otherwise make in written documents.
- Make sure that you do not open emails or attachments from unknown sources that could put your organization's system at risk.

WRITING PRACTICE

A. With the goal of writing that is concise and direct (a more appealing style for your reader), revise these correct sentences by using compound adjectives. *Do not change the meaning.* Keep your dictionary handy.

1. Denzel Washington is an actor who won an Academy Award. _____
   _____

2. I work in a building that has 100 stories. _____

3. Do you need a ladder that is 10 feet or one that is 20 feet to do the repairs? _____

4. My father is a man who works hard. _____

5. The case against the company that is based in Dallas was handled in Seattle. _____
   _____

B. Write a sentence using the following hyphenated and nonhyphenated words.

6. Re-creation
   _____

7. Recreation
   _____

8. Self-sufficient
   _____

9. High-powered/self-made

_____

10. Anti-intellectual

_____

_____

Date to submit this assignment: _____

PROOFREADING PRACTICE

Use proofreading marks or the online text to correct this article, which has errors related to this chapter as well as others.

Words That Respect Your Reader

Consider your the reading ability and background of your audience's before you write. If you are writing for a class taught by a college professor, you can write at a higher level than if you're message will be read by adults for whom english is a second language. It is equally important to avoid talking over the head's of your readers' or talking down to them. Readers' can tell when your are trying too hard too impress or when you are lecturing to them.. Avoid jargon words specific to a particular activity or line of work unless you are certain your readers will know what you are talking about. At a minimum, always define your terms.

Use three and four syllable words sparingly when you write. Why say utilize or incorporate when use will do? Long and unfamiliar words are hurdles that your readers must leap over to get to your meaning. Remember, the propose you want to serve, and keep it simple.

Certain words and phrases can convey a smug attitude. Obviously as anyone can see and in my estimation are example's of words that will turn off your readers, especially if your point is not as clear as you believe it to be. College's instructors will quickly detect a superior attitude if it appears in your writing. After all, your instructor's are looking to see if you can provide a straight-forward intelligent discussion of ideas in your writing assignments, not a show of your mental-superiority. Open-ness not smug self absorption is the way to win respect for your ideas.

How did you do? Excellent _____ Good _____
Need More Practice _____

chapter review

WORKSHEET 13.1

Use proofreading marks to correct the following sentences. They require a variety of punctuation marks covered in this chapter (including underlines to show italics) and in previous chapters.

1. He shouted Your house is on fire!

2. Why did FDR state The only thing to fear is fear itself?

3. Alonzo whispered Are you sure you have the right data?

4. Are you positive the numbers are correct he whispered again.

5. Do you know whether Jessica said Reserve a rental car?

6. If you use words like ain't and theirselves in some places you will be considered uneducated.

7. My classmate said Are you aware that many professionals use sloppy language all the time

8. What does the phrase negotiable instrument mean?

9. He texted us as follows We depart from O'Hare on American Airlines Flight 23 at 8 a.m. and arrive at Kennedy at 10:30 p.m.

10. Was Mr. Higgins the character in My Fair Lady who said Results are what count?

11. We need more tacos for the company party! Jim yelled.

12. This shipment the manager said will arrive in time for your January sale

13. Are you all right? asked Ann. Yes groaned her dad, as he lifted the unabridged version of the Oxford English Dictionary.

14. Bach's Suite No. 2 in B Minor is first on the program at the concert.

15. University of South Carolina Professor Benjamin Franklin is tired of people asking him, Why aren't you out flying your kite?

CHECK YOUR ANSWERS ON PAGE 462.

WORKSHEET 13.2

A. Decide whether to hyphenate these words and write the correct spelling or place a C in the blank. Then check your dictionary to see how they should appear.

1. brother in law   _____

2. vice president   _____

3. semi sweet   _____

4. up to date notebook   _____

5. third generation heir   _____

6. de escalate   _____

7. ex boyfriend   _____

8. re discover   _____

9. pre established   _____

10. per diem   _____

B. Insert hyphens where needed. Consult your dictionary when in doubt about whether an expression is a permanent compound. Write **C** beside the two sentences that don't need hyphens.

_____ 11. Buy your back to school laptop computer now and get free Windows based software.

_____ 12. If you're a charge account customer, you can save on clothes for going back to school.

_____ 13. He has a part time job planning never to be forgotten parties.

_____ 14. This seven foot tall basketball player understands the problem solving process.

_____ 15. The state of the art coffeemaker has a built in self cleaning system.

_____ 16. To get the lowest interest rate, you need to be prequalified for a home repair loan.

_____ 17. Studies show that the education system has a great impact on children's self esteem.

_____ 18. If you can postpone your vacation until mid August, I would really appreciate it.

_____ 19. The new director is a highly regarded former executive of a major financial firm.

_____ 20. I had planned to take a month long vacation this year, but the workload is too intense.

C. Use a vertical line (|) to show the preferred place to divide the following words at the end of a line. Three words should not be divided at all.

21. catalog	determined	effective
22. function	believe	horizontal
23. wouldn't	thousands	punctuation
24. aligned	impossible	interrupt
25. syllables	stopped	guesswork

CHECK YOUR ANSWERS ON PAGE 463.

WORKSHEET 13.3

Use proofreading marks to insert apostrophes or missing numbers where an apostrophe is incorrect. Write **C** beside the correct sentences. Draw a delete mark through incorrectly used apostrophes.

Example He's not aware that Winston Churchill was in his 80s in 1954.

_____ 1. I couldnt meet you at five oclock.

_____ 2. Dot your is and cross your ts is a way of saying, "youd better make it perfect."

_____ 3. MBAs are given preference when we recruit mid- or top-level management.

_____ 4. They experienced many ups and downs before achieving their astounding success.

_____ 5. We believe the last CFOs' convention was held in '11.

_____ 6. Dont use too many *ands* and *buts* in your writing.

_____ 7. Several MDs and RNs routinely have lunch here.

_____ 8. In tables or charts, its all right to use abbreviations like yd's, ft, or lb's.

_____ 9. During the 19th-century era known as "The Gay 90s, worker's suffered while the wealthy held lavish parties.

_____ 10. Three CPAs have offices in this building.

_____ 11. The word *committee* is spelled with two es.

_____ 12. "Wont you please help me with this work?" Timothy begged.

_____ 13. Only five As were recorded on the student's record.

_____ 14. In the early 2000's, email was not used as much as it is today.

_____ 15. Couldnt you make your 1s look less like 7s?

CHECK YOUR ANSWERS ON PAGE 464.

POSTTEST

Use proofreading marks to insert quotation marks, hyphens, and apostrophes and underline for italics where needed. Also insert any missing punctuation that you studied in preceding chapters of this unit.

1. As the result of yesterdays storm most subscribers lines lost power making even high capacity services unable to take care of their customers.

2. Make Jake aware of his problem by saying to him ask a friend for a frank opinion of whether you use double negatives all the time.

3. Albert Schweitzer said the following ethics is the maintaining of life at the highest point of development.

4. There is never a time in life when learning should stop said the luncheon speaker.

5. Please deliver the following papers to my hotel room the Daily News the New York Post and the New York Times.

6. The CEO wrote we are able to spread the cost over only the first and second quarter earnings not the whole year.

7. Until you learn to use the word misappropriation correctly choose a simpler word.

8. Please take Ms. Ellisons place she wont be able to join us.

9. Dont accept just anyones opinion about this 36 page report, its too important!

10. The instructor wants a report on Chapter 2: The Psychology of Fashion from the textbook Fashion Accessories.

CHECK YOUR ANSWERS ON PAGE 464.

Self-Study and Practice Tutorials

wordPOWER

Build your workplace vocabulary and improve spelling skills by completing the exercises in Appendix B on page 379.

Supplementary Practice Exercises

For additional practice, complete the Appendix C exercises for this chapter on page 421.

Perfecting Sentence Punctuation

recap—chapters 11–13

Use proofreading marks to correct the punctuation in the following sentences.

1. Please double-space your essay that is set the line spacing on 2.0.

2. The state postal abbreviations see chart, page 23 should be used on all envelopes.

3. My mother works hard at her job then she comes home to prepare dinner.

4. Phil worked overtime for three months so he was glad to get home early.

5. The decimal equivalents see Figure 4, page 80 will help you with the percentages.

6. What time will your plane arrive? Dale asked.

7. These DVD players last year's models are reduced.

8. The out of stock sale item was supposed to arrive by noon today.

9. Reverend Chamberlain a Unitarian minister will deliver the invocation at the Communications Club luncheon.

10. Before leaving for the airport, check the up to date weather report.

11. The new Food Carnival the one near the mall has the best selection of meats.

12. Martin was chosen Employee of the Year for the last two years.

13. The new product brochure in color and printed on heavy stock will increase sales, I'm sure.

14. The article Money Management in this morning's paper gave me some good ideas.

15. The hotel offered us first rate accommodations at a reduced rate in August.

16. The exhibit hours have been established booths open at 9 a.m. and close at 3 p.m.

17. My editor in chief's report asked for a high level review of the system failures in the last six months.

18. His use of inappropriate language stems from his lack of self respect.

19. Bessie Cambria the branch manager is coming to town please prepare for her visit.

20. After graduating from a four year college, consider getting a master's degree.

21. Please read the chapter entitled Uses for Quotation Marks in your text.

22. Our company is still too small to consider leasing a ten story office building.

23. We are so busy that many times the staff is here until after seven oclock.

24. Well be here today not tomorrow.

25. Bottled water avoid it for the environment's sake!

Name: _____ **Date:** _____

writing for your career

INTEROFFICE MEMOS

Interoffice memos (also called **memorandums**) are preprinted documents that contain an organization's logo and **guide words** (*Date, To, From, Subject*) at the top. Their principal use is for communicating within an organization. Although, like letters on printed letterhead, they have been largely replaced by emails, they are still used for certain types of communications. These uses include important announcements from managers to employees, such as high-level staff appointments and policy statements. Occasionally, memos are sent to people outside of an organization, usually in the case of ongoing projects. An example might be a **memo of transmittal**, which is a document that accompanies materials that are sent between two parties.

When considering the uses for a memo, the writer should consider the purpose of the message and how it will be used by the recipient. In the case of a policy statement, for example, the sender provides a formal document that can be printed for future reference by the recipient. The memo format also provides a permanent document that can be posted on a website

The preprinted parts of a memo allow it to be typed and formatted quickly. Most companies have preprinted memo forms with the company name and logo. Word processing programs also provide memo templates. Formatting is shown on page 285.

Formatting for Memos

Follow these guidelines when you type a memo:

1. Fill in the information next to the guide words by aligning text two spaces after the longest guide word.
2. Align the left margin of the message with the guide words.
3. Double-space after the "Subject" line and between paragraphs.
4. Do not place a signature at the bottom. Signing your name or initials next to the typed name at the top is optional.

Optional Memo Notations

Three types of notations might be included at the end of a memo: typist's initials, copy notations, and enclosure notations. The format for these is the same for both memos and letters. See Communications Connection for Chapter 9 on letters on page 180.

PACIFIC IMPORTS, INC.

MEMO

DATE: June 30, 20xx

TO: Sharon Alexander, Accounting Associate

CC: Yasmin Salazar, Director, Accounting Services

FROM: Ronald Leland, Director, Human Resources *RL*

SUBJECT: Welcome to Pacific Imports, Inc.

We are pleased to have you join our staff and hope you'll find your employment here enjoyable and personally rewarding. Because we are currently reprinting our official Employee Manual, I have summarized a few key policies to help you understand our operation and the importance of your job:

Security: Please wear your identification card at all times when on the company premises. Security guards at the main points of entry are required to check the identification of all employees.

Attendance: Employees are expected to be in their assigned departments and ready to begin work at 8:30 a.m. If you are unable to come to work, please call your department manager no later than 9 a.m. Please contact my office in the event of any extended absence from work.

Smoking: Employees are permitted to smoke on the terrace outside the cafeteria—and nowhere else in the building or on the grounds.

If you have any questions, please see my assistant Jim Harrison or me. Stop by my office at any time. I look forward to working with you.

writing for your career recap

A. Imagine that you work in the Human Resources Department of a company that is planning an office renovation and redecoration of the four floors (7, 8, 9, and 10) it occupies in its current location. For a period of six months, employees in your office will be relocated to a satellite office in the same area. Your supervisor has asked you to draft a memo notifying the employees of this temporary move, which will take place one month from the date of the memo.

Create a memo template with the name of your company and write a draft of the email. The points that need to be covered are listed below. You are to fill in the details, such as dates, names, and any other specific information that will enhance your communication. Consider that employees might be unhappy about being asked to move temporarily. Your tone and content should be used to address this concern.

- The reason for the relocation.
- The specific address of the temporary location.
- The length of time in the temporary location.
- The date of the move: Each floor will be moved on consecutive days beginning on a Monday and ending on a Thursday.
- Supplies (boxes and labels) will be delivered to employees the week prior to the move. All boxes must be packed and labeled the Friday before the move begins.
- Employees are not allowed to move any office equipment on their own; they may move personal items, such as plants, photos, and other office decorations.
- Management will do everything possible to minimize disruption of work and inconvenience to employees.
- More information will be distributed by email as the date of the move approaches.

Date to submit this assignment: _____

B. Write **T** (true) or **F** (false) in each blank.

_____ 1. Writing emails in the workplace requires using the same standards of English usage applied to other written communications.

_____ 2. In the workplace, it is customary to address all email recipients formally in the salutation.

_____ 3. Make email subject lines as long as necessary to communicate the purpose of your message.

_____ 4. Interoffice memos are never sent outside the office.

_____ 5. The preprinted words *Date, To, From,* and *Subject* at the top of a memo form are called guide words.

_____ 6. It isn't necessary to sign your name on an interoffice memo.

_____ 7. It isn't necessary to let the recipient(s) know who is being copied on correspondence.

_____ 8. Sign off emails with your first name only.

_____ 9. You have no control over whether an email you send is forwarded to others.

_____ 10. A signature block in an email should contain your full name and complete contact information.

Name: _____ Date: _____

_____ 11. Sending blind copies is a way to protect the privacy of email addresses on large mailings.

_____ 12. Interoffice memos are used only for formal communications to employees.

_____ 13. Templates are electronic forms for formatting memos.

_____ 14. It is best to use blind copies only when you have an important reason for doing so.

_____ 15. It isn't a good idea to send confidential messages via email.

_____ 16. It would not be appropriate to send a letter typed on letterhead as an email attachment.

_____ 17. Emails have largely replaced the use of printed interoffice memos.

_____ 18. It is never necessary to use the salutation "Dear" in an email.

_____ 19. Managers still use interoffice memos to send messages to their employees.

_____ 20. It is perfectly acceptable to send personal emails through the company email system.

Name: _____ **Date:** _____

unit five

Writing for Career Success

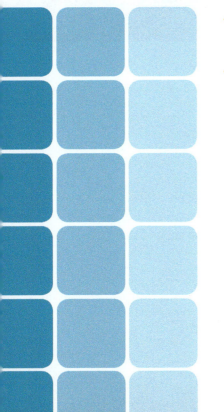

© Antiksu/Fotolia

After completing Chapter 14, you will be able to do the following:

- Write complete sentences and avoid fragments and comma splices.
- Write clearly and concisely and improve the style of your writing.
- Know how to construct sentences to achieve parallel parts and avoid misplaced modifiers.
- Apply the use of active and passive voice to achieve appropriate emphasis in your writing.

Polished Writing Style

career connection

GETTING THE INTERVIEW: PRESCREENING COMES FIRST

Employers use a variety of prescreening techniques to narrow down the field of job applicants. Being aware of and prepared for these techniques is just one more step in securing the position you want.

- **Online job application.** Employers look for related experience described with the right words. As any career changer will tell you, they don't spend much time thinking about the possibilities of candidate's with unrelated backgrounds.

- **Cover letter.** The screener is looking for a well-written document that is error-free and that provides a concise and well-crafted overview of the candidate's most relevant work experience for the job.

- **Resume.** The resume should be customized to reflect skills and experience that match the job posting as closely as possible. Employers look for keywords and are attuned to question gaps in employment, exaggerated claims, and dates that don't add up. They also look for educational credentials that match the employer's stated requirements.

- **Assessment tools.** These range from job-specific tests to broader instruments that measure personality traits. Tests may be written or Web-based, with the trend leaning toward online testing.

- **Phone interview.** Some employers conduct prescreening telephone interviews. They usually cover a few key questions that elicit job-related information while also giving the employer a chance to evaluate a candidate's communication skills, level of enthusiasm, and understanding of the position for which he or she is applying.

- **Salary expectations.** Be prepared for employers who also screen in advance for your salary requirements; some actually do demand that applicants name a figure up front.

Whatever prescreening techniques you encounter, try not to let them unnerve you. This variety of techniques provides opportunities throughout the job application process to advance your chances for consideration.

PRETEST

Revise these sentences so that they no longer have construction errors. If necessary, you may add information.

1. When you review the sentence faults explained in Chapter 10.

   _____

2. Use words that identify people by what they do, then you can avoid sexist language.

   _____

   _____

3. He worked on the report. He worked hard. He went home.

   _____

4. Although Angela spoke with her sister, she forgot to invite her to the party.

   _____

5. Sarah worked for the new company during her summer vacation in the sales department.

   _____

   _____

6. Topped with chocolate syrup, Janet ate the huge bowl of ice cream.

   _____

   _____

Change these passive voice sentences to active voice sentences:

7. The computer was turned on.

   _____

8. The best speech was delivered by the rookie.

   _____

9. We were the winners of the prize.

   _____

10. The film was given the highest praise by all the critics.

   _____

CHECK YOUR ANSWERS ON PAGE 464.

Polished Writing Style

Polished writing is writing that incorporates all of the principles of good writing you have learned in this course. You have learned the fundamentals of writing complete sentences, varying sentence structure to keep your reader alert and interested, and applying the rules of grammar to create clear, concise writing that gets across your intended message.

To wrap up the course, this chapter will provide some additional tips on writing style that will take your writing to the next level. If you always keep in mind that writing is a process and that good sentences build good paragraphs that create a whole, meaningful, and well-written communication, you won't find it very difficult to apply what you have learned in *English for Careers*.

Sentence Types and Construction

Sentences that are smoothly constructed convey your main idea in a concise and clear way. In Chapter 3, you learned about different types of sentences—simple, compound, complex, and compound-complex—and how varying sentence type adds meaning and interest to your writing. You have also learned about clauses and phrases and how to properly punctuate them. This section reviews some of those basics, but now you are looking at your writing from a different angle. You know how to construct a sentence that is correct—now you will look critically at your writing and use techniques to improve your writing style during the editing and revising stage of the writing process.

ADD VARIETY AND INTEREST

You will recall from Chapter 3 that varying sentence type adds variety and interest within a paragraph. The reader will be lulled into boredom with too many short, choppy sentences, and your writing style will come across as childish. Likewise, too many long, complex sentences bury the idea and confuse the reader. Balance is the key and this is achieved through varying sentence type and structure.

To achieve this balance, reread your draft and look for ideas that would be expressed better as one thought instead of two separate sentences and sentences that would flow more smoothly if combined. Also look for paragraphs where you have repeated the same sentence construction throughout. Here are some techniques that will add variety and interest to your writing style.

Combine Short, Simple Sentences

- Consider joining short, simple sentences of equal importance with a coordinating conjunction. The result might be a single smoothly written sentence. The examples that follow are exaggerations to make a point—a quick way for you to grasp the idea.

Original	Ellie likes her work. Robert hates his job.
Revised	Ellie likes her work, but Robert hates going to the office every day.

By combining two short, simple sentences and making one of the clauses dependent, your point is communicated more smoothly.

Original	Ellie likes her work. Robert hates his job.
Revised	Although Ellie likes her work, Robert hates going to the office every day.

Another option is to add a transitional expression.

Revised	Ellie likes her work; however, Robert hates going to the office every day.

Consider using a phrase, an adjective, or an adverb instead of only short clauses.

Original	Janet is wearing a new dress. She looks pretty. She approached Edward. Jane is shy.
Revised	Janet, looking pretty in her new dress, shyly approached Edward.

Vary Sentence Construction

Not only short, simple sentences need to flow more smoothly. Two sentences together with exactly the same construction don't read very well, whether they are long or short. The following revisions show several techniques for polishing writing by avoiding repetitive structure. You might think of other ways.

Original	You write in code. That is how you convey the information secretly.
Revised	By writing in code, you convey the information secretly.
Original	The dean's office is next to the reception room. It is on the first floor.
Revised	The dean's office is next to the reception room on the first floor.
Original	Measuring industrial output is comparatively easy. Measuring an education system's output is difficult.
Revised	While measuring industrial output is comparatively easy, measuring an education system's output is difficult.
Original	Some manufacturers engage in wholesale trade. They are not regarded as wholesalers. Their primary function is that of manufacturing.
Revised	Some manufacturers engage in wholesale trade. They are not, however, regarded as wholesalers because their primary function is manufacturing.

Revise Long, Complex Sentences

The preceding examples suggest ways to *join* ideas for more effective writing. Too much joining, however, can result in sentences that are too long and complicated for easy comprehension. Such writing, especially when combined with needlessly technical or long words, is called *gobbledygook*.

Gobbledygook is speech or writing with needlessly long words, superfluous words, or complicated sentence structure. Gobbledygook is pompous and hard to understand.

Research shows that big words and long sentences do not impress readers favorably. A simple language style that expresses ideas clearly, correctly, and concisely is more likely to get results in the workplace. Unfortunately, too much writing is gobbledygook. The technical, scientific, governmental, and legal professions are especially guilty of this type of writing. (Academic and business scholars have also been known to indulge in it.) These professions desperately need individuals who not only understand their field but can also explain it clearly in writing; maybe you can become one of them.

Gobbledygook needs more than revision—like a foreign language, it needs to be translated into understandable English.

Gobbledygook	Distributors of merchandise for profit in the Middle Ages kept numerical records of the merchandise they sold on "tally sticks," on which they produced a notch on a stick which was then broken in half, with the merchant retaining half and the other half being presented to the customer in order to have a record of the data for the merchant and the individual who made the purchase.

You can replace this gobbledygook with concise, straightforward writing. Separate the one long sentence into three clear sentences and use fewer and simpler words.

Translation	Merchants in the Middle Ages recorded sales on "tally sticks." The data was notched on a stick, which was then split in half. The merchant kept half and gave the matching half to the customer.

The last idea in the original paragraph can be understood by the reader from the context; therefore, it isn't necessary to include it. Here is another example.

Original	Please be advised that your inquiry concerning the availability of our recently advertised offer is being processed at this time. The products you requested will be sent to you via our express fulfillment service, which guarantees shipment within five business days.
Translation	Thank you for your order. It will be shipped within five business days.

People in today's workplace are busy and appreciate writing like the above that "cuts to the chase."

PRONOUN REFERENCE

When reviewing sentences for clarity, remember what you learned in Chapter 7 about pronoun reference. It is especially important to provide the reader with clear, immediate reference to the pronouns you use. When nouns become separated from the pronoun that refers back to them, take special care that the references are clear.

Each pronoun should mean precisely what you want it to mean to your reader. If necessary, rephrase a sentence or replace a vague pronoun with an appropriate noun.

Unclear   Deborah recommends Janice Daly to speak at the conference because she is a communication expert.

Did Deborah recommend Janice because Deborah is an expert, or is Janice an expert?

Clear   Deborah recommends Janice Daly to speak at the conference; Ms. Daly is a communication expert.

Unclear   If you are unable to provide the information by Friday's meeting, it will have to wait until the following week.

What will wait—the information or the meeting?

Clear   If you are unable to provide the information by Friday's meeting, the meeting will need to be rescheduled for the following week.

Make Clear Connections

You know that when a dependent clause is connected to an independent clause, the result is a complete sentence. Clauses may be joined by a coordinating conjunction (*and, but, for, nor, or, so, yet*); another type of conjunction used to join clauses is called a **dependent conjunction** (or **subordinate conjunction**). These conjunctions are used to introduce a phrase—a word group that cannot stand by itself as a sentence—and provide a smooth connection between ideas. They can replace punctuation in order to join ideas expressed in separate sentences. Another way to join ideas is by using transitional expressions, which you have also studied in previous chapters.

USE A DEPENDENT CONJUNCTION

The words below are often used as dependent conjunctions. The sentences following the list show the dependent conjunction in bold type; the phrase that it introduces is underlined.

after	even though	unless
although	if	until
as	since	when
because	so that	whenever
before	than	while

Business letters in the United States and Canada are less formal **than** in most other parts of the world.

Than is used as a dependent conjunction to introduce the phrase *in most other parts of the world.*

The fashion show will be a success if the PR firm gets adequate press coverage.

If is a dependent conjunction preceding the noun *PR firm* and the verb *gets.* To change emphasis, the dependent conjunction can be placed at the beginning of the sentence.

If the PR firm gets adequate press coverage, the fashion show will be a success.

Usually the dependent conjunction slightly changes the emphasis or meaning of the original sentence and might help express a particular idea.

Original	He thought he would be sick. Something was wrong with the potato salad.
Original	He thought he would be sick; something was wrong with the potato salad.
Revised	He thought he would be sick **because** something was wrong with the potato salad.
	Because something was wrong with the potato salad, he thought he would be sick.
Original	The picnic was fun. It rained in the afternoon.
Original	The picnic was fun; it rained in the afternoon.
Revised	The picnic was fun **although** it rained in the afternoon.
	Although it rained in the afternoon, the picnic was fun.

USE TRANSITIONAL WORDS AND PHRASES

You have learned how to use commas and semicolons to join independent clauses with transitional words and phrases. A quick review here examines how transitions help readers move effortlessly from one idea to the next *closely related* idea. Here are some common transitional words and expressions:

also	in addition	then
consequently	in fact	therefore
for example	moreover	thus
furthermore	nevertheless	yet
hence	otherwise	
however	that is	

In the following examples, you would choose your transitional word or phrase according to what you want your reader to understand.

Original	About 50 percent of our employees are engaged in the distribution of goods and services. About 20 percent are in production.

grammar**TIP**

Remember that when a transitional word or phrase connects *independent* clauses, insert a semicolon or a period—not a comma—before the transition. A comma would result in a comma splice.

Revised About 50 percent of our employees are engaged in the distribution of goods and services; **however**, 20 percent are in production.

OR

About 50 percent of our employees are engaged in the distribution of goods and services. **In addition**, about 20 percent are in production.

Original In the United States eye contact is extremely important. Americans don't trust someone who won't look them in the eye.

Revised In the United States eye contact is extremely important; **in fact,** Americans don't trust someone who won't look them in the eye.

OR

In the United States eye contact is extremely important. **In fact,** Americans don't trust someone who won't look them in the eye.

Original Order the new computers. You can find out about training later.

Revised Order the new computers; **then** you can find out about training.

OR

Order the new computers, and **then** you can find out about training.

Order the new computers. **Then** you can find out about training.

DECIDING WHEN TO JOIN IDEAS

grammar**TIP**

Use a comma *after* a transition of more than one syllable—except the short word *also*. Do not use a comma after one-syllable transitions, such as *yet, thus,* and *then*.

When two ideas are closely related, you decide whether to join or separate them, depending on what you want to convey to your reader. Which idea do you want to emphasize, or are they equal in importance? To develop an instinct for making the right choice, you should practice drafting and revising with a focus on sentence construction. In addition, routinely reading well-written communications will improve your good judgment and enable you to decide quickly.

Skillful business writers often use a dependent clause to deemphasize an idea they don't want the reader to focus on and use an independent clause to *emphasize* another idea.

Dependent Clause | Independent Clause

Although we don't give refunds on earrings, we'll be happy to exchange them for any other jewelry in the store.

Dependent Clause | Independent Clause

After we carefully reviewed your proposal, we find that it does not meet our needs at this time.

Dependent Clause | Independent Clause

When you write using this technique, you emphasize the positive and make the negative palatable.

DECIDING *NOT* TO JOIN IDEAS

Oscar Wilde, a witty British playwright of the late 1800s, wrote, "The English have really everything in common with the Americans except of course language." One of many examples of the differences between British and American English is the word for the mark that ends most sentences. In the United States, we say *period*; in Britain, it's a *full stop*.

Sometimes, the best way to get an idea across is to make a full stop, in other words, to change one sentence to two. How will you know when to do this? The flow of your words will tell you. Think about whether you have written a complete thought. Then analyze your intent: What part of the sentence do you want to emphasize? Will your emphasis be clear to the reader?

Practice deciding when to join or not join sentences by inserting missing punctuation in the following letter.

Dear Professor Cooper:

Thank you for the time and courtesy you extended to our representative Laura Mann at your college last month she enjoyed her visit with you.

At Laura's request, we have sent you the new edition of *Mathematics for Business* this was sent to you several weeks ago, and you should have it by now we do hope you'll look it over in addition your name has been placed on our mailing list to receive an examination copy of *Business Math: Practical Applications* a new edition of this book by Cleaves, Hobbs, and Dudenhef is expected off the press early next month.

We'll send your copy just as soon as it is available if there is any way we can be of help to you, Professor Cooper, please let us know best wishes for a happy holiday season we look forward to doing business with you in the future.

---

writingTIP

As you read the letter in the preceding exercise and other examples of well-written business letters throughout the text, notice the friendly, easy-to-understand style. This is the style to aim for in your business writing.

An example of a properly punctuated version is shown on page 465. You might have correctly punctuated yours differently.

GO TO PAGE 309 AND COMPLETE WORKSHEET 14.1.

Well-Placed and Parallel Parts

The late James McSheehy, a member of the San Francisco Board of Supervisors, addressed a group of women about his work on a finance committee. "Ladies," he said, "I have here some figures I want you to take home in your heads, which are concrete." Of course, Mr. McSheehy really meant that the *figures* were concrete.

MISPLACED WORDS

To avoid this kind of error in your writing, look for **misplaced words—** words that are not in the correct order—when revising and proofreading. If the words in a sentence are not in correct order, the reader or listener may be confused or amused. Either way, concentration on your message is lost.

Misplaced words often go undetected because the writer becomes "too close" to what is written. Once you have written, reread, and revised a draft, your eyes and brain may fail to pick up confusing sentence structure because you are not able to read objectively. Whenever time allows, it is a good idea to have a colleague or supervisor review your edited draft; another pair of eyes and point of view are always helpful.

To avoid the sentence fault of misplaced words, check each sentence and question whether words are in the best place for getting the message across.

Original	I have some figures that I want you to take home in your heads, which are concrete.
Revised	I have some figures, which I know are concrete, that I want you to take home in your heads.
Original	Irene hung a picture on the wall painted by Rembrandt.

Rembrandt painted the wall?

Revision 1	Irene hung a picture painted by Rembrandt on the wall.

What is on the wall—the painting or Rembrandt?

Final	The picture Irene hung on the wall was painted by Rembrandt.
	OR
	Irene hung a Rembrandt painting on the wall.

Unnecessary words are omitted, and additional information is included in one concise sentence.

Original	He only had $5 when he arrived in Kenansville.

No one else had $5, only *he*?

Revised	He had only $5 when he arrived in Kenansville.
Original	On the bulletin board of a factory building—WANTED: Worker to sew buttons on 4th floor.
Revised	WANTED ON 4TH FLOOR: Worker to sew buttons.

PARALLEL PARTS

Express parallel ideas—that is, similar sentence elements—in the same grammatical form.

This is known as **parallel construction**, which enables readers to understand immediately how two or more parts of a sentence are related. In the following examples, words that are *not parallel* are in boldface in the first sentence, and words that make the parts parallel are in boldface in the revision.

Original	The security guard chased the intruder **down** the hall, **out** the door, and **then they** ran into the yard.
Parallel	The security guard chased the intruder **down** the hall, **out** the door, and **into** the yard.
Original	He was **tall**, **muscular**, and **was able to run very fast**.

Make all three describing expressions parallel by using three adjectives and omitting the unneeded words.

Parallel	He was **tall**, **muscular**, and **fast**.
Original	His ambitions were **to join** a fraternity and **becoming** a football player.

Use *to* with a verb (the infinitive) before each ambition *or* use the *ing* form for each ambition.

Revised	His ambitions were **to join** a fraternity and **to become** a football player.
	His ambitions were **joining** a fraternity and **becoming** a football player.

GO TO PAGE 311 AND COMPLETE WORKSHEET 14.2.

Get to the Point

Do you know someone who makes a "beeline" for the snack table upon arriving at a party? This food fancier moves in a straight, unwavering path just as a bee flies directly to its chosen flower. Similarly, a well-written sentence makes a beeline to get to its point. Good writers know that their readers are busy and do not have time to sort through ideas, make assumptions, or ask follow-up questions. In the workplace, people usually react most favorably to a **direct writing style**; that is, a way of writing that directly states the action of the sentence.

In addition to your friend who makes a beeline for the refreshments, you may have other friends who eventually get there but take their time about it. In the same way, skillful business writers sometimes use an **indirect writing style**, stating the action indirectly, when a situation requires being tactful or de-emphasizing parts of a message.

VOICE OF VERBS

To write a sentence in the direct or indirect style, you need to know about **verb voice**. The way you construct a sentence can change verb *voice*—which may be *active* or *passive*.

Active Voice

A direct writing style uses **active voice**, which means that the subject *does* or *performs* the verb's action.

Carl ignored the boss.

The subject *Carl* did the action—*ignored*.

The United States won 110 medals at the 2008 Summer Olympics.

The subject *United States* did the action—*won*.

Passive Voice

An indirect writing style uses **passive voice**, which means that the subject *receives* the verb's action.

> The boss was ignored by Carl.

The subject *the boss* received the action—*was ignored*.

> One hundred and ten medals were won by the United States at the 2008 Summer Olympics.

The subject *medals* received the action—*were won*.

Since the required ingredients of a sentence are subject, verb, and independence, you can write complete sentences in the passive voice without mentioning who did the action.

> The letters were sent.

This sentence has a subject and a verb and is independent; it is passive because the subject *received* the action.

> One thousand fund-raising letters were sent.

This sentence is in passive voice because the subject is the receiver even though the doer of the action (the sender) is not named.

Choosing Active versus Passive Voice

Use active voice to convey information directly and clearly. Fewer words are usually required for the active voice; it is more efficient, and it takes the reader from point A to point B in a straight line. In the following sentences, there is no reason to use the passive voice.

Active	Jesse accurately prepared a spreadsheet of the accounts receivable.
Passive	The accounts receivable spreadsheet was prepared accurately by Jesse.
	The accounts receivable spreadsheet was prepared accurately.
Active	George presented the report to the stockholders.
Passive	The report was presented to the stockholders by George.
	The report was presented to the stockholders.

In many cases, there is good reason to use the passive voice. When you need to word a sentence tactfully or place the emphasis in a way that is less direct, use the passive voice. For example, you may want the reader to know about an error but do not want to say anything more about it. The passive voice can soften the impact of such news.

> An error was made on the report.

> The payment of your invoice was inadvertently delayed.

Use the passive voice if you don't know who is doing the action or if you want to emphasize the receiver of the action rather than the doer. The passive enables you to begin the sentence with the receiver; you can omit the doer or end with the doer. For example, the report is more important than the auditor in the following sentence.

Passive	A report was presented to the stockholders by the auditor.
	OR
	A report was presented to the stockholders.
Active	The auditor presented a report to the stockholders.

Distinguishing Active from Passive Voice

A quick test can help you detect the voice of a verb. If "by someone" makes sense after the verb, the voice is passive. If "by someone" is already there, then you *know* it's passive.

Passive	The book was purchased last week.
Test	The book was purchased (by someone) last week. ["By someone" makes sense after the verb.]
Active	Dorothy Larson bought the book today.
Test	Dorothy Larson bought (by someone) the book today. ["By someone" after the verb doesn't make sense.]

Dangling Phrases

Another problem to look for when revising and proofreading your work is known in grammar as the **dangling verbal**. Recall from Chapter 8 that a verbal is not a verb; it looks like a verb but isn't functioning as a verb.

A verbal may be one of the following:

- **An infinitive:** *to* plus a verb, such as *to work*, *to go*, *to eat*
- **A past participle:** *worked*, *gone*, *eaten*
- **A present participle:** *working*, *going*, *eating*
- **A combination:** *having worked*, *to have gone*, *to be eating*

A dangling verbal is a phrase containing a verbal that hangs loosely, or dangles, in a sentence.

RECOGNIZING DANGLERS

A dangling verbal phrase usually—but not always—opens a sentence, and a clause follows it. If the word group in question has a real verb, the word group is not dangling. The subject of the clause following a verbal phrase must tell who does the action referred to in the verbal phrase. If the subject doesn't tell who does the action of the verbal, the verbal phrase is dangling. The resulting sentence may amuse, confuse, or distract the reader.

| | Verbal Phrase   Subject |
| **Dangler** | To get the most out of our time, the session will include discussion of our day-to-day problems. |

The verbal is *To get*. It looks like a verb, but it isn't because it can't have a subject: You wouldn't say, "I to get the most out of our time." It would have to be "I *want* to get . . ." with *want* as the verb.

After noting that the sentence begins with a phrase containing a verbal, find the subject of the clause that follows the phrase; the subject is *session*. Then ask, "Is the *session* to get the most out of our time?" No, it's *we* who want to get the most out of our time. Therefore, the verbal phrase is dangling. To stop the dangling, the subject must identify *who* is to get the most out of our time.

Revision   To get the most out of our time, we will include in the session a discussion of our day-to-day problems.

                      Verbal Phrase   Subject

Dangler   Having made too many errors on the test, the personnel director did not hire Joe.

Since it was not the personnel director who made the errors, the opening phrase is dangling. Save the verbal (*having made*) from dangling by changing the subject to the one who did make the errors.

Revision   Having made too many errors on the test, **Joe** did not get the job.

Having made is a verbal—not a verb—because you can't give it a subject.

    OR   Because Joe made too many errors on the test, he did not get the job.

Dangler   While flying over the jungle at an altitude of 2,000 feet, the villagers could be seen hunting and fishing.

The opening phrase includes the verbal "flying." Notice that *flying* can't be a verb unless a helping verb precedes it. You can't say, "They flying over the jungle." The subject following the phrase is *villagers*. To decide whether the opener is dangling, ask, "Are the villagers flying over the jungle?" Since the answer is "no," correct the sentence so that the subject tells who is flying.

Revision   While we were flying over the jungle at an altitude of 2,000 feet, we could see the villagers hunting and fishing.

                      Verbal Phrase   Subject

Dangler   After looking at the cars for a while, the salesperson approached me.

After looking at the cars for a while is dangling. Was the salesperson looking at the cars? To make this sentence clear and avoid a dangler, the subject must be the one doing the looking.

Revision   After I looked at the cars for a while, the salesperson approached me.

Another way to correct a dangling verbal is to change it to a subject and verb—that is, a clause; clauses don't dangle.

Dangler   While taking an aerobics class at the gym, his clothes were stolen.

Since his clothes were not taking an aerobics class, change the dangling verbal phrase to a dependent clause. A dependent conjunction (*While*) is followed by a subject and a verb. Then the second clause does not have to be changed.

Revision   While he was taking an aerobics class at the gym, his clothes were stolen.

Do not try to correct a dangler by merely moving the beginning of the sentence to another place. The result is often a dangler in the middle or at the end of the sentence instead of at the beginning.

Dangler   His clothes were stolen while taking an aerobics class at the gym.

The sentence still reads as though his clothes were taking the class, but the verbal is now midsentence.

Dangler   Having been sick for two weeks, Enrique's father took him to the doctor.

Father is the subject; *Enrique's* is a possessive noun. The father was not sick for two weeks. Therefore, *having been sick for two weeks* is dangling. The correction below changes the opener to a dependent clause.

Revision   After Enrique had been sick for two weeks, his father took him to the doctor.

Dangler   Driving too fast through the busy intersection, the brake was applied quickly.

Revision   After driving too fast through the busy intersection, I applied the brake quickly.

After I had driven too fast through the intersection, I quickly applied the brake.

The verbal is changed to a dependent clause.

GO TO PAGE 314 AND COMPLETE WORKSHEET 14.3.

Checkpoint

Getting your message across as you intended doesn't always happen on the first draft. If you take the time to review and edit your drafts with a critical eye, you can recognize ways to improve your writing style and make your writing clearer, more interesting, and more meaningful to your reader. Making the effort to polish your written communications applies to everything you write. Faults with sentence variety, structure, passive versus active voice, misplaced words, danglers, and gobbledygook can derail a short message as easily as a long, complex document. Overcoming common sentence faults is a major step toward improving your workplace writing and increasing your opportunities for a successful career.

communications connection

PLANNING A SUCCESSFUL PRESENTATION

Do you know the reason so many people become frightened at the thought of standing before an audience and speaking? It's simple. To imagine yourself giving a speech in the abstract is scary. How will you know what to say? To whom will you be speaking? Will they be interested? How long will you have to speak? It's no wonder that the idea of public speaking is frightening when you don't have answers to all of these questions. This is where preparation comes in and where practice follows.

Confidence comes with carefully thinking through every aspect of a presentation and then scripting it and practicing it. You still might not feel comfortable, and you might be anxious until it's over, but preparation will eliminate a big reason for being fearful.

A successful presentation requires you to write a first draft in which you do the following: determine your precise objectives, outline the content—introduction, ideas, supporting facts, and specific examples—and conclude with a summary and action plan where appropriate.

Define Your Objective

Write out your objective, that is, what you want to accomplish as a result of the presentation. Your objective should be concise. If it can't be stated in one sentence, your thinking might not be clear. Work on it until you can boil your thoughts down to their essence and make one clear statement of what you want to do.

Here is an example:

> My objective is to convince supervisors and managers that the company should purchase QXR Software because it will save the company money and time and increase productivity.

Plan Your Presentation

Everything you say during the presentation must help you meet your objective. Plan what the presentation will include and how you will deliver it. Will you use note cards or a script? Either one can be used to list key points and key words that will trigger what you want to say. If you are doing a multimedia presentation, prepare your points and visuals as an integrated package that uses the visual medium to maximum effect.

In planning how you will develop and present your content, think about where you will make the presentation and what equipment and handouts you will need. Consider such details as whether you will be standing or sitting. Will there be a podium? Are you a member of a panel? If you will need equipment, such as a microphone, practice using it as you practice giving your speech aloud.

Know how much time you have and prepare and practice to ensure that you stay within the allotted time.

If you intend to provide handouts to your audience, make their development a part of your planning process. Some presenters use a printout of their slides as their handout.

Prepare the Content

To prepare your content, follow the traditional advice for structuring a speech: *Tell them what you're going to tell them (introduction), tell them (body), and tell them what you told them (conclusion).* Here is how it might work using the QXR Software presentation as an example:

Introduction   If you feel comfortable, begin with a story or joke relating to the subject. Then summarize the key points that you will be making, but don't go into detail:

- Last week I spent 10 minutes on what should have been a 15-second task: trying to retrieve a customer's lost file.
- I had to keep the customer on hold, which could have resulted in lost business.
- I did some research and discovered that a new, relatively inexpensive software package could eliminate this problem.

Body   Get down to business and tell them. Provide supporting facts that explain what the software is, how it works, and how it will save the company money and time and make their jobs easier. Each fact you state must support your objective. Use visuals if possible and give specific examples of what this software will do. Speak at a level that is appropriate to your audience. Avoid jargon, details, and vocabulary that some listeners may not understand. Explain and simplify as needed without making listeners feel foolish. Prepare handouts if they will help:

- What QXR software is: how it works; examples (with visuals)
- Its reputation; testimonials/success stories from users
- Cost/benefits for us: money, time, productivity
- Backup data verifying potential outcomes

Conclusion   Tell them what you've told them. Summarize what you explained and make specific recommendations. Avoid introducing new ideas in the conclusion.

- Why QXR is the best choice for our needs (review key points from the "body")
- Action plan: suggested time line for implementation—purchase, installation, and training
- Questions from the audience

WRITING AND SPEAKING PRACTICE

This assignment will give you the opportunity to practice your speaking and writing. First you will conduct an interview and take notes; then you will write about your findings.

To begin, choose a career field or a company that interests you and identify someone who is willing to be interviewed for approximately 30 minutes. Decide what your goal will be for the interview. Are you seeking general information about the industry or business to make a decision about pursuing it in the future? Are you exploring career options in the field? Are you interested in learning the specifics of a particular job? Is the company one that you would like to work for? Your goal is to target your interview to get information that will be valuable to you. You are the only one who knows exactly what that is.

You might start by doing some networking to find your interviewee—ask people you know or call or visit a company or organization and explain your purpose. Before the interview, prepare questions that will help you get the information you seek. Preparation might include doing some research on the Internet, reading some magazine articles, or talking with someone to get advice in advance.

Questions you might ask include the following: What kinds of job opportunities are available? What qualities are most important for success? What does the work consist of? What is a typical daily routine? What types of entry-level jobs are available? What are key qualifications for job seekers? What are the salary ranges? Are there advancement opportunities? What are the advantages and disadvantages of this kind of work? What kind of training is needed to qualify?

Be aware during your interview that you are not preparing a biography of your subject. People enjoy talking about themselves and telling their "life story," but it will be your job to steer the conversation to get the information you need. Take good notes during the interview. Then immediately afterward, summarize the information and prepare a five-minute presentation using the guidelines on pages 306 and 307.

Date to submit this assignment: _____

PROOFREADING PRACTICE

A well-written article has been altered to provide practice in correcting word and sentence errors based on the principles you have mastered so far. Correct the printed copy using proofreading symbols or go online to correct the document electronically.

The Power of Creative Thinking

Much of what we call progress in the world, came from seeing old ideas from new perspectives. Holding to the widely-accepted belief that the world was flat, the new world would not have been discovered by explorers in the fifteenth century. If no one had of challenged the notion that only men are smart enough to vote women would still be without this basic right.

Creative thinkers' examine information and are looking at data from all sides! They ask "What if?" How about if I tried this? "How can that be?" and wonder if that works, maybe I could try this.

Instincts are trusted by creative thinker. Do you sometimes just "have a hunch." Do you feel that something is right or wrong? In the dictionary a natural instinct is a feeling that seems to come from within. Something we all experience from time to time. Don't negotiate your way on natural instincts alone the world is far too complex. Don't forget creativity springs from internal "hunches". Combine hunches with a solid knowledge base, for example, creative artists often base their subject matter on real life. Creating a work of art for others to appreciate by relying on shared experiences expressed through the medium of their chosen art form and similarly, great actors often rely on instinct to interpret a role. They still follows the rules of the stage when performing. The lesson is this instincts, combined with intellectual knowledge and skill are a powerful combination.

How did you do? Excellent _____ Good _____
Need More Practice _____

chapter review

WORKSHEET 14.1

A. Use proofreading marks to revise these sentences.

                                                     but
    Example: Setting goals may be scary, it is necessary.
                                                      ^

1. You can do all the common things of life in an uncommon way. You will command the attention of the world.

2. An employee is asked to work overtime, that employee is entitled to compensation of one and one-half times the base hourly rate (Employee Handbook, page 25).

3. The manager was finishing the report. Her boss was calling the CEO to explain why it was late.

4. Getting a learner's permit is a first step. Then a new driver can practice driving.

B. Answer the following questions.

5. List six commonly used transitional words and expressions:

    _____ _____ _____ _____ _____ _____

6. If a transitional expression joins *independent* clauses, use a semicolon or a period before the transition. True _____ False _____

7. When a transitional word or expression joins independent clauses, use a comma to separate the clauses. True _____ False _____

8. Use commas before and after a transitional expression that does not connect independent clauses. True _____ False _____

C. Use proofreading marks to correct the punctuation in the following sentences. Write **C** beside the three correct items.

_____   9. He will not, however, take the blueprints to the laboratory until the end of next week.

_____   10. He will complete the blueprints today. Then he'll send them to the contractor.

_____   11. High achievers do mental rehearsals. They visualize themselves performing tasks successfully.

_____   12. High achievers can picture themselves doing something well; for example, they might visualize crossing the finish line of a marathon.

_____   13. Your mind never sleeps. Visualization is effective just before falling asleep since your mind probably continues to work on the desired achievement as you sleep.

_____   14. The instructor was right, however, in advising students to get a good night's sleep before the exam.

_____   15. We find that some of the merchandise is damaged. We are going to return the entire order.

D. Rewrite the following sentences to improve the sentence construction. Add and delete words where necessary for clarity and conciseness but take care to maintain the sense of the original sentence.

1. A college pennant is in the student's room. There is also a picture by Monet. Both of these hang on the wall. _____

    _____

2. A house sits far back among the trees, and it is in need of painting.

    _____

3. Dennis and Mike walked to the grocery store, from there they walked to the bakery, then they went to the flower shop. They were preparing for a party; it took them all afternoon. _____
_____
_____

4. An animal paced restlessly back and forth in the cage, it appeared to be a hyena. _____
_____

5. We realize that people who travel by airplane make a choice of an airline based on the quality of its service to the people who fly on that airline's planes, and we are extremely regretful that we have not been able to meet your expectations. _____
_____

6. We received your May statement. We are enclosing a check in payment. The check is for $635.23. _____
_____

7. I missed the final exam because I had been out late the night before, consequently, they wouldn't give me an "Incomplete" or "Withdrew" grade, they failed me. _____
_____
_____

8. For those of you who have small children and didn't know it, we have a nursery downstairs. _____
_____

9. We don't recommend that Mr. Nguyen go to Mr. Anderson's office uninvited because he is so busy. _____
_____

10. Despite our repeated reminders regarding nonpayment of your account, which is long overdue. _____
_____
_____

CHECK YOUR ANSWERS ON PAGE 465.

WORKSHEET 14.2

A. Find the misplaced words in each sentence and move them to where they belong. Write the correct sentence in the blank.

1. We sat there listening to his singing in awed silence. _____
_____

2. Ms. Griggs worked for CNN during her vacation in the Headline News Department. _____
_____

3. Genevieve Astor died in the home in which she had been born at the age of 96. _____

_____

4. The fire was brought under control before much damage was done by the fire department. _____

_____

5. The car was returned by the customer with the uneven paint job.

_____

B. Rewrite the following sentences so that the parallel ideas are parallel in construction; that is, they have the same grammatical form.

6. With the new software we hope to improve response time, reducing input errors, and see that system problems are identified more readily. _____

_____

7. Typing accurately can be more important than to type fast. _____

_____

8. Linda is a full-time securities analyst, and her husband is working part time as an insurance agent. _____

_____

9. We would appreciate learning your views on how to introduce change, controlling quality, and the motivation of employees.

_____

_____

10. Ophthalmologists and optometrists may examine eyes, and prescriptions for glasses and contact lenses may be issued by them also. _____

_____

C. Write **P** for lack of parallel parts, **M** for misplaced words, and **C** for correct.

_____ 1. Oranges are a valuable source of vitamins, which are not mentioned in your report.

_____ 2. The English teacher was sitting by the fireplace with his dog reading Shakespeare.

_____ 3. He is interested in science, math, and he likes to read good books.

_____ 4. Mr. Gorjus was frantically searching for the telephone number in his office that was missing.

_____ 5. The woman suggested that we fill out the form and to leave it with her.

_____ 6. Ad for a famous cosmetic: Lady Esther Dream Cream is recognized by leading dermatologists as highly effective in improving skin's texture, smoothness, and for counteracting aging.

_____ 7. I believe that playing a good game of chess is a better accomplishment than to play a good game of bridge.

_____ 8. Writing business documents requires excellent grammar, and they should be punctuated very well also.

_____ 9. Her hobbies are painting, to go to concerts, and reading blogs on the Internet.

_____ 10. A wholesaler's function is to buy in large quantities and sell in small quantities.

_____ 11. The father sat down in an easy chair to tell his children about his childhood after dinner.

_____ 12. According to a "Human Development Index" that includes incomes, education, and life expectancy, Norway ranks second in the world.

_____ 13. A major Norwegian industry is production and transporting oil and gas from offshore petroleum deposits.

_____ 14. Norway is heavily dependent on world trade conditions with a population under five million.

_____ 15. We would like to hear your ideas on motivating employees and how to introduce change.

_____ 16. Some employees react quickly, get things done promptly, and beat deadlines.

_____ 17. That program has too much sex, violence, and the language is bad.

_____ 18. Friendship means forgetting what one gives and remembering what one receives.

_____ 19. She believed him as well as having faith in him.

_____ 20. The old man sat on a bench next to his grandchild, smoking a cigar.

D. Type the number of each item in Part C that you marked **P** or **M**, and polish the sentence.

CHECK YOUR ANSWERS ON PAGE 466.

WORKSHEET 14.3

A. Write **A** next to the sentences with active voice verbs and **P** next to those with passive voice verbs.

_____   1. Antarctica is not owned by any country.

_____   2. Interested nations from around the globe have signed an agreement to preserve Antarctica as a zone of world peace.

_____   3. Military activity, nuclear testing, and disposal of radioactive waste are prohibited in Antarctica by the Antarctic Treaty.

_____   4. Constantly chattering penguins bellyride down icy slopes and dive into the placid waters of Antarctica.

_____   5. The Atlantic, Pacific, and Indian Oceans surround Antarctica.

_____   6. Antarctica is surrounded by parts of the Atlantic, Pacific, and Indian Oceans.

_____   7. When doing business in England, use the term *British* rather than *English*—except for referring to the language.

_____   8. A great many jobs now involve interactions with people living in various countries.

_____   9. Importers and exporters constantly move merchandise from one country to another.

_____   10. Some knowledge of geography, history, and foreign languages is needed for advancement in today's global marketplace.

_____   11. Companies such as Avon Products and the Fuller Brush Company used to employ sales representatives who sold products door-to-door.

_____   12. In today's economy and culture, few products can be sold that way.

_____   13. Many people who can afford to buy are at work, and some others won't open the door to a salesperson because of fear of crime.

_____   14. The plants were watered every day during your vacation.

_____   15. All freight charges must be verified before they are paid.

_____   16. He misspelled "Mississippi" in every paragraph.

_____   17. "Mississippi" was misspelled in every paragraph.

_____ 18. These tools are manufactured in Toronto.

_____ 19. Networking engineers take care of problems day or night.

_____ 20. She sold all her stock during a bear market.

B. If the sentence has a dangler, underline it and write **D** in the blank. Otherwise, write **C** for correct.

_____ 1. Having typed just half the report, the phone began ringing insistently.

_____ 2. On examining the goods, we found them to be defective.

_____ 3. Like many people living in Alaska, the summer months are our favorites.

_____ 4. Having recovered from his illness, his mother took him to Israel.

_____ 5. To keep the machine running in perfect condition, we oiled it once a month.

_____ 6. Before going to lunch, this report must be typed.

_____ 7. This report must be typed before going to lunch.

_____ 8. Walking quickly down the aisle, her skirt caught on a nail.

_____ 9. While doing the daily chores, a fire started in the farmer's barn.

_____ 10. Handing me the $50,000 order, his face broke into a broad smile.

_____ 11. Having produced a printout, the text was stored on the system.

_____ 12. While riding the bike down the street, the dog chased me.

_____ 13. Thinking about a bunch of new toys, Christmas was the only thing on the child's mind.

_____ 14. Upon landing in Dallas, his assistant picked him up at the airport.

_____ 15. Hoping to find a good communicator, employers often interview dozens of job candidates.

_____ 16. When looking up a word in the dictionary, notice its pronunciation as well as definitions.

_____ 17. Being in dilapidated condition, she bought the building cheaply.

_____ 18. If invited to dinner at a colleague's home, chocolates or flowers are a suitable gift for the hosts.

_____ 19. If you decide to give flowers, avoid white lilies as they suggest death.

_____ 20. To be a serious student of business, you should understand advertising, promotion, and marketing.

_____ 21. Confused by crowds rushing around the campus, a new student welcomes a familiar face with a sigh of relief.

_____ 22. After standing and repeating the pledge, the meeting began.

_____ 23. While walking home, a hundred dollar bill suddenly appeared before me.

_____ 24. While I was walking home, a hundred dollar bill suddenly appeared before me.

_____ 25. It began to rain after being on vacation for two hours, and it didn't stop for two weeks.

C. Rewrite these sentences so that the verbals are no longer dangling.

1. Being one of our most discriminating customers, we invite you to attend this private showing.

   _____
   _____

2. Turning the corner, the new building was right in front of him.

   _____

3. While using the computer, the cursor became stuck in the middle of the screen.

   _____
   _____

4. Unlike many high-tech millionaires in the 1990s, her talents in fine art and classical music resulted in her financial success.

   _____
   _____

5. Before having dinner with the woman he met through Ultimate Encounters Online, his table manners need improvement.

   _____
   _____

CHECK YOUR ANSWERS ON PAGE 468.

POSTTEST

Write the appropriate letter and number in the blank according to these instructions:

A Properly constructed sentence
B (1) Fragment or (2) Unclear pronoun
C (1) Run-on or (2) Comma splice
D (1) Lacks parallel parts (2) Has too many short, simple sentences (3) Has a dangling verbal
E (1) Misplaced words or (2) Gobbledygook

_____   1. Marianne is smart. She likes to study. She also likes her job.

_____   2. The new drug has proved to be highly effective it has no side effects.

_____   3. Mara overheard Beth talking to her boyfriend on the phone.

_____   4. He is an extremely capable worker, however, he lacks seniority.

_____   5. Annie told Caterina that she had a flat tire.

_____   6. Managers tend to promote people who can make decisions even at the risk of being wrong.

_____   7. He is very much interested in science, which he acquired from his cousin who is a chemist.

_____   8. Working accurately is more important than to work fast.

_____   9. The bank approves loans to reliable individuals of any size.

_____ 10. This is a beautiful sentiment from *The Diary of Anne Frank:* "Think of all the beauty still left in and around you, and be happy."

CHECK YOUR ANSWERS ON PAGE 469.

Self-Study and Practice Tutorials

wordPOWER

Build your workplace vocabulary and improve spelling skills by completing the exercises in Appendix B on page 382.

Supplementary Practice Exercises

For additional practice, complete the Appendix C exercises for this chapter on page 423.

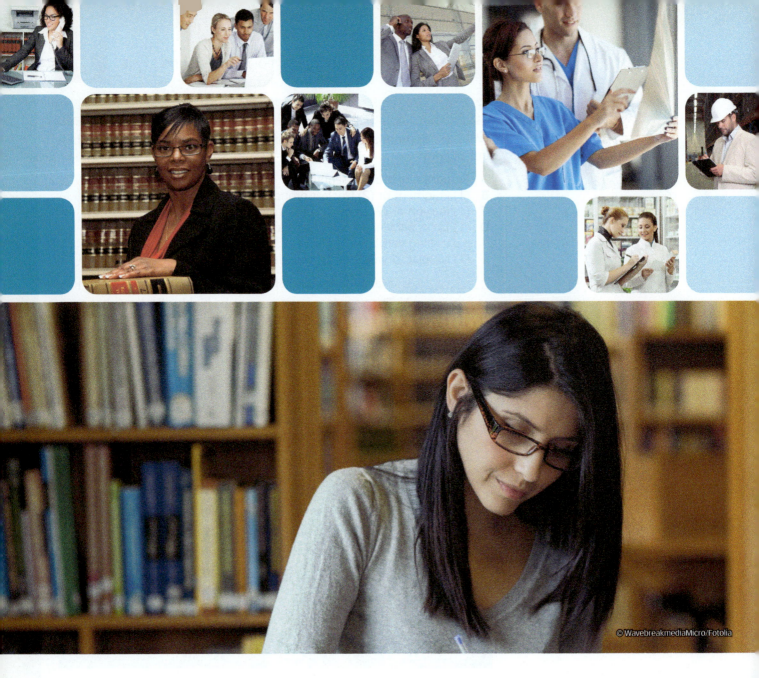

© WavebreakmediaMicro/Fotolia

After completing Chapter 15, you will be able to do the following:

- Correctly capitalize proper nouns.
- Correctly use abbreviations in workplace communications.
- Correctly express numbers in workplace communications.
- Correctly apply the rules of capitalization, abbreviations, and numbers when editing and proofreading your writing.

15

Capitalization, Abbreviation, and Numbers

career connection

THE INTERVIEW – PREPARATION AND FOLLOW-UP

Before a job interview, make sure you have the basic information you need to be prepared, and plan to express your appreciation for the interviewer's time afterwards. Here are some tips for before and after:

- Get basic information: the name, position title, and phone number of the contact person. Ask for the street address, floor, and directions to the location, if needed. Be sure you understand whether you are having a prescreening interview with a human resources representative or an interview with the hiring manager.

- Use the job description to prepare the key points you want to get across to the interviewer about your qualifications and skills.

- Be ready to answer typical interview questions by giving examples of your successes in handling specific situations at work or at school. Talking about yourself in specifics is a great way to get across your abstract qualities such as honesty, good judgment, teamwork, and initiative.

- Research the company in advance. Get a sense of its business philosophy, size, products, and services. Armed with this information, you can prepare questions to ask at the interview.

- Print several copies of your resume and any other required documents and place them in a folder to take with you. Also be sure to take a notebook and pen with you.

- Make sure you have a good sense of what the dress code is for the company. Wearing professional attire is always a safe bet.
- If you have any doubt about how to find the location of the interview, do a dry run to get a sense of how much time you need and avoid the possibility of getting lost on the way.
- During the interview, be sure to collect business cards or take note of names and position titles of the persons you talk to.
- Immediately after, follow up with thank-you emails or handwritten notes—both are not necessary, but either is appropriate. Expressing your appreciation and interest in the position can make a difference in the outcome.

PRETEST

Use proofreading marks to correct the capitalization, abbreviation, and number style errors in these sentences.

1. our english professor met reverend perez in this city last fall.

2. The team is trying to raise at least $1,000 dollars for new uniforms and equipment.

3. Did senator charles west from pennsylvania give a speech in northern maine?

4. to get to monroe college, go north on jerome avenue until you reach fordham road.

5. Rashid Ali PhD is the head of the arabic studies dept. at the University.

6. Please send me the brochures describing the east coast tours of Fall colors.

7. The trip to Denver, CO is planned for the spring.

8. Data indicates that 20% of total profits are earned in the 3rd quarter.

9. We are located at 1920 Tremont Ave., in the Bronx, NY.

10. I am writing to confirm your appointment for next Fri. at 2:30 p.m..

CHECK YOUR ANSWERS ON PAGE 469.

Capitalization Basics

Capitalization is one of three style points covered in this chapter to give you a well-rounded perspective on the details that must be perfect in business communications. As part of the editing and proofreading process, it is always wise to double-check capitalization as part of the routine when you check spelling.

NAMES OF PEOPLE

Names are often accompanied by other information about the person. This section provides the rules for these situations.

Professional and Official Titles

Capitalize a title that directly precedes a person's name.

> **Professor** Washington is my advisor.
>
> **Reverend** Juan Perez will give the invocation at the conference luncheon.

Do not capitalize the title if a comma separates it from the name.

> Our English **professor**, Dolores Denova, is an excellent instructor.
>
> The **captain**, Patrick O'Connor, will give a lecture on his historic maps.

Do not capitalize professional titles when used generally; do capitalize them when they identify a person's job title directly after the name.

> My **accountant** is David Rosenbaum, and I would recommend him enthusiastically.
>
> Joy Reid, **Manager of Production**, has been with the company for 20 years.

Capitalize an official title used directly before a person's name or used in direct address instead of the name. **Direct address** means you call a person by name or title in speech or writing.

Before the name	Did you know that **President** Jimmy Carter owned a peanut farm?
	A letter of recommendation was received from **Judge** Mary Genovese.
Direct address	We hope, **President Najeem**, that you will like this gift.

Generally, do not capitalize an official title when it is used as a general term of description.

> Maynard Jackson was elected **mayor** of Atlanta, Georgia, in 1973.

BUT   **Mayor** Michael Bloomberg of New York City served two terms and then was reelected for a third term.

> The **colonel**, Rachel Rothstein, is a West Point graduate.

No capital is used for *colonel* because a comma separates it from the name.

BUT   **Colonel** Rachel Rothstein graduated at the top of her West Point class.

Capitalize titles written after the name as part of the person's official identification.

The keynote speech will be delivered by Dr. Eugene Gilmore, **Director of Student Affairs**, University of Michigan.

Capitalize titles at the end of a letter:

> Sincerely yours,
>
> Rosalyn Amaro
> Vice President
> Human Resources Department

Educational Degrees

Educational degrees are usually abbreviated (see the "Abbreviations" section of this chapter). However, when they are spelled out, they should be capitalized when written directly after a person's name as part of his or her identification. Do not capitalize a spelled-out degree unless it immediately follows the person's name. Notice the comma before and after the degree following a name.

> Indi Chandra, **PhD**, specializes in management of nonprofit organizations.
>
> Jonathan Waller has a **master of arts** degree in speech pathology.
>
> Nina Chandra's **BS** is in animal husbandry.
>
> With an associate's level degree such as an **AA** or **AS**, you can qualify for many good jobs.
>
> Shirley J. Corley, **Doctor of Jurisprudence**, is the newest State Supreme Court judge.

Family Relationship Titles

Capitalize a family relationship title when used as part of the name or instead of the name.

> Do you think **Uncle George** will retire soon?
>
> Please tell **Grandmother** to give me a call.
>
> I attended **Aunt Jane's** 40th birthday party at the Town Club.

Do not capitalize general references to family titles.

> My **mother** teaches at the university.
>
> I believe my **cousin** Esther should apply for the job.
>
> I asked my **uncle** about the old days.
>
> My cousin Billy's **wife**, Janice, is an accountant.

GROUPS OF PEOPLE

Nationalities, Religions, and Languages

Capitalize names of nationalities and religions.

Dutch	Korean	British	English	French	Chinese
Catholic	Hindu	Jewish	Islam	Buddhism	Christianity

Racial and Ethnic Terms

Races named by color begin with lowercase letters, but sociological names of races and ethnic groups are capitalized.

white/Caucasian	black/African American
Latino/Hispanic	Asian American

TITLES OF PUBLICATIONS AND ARTISTIC WORKS

Capitalize the first word and all principal words of titles of books, films, plays, songs, and other artistic works.

> Chapter 8 is entitled "The Taming of the Apostrophe."

Do not capitalize short prepositions (such as *in, on,* and *of*) or conjunctions (such as *and, but,* and *or*) within titles unless they are the first word of a title or subtitle. (Longer prepositions such as *unless, between, beneath* should be capitalized.) Do not capitalize articles (*a, an,* and *the*) unless they are the first word of a title or subtitle.

> I saw the movie *Gone with the Wind.*
>
> I'm reading *The Seven Habits of Highly Effective People* to gain insights into success strategies.
>
> The best-selling book that year was *To Kill a Mockingbird.*

wordPOWER

Do not capitalize the second element in compound words in titles unless the word is a proper noun.

NAMES OF ORGANIZATIONS

Capitalize names of organizations and specific government groups.

Supreme Court	Fullerton College
Palm Springs Tennis Club	Department of Motor Vehicles
Royal Canadian Air Force	Arkansas Paper Mill

Except in legal documents and formal communications, do not capitalize words like *company, department,* and *college* when they are not part of a name.

> Melissa and Steven attend Seattle court reporting **schools**.
>
> This **company** will not issue common stock this year, but the Knott Company will.
>
> Give the papers to the **committee** at the **college**.

Capitalize names of departments within organizations when the reference is specific, but do not capitalize general references.

Specific	Our **Shipping Department** packed the order and shipped it via FedEx.
	Please submit your benefits forms to the **Human Resources Department** on the 8th floor.
General	Do not send a resume to an employer's **human resources department** without addressing it to a specific individual.
	I am looking for a position in the marketing or sales department of a large company.

NAMES OF LOCATIONS

Capitalize official names of specific places but do not capitalize general terms.

> We're going to the **city** of **Charleston** for the weekend.
>
> Our office is on **Victory Boulevard**.
>
> Our house is the first street after the main **boulevard**.
>
> Our summer house is in **Maine** on a beautiful stretch of the **Atlantic Ocean**.
>
> **North America** lies between two **oceans**.
>
> **Yosemite National Park** is a great place for a family vacation.
>
> We vacationed in a **national park** last year.

Regional Names

Capitalize regional names when they refer to specific geographical regions. Do not capitalize such terms when they are used to indicate general locations.

> Far East   West Coast   Midwest
>
> The sun sets in the **west**.
>
> Drive **south** along Main Street.
>
> He would like to settle in **Southern** California. [names a specific region]

Capitalize derivatives of regional names referring to people.

> I believe **Northerners** usually appreciate **Southern** hospitality.

Location Names

Capitalize words such as *town, city, state*, and *county* when they are part of the official name or if a governing body uses the geographic term officially; otherwise, do not capitalize them.

> New York State   Kansas City
>
> Mayor Jorgensen said the **City of Mayfield** is requesting bids for the new town hall.
>
> The **state** of Iowa is a great place to live, so we moved to Sioux City.
>
> The newspaper said the **city** budget is running high deficits.

CALENDAR DATES AND SEASONS

Capitalize days, months, and names of holidays; do not capitalize the names of seasons.

> The office will close for a week this summer from **Monday, June** 1, until **Friday, June** 5.
>
> Our **fall** sale begins right after **Labor Day**.
>
> We are planning to hire part-time workers during the **December holiday season**.

Capitalize names of historical periods; do not capitalize contemporary periods or the names of decades and centuries.

> The **twenty-first century** is only a decade old, yet the **millennium** celebrations seem like ancient history.
>
> The **Industrial Age** was a time when many new machines were invented.
>
> We grew up in the **information age**, which evolved into the **digital age** in which all kinds of media are a constant presence in our lives.

GO TO PAGE 335 AND COMPLETE WORKSHEET 15.1.

Abbreviations

Abbreviations are shortened forms of words and proper names. Generally avoid abbreviations in workplace communications, such as emails, letters, and reports. Spelling words out instead of abbreviating them helps create an image of thoroughness and accuracy. Common business abbreviations are appropriate (see page 330), however, and abbreviations may be used in informal communications and in documents such as forms, invoices, and technical reports.

COMPANY NAMES

writing**TIP**

If you question whether it is appropriate to use an abbreviation in a written document, remember the old adage of editors: When in doubt, spell it out.

Abbreviations of business organizations and other entities are usually based on the initials of the official name. When an abbreviation is pronounced as a word, for example, UNICEF (United Nations Children's Fund), it is called an **acronym**.

Spell out an organization's name the first time it is used and follow it with the abbreviation in parentheses. Thereafter in the same document, use just the abbreviation or acronym.

> The anticipated merger with **West Coast Information Systems (WCIS)** is progressing according to the planned schedule. **WCIS** has conducted its review of our financial statements, and a meeting is scheduled for July 29 to review its findings.

Note that this rule does not apply to an organization that uses only the acronym as its official name. In this case, use only the abbreviation. When in doubt, check the organization's website.

AT&T   CIA   FBI   AFL-CIO   CBS   NAACP

Abbreviate parts of company names when they appear in the official spelling.

writing**TIP**

In general, company names should always be written exactly as the company spells it on official documents, websites, and so on. When in doubt, always check. Getting names correct is a fundamental requirement in business communication.

Inc.   Co.   LLC

Marco's Painting Co.

Turner Broadcasting Systems, Inc.

PERSONAL AND ACADEMIC TITLES

Always abbreviate personal titles (Mr., Ms., Dr.) in front of names and academic degrees or designations following names. Separate the name and the abbreviation following the name with a comma.

> Mr.   Ms.   Dr.   Esq.   PhD   CPA   MD
>
> Jacqueline Ross, PhD
>
> Ronald Rosenberg, Esq.
>
> Ms. Sara Waller
>
> Dr. Spencer Blackman

Do not use both a personal title and an academic title together.

> Dr. Lynn Otero   or   Lynn Otero, MD

Abbreviate birth order designations (Jr. and Sr.); do not use a comma in front. The designations II and III are not abbreviations and do not require any punctuation.

> Carlton Thomas Jr.
>
> Carlton Thomas III

Spell out professional, military, and religious titles in written text.

> The Reverend Jonathan Flaherty was given the "Humanitarian of the Year" award.
>
> Captain Jeffrey Ortiz recently deployed to active duty in Afghanistan.
>
> Professor Mildred Murphy might be able to help you get the interview.

LOCATIONS

Spell out the names of geographic locations—parts of addresses, cities, counties, states, and regions—within the body of business communications.

> The subway construction on **Second Avenue** will continue for several years.
>
> Please do not send any packages to our **Jefferson Street** office after 4 p.m.
>
> Please send a copy of the contract to Mr. Peter Yu, Yu & Sons Construction, 1605 Abbott **Avenue, Des Moines, Iowa 50309**.

In the inside address of letters, it is optional to spell out or abbreviate parts of addresses.

> Street/St.   Avenue/Ave.   Boulevard/Blvd.

It is also optional in addresses to spell out or abbreviate parts of addresses.

Floor/Fl.   Suite/Ste.   Apartment is always abbreviated: Apt.

Word**POWER**

In the United States, *Esq.* (Esquire) is used only after an attorney's name—either male or female. In Great Britain, however, *Esq.* is a courtesy title equivalent to *Mr.* but is used *after* a man's name regardless of occupation.

writing**TIP**

In workplace writing, it is customary to use *Mr.* or *Ms.* or omit the personal title altogether.

In written text, spell out the above abbreviations.

> Please deliver the computers to Conference **Room** 304 for tomorrow's meeting.
>
> Our office is located at 204 E. Main Street, **Suite** 220.

On envelopes, use the two-letter state abbreviations. See your reference manual for a complete list of state abbreviations.

> Connecticut/CT   New York/NY   Michigan/MI

PERIODS AND COMMAS WITH ABBREVIATIONS

Periods

- Most common abbreviations do not require periods. This rule covers abbreviations, such as US for United States; academic titles, such as MA and PhD; and measurements, such as ft and lbs.
- Common abbreviations that *do* require a period include personal titles (Mr. and Ms.) and lower-case abbreviations, such as a.m. and p.m., etc., and e.g.
- Never use two periods when an abbreviation that ends in a period falls at the end of a sentence. This rule applies only to the period. Other sentence-ending punctuation—a question mark or exclamation point—should be used.

Commas

- Use commas to enclose the abbreviation of a college or professional degree that follows a name. Do not use periods in these abbreviations.

    > Millie S. Perry, PhD, and Brad Rosenberg, MD, will be the speakers at the convention in Visalia, Montana.

- Do not use a comma to separate a name from a birth order designation, such as Jr., Sr., II, and III (unless the person writes it that way).

    > Charles Davis Jr.
    >
    > Charles Davis III

- If a company name is followed by a designation that indicates the type of entity it is, such as Inc. or Ltd., do not set off this designation with a comma, unless the company writes it that way.

    > W. H. Jones Engineering Inc.
    >
    > Power Resources LL

DATES AND PERIODS OF TIME

Do not abbreviate names of days and months in the inside address of letters or in the body of business communications.

> The annual conference will take place in Orlando, Florida, **October 5–7**.
>
> Daily sessions will be held **Sunday**, from 1 to 5 p.m., and **Monday and Tuesday** from 8:30 a.m. to 5 p.m.
>
> Each speaker will have 45 **minutes** for presentation and 15 **minutes** for Q&A.
>
> The formal dinner will recognize VIPs and employees with 5, 10, and 15 **years** of service.

COMMONLY USED BUSINESS ABBREVIATIONS AND ACRONYMS

These abbreviations are acceptable in most workplace documents. Many are written with or without periods. The trend is to omit periods. Some of the following are acceptable in capital or lowercase, such as fax or FAX (facsimile).

APR	annual percentage rate
ASAP	as soon as possible
Attn:	attention
BTW or btw (email only)	by the way
CEO	chief executive officer
CFO	chief financial officer
CIO	chief information officer
COO	chief operating officer
COB	close of business
COD	collect, or cash, on delivery
EEO	equal employment opportunity
etc.	and so on (preferred)
Ext., ext., or ex.	when followed by a number for a telephone extension (ext. 32)
FAQ	frequently asked questions
FAX	facsimile
GDP	gross domestic product
HR	human resources
ID	identification
Inc., Corp., or Ltd	when part of a company name (incorporated, corporation, or limited)
IPO	initial public offering
LAN	local area network
PR	public relations
Q&A	question and answer
VIP	very important person

MEASUREMENTS

Write abbreviations of units of measure in lowercase letters with no periods.

pound/pounds	lb/lbs
foot/feet	ft
ounce/ounces	oz

In the body of communications, spell out units of measure when references are few; abbreviations may be used in text that is heavily devoted to a subject requiring such terms.

GO TO PAGE 336 AND COMPLETE WORKSHEET 15.2.

Numbers

Numbers are important to business, professional, and technical writing. Write them in figures on invoices, orders, requisitions, statistical documents, and tables within written documents. The following information—a consensus of the style used by most business writers—enables you to decide whether to spell out a number or use figures in emails, memos, letters, reports, and other workplace documents.

GENERAL RULES FOR EXPRESSING NUMBERS

- Spell out numbers for zero through ten; use figures for exact numbers over 10. If numbers under 10 and over 10 are used together, use figures for all.

  We need **five** computer engineers in our Akron office.

  We need **5** computer engineers, **25** clerks, and **30** assemblers in our Cleveland office.

- Spell out or use figures for approximate numbers that can be written in one or two words.

  Nearly **5,000** employees were laid off last year due to downsizing.

  We have hired over **two hundred** new employees this year.

- Use figures for rounded numbers of more than one or two words.

  We estimate that more than 250,000 people per month will visit our website.

- When a number begins a sentence, spell it out if you can do so in one or two words. If more than two words are required, rephrase the sentence.

  Six hundred crates were shipped to you yesterday.

  Yesterday **642** crates were shipped to you.

- To express millions or billions, combine figures with words to make reading easier.

  We produced **1.5 million** electric fans last year.

  Our gross profit last year was **$66 million**. [Do not add the word *dollars*.]

- When two numbers appear together, spell out the number that can be written with fewer letters.

  Lloyd designed **twenty 16**-unit apartment buildings.

  Frank designed **110 sixteen**-unit apartment buildings.

TIME

Use figures with *a.m.* and *p.m.* Use figures or words before *o'clock, morning, afternoon,* and similar words. Type *a.m.* and *p.m.* in lowercase letters, with no space after the first period. For time on the hour, omit the colon and zeros.

Yes	The teleconference will take place from **9 a.m.** through **5:30 p.m.**
	We should be there at **9 o'clock** in the evening.
No	nine p.m.
	9:00 p.m.

Use just one way to express time; avoid redundancy.

Yes	9 a.m.
	9 in the morning
	nine o'clock in the morning
No	9 a.m. in the morning

DATES

Use figures if the date follows the name of the month; do not use *th, nd, rd,* or *st* after the figure.

> The American Bankers Association will meet here again on **May 7, 2014**.

In military, international, and some government correspondence, write the date before the month; do not use a comma in this date style.

> The International Bankers Association will meet in Oslo on **7 May 2014**.

Use words or figures for centuries and decades.

> This book is about **nineteenth-century** poets.

In this sentence, *19th-century poets* is also correct.

Do not use an apostrophe when referring to a period of years in numbers.

> The 1990s (not 1990's)

MONEY

Use figures for amounts of money. The decimal point is unnecessary with even dollar amounts (no cents).

> Eduardo paid **$500** to join and **$25.50** a month to exercise at the gym.
>
> They need about **$150,000** to remodel the gym.

Use a dollar sign and decimal point for cents to be consistent with other amounts used in the same context. If other amounts are not involved, use figures for the number but spell out the word *cents*.

> We sold **1,000** cookies at **$.25** each, **42** pies at **$7.80** each, and two big cakes at **$50** each.
>
> The plugs cost **8 cents** each.

In legal documents, amounts are often spelled and then written in figures enclosed in parentheses. In ordinary correspondence, do not repeat numbers in this legal style.

> The fee for use of said property is to be **Two Hundred and Fifty Dollars ($250.00)** a month.

BUT

> We paid **$250** for those tickets.

ADDRESSES

For numbered street names, follow the exact style as written by the correspondent or municipality.

> The store is on **Sixth Street**.
>
> Professor Maxey of Oroville moved to **11th Avenue** in Newport.

Use figures for address numbers except *One.*

> Their new suite of offices is at **One Lake Street**.
>
> The Atlanta factory is at **8 Leland Avenue**.

PERCENTAGES AND FRACTIONS

In written text spell out the word *percent* but use figures for the number. Use the % sign in statistical and technical documents and in tables.

The unemployment rate was **5 percent** that year.

Spell out a common fraction or mixed number (fraction and whole number) when it is the only one in the sentence.

Our profits are **four and a half** times those of last year.

We have received only **one-fourth** of our order.

Use figures for less common fractions or when several fractions are in a sentence.

The specifications for the blue widgets are **3/8** of an inch and for the purple widgets, **4/5** of an inch.

MEASUREMENTS

Express fractions in measurements as numerals or decimals; be consistent in each document.

Please purchase **5 1/2** more yards of fabric. [or 5.5]

In business letters and reports, spell out measuring words, such as *feet*, *pounds*, and *inches*; use figures for the numbers.

The boards are **5 by 6 by 2 inches.** [Use *by*, not *x*.]

Each one weighs **6 pounds 4 ounces** and is **8 feet** long.

When abbreviations for measurements are used, do not end them with a period.

lbs   ft   yds

BOOKS

Use figures for numbers of pages, chapters, volumes, and so on.

The information you need is on **page 202** in **Chapter 5.**

COMMAS IN NUMBERS

- The comma is optional in four-digit numbers, but recommended for clarity. Commas are required in numbers of more than four digits.

  10,000   1,000,000   2,000 or 2000

- When four-digit numbers are listed along with numbers in the ten thousands and higher, use the comma in all of them for consistency.

  Sales figures for the past three years were **5,000** in the first year, **7,900** in the second year, and **10,200** in the third year.

- Do not use commas in numbers that "identify," such as addresses, serial numbers, page numbers, and so on.

  page 1247   19721 Victory Boulevard   No. 23890

GO TO PAGE 337 AND COMPLETE WORKSHEET 15.3.

Checkpoint

Attention to the rules of capitalization, abbreviation, and number expressions is an important part of the writing process. The proofreading stage is the point to check names, numbers, and all the style and usage points covered in this chapter. The process of rechecking often involves more than applying the rules correctly; for example, you might need to check source materials against your document for accuracy. A number that is expressed correctly but mistyped is an egregious error. Many of the rules you learned here are already a part of your usage vocabulary; others you will need to review and rely on more extensive coverage in your reference manual.

communications connection

DEVELOPING PRESENTATION SLIDES

Continue the work you began in Chapter 14 by developing a slide show to supplement your presentation. PowerPoint is the slide presentation software program used in most work settings. If you have access to this software, use it or any other similar program. However, you do not need to have the software to prepare the text for presentation slides. You can create boxes and insert text using your word processing program.

If you are using a software program, you can take advantage of predesigned templates.

Use Slides to Supplement Your Words

Audiences expect slides to provide short bites of information that are augmented by the speaker. Therefore, the text you put on slides should hit key points—it should not be a script for your oral presentation. Your script should be typed in large type on white paper or written on note cards if you feel comfortable speaking from memory while looking at notes as a guide. Avoid reading a presentation word for word from a script. Looking down at a written speech makes it extremely hard to achieve a high level of audience rapport. It is important to look at your audience, speak in a natural tone and rhythm, and work to make a connection with your listener. With practice, you will be able to speak without relying on reading.

You can outline your presentation on the slide template or make notes on paper. This will help you decide what you are going to say and what points you want to highlight on the slides. The key is to use as few words as possible on the screen—you don't want to overload your audience or encourage them to read the slides at the expense of listening to you. You might also opt to create a storyboard.

A storyboard is a method of writing in two columns, one for graphics and one for the points about each image, as shown in the following example:

	Script Notes	Slide Text
Slide 1	• Develop a fitness plan that fits your needs and interests. • Make it enjoyable and part of your lifestyle. • Don't use exercise as a quick fix.	IMPORTANT CONSIDERATIONS • Have you been active or sedentary? • What activities do you like? • What is your fitness level?

This is an excellent way to avoid having the slide show become a "script" of your spoken message. Notice in the example how the points to be covered in the "script" column relate to the questions on the slide, but they do not duplicate each other.

The speaker will discuss the three general points and augment each point with a question that personalizes the content for the audience. The speaker can opt to have the questions "build" on the slide, that is, appear one after the other on the same slide. Another option would be to put each question on a different slide with images.

A rule of thumb for the amount of text per slide is one key point for each line of text, not more than six to eight words per line, and no more than six lines per slide.

Use Color and Design Skillfully

Slide presentation templates provide predesigned background color combinations and attractive graphics. Unless you are a design "wizard" yourself, rely on these to make an attractive presentation. Select type colors that provide sharp contrast for reading and that are appropriately conservative or "jazzy," depending on the purpose of your presentation and the audience's expectations. Use visual aids that include images such as photographs or clip art that are appropriate for the audience and subject matter. Do not use images for purely decorative or entertainment purposes in a business setting.

Select a type font and background and use them for all of the slides. Some variations in format (color and size of type) can be used for titles, but consistency is important for visual attention and understanding. For example, if you are using a headline at the top and bullet points, don't switch to paragraphs with no headline.

- Follow the rule of parallel structure for items listed in a series.
- Avoid using all-capital letters for emphasis; instead, use a larger or different style font.
- Avoid fancy fonts that are hard to read.
- Limit lines of text on each slide to no more than six to eight, depending on the size of the font you are using.
- Print the slides and proofread them for spelling, consistency, style, language usage, punctuation, and capitalization.

WRITING AND SPEAKING PRACTICE

Using the example of how to prepare a storyboard, prepare slides to supplement the five-minute presentation you developed based on your career exploration interview. Prepare your storyboard at the computer or use pen and paper. Draft, edit, and revise the text that will appear on slides, making sure the length is within the guidelines suggested in this chapter. Practice speaking from your script, which may be in the form of notes or sentences. Time your presentation and be ready to share it with your class at your instructor's request.

Date to submit this assignment: _____

PROOFREADING PRACTICE

Correct the following email using proofreading symbols or go online to correct the document electronically.

Dear mr. Arroyo:

This is to follow up on our discussion about the event for our Jackie Thompson's new book, "the Perfect Dinner Party." All of us at BBP are so excited about holding the launch just in time for the Holidays. As discussed, we would like to schedule the party for December 21st, at the Yale Club—the authors Alma Mater where she earned a Ph.D in film—located on Vanderbilt Ave across from grand central terminal. As Best Book Publishing is a new Company we hope Miss Thompson's book will be a bestseller and that this event can help us improve our Branding in the NY publishing world.

Just a little history about BBP We opened our doors 2 years ago on July 1st. As I'm sure you know on a Summer weekend on the east coast the publishing movers-and-shakers had taken off for the Beaches. We gave a party at a supporters home in the hamptons on Long Island, but we were one of dozens of places to go that weekend, and attendance was sparse. We have not given a party since therefore the launch of PDP is our chance to hit the bigtime. 200 guests are the minimum we want to attract. If you can brign in more, we'll spend up to 25 thousand dollars on this important exciting event.

As we discussed, we are open to either the 21st or the twenty-second of Dec. The book will be in bookstores by 12/19 and Jackie's book tour starts in Philadelphia, Pa on Dec. 24.

Can you call to give me an update by November 1st? The best time to catch me is in the before 9 a.m..

Sincerely,

Jeannette Kraft
Marketing Manager

How did you do? Excellent _____ Good _____

Need More Practice _____

chapter review

WORKSHEET 15.1

Use proofreading marks to correct capitalization in the following sentences.

Example: susan is an occupational therapist in new york state.

1. chairman O'Reilly flew via united airlines to uganda on veteran's day.

2. world war II preceded the era known as the fabulous fifties.

3. my uncle was the first to do accounts payable auditing for department stores.

4. if you speak german and have a master's degree, you might qualify for that job.

5. although she has a bs and an ma degree, she does not have a doctorate.

6. The salutation is "dear credit manager"; the complimentary close is "sincerely."

7. the atomic age began on August 5, 1945, when the atomic bomb was dropped on the city of hiroshima.

8. we flew on american airlines last summer with the president of israel and the senator from south Dakota.

9. winston churchill wrote *triumph and tragedy*, an important book about world war II.

10. the judge said that the supreme court decision was favorable to my company.

11. i will know chinese well enough by september to take a university course in chinese literature.

12. the atlantic ocean beaches make the east coast one of the most scenic regions of the united states.

13. Let me know if you would like to plan your visit for the summer or fall; both are beautiful in new England.

14. Dr. lalitha, a hindu woman from the south of india, received her md from an American university.

15. the salutation of the letter is "dear customer," and the complimentary close is "sincerely yours."

Use proofreader's marks to change capitalization as needed in these sentences.

16. If the Sales Manager calls, please ask her to send me the report immediately.

17. Jose Rodriguez, General Manager of Horizon apartments, would like to speak before the city Council at its Monthly Session.

18. Our Department plans to hire a General Manager to oversee the Accounting and Auditing departments of the Company.

19. We drove East last Summer until we reached Kansas city.

20. I believe governor Shawn A. Taylor is the person best suited to run for the senate as an independent in the next General Election.

CHECK YOUR ANSWERS ON PAGE 469.

WORKSHEET 15.2

Circle the correct form—the spelled-out word or abbreviation—in parentheses.

1. Our regional office in Boston, (MA/Massachusetts) is not far from Harvard University where I earned my (master's/Master's) degree.

2. Each member of the Accounting (Dept./Department) is getting an extra (week/wk) vacation as a bonus.

3. After receiving her (bachelor's/ Bachelor's) degree in criminal justice, Michele moved to Tom's River, (NJ/ New Jersey).

4. Everyone in the (dept./ department) has to attend the meeting in the (NY, New York) office.

5. Please contact the owner, (David Wallace, III/David Wallace III), and let him know that we are interested in bidding on the construction contract.

6. Our office is moving from (Parkhurst Ave./Parkhurst Avenue) because our new (Chief Operating Officer/COO) owns the (building/bldg.)

7. We will be closed (Fri./Friday and Sat./Saturday) for inventory, but you can mail your application to us at 201 Willow (Blvd./Boulevard, Ste./Suite) 11E, West Palm Beach, (FL, Florida) 33401.

8. Before writing for information, I suggest you review our (Frequently Asked Questions/FAQs) on the company website.

9. (Carol Quinones, MD/Dr. Carol Quinones, MD) teaches in the medical department at (UCLA/the University of California, Los Angeles (UCLA)).

10. Refer to (page 5, p. 5) for charts showing the (no./number) of students who have a 4.0 (GPA/grade point average).

11. The police chief is planning to promote (Cpt. Loretta Barker/Captain Loretta Barker) in (Sept./September).

12. (Edward Brown, Ph.D,/Edward Brown PhD/Edward Brown, PhD,) has a brother in the legal profession named (Bill Brown, III/Bill Brown III).

13. Please arrange to arrive at my office about 30 (mins./minutes) before the meeting, which starts at (8:30 a.m./8:30 a.m..)

14. According to (Internal Revenue Service (IRS)/IRS) regulations, income tax forms must be signed by the person hired to prepare them.

15. The position was offered to (Prof. Robinson/Professor Robinson), but he isn't sure he wants to leave (NYC/New York City).

16. We will need six limousines to move the (very important persons/ VIPS/VIPs) from the reception to the main event.

17. (OSHA/The Occupational Safety and Health Administration (OSHA)) does not set limits on how many (lbs/pounds) of weight an employee should be asked to lift.

18. You can reach the (CFO/Chief Financial Officer) on (ext. 0702/extension 0702) before noon.

19. Would it be possible for you to send the document by (FAX/FACS) before 4 p.m. on (Mon./Monday)?

20. The (U.S. Foreign Service/US Foreign Service) offers exciting career opportunities.

CHECK YOUR ANSWERS ON PAGE 470.

WORKSHEET 15.3

Circle the correct form of the two number styles in parentheses.

1. If you look on (page 5, page five), you will find the chart that summarizes the questionnaire answers.

2. The budget will be reduced by at least 25 to 30 (%, percent) by the end of the (3rd, third) quarter.

3. The office space will not be ready until October (first, 1).

4. Because of the recession, our sales revenues have declined dramatically; therefore, as of (July 15, July 15th) all sales representatives will experience a 15 (%, percent) decrease in their annual sales bonuses.

5. We will need about (12, twelve) additional chairs in the conference room.

6. (July 26, July 26th) is my last day in the office before leaving on vacation.

7. This meeting will give us an opportunity to discuss points (#3 and 4, #3 and #4) of my proposal.

8. (21, Twenty-one) is the customary age for being served alcohol, and (16, sixteen) is customary for driving.

9. The company needs to increase production by (two and a half times, 2½ times) the current output in order to break even next year.

10. We invested ($20,000/$20,000 dollars) in the franchise, and it was well worth it.

11. We purchased (5, five) different varieties of flowers.

12. (One hundred twenty/120) people have applied for the position.

13. My technology stocks increased (15 percent, 15%) in the last year.

14. We must receive a reply to our offer within the next (thirty, 30) days, or it will be withdrawn.

15. Please revise the description of item (#3, number 3) to make it clearer.

16. If you cannot supply the full amount, would it be possible to send (one-half/1/2) of the order this week?

17. The room would look best with small (8- by 10-foot/8 × 10-foot) rugs in a bright color.

18. Look on (page five/page 5) of the annual report for the budget figures.

19. The technology bubble of the (1990s/1990's) came as a surprise to some very sophisticated economists.

20. The weight limit is (fifty/50) (lbs/pounds).

CHECK YOUR ANSWERS ON PAGE 470.

POSTTEST

1. Please pay the ($35/$35.00) fee for the luncheon by (Fri./Friday), Feb./February) (first/1ˢᵗ/1).

2. The (NAACP/National Association for the Advancement of Colored People (NAACP)) is the oldest (civil rights/Civil Rights) organization in the country.

3. The population of the (US/U.S. United States) is over (300 million/ 300,000,000).

4. The Company is worth close to (two hundred fifty thousand, $250,000).

5. We must leave no later than (four p.m., 4 p.m.) to get to (O'Hare airport/O'Hare Airport) on time.

6. The address is (18626 Anglin/18,626 Anglin) right off Seven Mile Road in Detroit, (MI, Michigan).

7. The meeting will begin promptly at (4 pm/4 p.m.) in Conference (Rm./Room) 1038.

8. We are planning a tour of a(n) (LA, Los Angeles) film studio for ($25/$25.00) per person.

9. Please prepare a (four- or five-minute/4- or 5-minute) presentation about your history with the company.

10. I will collect questions from the audience for the (Q&A/FAQ) period at the end of the session.

CHECK YOUR ANSWERS ON PAGE 471.

Self-Study and Practice Tutorials

wordPOWER

Build your workplace vocabulary and improve spelling skills by completing the exercises in Appendix B on page 383.

Supplementary Practice Exercises

For additional practice, complete the Appendix C exercises for this chapter on page 427.

Writing for Career Success

recap—chapters 14 and 15

Test your mastery of Unit 5 by completing these exercises. Your instructor will provide the answer key or have you submit your work for scoring.

A. POLISHED WRITING STYLE

Number right: _____ **out of 20**

Combine these short, simple sentences into one smooth sentence.

1. Ellen went to business school. She majored in Computer Information Systems. _____
_____

2. Chris plays football. He is on the junior varsity team. _____

3. The shoe store at the mall had a sale. It was an end-of-summer sale. _____
_____

4. The hamburger was juicy. It was covered with onions. _____

5. The clock was ticking loudly. It gave Marissa a headache. _____
_____

Underline the misplaced words in the following sentences.

6. The student came to the school with no textbooks.

7. The rosebush was pruned by the gardener with the thorns.

8. Sally searched for her purse in the English classroom, which was misplaced this afternoon.

9. The parking lot was repaved by the contractor with the speed bumps.

10. My bike is in the garage with two flat tires.

Revise the following sentences to make the parts parallel.

11. Amanda is an attorney, spends time cooking, and she loves to ski.

_____

12. Laurie is an honor society member, a cheerleader, and sings in the school choral group.

_____

13. The play was entertaining, made us laugh, and was mysterious.

_____

14. The research specialist's talk was motivating and challenged us.

_____

15. You must write clearly and with conciseness as well as making sure you are accurate.

_____

Name: _____ **Date:** _____

Correct danglers in the following sentences and change passive voice to active.

16. Having taken too many sick days, the supervisor was forced to fire Ralph.

_____

17. Our company was outsold by the competition for three quarters straight.

_____

18. Biting quickly on the bait, the young fisherman caught his first fish.

_____

19. Torn around the edges, the teacher read from his old textbook.

_____

20. The session on setting performance goals was conducted by an expert on business psychology.

_____

B. CAPITALIZATION, ABBREVIATIONS, AND NUMBERS

Number right: _____ **out of 20**

Use proofreading marks to correct errors. Refer to your reference manual in addition to Chapter 15.

1. The national September 11 memorial is a tribute of remembrance and honor to the nearly three thousand people killed in the terrorist attacks at the world trade center site.

2. The communications department in my company recommends says *Sincerely Yours* (or *Sincerely*) is still frequently used in business letters.

3. To get to the Stadium for Friday's game, drive East on I-94 to the Brentwood exit and get off at Northern Blvd.

4. When you get to the 15th Fl., see the receptionist who will introduce you to Cpt. Feldman, the Bureau chief.

5. The Annual Board meeting on Dec. 1st in Downtown Chicago, Il. Will be the last one befor the New Year.

6. The CEO and all of the Company Officers will be in attendance.

7. They are flying to Chicago on the corporate jet, and the general manager of the Midwest regional office will meet them at O'Hare Airport.

8. Mr. Bryant, director of education, is planning to expand his chain of Business Schools in the south and southwest.

9. The cost of building new facilities will run approximately $10 million dollars, and will need the support of City zoning officials.

10. Norfolk, a large U.S. Navy port, is a great place to visit in the Summer.

11. We ordered 30 lbs. of prime rib for the reception honoring Prof. Louis Bennis, III, who won the National Book award for his bestseller, *the History of Academic Excellence in the United States.*

12. The graduate student will receive her MA in the Spring and hopes to begin work on her Doctorate in the fall.

13. Michael Bloomberg, mayor of NYC, created a controversy when he proposed eliminating large-size soft drinks, e.g., coke and other sugary beverages..

14. In the view of some new Yorkers, a visit to Yankee stadium and the amount of sixteen-oz. sugar drinks consumed is not the business of the City Government.

15. The retirement dinner for Paul Archer will take place on Friday evening, July 3, at 6 pm in the Fern room of the Garden court Hotel.

16. Turn your paper in to your Professor before the 10th of May in order to get credit and maintain your GPA.

17. The book, *Gone With the Wind,* is one of my favorites; I have read it at least 5 times.

18. My accountant advised me, "do not sell your stock at this time" do you think I made a mistake by ignoring his advice?

19. Jeremy Ross, Jr will arrive in Atlanta, GA on flight 225 at 7:30 pm.

20. We are excited to offer you the position of assistant manager, Accounts Receivable with a starting salary of $35 thousand dollars, and would like you to begin work on Oct. 1st.

Name: _____ Date: _____

writing and speaking for your career

DELIVERING YOUR PRESENTATION

After your script notes and visuals are prepared, leave them for a while and come back later for one final review. If possible, have someone review it with you. Ask yourself these questions:

- Does it flow in a clear, organized way?

- Is it accurate? (Your credibility is at stake.)

- If you are using slides, are spelling, grammar, and punctuation correct? Any inaccuracy reflects poorly upon the professionalism of your entire effort.

- Is it concise yet complete?

- Is the tone and level appropriate for the subject matter and audience—that is, formal versus informal, humorous versus serious, introductory versus advanced, objective versus persuasive?

- If information is from another source, did you credit the source? If not, you may have committed **plagiarism**, which is the unlawful use of copyrighted work. Always identify the title and author of your source.

Once you have completed your review, practice until you feel comfortable with your delivery. During the first round of practice, focus on fitting your content into the amount of time you have without rushing or leaving a void. Look for a balance of time and content that allows you to speak at a normal, conversational rate of speed and connect with your audience. If you tend to speak too fast, especially when you're nervous, practice deep breathing and slowing down.

Next, focus on practicing techniques for building rapport with your audience. If you are not going to be using a microphone, practice speaking clearly and loudly enough to be heard in the back of the room. Plan to make direct eye contact with as many listeners as possible, dress appropriately, have good posture, and vary your tone of voice and volume appropriately for the content. Above all, speak clearly, distinctly, and enthusiastically.

If you are using slides, it is important to be comfortable with the equipment and your position while speaking in relation to the screen on which they are projected. Whenever possible, preview the site of your presentation and do at least one run-through there. If the screen is behind you, be conscious of the need to always face your audience; do not turn around to view the slides—and never read from them.

Finally, decide whether it makes sense and whether you feel comfortable taking questions during your talk or at the end of your talk. If you worry that questions will make you run overtime or sidetrack your thinking, ask the audience to hold their questions until the end.

Finally, put it all together—practice your delivery, timing, and techniques until you feel ready to deliver your presentation. If you can practice in front of one or more people who are representative of your audience, so much the better.

writing and speaking for your career recap

A. **Deliver your presentation to your classmates at your instructor's request.**

B. **Write T (true) or F (false) in each blank.**

_____ 1. Use your slides as a script for your presentation.

_____ 2. Never begin a presentation with a joke; if your boss doesn't think it's funny, you'll probably get fired.

_____ 3. The most comfortable presenters are those who can speak extemporaneously—in other words, "just wing it."

_____ 4. Colorful slides with lots of pizzazz are not necessarily the best way to hold an audience's attention.

_____ 5. Don't waste paper and time preparing handouts before giving a presentation.

_____ 6. So that you'll sound natural and be more relaxed, practice your timing and techniques before making a presentation to your colleagues.

_____ 7. Avoid direct eye contact with your audience, as you might encourage them to start asking questions.

_____ 8. If you have a new idea for improving sales of your company's products, tell the audience about it in your conclusion.

_____ 9. Making a good presentation to supervisors and coworkers can improve your chances for promotion.

_____ 10. This is the hardest exercise in the whole course.

Name: _____ **Date:** _____

Appendix A

Writing, Editing, and Proofreading Guidelines

WRITING GUIDELINES

The Writing Process

Step 1: Plan

Goal: To think through what you want your document to say and do

✓ Identify your audience and its information needs.
✓ Identify your goals and purpose.
✓ Identify the scope of information to include in your document.
✓ Identify the format and medium for your document.

Step 2: Gather and Organize Information

Goal: To cover your topic logically and provide accurate information

✓ Decide what primary and secondary topics to include.
✓ Gather information and assess its accuracy and completeness.
✓ Organize information logically.

Step 3: Write

Goal: To create a first draft that achieves your purpose

✓ Develop main points in logical paragraphs with supporting ideas and details.
✓ Write to communicate concisely and clearly.
✓ Format information and parts of the document according to business standards.
✓ Use highlighting techniques—headings, boldface, bullets, numbering, and so on for ease of reading and visual appeal—where appropriate.

Step 4: Revise

Goal: To improve the content, writing style, structure, and format of your document

✓ Evaluate the overall content and organization; revise so that the order of information is clear and logical and content is focused; add or delete information as necessary.
✓ Evaluate the paragraphs; revise so that each is strong and organized in a coherent manner.
✓ Evaluate the sentences; revise so that important details are included, extraneous words are deleted, and emphasis is correct and logical. Correct sentence construction errors.

✓ Evaluate word usage; revise so that meaning is clear and concise and tone is appropriate for the audience. Correct grammar and usage errors.

✓ Evaluate wording of titles, headings, lists, and special features, such as captions or table titles, for parallel construction.

Step 5: Edit and Proofread

Goal: To eliminate errors in spelling, grammar, punctuation, and formatting

✓ Check for typographical or spelling errors.

✓ Check for words accidentally omitted or inserted during the revision process.

✓ Check for errors in grammar, punctuation, and capitalization.

✓ Check numbers, names, dates, and other data for accuracy and consistent expression.

✓ Check format and appearance of page layout, including margins, line spacing, titles, and headings.

✓ Check standard parts (as required for the type of document) for accuracy, completeness, and correct formatting.

EDITING GUIDELINES

Editing Paragraphs and Sentences

During Step 4 of the writing process, review each paragraph to look for ways to improve the details of the message. If your corrections are heavy, you might need to repeat this step more than once. Ask yourself these questions as you review your draft:

- Does the opening paragraph capture the reader's attention?
- Does it clearly state the purpose?
- Does it focus on the reader's point of view?
- Does each middle paragraph state a main point and develop it logically?
- Do paragraphs contain sentences that form a clear organizational structure and logical flow of ideas?
- Is the last paragraph a concise conclusion?
- Does it leave the reader with an understanding of how to respond?

Editing Grammar and Sentence Structure

Review each sentence critically and look for the following:

- Are sentences grammatically complete? Are there any run-on sentences, comma splices, or fragments?
- Are phrases and clauses arranged to emphasize the most important ideas? Would some ideas come across more effectively if they were moved to the beginning or the end of the sentence?
- Are modifying words, phrases, and clauses as close as possible to the sentence elements they modify?
- Are elements in series and listed items presented in parallel form?

- Is there variation in sentence length and structure?
- Are there places where sentences in succession all have the same structure?
- Are sentences too long or too short?
- Is the same rhythm repeated without variety, creating a monotonous tone?
- Are most sentences in the active voice?
- Is the passive voice used appropriately for emphasis?

Editing Words

Consider the language used and ask these questions:

- Does each word contribute to clarifying the message?
- Are there "wordy" phrases that could be more concise?
- Are words in the proper order? (Sometimes word order is inadvertently changed while revising.)
- Is word usage precise and appropriate?
- Does the choice of words fit the intended tone and degree of formality for the intended audience?
- Are pronoun references clear? Do you need to remove a pronoun and repeat the reference, provide a missing reference, or revise a sentence to avoid pronoun confusion?
- Are there any "big words" that should be replaced with more common terminology for clarity?
- Are there technical words, abbreviations, or business jargon that need definition to ensure the reader's understanding?
- Are there any negative words or phrases that could be changed to make the message sound more positive?
- Do any words reflect bias or other lack of consideration for the reader?

PROOFREADING GUIDELINES

Checking for Errors

A good technique for uncovering errors you missed in previous readings is to read each sentence out loud to yourself or with a partner. Taking time between readings—hours or even days if your deadline allows—will help you take a fresh look at your work.

- Are there any typographical or spelling errors or omitted words?
- Are there any errors in grammar, punctuation, capitalization, abbreviation, numbers, or word usage?

Checking Accuracy and Consistency

- Are figures, names, and numerical data correct and consistent?
- Is information such as dates and times correct?

Checking Format and Appearance

- Does the document have the standard elements required?
- Are the elements formatted correctly?
- Are spacing and margins correct and consistent?

Appendix B

Word Power: Vocabulary and Spelling

HOW TO USE THIS APPENDIX

This material is designed to give you "word power." After each chapter in the book, you should complete two vocabulary-building activities. It is worth taking the time to build an extensive business, professional, technical, and general vocabulary that will enhance your chances for future success. An extensive vocabulary pays off in job and social success as well as in managing personal affairs. Chances are your career and even your specific job might have its own specialized language that you have to learn, but no matter what career you choose, you will benefit from being familiar with the words defined here.

WORD POWER

Word Power lists the definitions of current business, professional, and technical terms from A to Z. In addition to the career applications of the words listed, you will find a vast number of terms that will help you make decisions about "real-life" matters, such as banking, investments, home ownership, insurance, attorneys' services, credit, and government. You will find it easier to understand information and advice about these matters when you have a command of the precise terminology.

For some of the words, not all definitions are provided. For example, look up *audit*. You'll find several definitions in your dictionary besides the one given here. The idea is to work your way through these word lists over time as you complete this course and then continue to increase your workplace vocabulary through reading business, financial, and technical news in print newspapers, print and online magazines, and Internet sources of news, business, financial, and technical information.

After reviewing the Word Power list, go to the Word Power Play and complete the matching exercise from memory. Have fun with it—use the process of elimination and test your ability to retain information. Then check your answers and review the definitions again. You will find the answers in Appendix F.

WORD POWER BUILDER LISTS

You probably already know many of the words listed here. In that case, make sure you spell and pronounce them correctly. Follow the instructions asking you to circle the unfamiliar words, look them up, and then write down the meaning. The act of writing will help you retain the information. The goal is to become sufficiently familiar with most of them so that you'll understand them in print or conversation and use many of them in your communications.

These lists contain many commonly misspelled words. Be sure you know the spelling and pronunciation of each word as well as the meaning. The 1–3–2–1 Plan is an efficient method for mastering correct spelling of an entire list of words. Here's how it works:

1   Ask someone to dictate the words. After writing or typing them *once*, note those you misspelled or were unsure of.

3   Correctly say and spell aloud each misspelled word. Then write or type the misspelled words *three* times each. Use the dictionary if in doubt about pronunciation.

2   Next, correctly write each previously misspelled word *twice*.

1   Now use an audiotape or ask someone to dictate the originally misspelled words to you, and write each one once. After checking the

spelling of each word, list any words you misspelled or felt unsure of. Practice these, using the 1–3–2–1 Plan again.

Follow the same procedure with the other lists.

To get the most out of this appendix, use it in conjunction with the advice given in Chapter 1: read, read, read. Vocabulary building is easier when you don't have to concentrate on it. Words take on life in context, and you will be surprised how often you will see a new word in print after have you have focused on it for the first time. We hope you will leave this course with a new sense of curiosity and enthusiasm for broadening the basic element of your communication skills: the ability to use words effectively—an achievement that begins and ends with *word power*!

CHAPTER 1: Word Power   *Account Executive–Blogger*

1. **account executive** Person who manages a customer's account in a business, such as an advertising agency or a financial services organization.
2. **acknowledgment** The signature of a person filing a document attesting that the contents are true and/or that the document is signed by his or her free act and deed.
3. **affidavit** Written statement sworn to before a notary public—a person authorized by law to administer oaths.
4. **amortization** The payment of a debt over time or the writing off of an asset against expenses over the period of its useful life.
5. **annual report** Yearly message to stakeholders providing information about the financial status and progress of an organization.
6. **antitrust legislation** Laws against monopoly-type business practices that result in a business making unfair profits.
7. **appraisal** Analysis of employee performance, system capability, and various other needs in a business.
8. **APR** annual percentage rate—what a borrower must pay in interest on a debt.
9. **arbitration** The settlement of a dispute between two groups by an appointed third party.
10. **arrears** An unpaid amount that is overdue.
11. **assets** Tangible or intangible resources and valuables (that can be converted to cash or cash itself) owned or controlled by an individual or company; must be listed on a balance sheet or financial statement.
12. **attachment** A court order authorizing seizure of property for failure to meet obligations.
13. **audit** Examination of an organization's records to determine accuracy and compliance with governing laws, regulations, and policies; such an examination is made by an auditor.
14. **back office** The part of a business devoted to basic functions such as hiring and paying employees, processing invoices, and managing information technology.
15. **bandwidth** In modern business jargon, the resources needed to complete a task or project.

16. **bar code** An imprinted code that can be read by a computerized scanner designed for that purpose.

17. (a) **bear market** The stock market when prices are declining and many stockholders are selling their stock because they think prices will continue to decrease. These sellers are called *bears*.

   (b) **bull market** The stock market when prices are increasing and many stockholders are buying stock because they expect prices to continue to increase. These buyers are called *bulls*.

18. **beneficiary** A person designated to receive benefits on the death of the primary holder of an asset.

19. **blog** A website that contains an online personal journal with reflections, comments, and often hyperlinks provided by the writer; also the contents of such a site.

20. **blogger** Someone who writes or edits a blog.

WORD POWER PLAY 1

Match the word to its definition by inserting the appropriate number in the blank.

1. account executive	12. attachment
2. acknowledgment	13. audit
3. affidavit	14. back office
4. amortization	15. bandwidth
5. annual report	16. bar code
6. antitrust legislation	17a. bear market
7. appraisal	17b. bull market
8. APR	18. beneficiary
9. arbitration	19. blog
10. arrears	20. blogger
11. assets	

a. _____ A person designated to receive benefits on the death of the primary holder of an asset.

b. _____ An imprinted code that can be read by a computerized scanner designed for that purpose.

c. _____ A pessimistic stock market. Stock prices are declining, and stockholders are selling.

d. _____ Percentage rate paid annually in interest on a debt.

e. _____ A court order authorizing seizure of property for failure to meet obligations.

f. _____ Payment of a debt over time or the writing off of an asset against expenses over the period of its useful life.

g. _____ Analysis of employee performance, system capability, and various needs in a business.

h. _____ A written statement sworn to before a person authorized to administer oaths.

i. _____ A debt that is overdue and still unpaid.

j. _____ Laws against monopoly-type business practices.

k. _____ The settlement of a dispute between two groups by an appointed third party.

l. _____ Tangible and intangible resources that can be converted to cash and must be listed on a balance sheet.

m. _____ Examination of an organization's records to determine accuracy and compliance with governing laws, regulations, and policies.

n. _____ The part of a business devoted to basic functions such as hiring and paying employees, processing invoices, and managing information technology.

o. _____ The signature of a person attesting that the contents of a document are true and/or that the document is signed by his or her free act and deed.

p. _____ Someone who writes or edits a blog.

q. _____ Person who manages a customer's account in an advertising agency or a financial services organization.

r. _____ In modern business jargon, the resources needed to complete a task or project.

s. _____ Annual message to stakeholders about the corporation's progress.

t. _____ An online personal journal with reflections, comments, and often hyperlinks provided by the writer; also the contents of such a site.

u. _____ Stock market prices are increasing; stockholders are buying and expect prices to continue to increase.

CHECK YOUR ANSWERS ON PAGE 472.

WORD POWER BUILDER 1

Circle the words that are unfamiliar to you and those that you have trouble spelling. Create a list called "English for Careers Word Power Builder" in a notebook or word processing document. This will be used as your personal vocabulary-building list throughout the course. Look up the meaning of the unfamiliar words and then write a sentence using the word.

abbreviate	admissible	analysis
absence	advantageous	announcement
absurd	aggressive	ambassador
acceptance	align	appearance
accommodate	allotted	approximately
accessible	altogether	aromatic
acerbic	amateur	ascertain
acquaintance	ambiguous	
adjournment	amendment	

21. **bonus** Money paid to an employee in addition to the employee's base salary, often for achieving specified goals.

22. **brand** A name, term, sign, symbol, design, or a combination of all used to uniquely identify a business or individual's products or services and differentiate them from competitors.

23. **break-even analysis** The method of determining the exact point at which the money coming into a company equals the costs associated with producing the revenue.

24. **business jargon** Specialized terminology pertaining to a specific type of work.

25. **business plan** A written document that describes a business and its objectives, strategies, market, and financial forecast.

26. **certification** A designation earned by a person to assure qualification to perform a job or task; often conferred through examination.

27. **capital** Money invested in a business enterprise.

28. **certified check** A check issued by a bank that guarantees to the recipient that sufficient funds are available and that the check is valid.

29. **COLA** Cost-of-living adjustment for wages or Social Security payments.

30. **collateral** Borrower's property held by a lender as security for payment of a loan.

31. **conference call** A telephone call which allows three or more people to take part at the same time; also called a *teleconference*.

32. **consumer price index (CPI)** A monthly survey of changes in consumer prices; it is used to measure inflation.

33. **copyright** Legal protection of documents, computer software, films, and other creative works of authors, composers, artists, and so on.

34. **corporation** An entity formed to act as a single person although constituted by one or more persons, operating under a charter granted by a state and authorized to do business under its own name.

35. **creditor** A person or institution to whom a debt is owed.

36. **cybersecurity** Measures taken to protect a computer or computer system against unauthorized access or attack.

37. **damages** Money that a defendant pays a plaintiff in a civil case if the plaintiff has won. Damages may be compensatory (for loss or injury) or punitive (to punish and deter future misconduct).

38. **de facto** Latin, meaning "in fact" or "actually"; something that exists in fact but not as a matter of law.

39. **defendant** An individual (or business) against whom a lawsuit is filed.

40. **demographic profile** Characteristics of a particular segment of the population.

WORD POWER PLAY 2

Match the word to its definition by inserting the appropriate number in the blank.

21. bonus
22. brand
23. break-even analysis
24. business jargon
25. business plan
26. certification
27. capital
28. certified check
29. COLA
30. collateral

31. conference call
32. consumer price index (CPI)
33. copyright
34. corporation
35. creditor
36. cybersecurity
37. damages
38. de facto
39. defendant
40. demographic profile

a. _____ A designation earned by a person to assure qualification to perform a job or task; often conferred through examination.

b. _____ Check guaranteed by a bank to be worth the amount for which the depositor wrote it.

c. _____ Legal protection of creative work produced by authors, composers, artists, and so on.

d. _____ A written document that describes a business and its objectives, strategies, market, and financial forecast.

e. _____ A person or institution to whom a debt is owed.

f. _____ Characteristics of a particular segment of the population.

g. _____ Latin, meaning "in fact" or "actually"; something that exists in fact but not as a matter of law.

h. _____ Cost-of-living adjustment for salaries and Social Security payments.

i. _____ An individual (or business) against whom a lawsuit is filed.

j. _____ Money paid to an employee in addition to the employee's base salary, often for achieving specified goals.

k. _____ A name, term, sign, symbol, design, or a combination of all used to uniquely identify a business or individual's products or services and differentiate them from competitors.

l. _____ Money paid by the defendant to the plaintiff in a civil case if the plaintiff has won.

m. _____ Terminology specific to a field of work.

n. _____ Money invested in a business enterprise.

o. _____ A monthly survey of changes in consumer prices used to measure inflation.

p. _____ Measures taken to protect a computer or computer system against unauthorized access or attack.

q. _____ Borrower's property held by a lender until debt is paid.

r. _____ A business entity formed to act as a single person operating under a charter granted and authorized to do business under its own name.

s. _____ A telephone call which allows three or more people to take part at the same time.

t. _____ The method of determining the exact point at which the money coming into a company equals the costs associated with producing the revenue.

CHECK YOUR ANSWERS ON PAGE 472.

WORD POWER BUILDER 2

Circle the words that are unfamiliar to you and those that you have trouble spelling and enter them in your "English for Careers Vocabulary Builder" list. Look up the meaning of the unfamiliar words and then write a sentence using the word.

bargain	bazaar	bookkeeping
bachelor	beginning	boundary
balloon	believe	bouquet
bankruptcy	belief	brilliant
basically	belligerent	broccoli
battalion	beneficial	buoyant

CHAPTER 3: Word Power *Disburse–Fiscal Year*

41. **disburse** To pay out money from a large fund, such as a treasury or public fund.

42. **direct mail** Advertisements mailed directly to homes or businesses.

43. **disposable income** Money earned that is left over after payment of recurring obligations and debts.

44. **diversification** To expand a commercial organization and make it more varied by engaging in additional or different areas of business.

45. **dividend** A payment to a stockholder of a portion of the corporation's profits.

46. **dot-com** A company that markets its products or services usually exclusively online via a website.

47. **Dow Jones Industrial Average** (also called simply the "Dow" or "Dow Jones") The daily average of the closing prices of specific stocks on the New York Stock Exchange. This figure is widely publicized and indicates current stock market trends.

48. **document sharing** A system that allows people in different places to view and edit the same document at the same time on their computers.

49. **email blast** Mass mailing of an email within an organization or community.

50. **electronic funds transfer** Transfer of money from one bank account directly into another through the use of electronic communications systems.

51. **ethics** Moral principles, such as the honesty and integrity required of employees in business and professions.

52. **equity** The net value of assets minus liabilities.

53. **euro** The currency unit used in many of the European Union countries.

54. **exchange rate** Price of one country's money in relation to the price of another's; for example, the rate at which pesos, euros, francs, yen, rupees, and so on can be exchanged for dollars.

55. **exemption** In relation to taxes, an amount of income or other value not subject to taxation, such as reduced taxation for support of dependents.

56. **FAQ** Frequently asked questions.

57. **FDIC** Federal Deposit Insurance Corporation. A U.S. government corporation that protects bank deposits that are payable in the United States up to $250,000.

58. **financial adviser** A specially trained and licensed professional who advises clients on managing and investing financial assets.

59. **financial statement** Documentation that presents a complete picture of the finances of a business or individual.

60. **fiscal year** A 12-month period when an organization's annual financial records commence and conclude; this period does not necessarily follow the calendar year.

WORD POWER PLAY 3

Match the word to its definition by inserting the appropriate number in the blank.

41. disburse	51. ethics
42. direct mail	52. equity
43. disposable income	53. euro
44. diversification	54. exchange rate
45. dividend	55. exemption
46. dot-com	56. FAQ
47. Dow Jones Industrial Average	57. FDIC
48. document sharing	58. financial adviser
49. email blast	59. financial statement
50. electronic funds transfer	60. fiscal year

a. _____ Moral principles required of business and professional employees.

b. _____ To pay out money from a large fund.

c. _____ Documentation of the finances of a business or individual.

d. _____ Transfer of money from one bank account directly into another through electronic communications systems.

e. _____ A system which allows people in different places to view and edit the same document at the same time on their computers.

f. _____ Daily average of closing prices of 30 stocks traded on the New York Stock Exchange.

g. _____ Advertisements mailed directly to homes or businesses.

h. _____ Currency used in the European Union.

i. _____ Frequently asked questions.

j. _____ Money earned that is left over after payment of recurring obligations and debts.

k. _____ Income or other value excluded from taxation.

l. _____ Mass mailing of an email.

m. _____ Value of a country's currency (money) in relation to the value of another country's currency.

n. _____ The expansion of an organization's business interests.

o. _____ Federal Deposit Insurance Corporation.

p. _____ A 12-month period of financial accounting that does not necessarily follow the calendar year.

q. _____ Specially trained professional who advises clients on handling financial matters.

r. _____ Payment to a stockholder of a portion of the corporation's profits.

s. _____ A company that markets its products or services online via a website.

t. _____ The net value of assets minus liabilities.

CHECK YOUR ANSWERS ON PAGE 472.

WORD POWER BUILDER 3

Circle the words that are unfamiliar to you and those that you have trouble spelling and enter them in your "English for Careers Vocabulary Builder" list. Look up the meaning of the unfamiliar words and then write a sentence using the word.

calendar	chronic	confidently
camouflage	collaborate	connoisseur
camaraderie	commencement	conscience
campaign	commission	copyright
candidate	compelled	curiosity
carriage	concede	curriculum
ceiling	condemn	customary
chargeable	confidentially	

61. **foreclosure** A lender taking over property when a debtor is not making payments on the mortgage.

62. **401k** A retirement plan for employees that allows contributions from wages to be exempt from federal income tax, provided funds remain in the plan until retirement.

63. **411** Information; mostly used in text messaging, as in "Have you got the 411 on that?" Derived from the telephone number for information.

64. **fringe benefits** or **benefits** Paid vacations, insurance coverage, pension plans, part-time college tuition fees, and so on given to employees in addition to salary or wages.

65. **Fannie Mae** (Federal National Mortgage Association) A congressionally chartered corporation that purchases residential mortgages from financial institutions and secures them for sale into the capital markets.

66. **FASB** Financial Accounting Standards Board. Sets accounting standards for US firms.

67. **garnishment** A legal withholding of part of a debtor's future wages for payment of a debt owed to a creditor.

68. **glass ceiling** Perceived or actual invisible barrier that prevents career advancement beyond a certain level for reasons of gender, age, race, ethnicity, or sexual orientation.

69. **goodwill** An intangible asset of a business derived from its good reputation.

70. **google** To use the Google search engine to obtain information on the Internet.

71. **graphics** Visual display of data such as graphs, charts, and diagrams.

72. **gross** The total before deductions, such as gross income or gross profit.

73. **hacker** A person who infiltrates other people's computer data.

74. **income statement** Documentation of the financial status, such as sales, expenses, and profit or loss of a business on a periodic basis.

75. **infomercial** A long television commercial made to seem like an informative talk show (information plus commercials).

76. **injunction** A court order preventing one or more parties from taking some action that is in dispute. A **preliminary injunction** is often issued to allow fact-finding so that a judge can determine whether a permanent injunction is justified.

77. **insolvent** Unable to pay one's debts (**broke**—slang).

78. **interface** The interaction between a computer and the user; usually refers to "user interface," which consists of the system functions, graphic display formats, and other features of program or application.

79. **intranet** A website with access restricted to a limited group of authorized users (such as employees of a company).

80. **itinerary** A detailed written schedule of activities, commonly used for travel and group activities.

WORD POWER PLAY 4

Match the word to its definition by inserting the appropriate number in the blank.

61. foreclosure
62. 401k
63. 411
64. fringe benefits or benefits
65. Fannie Mae
66. FASB
67. garnishment
68. glass ceiling
69. goodwill
70. google

71. graphics
72. gross
73. hacker
74. income statement
75. infomercial
76. injunction
77. insolvent
78. interface
79. intranet
80. itinerary

a. _____ A long television commercial.

b. _____ Visual display of data, including graphs and charts.

c. _____ Legal deduction of wages from a debtor's salary for payment to a creditor.

d. _____ Unable to pay one's debts.

e. _____ Invisible barrier that usually prevents job promotions.

f. _____ Written schedule for travel and activities.

g. _____ A court order preventing one or more parties from taking an action that is in dispute.

h. _____ Debtor losing property because of inability to pay debts.

i. _____ Benefits given to employees in addition to salaries.

j. _____ Documentation of the financial status of a business on a periodic basis.

k. _____ A retirement plan for employees.

l. _____ A website with access restricted to a limited group of authorized users.

m. _____ Federal National Mortgage Association.

n. _____ Person who infiltrates other people's electronic data.

o. _____ An intangible asset of a business derived from its good reputation.

p. _____ Text messaging language for "information."

q. _____ To use the Google search engine to obtain information on the Internet.

r. _____ The total before deductions.

s. _____ Financial Accounting Standards Board.

t. _____ The interaction between a computer and the user.

CHECK YOUR ANSWERS ON PAGE 473.

WORD POWER BUILDER 4

Circle the words that are unfamiliar to you and those that you have trouble spelling and enter them in your "English for Careers Vocabulary Builder" list. Look up the meaning of the unfamiliar words and then write a sentence using the word.

debatable	definitely	disappointed
deceive	dependent	disapprove
deductible	desperate	disastrous
default	develop	discretion
deterrent	diligent	disguise
deferred	dilemma	dissatisfied
deficient	dimension	
deluge	disappearance	

CHAPTER 5: Word Power   *Joint Venture–Negotiable Instruments*

81. **joint venture** A collaboration between two parties to mutually accomplish a business objective.

82. **judgment** The decision of a court resolving a dispute between the parties to a lawsuit.

83. **liabilities** The obligations or debts of a business or an individual.

84. **libel** A written or oral defamatory statement or representation, usually published, that conveys an unjustly unfavorable impression of its target.

85. **lien** Claim against property preventing the owner from selling it until a debt (such as taxes) is paid.

86. **limited liability company (LLC)** A business formation that, under state law, provides the limited liability features of a corporation and the tax efficiencies and operational flexibility of a partnership.

87. **line of credit** A commitment by a lender to lend up to a certain amount of money to a business.

88. **liquid assets** Assets of a business that can be converted to cash within a relatively short period of time.

89. **list price** The advertised or recommended retail price of a product.

90. **litigation** A legal process for resolving a dispute; participants (plaintiffs and defendants) in lawsuits are called **litigants**.

91. **markup** The difference between the cost price and the selling price in a retail business.

92. **merit rating** Rating employees by measurable job performance benchmarks so that fair decisions may be made about raises, promotions, and so on.

93. **monopoly** Exclusive control of the supply of a commodity or service.

94. **mortgage** Pledge of property (real estate) as security for a loan.

95. **multinational corporation** A company with subsidiaries or branches in many nations.
96. **multitasking** The simultaneous execution of more than one task by a computer or a person.
97. **mutual fund** An investment in a fund that invests shareholders' money in various stocks or bonds.
98. **NASDAQ** American stock exchange that is the second-largest stock exchange in the world after the New York Stock Exchange; has more trading volume than any other electronic stock exchange in the world.
99. **navigate** While online, clicking on hypertext links (or paths) that take you from one Web page to another.
100. **negotiable instruments** Documents in which ownership is easily transferred to another person, for example, stock certificates or checks made out to "cash."

WORD POWER PLAY 5

Match the word to its definition by inserting the appropriate number in the blank.

81. joint venture
82. judgment
83. liabilities
84. libel
85. lien
86. limited liability company (LLC)
87. line of credit
88. liquid assets
89. list price
90. litigation

91. markup
92. merit rating
93. monopoly
94. mortgage
95. multinational corporation
96. multitasking
97. mutual fund
98. NASDAQ
99. navigate
100. negotiable instruments

a. _____ A written or oral defamatory statement or representation, usually published, that conveys an unjustly unfavorable impression of its target.

b. _____ A claim against property that prevents the owner from selling it until a debt (such as taxes) is paid.

c. _____ American stock exchange with largest electronic trading volume.

d. _____ Difference between a retailer's cost price and the selling price.

e. _____ The advertised or recommended retail price of a product.

f. _____ Rating employees by their job performance.

g. _____ Pledge of property as security for a loan.

h. _____ Documents easily transferred to another person or organization.

i. _____ Fund that invests shareholders' money in various stocks or bonds.

j. _____ A commitment by a lender to lend up to a certain amount of money to a business.

k. _____ Exclusive control of a commodity or a service.

l. _____ A company with branches in many nations.

m. _____ A business collaboration between two parties.

n. _____ Assets of a business that can be quickly converted to cash.

o. _____ Doing several tasks all at the same time.

p. _____ A court's decision resolving a lawsuit.

q. _____ A business that has the limited liability of a corporation and the tax efficiencies and operational flexibility of a partnership.

r. _____ To move around on the Internet using hypertext links on websites.

s. _____ A legal process for resolving a dispute.

t. _____ The obligations or debts of a business or an individual.

CHECK YOUR ANSWERS ON PAGE 473.

WORD POWER BUILDER 5

Circle the words that are unfamiliar to you and those that you have trouble spelling and enter them in your "English for Careers Vocabulary Builder" list. Look up the meaning of the unfamiliar words and then write a sentence using the word.

economics	enforceable
eerie	enormous
efficiency	enthusiastically
eighth	entrepreneur
eligible	enumerate
eliminate	environment
embarrass	equipped
emphasize	erroneous
en route	esoteric
encouragement	especially
endorsement	espionage

101. **net** Amount remaining after all deductions are made; for example, net profit is the balance after all expenses have been deducted from gross profit.

102. **net worth** The net value of assets minus liabilities.

103. **networking** The cultivation of productive relationships for employment or business.

104. **New York Stock Exchange (NYSE)** Largest stock exchange in the United States; it's on Wall Street in New York City.

105. **operating expenses** The expenses of a business not directly associated with the making of a product or providing of a service, such as administration, employee benefits, and rent.

106. **outplacement** A company's assistance in finding jobs for its employees who have been terminated.

107. **outsource** Using outside sources for labor, parts, and various services instead of personnel and services within the company.

108. **overhead** General costs of running a business, such as taxes, rent, heating, lighting, and depreciation of equipment.

109. **partnership** A legal arrangement of two or more persons as owners of a business.

110. **PDF (Portable Document Format)** A method of formatting documents that allows them to be universally read on a computer screen or printed regardless of the user's equipment; word processing files are often converted to PDF files for transmission; the PDF format cannot be manipulated by the receiver.

111. **per capita** Equally to each individual; usually applied to a national population.

112. **per diem** By the day; for example, a consultant's fee is often based on a specified rate per day.

113. **plaintiff** A person or business that files a formal complaint with the court.

114. **public offering** The sale of a company's shares of a stock to the public in the financial market.

115. **quorum** The number of members of an organization required to be present to have a formal meeting at which business is transacted.

116. **radar screen** In modern business jargon, refers to the range of interests that a company or individual is focused on or has taken notice of; that is, something is either "on the radar screen" or "not on the radar screen."

117. **requisition** A written request, made within an organization, for supplies or equipment.

118. **retainer** A fee paid to a lawyer or other professional for services to be rendered in the future.

119. **Securities and Exchange Commission** The federal governmental agency that oversees and regulates the stock and securities exchanges.

120. **shareholder** Shareholder and stockholder have the same meaning— one who owns stock (or shares) in a corporation.

WORD POWER PLAY 6

Match the word to its definition by inserting the appropriate number in the blank.

101. net
102. net worth
103. networking
104. New York Stock Exchange (NYSE)
105. operating expenses
106. outplacement
107. outsource
108. overhead
109. partnership
110. PDF

111. per capita
112. per diem
113. plaintiff
114. public offering
115. quorum
116. radar screen
117. requisition
118. retainer
119. Securities and Exchange Commission
120. shareholder

a. _____ By the day.

b. _____ Amount remaining after deductions.

c. _____ A company's assistance in finding jobs for terminated employees.

d. _____ The range of interests that a company or individual is focused on or has taken notice of.

e. _____ General costs of running a business.

f. _____ Use of outside sources for labor instead of the company's own employees.

g. _____ Equally to each individual.

h. _____ The federal governmental agency that oversees and regulates the stock and securities exchanges.

i. _____ The net value of assets minus liabilities.

j. _____ A method of formatting documents that allows them to be read or printed universally.

k. _____ The sale of a company's shares of stock to the public in the financial market.

l. _____ One who owns shares in a corporation.

m. _____ The cultivation of productive relationships for employment or business.

n. _____ The expenses of a business not directly associated with the making of a product or providing of a service.

o. _____ Fee paid to a lawyer or other professional for services to be rendered in the future.

p. _____ A legal arrangement of two or more persons as owners of a business.

q. _____ The number of members who must be present in order to have a formal meeting.

r. _____ Written request for supplies, equipment, or materials made within an organization.

s. _____ Largest stock exchange in the United States.

t. _____ A person or business that files a formal complaint with the court.

CHECK YOUR ANSWERS ON PAGE 473.

WORD POWER BUILDER 6

Circle the words that are unfamiliar to you and those that you have trouble spelling and enter them in your "English for Careers Vocabulary Builder" list. Look up the meaning of the unfamiliar words and then write a sentence using the word.

fascism	foreign	fictitious
feasible	foreseeable	fraudulent
February	forfeit	freight
feint	forth (forward)	frieze
fiscal	fortunately	fulfill
flexible	forty	fundamentally
fluorescent	fourth (after third)	furor

CHAPTER 7: Word Power   *Share–Workaholic*

121. **share** A single unit of ownership in a corporation, mutual fund, or any other organization.

122. **simulation** The use of a model to imitate a situation in order to estimate the likelihood of various possible outcomes.

123. **slander** Untrue malicious and defamatory statements about someone that harm the person's reputation. (**Libel** refers to untrue *written* remarks.)

124. **Small Business Administration (SBA)** The federal governmental agency that guarantees loans made by banks to small businesses.

125. **solvent** Having the funds necessary to pay all debts.

126. **spreadsheet** A computer application used for entering, calculating, and storing financial or numerical data; can also be used for entering text data in rows and columns.

127. **startup** A new company that is just beginning to operate as a business.

128. **statute** A law passed by a legislature.

129. **stock** A unit of investment in a corporation. Stockholders are entitled to vote on various corporate matters and to share in the company's profits—based on the amount of stock they possess.

130. **tariff** A tax, called a **duty**, on imported items.

131. **turnaround time** Time elapsed between starting a task and completing it.

132. **turnover** Replacement of employees who have left an organization or merchandise that has been sold.

133. **unhappy camper** Someone who has complaints about his or her employer or work situation; an unsatisfied customer.

134. **URL** (Uniform Resource Locator) The global address of documents and other resources on the World Wide Web.

135. **users** (also called **end users** or **visitors**) Persons who use a computer system or access a website.

136. **watchdog** A person or organization that monitors the practices of companies to ensure they are not acting illegally.

137. **World Wide Web** (or **Web**) A way of transmitting and accessing information over the medium of the Internet through the use of graphics and documents that are connected by hyperlinks.

138. **Wikipedia** An online encyclopedia written collaboratively by its users and originators (www.wikipedia.org).

139. **webmaster** One who organizes or updates information on a website.

140. **workaholic** A person who is addicted to work at the expense of other activities that define a balanced lifestyle.

WORD POWER PLAY 7

Match the word to its definition by inserting the appropriate number in the blank.

121. share
122. simulation
123. slander
124. Small Business Administration
125. solvent
126. spreadsheet
127. startup
128. statute
129. stock
130. tariff

131. turnaround time
132. turnover
133. unhappy camper
134. URL (Uniform Resource Locator)
135. users (end users or visitors)
136. watchdog
137. World Wide Web (or Web)
138. Wikipedia
139. webmaster
140. workaholic

a. _____ A means for transmitting and accessing information over the medium of the Internet.

b. _____ Untrue, malicious, and defamatory statements about someone that harm the person's reputation.

c. _____ One who organizes or updates information on a website.

d. _____ The use of a model to imitate a situation in order to estimate the likelihood of various possible outcomes.

e. _____ Time elapsed between starting and completing a task.

f. _____ Someone who has complaints about his or her employer or work situation; an unsatisfied customer.

g. _____ Having funds needed to pay all debts.

h. _____ An online encyclopedia written collaboratively.

i. _____ Investment in a corporation entitling the investor to vote and to share in profits.

j. _____ A new company.

k. _____ Replacement of employees who have left an organization or merchandise that has been sold.

l. _____ A person or organization that monitors the practices of companies to ensure that they are not acting illegally.

m. _____ Tax, often called a *duty*, on imported items.

n. _____ A computer application used for entering, calculating, and storing financial or numerical data; it can also be used for entering text data in rows and columns.

o. _____ The global address of documents and other resources on the World Wide Web.

p. _____ A person who is addicted to work at the expense of other activities that define a balanced lifestyle.

q. _____ A unit of ownership in a corporation.

r. _____ The federal governmental agency that provides support to small businesses across the nation.

s. _____ Persons who use a computer system or access a website.

t. _____ A law passed by a legislature.

CHECK YOUR ANSWERS ON PAGE 473.

WORD POWER BUILDER 7

Circle the words that are unfamiliar to you and those that you have trouble spelling and enter them in your "English for Careers Vocabulary Builder" list. Look up the meaning of the unfamiliar words and then write a sentence using the word.

genealogy	grammar	guarantee
generalize	granddaughter	guaranty
gigantic	grandeur	guardian
gnash	grateful	guesstimate
government	grievance	guidance
governor	grieve	guitar
graffiti	grievous	

According to the *Microsoft Encarta College Dictionary*, a maven is an "expert or a knowledgeable enthusiast of something." Be a word maven by seeing how many of the business terms you can recall from Word Power 1–7 without looking back at the definitions. Then go to page 474 and use the key to complete the ones you missed. Keep in mind that in some cases you might have selected different words that also make sense in the sentence.

1. The _____ is located on Wall Street in New York City in a building that is designated as a National Historic Landmark.

2. Before opening an account with a credit card company, it's a good idea to shop around for the best _____.

3. To receive _____ as a CPA, an accountant must pass a state test.

4. The company's _____ provides details about its _____ operations over the last _____ year.

5. The _____ for processing orders has increased due to staff _____ and _____ on the production line.

6. The _____ of Facebook _____ was a disappointment to some _____ who saw the value decrease in the initial stages.

7. If you are traveling to Europe, be sure to check the _____ on the _____ before planning your trip.

8. We did not pay our employees a _____ this month because of the cost of _____ work that they could not handle.

9. My best friend and I formed a business _____ and hired a _____ who is an expert on helping _____ companies develop sound _____.

10. Our _____ is very well versed in _____, and our computer system has never been victimized by a _____.

11. During the _____, we informed the _____ that their _____ would be well taken care of because of the _____ that sent the stock price soaring.

12. During the housing crisis, _____ payments ballooned, causing rampant home _____ throughout the country.

13. The rising cost of _____, increased the company's _____ and forced the owners to increase their products' _____ and sell some of their _____.

14. After the car accident, the insurance company issued a _____ to pay for _____.

15. If your company offers employees a _____ as one of its _____, you will need to name a _____.

16. The _____ of the group of displaced workers indicates that adding resume writing to the _____ of _____ services will be helpful.

17. One of the symptoms of becoming a _____ is finding yourself focusing exclusively on work with no thought of leisure activities on your _____.

18. _____ prohibits a _____, so in recent years _____ have pursued _____.

19. The lawyer was given a _____ and will file suit for _____ on behalf of the _____ who was the victim of a series of false statements by the _____.

20. The female chief executive was able to break through the _____ by _____ with her colleagues and peers in the profession.

WORD POWER BUILDER 8

habeas corpus	headhunter	hindrance
handkerchief	healthful	hindsight
haphazard	hemorrhage	hoping
happiness	hence	humorous
harass	hesitant	hygiene
hazardous	hierarchy	hypocrite

CHAPTER 9: Word Power   *Homophones*

English has hundreds of **homophones** (words that sound alike but are spelled differently, such as *right, write,* and *rite*). Only careful proofreading catches most homophone errors because computer spell-checkers overlook words that are spelled correctly but used incorrectly in a sentence. Review the following list of common homophones that often cause embarrassing errors.

accept	agree to receive
except	excluding, as in *everyone except me*
access	ability to enter, obtain, or use something
excess	more than is needed or wanted
ad	short for advertisement; one *d* like advertisement
add	to join; two *d*'s as in *addition*
affect	verb meaning to change, to influence, to pretend (His limited education will affect his ability to do the job.)
effect	verb meaning to bring about or to result in (We can effect no changes without your approval.)
effect	a noun that means result (We all know the effect would be disastrous.)
alot—no such word	do not write this "nonword"! Your spell checker will alert you to this error.
allot	with two *l*'s, the word is correct when it means to distribute
a lot	correctly written as two words; use this expression only in conversation or informal writing; instead use *a great deal, very much,* or *many*. Of course, *a lot* also refers to a small piece of land.
alright	avoid this spelling
all right	this spelling is preferred: two *l*'s; two words

alter	change (The groom said, "Don't try to alter me after we leave the altar.")
altar	a place for sacred rituals
bazaar	a sale or marketplace (note three *a*'s)
bizarre	odd; grotesque; strange (note two *r*'s)
capital	wealth; a city that is the capital of a state; an upper-case letter; execution, as in *capital punishment*
capitol	a building where legislators make laws
cite	summon to court; to honor; to quote
sight	ability to see; a thing regarded as worth seeing; something ludicrous or disorderly in appearance
site	noun meaning a location
coarse	rough; of poor quality; crude
course	school subject; portion of a meal; place where golf is played; a direction taken
counsel	lawyer; advice or to give advice
council	group that meets to discuss, plan, or decide action
die, dying	to pass from life
dye, dyeing	to change a color, such as fabric or hair
dissent	disagreement
descent	a downward movement; the verb is *descend*
here	at this place
hear	*ear* is in *hear*; proofread carefully to avoid careless *here/hear* errors
heir	person who inherits (A female who inherits is an heiress.)
air	referring to atmosphere; pronounced like *heir*
illicit	not legal; prohibited; improper
elicit	to draw forth or to bring out
principle	a rule; a fundamental truth; a law
principal	main or most important; the chief administrator of a school

WORD POWER PLAY 9

Write the correct word in the blank without looking at the definitions.

accept/except	1. We'll _____ deliveries every day _____ Sunday.
ad/add	2. We'll _____ the figures before we place the _____ in the newspaper.
dyeing/dying	3. I'm _____ to hear what he'll say after finding out that I've been _____ my hair.
descent/dissent	4. Peaceful _____ should be encouraged.
	5. The _____ from Mt. Baldy will be difficult.
bazaar/bizarre	6. His behavior was so _____ that she left him at the _____.

coarse/course

7. Her _____ manners were distasteful to him, but the professor couldn't exclude her from the _____.

site/sight/cite

8. A magnificent _____ was selected for the new theater.

9. We could _____ several examples of unfair taxation.

10. What a _____ he was with his torn clothing!

council/counsel

11. Richard is the _____ for the defense.

12. The City _____ meets every Friday morning.

access/excess

13. Do you have _____ to the _____ funds?

affect/effect

14. How does the hot weather _____ you?

15. What _____ does the heat have on you?

capital/capitol

16. Is the _____ in the downtown section of the _____?

a lot/allot

17. We cannot _____ any funds for the company to purchase _____ for the new parking structure.

principle/principal

18. An important _____ for students to remember is to be respectful to the _____.

elicit/illicit

19. We are trying to _____ the full details concerning the _____ business deal.

CHECK YOUR ANSWERS ON PAGE 474.

WORD POWER BUILDER 9

Circle the words that are unfamiliar to you and those that you have trouble spelling and enter them in your "English for Careers Vocabulary Builder" list. Look up the meaning of the unfamiliar words and then write a sentence using the word.

idiosyncrasy	initiative	itemize
illegal	inaccurate	interference
illuminating	incredible	interpretation
imaginary	indigenous	itinerary
immediately	ingenious	intolerable
impromptu	innuendo	irrational
improvement	inoculation	irrelevant
incidentally	insistence	inscrutable
indispensable	intangible	

CHAPTER 10: Word Power *Commonly Confused Words*

Although the following pairs of words on the left are similar in appearance, spelling, and pronunciation, they differ greatly. Be sure to observe the distinctions in your reading, writing, and speech.

beside	by the side of; near; next to
besides	in addition to
choose	present tense; pronounce the *oo* as in *pool*
chose	past tense of *choose*; pronounce the *o* like the alphabet sound of *o*
compliment	to praise
complement	something that completes
conscience	the part of us that hurts when we do wrong
conscious	alert; awake; aware
defer	to put off or to postpone (accent on the second syllable)
differ	disagree
desert	accent on first syllable—a hot, arid land
desert	accent on second syllable—to leave behind or to abandon
dessert	last course of a meal (Taking seconds on dessert is the memory hook for spelling this word with two s's.)
device	a machine, tool, or method to achieve or do something (rhymes with *rice*)
devise	to plan or figure out (rhymes with *rise*)
eligible	have the qualifications to participate
illegible	not readable or difficult to read
eminent	recognized for accomplishments; outstanding; famous
imminent	about to happen
envelope	paper container for sending mail
envelop	to wrap or surround
irregardless	Not a word. Do not say it or write it! Instead, use *regardless*.
regardless	no matter what else happens
fiscal	pertaining to financial affairs
physical	pertaining to the body
guise	a false outward appearance
guys	informal word for men or boys
it's	with the apostrophe—contraction for *it is* or *it has*
its	no apostrophe—shows possession; for example, *Its wings were flapping.*
led	past tense of lead, as in *He led the parade.*
lead	to guide; to direct operations or activity, as in *He'll lead it again tomorrow.*
minor	under 18; unimportant
miner	worker in a mine

WORD POWER PLAY 10

Write the correct word in the blank.

eminent/imminent

1. A storm is _____.
2. The _____ statesman Winston Churchill is admired for his eloquent use of the English language.

regardless/irregardless

3. He plans to attend _____ of the weather.

eligible/illegible

4. He is not _____ to study calligraphy because his handwriting is _____.

devise/device

5. Can you _____ a _____ that is less expensive?

desert/dessert

6. Please don't _____ me if I don't stay for _____, for this _____ heat has made me very tired.

choose/chose

7. Did you _____ the same books that I _____?

defer/differ

8. My roommate was able to _____ her student loan payments, but our circum-stances _____, so I cannot do the same.

conscience/conscious

9. My _____ is clear because he was _____ and not in pain after the accident.

beside/besides

10. No one _____ Mr. Jefferson ever parks _____ me.

envelop/envelope

11. When he walks in, I'll _____ him in my arms and place the _____ in his hand.

fiscal/physical

12. During this _____ year, we won't have the funds to construct a _____ education building at the high school.

compliment/complement

13. She _____ us on the quality of the fabric and the way the color of the curtains _____ the new sofa.

guys/guise

14. She hides her true feelings under the _____ of friendliness toward _____ she really doesn't like.

it's/its

15. _____ not a good idea for a startup company to stray from _____ basic business plan.

minor/miner

16. A _____ problem with the equipment turned out to be a dangerous situation for the _____.

CHECK YOUR ANSWERS ON PAGE 475.

WORD POWER BUILDER 10

Circle the words that are unfamiliar to you and then look up the meaning and practice spelling them.

jackpot	jeep	jitney
jagged	jeer	job lot
java	jetliner	journal
jaywalk	jettison	joystick
jealous	jewelry	judgment
jeopardize	jicama	justifiable
jargon	jillion	

CHAPTER 11: Word Power *More Commonly Confused Words*

Hasty proofreading can cause errors—especially with the following words that are easily mistaken for each other. Carefully check your writing for these kinds of "quiet mistakes."

lose	to misplace or leave something behind
loose	not tight or not fastened
moral	a concept of right behavior
morale	spirit; sense of common purpose
perquisite	a privilege, a benefit, a payment, or a profit in addition to salary; this word is usually used in the abbreviated form *perk* or the plural *perks*
prerequisite	something required beforehand, such as taking a beginning class before being permitted to enroll in the advanced class
persecute	to mistreat or injure, often because of a belief or a way of life
prosecute	to take legal action against someone accused of a crime
personnel	employees of a particular company or others who make up a group
personal	private
perspective	ability to see objects in terms of their relative distance from one another or to consider ideas in terms of their relative importance to one another
prospective	expected; likely to happen in the future
proceed	to go ahead, advance, or continue
precede	to go before; to be earlier
proceeds	the money or profits derived from a business transaction; pronounced PRO ceeds
quit	cease; give up employment; admit defeat
quite	positively; completely
quiet	without noise
reality	what is real or true
realty	real estate; property

reason is because	avoid this phrase; it is non-Standard English
reason is that	use *reason is that* or simply *because* without the word *reason*
respectfully	with respect
	Note: do not use *respectfully* as a closing for typical business letters—unless a letter is to someone warranting an unusual degree of respect, such as a high-ranking official or religious leader
respectively	in the order named
rye	a grain or seeds used for making flour or whiskey
wry	twisted; perverse; ironic (read the dictionary entry for *wry*)
suit	clothing consisting of a matched outfit; a legal action (in business writing, use the complete word *lawsuit*)
suite	group of items forming a unit, such as matched furniture, or a group of adjoining rooms or offices
then	at that time; next
than	used in comparisons, such as *better than*, *rather than*, *more than*, and so on
through	across or from one side to another
thorough	with attention to detail; complete
were	past tense form of the verb *to be*; the plural form of *was*.
we're	contraction of *we are*
whether	indicates a choice
weather	climate condition

WORD POWER PLAY 11

Select the appropriate word for each blank without looking at the definitions.

personal/personnel

1. Don't open an envelope marked _____ unless it is addressed to you.

lose/loose

2. The lamp broke because the wires were _____.

than/then

3. His work is usually better _____ anyone else's.

thorough/through

4. The editor did a _____ job of going _____ the author's manuscript.

suit/suite

5. When working in the executive _____, most people will wear a _____.

weather/whether

6. It doesn't matter _____ the _____ is cold or hot, you must still dress for success.

suit/suite

7. During the summer months, you should wear a _____ to work except for casual Fridays.

prosecute/persecute

8. Mr. Chandra would be the best attorney to _____ this case.

that/because

9. The reason Sarah was promoted is _____ she now has an MBA.

weather/whether

10. Do you know _____ the _____ will change tonight?

proceeds/proceed

11. Some of the _____ from Friday's sale will be donated to charity.

rye/wry

12 Can you pick me up a loaf of _____ bread at the grocery store?

we're/were

13. _____ sure he receives many perks.

proceed/proceeds

14. Are you going to _____ with the evaluation?

moral/morale

15. The _____ of the staff is my paramount concern.

personal/personnel

16. The supervisor spends too much time talking about _____ issues with the office _____.

prospective/perspective

17. The _____ instructor wanted a very high salary.

perquisite/prerequisite

18. The _____ courses he required were reasonable.

moral/morale

19. The _____ is good in this company because the executives make _____ decisions.

we're/were

20. Where _____ you when we _____ doing all the work?

perspective/prospective

21. Seen in _____, the incident was not too serious.

respectfully/respectively

22. I _____ disagree with your decision.

quit/quite/quiet

23. Please keep _____ about my plan to _____ the job until I am _____ sure that I'll go through with it.

we're/were

24. _____ wondering if you were serious about working late.

weather/whether

25. We will stay _____ you join us or not.

thorough/through

26. We need to do a _____ job even if we work _____ the night.

persecuted/prosecuted

27. They were _____ because of their beliefs.

moral/morale

28. _____ is high in this department.

proceed/precede

29. The attorney was asked to _____ with the trial.

suit/suite

30. The décor in the executive _____ is quite luxurious.

lose/loose

31. If his mistake is discovered, he will _____ his job.

personal/personnel

32. Job interviewers must be cautious about asking _____ questions of applicants.

we're/were

33. _____ going where the jobs are.

then/than	34. _____ he said that I look better _____ ever.
that/because	35. The reason for the secrecy is _____ he works in the financial industry.
realty/reality	36. Some of the most popular programs on television today are _____ shows.

SEE ANSWERS ON PAGE 475.

WORD POWER BUILDER 11

Circle the words that are unfamiliar to you and then look up the meaning and practice spelling them.

khaki	kinesiology	kopek
kaleidoscope	kleptomaniac	kumquat
kibitz	knead	kung fu
kilo	knowledgeable	kook (slang)
kilometer	knuckleball	

CHAPTER 12: Word Power *Homonyms and Homophones*

Avoid embarrassing errors in your writing by remembering the different meanings of these *homonyms* (spelled similarly) and *homophones* (sound alike but spelled differently). You'll also find useful words for vocabulary growth. Keep your dictionary handy for further information.

appraise	to estimate the value of an item
apprise	to inform
bloc	a group of persons or countries combined to achieve a purpose
block	a large solid piece of a heavy material; see dictionary for multiple meanings
canvas	coarse cloth
canvass	to ask for votes, opinions, information
everyday	ordinary
every day	each day
foreword	an introduction to a written work
forward	toward the front
halve	verb meaning to reduce to half
half	one of the two equal parts of something
have	possess
key	a device used for unlocking; an instrumental or deciding factor
quay	(pronounced the same as key) concrete or stone water-front structure
lesson	something to learn
lessen	decrease

marquee	a roof-like projecting structure over an entrance
marquis	(*quis* pronounced *key*) royalty ranking above a count
marquise	(pronounced *keez*) wife or widow of a marquis
naval	referring to the navy
navel	small scar in the abdomen; a kind of orange
ode	a dignified poem
owed	responsibility to repay
peak	the top
peek	a brief or concealed look at something
pique	to be annoyed
reign	royal power
rain	water from the sky
rein	means of controlling an animal
serge	a strong fabric
surge	a sudden, strong increase, as in power or water
stationery	writing paper
stationary	unmovable
taught	past tense for teach
taut	tightly pulled or stretched
their	belonging to them
there	at that place
they're	contraction of they are
throes	spasm or pangs of pain
throws	tosses
vise	a device for holding an object so that it can be worked on
vice	an evil action or habit
waive	to give up or postpone
wave	to signal by moving a hand or an arm
wary	cautious
wear	damage as a result of using a product

WORD POWER PLAY 12

Write the correct word in the blank without looking at the definitions.

appraise/apprise

1. After we _____ you of the cost, you can decide whether you want Mr. Gold to _____ the ring.

bloc/block

2. The European _____ wants to _____ further action.

canvass/canvas

3. We will _____ the fashion editors to find a magazine that will feature our newest designer _____ bag.

every day/everyday

4. I wear my _____ clothes _____.

foreword/forward

5. Read the _____, and then tell the members about going _____ with the project.

halve/half/have

6. To _____ a smaller cake, simply _____ the slices. Then serve the cake with coffee and hope only _____ the people stay to eat.

key/quay

7. You don't need a _____ until you arrive at the _____.

lesson/lessen

8. A _____ is something we sometimes learn the hard way. If we try to do the right thing, perhaps we'll _____ the consequences.

marquis/marquise/marquee

9. The actors who play the _____ and the _____ will have their names on the theater _____.

navel/naval

10. It isn't advisable to wear clothing that exposes one's _____ when attending a party at a _____ base.

ode/owed

11. Did you know that an _____ is a lovely poem expressing romantic emotion? After her bad behavior at the prom, she _____ him one.

proceed/precede

12. His speech will _____ the meal, and when he finishes speaking, we will _____ to the refreshment tables.

rain/reign/rein

13. The Triple Crown winner ran in the _____, and the jockey had to control the _____ so that his horse would not miss the chance to _____ supreme in the world of racing.

peek/pique/peak

14. The mountain _____ will be in sight and will _____ your curiosity about the view, but you must not _____ until you reach the top.

some time/sometime

15. I would like to meet with the volunteers _____ next week if you can set aside _____ on my calendar.

stationery/stationary

16. We have a large supply of _____ in the desk that is _____; that is, fastened to the floor.

taut/taught

17. I was _____ that one of the meanings of _____ is emotionally tense.

vise/vice

18. A _____ is closed with a screw or a lever and holds the object being worked on. It is totally different from a _____, which is a negative activity.

wary/wear   19. Be _____ of the _____ and tear on your new tools when you lend them to friends.

waive/wave   20. If you _____ your right to be first at the buffet, you might as well _____ good-bye to the best appetizers.

CHECK YOUR ANSWERS ON PAGE 475.

WORD POWER BUILDER 12

Circle the words that are unfamiliar to you and then look up the meaning and practice spelling them.

laboratory	length	library
larceny	leverage	lucrative
launch	liaison	luscious
leisure	liqueur	
legitimate	likelihood	

CHAPTER 13: Word Power *Similar Word Pairs*

The following pairs of words often cause confusion; some are similar in meaning, and others are similar in spelling but differ considerably in meaning.

anxious	worry or fear
eager	looking forward to something
disinterested	impartial; one who listens to all sides of an issue; can also mean *uninterested*
uninterested	not interested or lacking enthusiasm
enthusiastic/enthusiasm	strong excitement
emigrate	to move out of a country
immigrate	to move into a country
explicit	clearly expressed
implicit	not stated but understood—"between the lines"
flammable/inflammable	These two words mean the same: *can burn.*
nonflammable	cannot burn; the opposite of *flammable* and *inflammable*
farther	refers to actual distance
further	refers to figurative distance, e.g., to a greater degree
indigenous	people, wildlife, plants, and culture, native to a particular area
indigent	poor or needy
less	a more limited number or amount that can't be counted; of lower rank, degree, or importance; of reduced size, extent, or degree

fewer	a smaller number or amount that *can* be counted
imply	the speaker or writer "implies" something by what is said, done, or written
infer	the listener or reader "infers" a meaning from another's words or actions
last	final, concluding
latest	most recent, newest, current
per annum	by the year, annually (Latin) or a yearly salary
per diem	by the day (Latin) or a daily salary (These terms refer to wages.)
rsvp	French abbreviation for *Respond if you please* or *Please respond.*
please rsvp	Do not use this expression: it's redundant (saying the same thing twice).
principal	main or most important; a person who has control or authority
principle	a fundamental law, doctrine, or assumption
raise	to lift something to a higher level
rise	to move upward or increase
simple	easy to understand
simplistic	using poor judgment by making complex ideas sound deceptively easy
percent	a portion; used to express a specific amount
percentage	a portion; used to express the general concept
take	to carry away from
bring	to carry to
passed	went beyond or through
past	a period of time before the present
rational	having reason or understanding
rationale	an underlying reason

WORD POWER PLAY 13

Insert the appropriate word in each blank. Use your dictionary when needed. Have fun with this "power play" through a number of interesting words.

anxious/eager
1. We are _____ to see you, but we are _____ about your health.

disinterested/uninterested
2. Although he is a _____ observer, he is not _____ in the outcome.

enthusiastic/enthusiasm
3. We are _____ about this new project, and our _____ shows.

implicit/explicit
4. _____ orders were not given; however, there was _____ acceptance of the orders by the entire staff.

per annum/per diem

5. His _____ is enormous, but her _____ is low.

flammable/inflammable

6. _____ blankets are illegal in this city's hospitals.

inflammable/nonflammable

7. Only _____ blankets may be used.

farther/further

8. To succeed _____ in your career, you must go _____ in your studies.

indigenous/indigent

9. _____ food is available for the _____ workers and their families.

emigrate/immigrate

10. To _____ is to leave a country, while to _____ means to move to another country.

less/fewer

11. We bought _____ apples than planned and made _____ money.

infer/imply

12. The speaker _____, and the listener _____.

take/bring

13. If you cannot _____ the report to the printer, would you please _____ it to me so I can do it after work.

simple/simplistic

14. The problem is not _____ to solve and his _____ solution will make it worse.

please rsvp/rsvp

15. We hope you will _____ by September 1 to let us know whether you can attend.

proceed/proceeds

16. Let's _____ with the rehearsal and divide the _____ from admission to the performance.

principle/principal

17. The _____ instituted rules that were designed to help students learn the _____ of respect and cooperation.

raise/rise

18. In order to see a _____ in production, we must _____ the quotas and offer a bonus.

passed/past

19. In the _____ I would never have _____ up an opportunity to travel.

rational/rationale

20. A _____ person can present a _____ for the most risky decisions.

CHECK YOUR ANSWERS ON PAGES 476.

WORD POWER BUILDER 13

Circle the words that are unfamiliar to you and then look up the meaning and practice spelling them.

maintenance	Mediterranean	naïve
manageable	memorize	necessary
management	messenger	neighbor
maneuver	millennium	ninth
marriage	miscellaneous	ninety
media	mischievous	notable
mediator	misspelling	noticeable
medieval	mortgage	nuclear

CHAPTER 14: Word Power *9–13 Review*

Choose the correct word from the choices given in parentheses and write it in the blank.

1. We cannot _____ any more funds to this project. (alot/allot/a lot)

2. The _____ professor prepared the _____. (eminent/imminent, bibliography/biographical)

3. Yesterday we _____ to _____ the legal action. (choose/chose, differ/defer)

4. Even though his writing is _____, he is _____ to win the prize. (eligible/illegible)

5. _____ going to _____ to _____ home before the _____ begins. (We're/Were, proceed/precede, there/their, reign/rein/rain)

6. She _____ the company for a _____ tent, which had been _____ for more than $1,000. (ode/owed, canvas/canvass, appraised/apprised)

7. _____ a fundamental _____ that when you tour the _____ building, you don't try to _____ or lobby our officials about your pet project. (It's/Its, principle/principal, capital/capitol, elicit/illicit)

8. _____ doing a _____ job of refurbishing the _____. (Were/We're, through/thorough, suit/suite)

9. With a _____ grin, he asked what the _____ would have been if he had concealed his true character with a _____ of friendliness. (rye/wry, perks/perquisites/prerequisites, guys/guise)

10. He _____ the coal _____ to the building where the _____ is stored in _____ bags. (led/lead, minor/miner, canvas/canvass)

11. _____ of the company's _____ situation, we cannot in good _____ encourage _____ irresponsibility. (Regardless/Irregardless, fiscal/physical, conscious/conscience)

12. During the next _____ year, we cannot _____ funds to rebuild the historic _____ in the _____ city. (physical/fiscal, allot/alot, alter/altar, capitol/capital)

13. Your _____ is needed at this time. (advice/advise)

14. We worked _____ the night to do a _____ job of taking inventory before the start of the sale. (through/thorough)

15. I know you are _____ in the results of this survey, but would you please randomly select ten _____ parties to complete the questionnaire? (uninterested/disinterested)

16. If you want to take a larger _____ of the work, we can give you a 10 _____ increase in salary. (percent/percentage)

17. Although you _____ the test, we have concerns about whether your _____ experience warrants a promotion. (past/passed)

18. The _____ point made by the speaker was that decisions based on solid _____ are less likely to end in regret. (principal/principle)

19. If you do not want to _____ with the project, we will not be able to donate the _____ to charity. (proceed/proceeds)

20. We have _____ new products than our competitor and have made _____ money as a result. (less/fewer)

CHECK YOUR ANSWERS ON PAGE 476.

WORD POWER BUILDER 14

Circle the words that are unfamiliar to you and then look up the meaning and practice spelling them.

observant	oppression	per annum
occasionally	opponent	perceive
occupation	optimistic	perceptible
occurred	outrageous	plausible
odyssey	override	prominent
occurrence	ozone	queue
omission	pamphlet	questionnaire
omitted	participant	quota

CHAPTER 15: Word Power *Speaking with Confidence*

Being sure that you are pronouncing words correctly increases your confidence in the workplace. Whether you are speaking formally or informally, use words correctly and be aware of your pronunciation. If you are not a native speaker of English, listeners will be understanding if you mispronounce a word; native English speakers, however, are subject to being judged more harshly.

The frequently mispronounced words following are spelled to show correct pronunciation; the syllable receiving the most emphasis is capitalized. The common mispronunciations or acceptable alternative pronunciations are in parentheses *after* the sample sentence.

accessories	ak SES uh rees—The interior designer recommended that the accessories be selected last. (uh SES a rees)
affluence/affluent	AF loo ens/AF loo ent—Palm Beach, Florida, and Beverly Hills, California, are examples of affluent communities. (a FLOO ens, a FLOO ent are also acceptable)
applicable	AP lik uhbul—This information is not applicable to our dilemma. (uh PLIK uhbul is also acceptable)
asked	askt—He asked the four questions. (ast or axt)
athletics	ath LET iks—Participation in athletics contributes to good health. (ath uh LET iks)
debris	de BREE—After the storm, debris was everywhere. (Dee BREE)
debut	day bYOO—She made her debut in a British film. (DEB yoot)
Des Moines	de MOYN—The site for our new factory is in Des Moines. (des MOYNS)
entrée	ON tray—The interviewer ordered the cheapest entrée on the menu. (EN tree)
etcetera	et SET e ra or et SET ra (usually abbreviated as etc.)—The king of Siam was fond of saying "etcetera, etcetera, etcetera." (ek SET era)
February	FEB ru er ee—Valentine's Day is February 14. (FEB u airy is also acceptable)
genuine	JEN u in—The stock certificates are genuine. (JEN u wine)
gourmet	goor MAY—A diet of burgers and fries doesn't qualify one as a gourmet. (goorMET)
grievous	GREEV us—A grievous crime has been committed. (greev e us)
height	HITE—The height of the new building has not been decided. (hithe)
hostile	HOS til—His hostile attitude made us uncomfortable. (HOS tile)
Illinois	ill e NOY—The salesman's territory is the entire state of Illinois. (ILL i noys)
incomparable	in COMP er uh bul—Our products are incomparable. (in com PARE able)
irrelevant	ir REL a vint—The course is irrelevant to my major but is related to my hobby. (ir REV a lint)
irrevocable	i REV uh kuh bul—An irrevocable decision cannot be revoked. (i ree VOKE a ble)

Italian	i TAL yin—If you move to Rome, you'll need to learn Italian. (eye TAL yin)
jewelry	JOO el ree—Many jewelry manufacturers are still on 45th Street. (JOO ler ee)
lackadaisical	LAK uh DAY zuh kul—Employers don't hire applicants who appear lackadaisical. (lax uh DAY zuh kul)
library	LI brer ee—Be sure to pronounce both r's in library. (LI berry)
lieu	LOO—In lieu of means instead of or in place of. (LEE oo)
mischievous	MIS chiv us—Some children are mischievous on Halloween. (mis CHEEV e us)
naïve	ni EEV—He is naïve to think he will get a raise without asking for it. (NAVE)
picnic	PIK nik—I look forward to meeting your husband at the company picnic. (PIT nik)
picture	PIK cher—Pictures of past presidents hang in the gallery. (PITCH er)
preface	PRE fis—Have you read the preface to this book? (PREE face)
preferable	PREF er uh bul or PREF ra bul—I think the old equipment would be preferable to the new. (pre FER uh bul)
probably	PROB ub lee—Two baristas will probably serve coffee at the meeting. (PROB lee)
pronunciation	pro NUN see A shun—Pronounce the second syllable nun. (pro NOUN see A shun)
realty	REE ul tee—Several new realty offices opened last year in Fairbanks, Alaska. (REEL uh tee is also acceptable)
relevant	REL uh vint—Mr. Goldman included only relevant statistics in his report. (REV uh lint)
statistics	sta TIS tiks—The sales statistics are included in Ms. Gomez's report. (suh TIS tiks)
subpoena	suh PEE nuh—A subpoena was issued for the murder witness. (sub PEE nuh is also acceptable)
subtle	SUH tl—George was so subtle that Jesse didn't understand he had been fired. (SUB tl)
superfluous	su PER floo us—Those items are superfluous and should be returned. (su PERF e lus or sooper FLU us)
vehicle	VEE i kul—Do not pronounce the h in vehicle. (vee HICK el)
versatile	VER suh tl—A versatile object can be used for various purposes. A versatile person can do many different things. (VER suh tile)
visa	VEE zuh—The word *visa* came into the English language from French in the early 1800s. (VEE suh)

WORD POWER PLAY 15

Say each word aloud before responding to these questions.

A. How many syllables does each word have?

1. grievous   _____
2. superfluous   _____
3. mischievous   _____
4. probably   _____
5. naïve   _____

B. Which letters are silent in these words?

6. Des Moines   _____
7. Illinois   _____
8. debris   _____
9. subtle   _____
10. vehicle   _____

C. Write **T** (true) or **F** (false) in the blank.

_____ 11. Pronounce *affluent* with the accent on the first syllable.

_____ 12. The *i* in *versatile* is pronounced the same as the alphabet sound of *i*.

_____ 13. When saying *preferable*, the accent is on the first syllable.

_____ 14. The capital *i* in *Italian* sounds like the alphabet sound of *I*.

_____ 15. *Height* ends with a *th* sound.

_____ 16. Pronounce *jewelry JOOL e ree*.

_____ 17. *Realty* should be pronounced *reel i tee*.

_____ 18. The second syllable of *pronunciation* sounds different from the second syllable of *pronounce*.

_____ 19. The second syllable of *hostile* is pronounced like the word *tile*.

_____ 20. The first syllable of *statistics* sounds like *sis*.

_____ 21. To remember how to pronounce and spell *irrelevant* and *relevant*, notice that the *l* goes before the *v*.

_____ 22. *Picture* is pronounced the same as the word for a baseball player who pitches.

_____ 23. *Irrevocable* has the primary accent on the third syllable.

_____ 24. The second syllable of *preface* is pronounced like the word *face*.

_____ 25. When identifying the nationality of a native of Italy, the first syllable should sound like the word *eye*.

CHECK YOUR ANSWERS ON PAGE 476.

WORD POWER BUILDER 15

Circle the words that are unfamiliar to you, and then look up the meaning and practice spelling them.

relevant	tariff	wholly
reference	tedious	workable
recurrence	tournament	write-off
referred	ultimately	yield
relegate	vacillate	zealous
silhouette	vacuum	
subsidize	weird	

Appendix C

Supplementary Practice Exercises

Complete these exercises to practice what you learned in the chapters. Doing so will help you achieve mastery of the grammar concepts you learned so that application in your writing and speaking will become automatic.

Chapter	Exercise	Number Right	Total	Date Completed
CHAPTER 1 **References and Resources** **Pages 390–392**	**1-A** Dictionary Practice		10	
	1-B Spelling		20	
	1-C Dictionary Code		20	
	1-D Using Your Thesaurus		10	
	1-E Using Your Reference Manual		10	
CHAPTER 2 **The Parts of Speech** **Pages 393–396**	**2-A** Nouns		10	
	2-B Pronouns		15	
	2-C Verbs		10	
	2-D Adjectives		15	
	2-E Adverbs		15	
	2-F Conjunctions and Prepositions		20	
	2-G Identifying the Parts of Speech		20	
CHAPTER 3 **Sentence Fundamentals** **Pages 396–400**	**3-A** Complete Sentences and Fragments		20	
	3-B Comma Splices and Run-ons		20	
	3-C Dependent Clauses		10	
	3-D Dependent and Independent Clauses		10	
	3-E Sentence Types and Punctuation		10	
CHAPTER 4 **Nouns: Forming Plurals** **Pages 400–402**	**4-A** Regular Noun Plurals		20	
	4-B Irregular Noun Plurals		20	
	4-C Singular and Plural Nouns		10	
	4-D Plurals of Proper Nouns		10	
	4-E Plurals of Compound Nouns		10	
CHAPTER 5 **Nouns: Forming Possessives** **Pages 403–404**	**5-A** Possessive Nouns		10	
	5-B Singular and Plural Possessives		20	
CHAPTER 6 **Pronouns: Types and Their Uses** **Pages 404–406**	**6-A** Personal Pronouns		20	
	6-B Pronoun Usage		20	
	6-C Possessive Pronouns		20	
	6-D Who/Whom and Who/That		20	

Chapter	Exercise	Number Right	Total	Date Completed
CHAPTER 7 **Pronouns: Agreement and Writing Principles** Pages 407–408	**7-A** Pronoun Agreement		20	
	7-B Pronoun Agreement (Its/Their)		10	
CHAPTER 8 **Verbs: Types, Tenses, and Forms** Pages 408–410	**8-A** Verb Tense		25	
	8-B Irregular Verbs		15	
	8-C Verb Forms		15	
CHAPTER 9 **Subject-Verb Agreement** Pages 410–411	**9-A** Subjects and Verbs		20	
	9-B Subject-Verb Agreement		15	
CHAPTER 10 **Adjectives and Adverbs** Pages 411–414	**10-A** Articles		20	
	10-B Pointing Adjectives		15	
	10-C Double Negatives		20	
	10-D Comparative Forms of Adjectives		15	
	10-E Adjectives and Adverbs		20	
CHAPTER 11 **Punctuation: The Comma** Pages 414–419	**11-A** Commas with a Series of Items or Adjectives		20	
	11-B Commas with Clauses		20	
	11-C Commas with Introductory Words and Expressions		20	
	11-D Commas with Nonessential Expressions		20	
	11-E Commas with Quotations		20	
	11-F Commas with Names, Dates, and Places		20	
CHAPTER 12 **Punctuation: The Semicolon, Colon, and Other Marks** Pages 419–420	**12-A** The Semicolon and Colon		15	
	12-B The Colon		10	
CHAPTER 13 **Punctuation: The Fine Points** Pages 421–423	**13-A** Quotation Marks		15	
	13-B The Hyphen		15	
	13-C The Apostrophe		20	
	13-D Parentheses, Brackets, and Dashes		15	
CHAPTER 14 **Polished Writing Style** Pages 423–427	**14-A** Pronoun Reference		10	
	14-B Sentence Variety		20	
	14-C Misplaced Words and Parallel Parts		10	
	14-D Active and Passive Verbs		20	
	14-E Identifying Danglers		15	
CHAPTER 15 **Capitalization, Abbreviations, and Numbers** Pages 427–430	**15-A** Capitalization		20	
	15-B Abbreviations		20	
	15-C Numbers		20	

CHAPTER 1   *References and Resources*

EXERCISE 1-A: DICTIONARY PRACTICE

Use your dictionary and briefly state the meaning of each of the following:

1. embryology _____
2. geology _____
3. seismologist _____
   _____
4. therapeutic _____
   _____
5. oxymoron _____
   _____
6. egocentric _____
7. neurosis _____
8. agoraphobia _____
   _____
9. anthropology _____
10. demographics _____

CHECK YOUR ANSWERS ON PAGE 477.

EXERCISE 1-B: SPELLING

Rewrite the misspelled words, using your dictionary as needed. Write **C** beside correctly spelled words.

1. absense _____
2. accuracy _____
3. analyse _____
4. attendence _____
5. britian _____
6. cemetary _____
7. changable _____
8. changeing _____
9. comeing _____
10. defered _____
11. dineing _____
12. excelince _____
13. existance _____
14. fourty _____
15. credible _____
16. grievious _____
17. inevitable _____
18. lonliness _____
19. ninty _____
20. omited _____

CHECK YOUR ANSWERS ON PAGE 477.

EXERCISE 1-C: DICTIONARY CODE

Draw vertical lines to show where the syllables are divided. In the blank, write the number of syllables in each word.

1. September _____
2. wonderful _____
3. merriment _____
4. methodology _____
5. totality _____

Write the part or parts of speech for each word.

6. motor _____
7. metal _____
8. facility _____
9. grandeur _____
10. make _____

Pronounce each word and then check your answers.

11. maudlin _____
12. nuclear _____
13. literature _____
14. spastic _____
15. bastion _____

Find the language or languages of derivation and write them in the blanks.

16. fanatic _____
17. syllogism _____
18. phonetic _____
19. oration _____
20. milieu _____

CHECK YOUR ANSWERS ON PAGE 477.

EXERCISE 1-D: USING YOUR THESAURUS

Replace the words in bold with words that express the same meaning more tactfully or in more businesslike terms.

1. The cleaning fluid has a **very foul smell**. _____
2. We feel that we were **duped** by the way your offer was worded. _____
3. Wearing revealing clothing to the office is **stupid**. _____
4. We have decided to **reject** your offer of $6,000 for the artwork. _____
5. The numbers in this research report appear to be **bogus**. _____
6. Can you please direct us to a **cheaper** source for the material? _____

7. The design samples for the book cover are very **ugly**. _____

8. The **childish** behavior of your sales staff needs to be dealt with. _____

9. Don't allow yourself to **get mad** in front of clients. _____

10. This holiday season we are going to **kill** the competition. _____

CHECK YOUR ANSWERS ON PAGE 478.

EXERCISE 1-E: USING YOUR REFERENCE MANUAL

Using your reference manual, fill in the blank with the letter of the correct answer or phrase that best completes the meaning of the sentence.

_____ 1. "Dear Mr. Jones" is an example of the standard way to address the recipient of a business letter. This is known as the a) greeting b) salutation c) opening.

_____ 2. An agenda is a business document used to a) list travel plans b) provide minutes c) list topics to be discussed.

_____ 3. An email sent to a recipient whose name does not appear in either the "To" or the "cc" part of the email template is known as a) blind copy b) carbon copy c) confidential copy.

_____ 4. A standard way of writing citations that give credit to the sources used to prepare a report or other informational document is a) endnotes b) footnotes c) text notes d) all of these are acceptable ways to write citations.

_____ 5. A block style letter is one that is formatted a) with some parts indented b) without a signature c) with all elements flush with the left margin.

_____ 6. When a preprinted memo form is used to send a communication, the signature of the sender is not required. a) true b) false

_____ 7. It is customary to use periods with all abbreviations written in all-capital letters. a) true b) false

_____ 8. You should always capitalize words that refer to specific geographical regions. a) true b) false

_____ 9. Names of the seasons of the year should not begin with a capital letter except at the beginning of a sentence or when used as part of a title. a) true b) false

_____ 10. When a number is the first word of a sentence, it should always be written as a word instead of in figures. a) true b) false

CHECK YOUR ANSWERS ON PAGE 478.

CHAPTER 2   *The Parts of Speech*

EXERCISE 2-A: NOUNS

Underline the nouns in the following sentences.

1. The professor gave the students a challenging assignment.
2. Some commuters drive more than 20 miles to work each day.
3. The proposals were due in two weeks.
4. The syllabi contain all the information for each subject.
5. Tina and Rose sent in their applications for a student loan.
6. Will was embarrassed when his stomach growled during math class.
7. Correct your errors before sending emails.
8. The instructor announced the examination schedule for midterms.
9. Larry rearranged the textbooks, notebooks, and papers in his backpack.
10. The classroom contained 20 computers and 5 printers.

CHECK YOUR ANSWERS ON PAGE 478.

EXERCISE 2-B: PRONOUNS

Underline the pronouns in the following sentences.

1. She announced that anyone could attend the seminar.
2. Your insurance will cover his hospital bills.
3. John and I received our applications in the mail.
4. Who will accept the award for him?
5. Something was missing from the top of her file cabinet.
6. Everyone in the audience clapped loudly after her presentation.
7. He tried to unscramble the puzzle, but nothing made sense.
8. You must think about the correct way to approach your boss about a raise.
9. Those of you who were absent must turn in your assignments.
10. Whomever you select as chairperson will choose the new committee members.
11. Somebody in the audience dropped his or her wallet on the floor.
12. Since everyone was anxious to leave, no one heard the teacher give the assignment.
13. I thought the responsibility was mine, but Betty said it was hers.
14. We are renting a truck and moving ourselves to our new office space.
15. Everything in the store will be sold at the annual sidewalk sale.

CHECK YOUR ANSWERS ON PAGE 478.

EXERCISE 2-C: VERBS

Underline the complete verb in the following sentences. Remember to include any helping verbs as part of the complete verb.

1. The Admissions Director welcomed each student.
2. Martha will be attending the orientation program on Monday.
3. Bill was eager to see his new class schedule.
4. The counselor has handed each new student a college catalog.
5. The admissions office required a high school transcript.
6. Stacey will be a student for the first time in ten years.
7. The butterflies were jumping in Maria's stomach on the first day of class.
8. The professor's friendly smile brightened the student's entire day.
9. The young man's laughter echoed throughout the Student Union.
10. The new students were looking forward to the first day of the semester.

CHECK YOUR ANSWERS ON PAGE 479.

EXERCISE 2-D: ADJECTIVES

Underline the adjectives in the following sentences.

1. The irritated caller harassed the busy receptionist.
2. The tired and thirsty workers appreciated the cold lemonade.
3. The noisy water pipes rattled throughout the law offices.
4. The blue ballpoint pen rolled off the wooden desk.
5. The teacher gave Keith a few ideas for his speech.
6. The efficient assistant typed the ten-page report.
7. Mr. Thomas had a magnificent view of the inner harbor from his office window.
8. Twenty-five new students enrolled in the course.
9. The heavy paper jammed the laser printer.
10. The grouchy administrator needed a fresh cup of brewed coffee.
11. Several people rushed into the classroom as the bell rang.
12. The elegant executive greeted the new clients with a firm handshake.
13. The pages in that old book are faded and torn.
14. Do you have enough time to complete the test?
15. Her paper contained no errors.

CHECK YOUR ANSWERS ON PAGE 479.

EXERCISE 2-E: ADVERBS

Underline the one adverb in the following sentences.

1. Ron finally proposed to Mary.
2. Jonas worked diligently on his homework.

3. The report is due immediately.
4. The new computer is very expensive.
5. Turner worked well with the other employees.
6. Mr. Jones really wanted a raise.
7. Cynthia is an extremely talented singer.
8. Michael almost lost his contract.
9. The job applicant was dressed appropriately.
10. These figures are added accurately.
11. Many products are cheaply manufactured.
12. Mr. Johnson never arrives on time.
13. The clerk was working hard on the filing project.
14. The most outstanding employee of the year received an award today.
15. The paper was too messy to read.

CHECK YOUR ANSWERS ON PAGE 479.

EXERCISE 2-F: CONJUNCTIONS AND PREPOSITIONS

Part 1: Underline the conjunctions in the following sentences.

1. Although Andy attended the conference, he didn't see me.
2. Shannon left class when the teacher was finished lecturing.
3. They waited under the tree until the rain stopped.
4. Ryan studied hard so that he would pass the test.
5. Can you work late tonight, or would you prefer to come in early?
6. The couple wanted to go to the movies, but it was too late.
7. The crowd waited in the lobby while the elevator was being repaired.
8. Al and Jeremy hurried to the office since the meeting was about to begin.
9. The employees didn't know if they had received a raise.
10. The instructor praised the students whenever they answered the questions correctly.

Part 2: Underline the prepositional phrases in the following sentences.

11. Please put the laptop on the desk.
12. The secretary put the papers in the folder.
13. The sun broke through the clouds.
14. The flowers were blooming along the path.
15. The store owners lived above the business.
16. The clerk bumped into the file cabinet.
17. Louise moved her car across the street.
18. Everyone except Luther will be going on the business trip.
19. Several people were talking during the lecture.
20. We found the birth certificate beneath the other papers.

CHECK YOUR ANSWERS ON PAGE 479.

EXERCISE 2-G: IDENTIFYING THE PARTS OF SPEECH

Identify the underlined words as either nouns, verbs, or adjectives by writing **N**, **V**, or **A** in the blank.

_____ 1. She put her money in the <u>bank</u>.

_____ 2. Jim was training to be a <u>bank</u> teller.

_____ 3. The store's motto was, "You can <u>bank</u> on us!"

_____ 4. In what <u>time</u> zone do you live?

_____ 5. I will <u>time</u> the runners.

_____ 6. Do you have the <u>time</u> to read this assignment?

_____ 7. The baseball game's final <u>score</u> was 7 to 5.

_____ 8. Lincoln <u>scored</u> the winning touchdown.

_____ 9. The caddie kept the <u>score</u> card during the golf match.

_____ 10. The <u>swim</u> coach taught Darla the backstroke.

_____ 11. He will <u>swim</u> each morning to keep in shape.

_____ 12. The long <u>swim</u> across the lake was exhausting.

_____ 13. Martin <u>shops</u> for bargains.

_____ 14. The <u>shop</u> manager retired after 30 years.

_____ 15. That new <u>shop</u> has good bargains.

_____ 16. Mrs. Brown's <u>garden</u> contains more than one hundred flowers.

_____ 17. The <u>garden</u> furniture needs painting.

_____ 18. Mother said she will <u>garden</u> after breakfast.

_____ 19. The cashier could not read the amount on the <u>price</u> tag.

_____ 20. We must <u>price</u> the furniture at several stores.

CHECK YOUR ANSWERS ON PAGE 480.

CHAPTER 3 *Sentence Fundamentals*

EXERCISE 3-A: COMPLETE SENTENCES AND FRAGMENTS

Identify the complete sentences and fragments by placing a **C** or an **F** in the blank.

Example: When the bell rang for class. _____F_____

_____ 1. The payroll clerk computed the salaries.

_____ 2. While the payroll clerk computed the salaries.

_____ 3. Provided you can begin the job Monday.

_____ 4. You can begin the job on Monday.

_____ 5. The instructor's lecture lasted the whole hour.

_____ 6. Since the instructor's lecture lasted the whole hour.

_____ 7. The boss handed George his paycheck.

_____ 8. Unless the boss handed George his paycheck.

_____ 9. The employees left the office at 5 o'clock.

_____ 10. After the employees left the office at 5 o'clock.

_____ 11. As Mr. Harrison accepted the award.

_____ 12. Mr. Harrison accepted the award.

_____ 13. The president read all the reports in two hours.

_____ 14. Although the president read all the reports in two hours.

_____ 15. Because Mr. Schaffer handed in his resignation.

_____ 16. Mr. Schaffer handed in his resignation.

_____ 17. All the class members passed the final exam.

_____ 18. Until all the class members passed the final exam.

_____ 19. Marsha spoke with the new professor.

_____ 20. If Marsha spoke with the new professor.

CHECK YOUR ANSWERS ON PAGE 480.

EXERCISE 3-B: COMMA SPLICES AND RUN-ONS

Place a **C** in the blank if the word group is a complete sentence, **CS** if it is a comma splice, and **R** if it is a run-on.

_____ 1. The secretary handed the report to the supervisor, he read it quickly.

_____ 2. When the secretary handed the report to the supervisor, he read it quickly.

_____ 3. The secretary handed the report to the supervisor he read it quickly.

_____ 4. While the lawyer prepared the case, her assistant checked the reference sheets.

_____ 5. The lawyer prepared the case her assistant checked the reference sheets.

_____ 6. The lawyer prepared the case, her assistant checked the reference sheets.

_____ 7. The corporation expanded its holdings; it now oversees $2 billion a year.

_____ 8. Since the corporation expanded its holdings, it now oversees $2 billion a year.

_____ 9. The corporation expanded its holdings, it now oversees $2 billion a year.

_____ 10. The corporation expanded its holdings it now oversees $2 billion a year.

_____ 11. The reporter wrote the award-winning story it was published in over 200 newspapers.

_____ 12. The reporter wrote the award-winning story; it was published in over 200 newspapers.

_____ 13. The reporter wrote the award-winning story, it was published in over 200 newspapers.

_____ 14. The company jet flew to London, all the major executives were aboard.

_____ 15. When the company jet was flown to London, all the major executives were aboard.

_____ 16. The company jet was flown to London all the major executives were aboard.

_____ 17. When the mayor spoke to the council, all the members listened.

_____ 18. The mayor spoke to the council, all the members listened.

_____ 19. The mayor spoke to the council all the members listened.

_____ 20. The mayor spoke to the council; all the members listened.

CHECK YOUR ANSWERS ON PAGE 480.

EXERCISE 3-C: DEPENDENT CLAUSES

Underline the dependent clause in each sentence.

1. After the workers finished the project, they all received bonuses.
2. The sun was shining brightly until the clouds moved in.
3. Because the biscuits were hard, the family refused to eat them.
4. Since Susan left town, there is not a great swimmer on the team.
5. When salespeople are successful, the company reaches its goal.
6. Although we had a wet spring, the water table is still low.
7. Esther and David are planning to get married soon even though they have no money.
8. John F. Kennedy delivered many great speeches when he was president.
9. Even though his supervisor gave clear directions, Mark still made several mistakes on his report.
10. Since wrong answers will be subtracted from the total number of correct responses, do not guess.

CHECK YOUR ANSWERS ON PAGE 480.

EXERCISE 3-D: DEPENDENT AND INDEPENDENT CLAUSES

Revise the following sentences to make one of the clauses a dependent clause and connect it to an independent clause.

1. John is an excellent student. John gets good grades. _____
   _____

2. The manager of the store trains the employees very well. The store has the highest sales in the district. _____
   _____

3. The short story was very dramatic. The students in the English Composition class responded enthusiastically. _____

_____

_____

4. Modern psychologists do not all agree with Sigmund Freud's theories. Freud was a pioneer in the field of psychology. _____

_____

_____

5. Political activist C. Delores Tucker attacked the moral standards of hip-hop music in the 1990s. The public had mixed views on the subject.

_____

_____

6. Bobby Flay prepared six different pork belly dishes. He is one of the Food Network's top stars. _____

_____

7. The Accounting Department will issue new expense forms this week. Many people are confused about how to tabulate mileage reports.

_____

_____

8. American Indians were stereotyped in films of the 1940s and 1950s. Very few sympathetic portrayals were presented. _____

_____

_____

9. We cannot issue paychecks on the 15th of this month. Our checks are late coming from the home office. _____

_____

_____

10. Bob and Art are undecided. They will need to make a bid on the house by close of business tomorrow. _____

_____

CHECK YOUR ANSWERS ON PAGE 481.

EXERCISE 3-E: SENTENCE TYPES AND PUNCTUATION

Match the word to its definition by writing the appropriate letter in the blank.

_____ 1. A sentence that has only one independent clause.

_____ 2. A sentence that ends in an exclamation point.

_____ 3. A sentence that has at least two independent clauses.

_____ 4. A sentence that ends in a question mark.

_____ 5. A sentence that makes a request not requiring a response.

_____ 6. A sentence that ends in a period.

_____ 7. A shortened form of a question.

_____ 8. A sentence that has one independent clause and one or more dependent clauses.

_____ 9. A sentence that has at least two independent clauses and one or more dependent clauses.

_____ 10. A sentence that sounds like a question but is a statement.

A. complex sentence

B. statement

C. exclamatory

D. simple sentence

E. interjection

F. compound sentence

G. direct question

H. compound-complex sentence

I. courteous request

J. indirect question

K. elliptical question

CHECK YOUR ANSWERS ON PAGE 481.

CHAPTER 4	*Nouns: Forming Plurals*

EXERCISE 4-A: REGULAR NOUN PLURALS

Make the following singular nouns plural.

Example: writer _____writers_____

Singular	Plural
1. baby	_____
2. alloy	_____
3. daisy	_____
4. play	_____
5. rally	_____
6. country	_____
7. church	_____
8. tax	_____
9. wish	_____
10. glass	_____
11. veto	_____
12. echo	_____
13. radio	_____
14. alto	_____
15. leaf	_____
16. roof	_____
17. shelf	_____
18. wife	_____
19. chief	_____
20. dwarf	_____

CHECK YOUR ANSWERS ON PAGE 481.

EXERCISE 4-B: IRREGULAR NOUN PLURALS

Part 1: Write the plural of the following nouns. Use a dictionary if needed. If two plurals are acceptable, write the preferred spelling.

Example: basis _____bases_____

Singular	Plural
1. thesis	_____
2. bacteria	_____
3. analysis	_____
4. stimulus	_____
5. alga	_____
6. sheep	_____
7. hypothesis	_____
8. curriculum	_____
9. memorandum	_____
10. fungus	_____
11. antenna	_____
12. appendix	_____
13. syllabus	_____
14. crisis	_____

Part 2: Write **S** or **P** in the blank to indicate if the following words are singular or plural; write both letters if applicable.

Example: fungi ____P____

15. data	_____
16. crisis	_____
17. media	_____
18. alumni	_____
19. algae	_____
20. bacteria	_____

CHECK YOUR ANSWERS ON PAGE 482.

EXERCISE 4-C: SINGULAR AND PLURAL NOUNS

Write **S** or **P** to indicate if the following nouns are usually singular or plural.

1. economics	_____
2. statistics	_____
3. news	_____
4. goods	_____
5. thanks	_____
6. scissors	_____
7. civics	_____

8. measles   _____

9. proceeds   _____

10. mathematics   _____

CHECK YOUR ANSWERS ON PAGE 482.

EXERCISE 4-D: PLURALS OF PROPER NOUNS

Write the plurals of the following proper nouns.

Singular	Plural
1. Bush	_____
2. Kelly	_____
3. Jones	_____
4. Hartman	_____
5. James	_____
6. Rodriguez	_____
7. Chen	_____
8. Williams	_____
9. Booth	_____
10. Morgenthau	_____

CHECK YOUR ANSWERS ON PAGE 482.

EXERCISE 4-E: PLURALS OF COMPOUND NOUNS

Part 1: Write the plural form of the following compound nouns.

Singular	Plural
1. get-together	_____
2. post office	_____
3. runner-up	_____
4. chief of police	_____
5. son-in-law	_____
6. nurse's aide	_____
7. photocopy	_____
8. hand-me-down	_____
9. chairperson	_____
10. letter of recommendation	_____

CHECK YOUR ANSWERS ON PAGE 482.

CHAPTER 5   *Nouns: Forming Possessives*

EXERCISE 5-A: POSSESSIVE NOUNS

Complete the following sentences by writing a possessive noun in the blank.

1. Two _____ derby hats were left behind in the cloak room.
2. Our _____ insurance policy is very expensive.
3. The _____ communication skills are important to the success of the company.
4. The five _____ calculations were amazingly accurate.
5. A _____ postponement of construction is in our best interest.
6. A _____ salary can be calculated if you know the hourly rate and hours per week.
7. The new _____ training program begins on Monday.
8. The _____ weight was a key factor in getting the modeling contract.
9. The _____ appearance should not be a barrier to consideration for the position.
10. The _____ grade point averages were a factor in their college admissions.

CHECK YOUR ANSWERS ON PAGE 483.

EXERCISE 5-B: SINGULAR AND PLURAL POSSESSIVES

Write **S** or **P** in the first blank to indicate if the word is singular or plural and then write the possessive form in the second blank. Write both letters if the item could be singular or plural.

Example: authors   _S/P_   _author's/authors'_

	Singular or Plural	**Possessive**
1. childs	_____	_____
2. customers	_____	_____
3. students	_____	_____
4. judges	_____	_____
5. afternoon	_____	_____
6. factories	_____	_____
7. secretaries	_____	_____
8. months	_____	_____
9. European	_____	_____
10. children	_____	_____
11. Virginia	_____	_____
12. men	_____	_____
13. Macy's	_____	_____
14. company	_____	_____

15. accountants   _____   _____
16. industries   _____   _____
17. years   _____   _____
18. woman   _____   _____
19. employee   _____   _____
20. waiters   _____   _____

CHECK YOUR ANSWERS ON PAGE 483.

CHAPTER 6	*Pronouns: Types and Their Uses*

EXERCISE 6-A: PERSONAL PRONOUNS

Underline the correct pronoun for each sentence.

Example: Please give (I, <u>me</u>) your answer.

1. Bob and (I, me) went to the movies.
2. Give (we, us) the new course outlines.
3. (They, Them) worked hard to complete their assignments.
4. Please pass the test papers to (I, me).
5. (We, Us) teachers are looking forward to vacation.
6. The secretary handed (he, him) the messages.
7. It was (they, them) who were late for class.
8. Bring your baked goods to (we, us) on Saturday morning.
9. Give your answer to (I, me) by this afternoon.
10. (He, Him) will be attending the conference in Atlanta.
11. Mr. Johnson presented the award to (she, her).
12. John sat behind (we, us) at the football game.
13. It was (she, her) who answered the telephone.
14. Jerry sat between George and (I, me) on the bus.
15. The speakers will be Mr. Benjamin and (I, me).
16. The teacher introduced Tracey as well as (I, me) to the class.
17. Holly and (she, her) stayed after class.
18. (We, Us) graduates will proceed down the aisle when the music begins.
19. The ballots were given out to (we, us) students during first period class.
20. His friend and (he, him) left class before dismissal time.

CHECK YOUR ANSWERS ON PAGE 483.

EXERCISE 6-B: PRONOUN USAGE

Part 1: Underline the correct pronoun to complete the following sentences.

1. The manager and (he, him, himself) waited for the paychecks to arrive from the Payroll Department.

2. No one works harder in class than Michael and (she, her, herself).
3. The student council members (themselves, theirselves) made all the food for the bake sale.
4. She arrived in class earlier than (he, him).
5. Please send the downloaded files to (me, myself).
6. Barry is just as good a student as (he, him).
7. The other workers left earlier than (I, me, myself).
8. The barber gave (hisself, himself) a haircut.
9. The committee members (theirselves, themselves) decided to have another meeting in two weeks.
10. We gave (ourselves, ourself) tests on speaking Spanish.

Part 2: Six of the following 10 sentences contain an error in pronoun usage, and four are correct. Circle the incorrect pronoun and write the correct one in the blank; write **C** for the sentences that are correct.

_____ 11. The author himself autographed the novel.
_____ 12. Salinda does not type as fast as myself.
_____ 13. Mr. Cone has spoken to the trainees more often than him.
_____ 14. I myself worked till the project was completed.
_____ 15. The executives may find theirselves working overtime tonight.
_____ 16. John granted hisself a leave of absence from the office.
_____ 17. No other student completed the test as quickly as she.
_____ 18. It was him who welcomed us to the conference.
_____ 19. Tina hurt herself during the fire drill.
_____ 20. Ann knows her legal terminology better than me.

CHECK YOUR ANSWERS ON PAGE 483.

EXERCISE 6-C: POSSESSIVE PRONOUNS

Underline the correct pronoun in each sentence.

1. The dog buried (its, it's) bone in the backyard.
2. Do you know (whose, who's) book is on the desk?
3. Is (you're, your) mother coming to graduation?
4. (No ones, No one's) project received a grade lower than a "B."
5. Is (yours, your's) the exam that has been graded already?
6. (Whose, Who's) going to attend the seminar this afternoon?
7. Almost (everyones, everyone's) job was threatened by the strike.
8. (Their, They're) going with us to the retreat.
9. The new iPad is (mines, mine).
10. The newly renovated building on Third Street is (our's, ours).
11. (Its, It's) too late to begin the project now.
12. (Who's, Whose) working overtime tonight?
13. If (you're, your) running out of disk space, delete your old documents.

14. (Somebodys', Somebody's) child was crying in the lobby.

15. I hope (your's, yours) is the one selected by the judge.

16. Are you the one (whose, who's) car is double-parked?

17. Is the accident report (anyone's, anyones) business other than the person involved?

18. We will be going to (they're, their) house after the show is over.

19. (My, Mine) children will be in high school next fall.

20. The organization changed (their, its) name.

CHECK YOUR ANSWERS ON PAGE 484.

EXERCISE 6-D: WHO/WHOM AND WHO/THAT

Underline <u>who</u>, <u>whom</u>, or <u>that</u> to complete each of the following sentences.
Example: The man (who, <u>whom</u>) you just met is my father.

1. Mr. Brooks, (who, whom) is a technical support manager, received a promotion.

2. Do you know (who, whom) is working overtime?

3. The suspects (who, that) the police arrested were driving Frank's stolen car.

4. Give the extra food to (whoever, whomever) can use it.

5. Dr. Holley, (who, whom) was elected state senator last week, is also my internist.

6. (Who, Whom) will you ask to speak to the class?

7. Mr. Harris, (who, whom) I mentioned in my letter, will be arriving next week.

8. The young man, (who, whom) is getting married today, works in Richard's office.

9. The contest winner (who, that) will be chosen today will win a trip to Europe.

10. (Who, Whom) spoke to Mr. Anderson before he left?

11. The baseball manager, (who, whom) the umpire threw out of the game, complained to the team.

12. Give the receipt to the person (who, that) paid for the package.

13. The new stock analyst, (who, whom) was just hired, will start next week.

14. The new city manager, (who, whom) no one has met, will be in the office this afternoon.

15. He is the applicant (who, whom) I am sure you will want to meet.

16. (Whoever, Whomever) signs up first will be given the opportunity to go to the conference.

17. I am the teacher (who, that) will be teaching the career development class next quarter.

18. (Whoever, Whomever) you choose for the position should have good computer skills.

19. I wonder (who, whom) will do my work while I am on vacation.

20. The woman (who, whom) I met on the bus is Theresa's mother.

CHECK YOUR ANSWERS ON PAGE 484.

CHAPTER 7   *Pronouns: Agreement and Writing Principles*

EXERCISE 7-A: PRONOUN AGREEMENT

Underline the correct form of the pronoun in the following sentences.

Example: (<u>Anything</u>, Any thing) you purchase is 30 percent off.

1. (Everyone, Every one) of the students needed more time to finish the test.
2. (Someone, Some one) left (his, their, his or her) notebook in class.
3. Do you know if (anybody, any body) is planning on going to the picnic?
4. The teacher asked if (somebody, some body) would carry the textbooks to the office.
5. (Anyone, Any one) of the students' essays could be published in the literary magazine.
6. (Everything, Every thing) seems to be going wrong today.
7. The police could find (nobody, no body) (who, whom) had witnessed the crime.
8. (Everyone, Every one) (who, that) attended the presentation stood up and applauded after Barbara finished her speech.
9. (Something, Some thing) made a loud crashing noise in the hall during class.
10. (Anything, Any thing) you plan for the conference will be fine with me.
11. Few of the students had (his or her, their) dictionaries with them.
12. Each of the teachers assigned (his or her, their) classes a project today.
13. Everyone in the cast gave (his, their, his or her) best performance.
14. If a customer complains about (his, his or her, their) purchases, send a report to customer care.
15. The team members gave (his or her, their) best effort to get the job done.
16. Several speakers complimented (his, their) audience.
17. Anybody can still add (his or her, their) name to the list.
18. Someone must volunteer (his or her, their) name to the list.
19. Both my sons lost (his, their) keys on the same day.
20. Students did not raise (his or her, their) hands to answer the question.

CHECK YOUR ANSWERS ON PAGE 484.

EXERCISE 7-B: PRONOUN AGREEMENT (ITS/THEIR)

Underline either <u>its</u> or <u>their</u> to complete each of the following sentences.

1. The company gave (its, their) gift to the college building fund.
2. Each group has (its, their) own type of music.
3. The team celebrated (its, their) first victory.
4. The herd of bison thundered (its, their) way across the plain.

5. The orchestra will play (its, their) first performance on Sunday.
6. The band had to change (its, their) uniforms after the game because of the muddy field.
7. The faculty angrily returned to (its, their) offices.
8. The union won (its, their) attempt to represent the employees.
9. The counseling staff disagreed about endorsing (its, their) president's position.
10. The jury pondered (its, their) verdict a long time before announcing it to the judge.

CHECK YOUR ANSWERS ON PAGE 485.

CHAPTER 8   *Verbs: Types, Tenses, and Forms*

EXERCISE 8-A: VERB TENSE

Part 1. Underline the verb in the following sentences. Then fill in the blank with the tense of the verb: present, past, or future.

Tense

1. Dawn looks forward to class every morning.   _____
2. Frankie will sing in the concert on Saturday.   _____
3. The justice system provides free legal advice.   _____
4. The audience misunderstood the presenter's conclusion.   _____
5. Pamela consulted a career counselor.   _____
6. We will fly to Orlando next Wednesday.   _____
7. During the week, Brian stays in the city.   _____
8. Harry and his business partner were in debt.   _____
9. The manager explained the new policy.   _____
10. The contractor will paint the office this afternoon.   _____
11. Anthony takes a course in Arabic on Thursdays.   _____
12. Mark needs a ride to the banquet this evening.   _____
13. Christy earned a master's in business administration.   _____
14. Everyone appreciates getting a bonus vacation day.   _____
15. The teacher will talk with me after class.   _____

Part 2. Underline the correct form of the verbs in the following sentences.

16. Barney has (took, taken) several courses in accounting.
17. Greg has (ate, eaten) pizza for dinner every night this week.
18. During the party the guests (drank, drunk) a toast to the award winner.
19. Mr. Shah (processes, processed) the payroll checks each Thursday.
20. When Tiffany enrolled in college, she (chose, had chose) the medical assistant program.
21. The temperature has (began, begun) to get colder.

22. The furniture has (wore, worn) well over the years.
23. The professor had (took, taken) a leave of absence from his classes.
24. The telephone had (rang, rung) ten times before the operator picked it up.
25. The children had (drank, drunk) all the lemonade and yelled for more.

CHECK YOUR ANSWERS ON PAGE 485.

EXERCISE 8-B: IRREGULAR VERBS

Select the correct form of the verb in the following sentences.

1. Mr. Yearby has (wrote, written) a letter to the editor.
2. The burglar had (threw, thrown) the furniture around the room.
3. The choir (sang, sung) three hymns during the service.
4. The total liability was (hid, hidden) in the complex language of the contract.
5. The water should have (froze, frozen) quickly in the new freezer.
6. Everyone had (forgot, forgotten) what time the program was scheduled to start.
7. The artist had (drew, drawn) a sketch of the book cover.
8. The client has (forgot, forgotten) the contract terms.
9. The mayor (threw, thrown) the first ball of the game to the pitcher.
10. We have (sang, sung) that song fifty times during rehearsal.
11. The applicant had (took, taken) the exam required for employment.
12. The teachers have (hid, hidden) the tests from the students.
13. The speaker's opening story was (drew, drawn) from an experience in his past.
14. Peter had (broke, broken) one of the computer monitors.
15. The employee has (withdrew, withdrawn) her application for a transfer.

CHECK YOUR ANSWERS ON PAGE 485.

EXERCISE 8-C: VERB FORMS

Insert a correct form of the verb shown in parentheses to complete each of the following sentences. Use being verbs and helping verbs where appropriate. Some items have more than one correct answer.

1. How many of you (go) _____ to the meeting tomorrow morning?
2. Marissa (elect) _____ president at last night's meeting.
3. We (wait) _____ for your answer before proceeding to draw up the agreement.
4. Is anybody (go) _____ with me?
5. You (require) _____ to sign in when you enter the building after hours.

6. The baseball team (go) _____ to Montreal next week.

7. Doctor Swenson (speak) _____ at the physician's conference in Norfolk.

8. The shipment of textbooks (<u>expect</u>) _____ next week.

9. The teachers (have) _____ tutoring sessions after school.

10. Keith (make) _____ waffles for breakfast.

11. The proofs for the annual report (review) _____ right now by the editors.

12. The copy machine (repair) _____ by noon.

13. During the summer the children (sleep) _____ later than usual each morning.

14. You (choose) _____ to represent our department at the conference.

15. We (like) _____ to nominate Mr. Rodriguez as the employee of the month.

CHECK YOUR ANSWERS ON PAGE 485.

CHAPTER 9	*Subject-Verb Agreement*

EXERCISE 9-A: SUBJECTS AND VERBS

Circle the subject and underline the verb in the following sentences.

1. The morning sun rose at 6 a.m.
2. The hungry wolves howled throughout the valley.
3. Do you have a completed resume?
4. Gourmet cooking is Martina's favorite hobby.
5. Please answer his question immediately.
6. The daily newspaper is delivered each morning.
7. There are 25 students in the communications class.
8. Both mother and son were found safe before nightfall.
9. The job placement director sent Andrew on three job interviews.
10. Did you buy a ticket for the afternoon or evening performance?
11. Across the street from our office is our favorite restaurant.
12. Early sign-ups for Little League will be held next Sunday.
13. Across the countryside word spread about the fire.
14. Mr. Overton, along with his wife, attended the mayor's conference in San Francisco.
15. The toy manufacturer recalled the new product because of sharp edges.
16. The boy and his grandfather strolled through the city park.
17. Advancement courses are taught for all employees on Wednesday evenings.
18. Along the Outer Banks, residents were warned of the approaching hurricane.

19. In the morning Sidney will learn his test scores.
20. All during August the football team practiced in the hot sun.

CHECK YOUR ANSWERS ON PAGE 486.

EXERCISE 9-B: SUBJECT-VERB AGREEMENT

Underline the verb that is correct in the following sentences.

1. Juanita (call, calls) her mother each night before bedtime.
2. Some of the children at the summer camp (has, have) been sick.
3. Antoinette and her sisters (runs, run) the small bakery down the street.
4. Neither of my sisters (has, have) cleaned her room.
5. Here (is, are) the hotdog and soda you asked for.
6. My grandfather, as well as my mother, (loves, love) to watch the evening news.
7. Each of the members on the team (is, are) contributing to the project.
8. (Has, have) your mother and father been by to visit?
9. The House and the Senate (is, are) still fighting over the legislation.
10. Many a father and son (is, are) involved in Little League.
11. That is the student who (talks, talk) during class.
12. Here (is, are) the supplies you need.
13. Their mother, who (is, are) an optometrist, examined me for contact lenses.
14. Several groups (was, were) touring the monument when the lightning struck.
15. The lawyer (does, do) want to represent the client in this case.

CHECK YOUR ANSWERS ON PAGE 486.

CHAPTER 10   *Adjectives and Adverbs*

EXERCISE 10-A: ARTICLES

Circle the article *a* or *an* to put in front of the following words.

1. (a, an) white car
2. (a, an) hospital
3. (a, an) edition
4. (a, an) honest reply
5. (a, an) big mistake
6. (a, an) ten percent raise
7. (a, an) increase in sales
8. (a, an) agreed amount
9. (a, an) M & M candy lover

10. (a, an) one-way street
11. (a, an) heavy package
12. (a, an) angry customer
13. (a, an) unknown author
14. (a, an) open door
15. (a, an) USC football player
16. (a, an) early riser
17. (a, an) universal policy
18. (a, an) holiday greeting
19. (a, an) omelette
20. (a, an) UPS delivery

CHECK YOUR ANSWERS ON PAGE 487.

EXERCISE 10-B: POINTING ADJECTIVES

Underline the correct word to complete the following sentences.

1. These (kind, kinds) of rumors cause marriages to break up.
2. Margaret wanted to buy (this, those) brand of photocopy paper.
3. The manager wanted (them, those) reports to be distributed yesterday.
4. These (type, types) of situations are awkward for us.
5. (These, Them) textbooks are needed in class today.
6. Unfortunately, I make this (types, type) of error often.
7. (That, Those) sort of clothing should not be worn in the office.
8. Pedro does not like these (types, type) of shoes.
9. Priscilla wanted to save these (kind, kinds) of articles.
10. The supervisor wanted (them, those) employees to work overtime.
11. Those (kind, kinds) of memos must be typed before noon today.
12. (This, This here) restaurant is my favorite.
13. The teacher is looking for these (type, types) of ideas.
14. Those (kind, kinds) of remarks will not improve our customer relations.
15. (That, That there) student received an A+ on his English final.

CHECK YOUR ANSWERS ON PAGE 487.

EXERCISE 10-C: DOUBLE NEGATIVES

Underline the correct word for each sentence. Remember to avoid two negatives in the same sentence.

1. The student didn't do (anything, nothing) wrong.
2. Mary doesn't want (no, any) chicken.
3. The store (can't, can) hardly keep those shoes in stock.
4. Stanley hasn't gone (nowhere, anywhere) in this new car.
5. I won't (never, ever) speak to Helen again.

6. Since you are on a diet, you don't need (no, any) ice cream.
7. Johnny doesn't know (nothing, anything) about politics.
8. Mrs. French won't go (nowhere, anywhere) without her dog.
9. There was hardly (no, any) difference between the two bids on the contract.
10. Linda said she wouldn't (never, ever) cheat on her fiance.
11. Nobody (can, can't) leave class early today.
12. Susan hardly (ever, never) drives anymore.
13. Don't put (no, any) gravy on the potatoes.
14. Mr. Langley doesn't need (no, any) help with the proposals.
15. I shouldn't go (anywhere, nowhere) with all this work to do.
16. Bob (can't, can) barely see in the fog.
17. Mr. Bowles can't get (any, none) of his report written with all the noise.
18. The baseball player (could, couldn't) never hit the curve ball.
19. Our family doesn't (never, ever) go to that restaurant to eat.
20. That child shouldn't eat (no, any) more candy.

CHECK YOUR ANSWERS ON PAGE 487.

EXERCISE 10-D: COMPARATIVE FORMS OF ADJECTIVES

Underline the appropriate adjective for each sentence.

1. Mrs. Brown is the (nicer, nicest) of all the teachers I have had.
2. Mr. Little is the (kindest, kinder) of the two gentlemen.
3. Julia is a (harder, more hard) worker than her brother.
4. The Browns' youngest daughter is the (more successful, most successful) of the four children.
5. Alison is the (most friendliest, friendliest) person in our neighborhood.
6. Benjamin received the (worse, worst) grades in the class.
7. Bernadette is among the (most strong, strongest) athletes.
8. Mr. Casperini has (the most unique, a unique) style of classroom instruction.
9. This soup tastes (worser, worse) than the special we were offered last week.
10. Who's the (better, best) lawyer, Rose or Chandra?
11. Raymond is the (older, oldest) of all his brothers and sisters.
12. This is the (most unusual, most unique) home I've ever seen.
13. The view from the top of the Empire State Building is the (more beautiful, most beautiful) of any in the city of New York.
14. Which is (more, most) expensive, the airfare to Spain, France, or Italy?
15. Would email or fax be (better, best) for this message?

CHECK YOUR ANSWERS ON PAGE 487.

EXERCISE 10-E: ADJECTIVES AND ADVERBS

Decide which is needed—an adjective or an adverb—in the following sentences. Then underline the correct word from the choices given.

1. She did (good, well) on the driver's test.
2. Marilyn's new dress looks (good, well) with her new shoes.
3. The paintings on the walls are (sure, very) pretty.
4. The car runs (smoother, more smoothly) than it did before.
5. He drives (more careful, more carefully) now.
6. Those cookies tasted (delicious, deliciously).
7. If you do (good, well) on the test, you'll be accepted at the college.
8. The driver felt (bad, badly) about the accident.
9. The film seemed to move (slow, slowly).
10. The band played so (loud, loudly) that we couldn't hear the sirens.
11. My sister feels (good, well, either good or well) today.
12. Edna did (good, well) in the interview.
13. He (sure, surely) didn't treat her well.
14. Can you work (quicker, more quickly)?
15. The students worked (real, really) hard on their science project.
16. Our doctor always writes his prescriptions (clear, clearly).
17. He works (neat, neatly) and fast.
18. That hat looks (good, well) on you.
19. I am (sure, surely) working hard on the project.
20. I have learned all the answers (well, good).

CHECK YOUR ANSWERS ON PAGE 487.

CHAPTER 11 — *Punctuation: The Comma*

EXERCISE 11-A: COMMAS WITH A SERIES OF ITEMS OR ADJECTIVES

Insert a comma where needed in the following sentences. If no comma is needed, write **C** at the end of the item.

Example: Mason wiped the hot, sticky sauce off his fingers.

1. The elderly residents stayed inside because of the hot humid weather.
2. They drove the old grey dump truck to the junkyard.
3. Tommy took a bite of the chocolate chewy candy bar.
4. The recipe requires two eggs one stick of butter and two cups of flour.
5. Her father's bright cheery smile cheered up Melissa.
6. Linda longed for a day to enjoy the warm gentle ocean breezes.
7. The dentist told Sam he could not eat any hard crunchy foods.
8. The FBI accepts only intelligent competent applicants.

9. Elena wants ketchup mustard and relish on her hotdog.

10. Margaret's accurate efficient accounting skills led to her promotion.

11. Many soldiers were killed during the long fierce battle.

12. The friendly honest stranger returned my briefcase.

13. When Kerry got the cast off her foot, she wanted to run jump and dance.

14. The boss's note told Joanie to draft the letter proofread it and hold it for his review.

15. Keith's daring competent actions during the fire were praised by the mayor.

16. His ridiculous comic behavior made everyone laugh.

17. Patricia craved the hot salty taste of the freshly roasted peanuts.

18. The owner gave the first five customers a rose a $100 gift certificate and a big smile.

19. The city's new operating system accounting procedures and auditing process will be installed this week.

20. The novice skateboarder skinned his knee bruised his arm and broke his front tooth in the accident.

CHECK YOUR ANSWERS ON PAGE 488.

EXERCISE 11-B: COMMAS WITH CLAUSES

Insert any necessary commas in the following sentences. Write **C** at the end of the item if no commas are needed.

Example: I want to go to the movies, yet I also have to finish my essay.

1. Please give me your test paper and you may then begin reading Chapter 5.

2. Susan baked some chocolate-chip cookies and she gave some to all the people in our group.

3. We were ready to go to class but Deborah couldn't get the car started.

4. Brenda worked quickly yet the class ended before she completed the test.

5. The assistant answered the telephone but no one was on the line.

6. The baseball player hit the ball hard and he ran quickly to first base.

7. I don't want to study but I don't want to fail the test.

8. Alex does not want to go to the meeting nor will he send anyone in his place.

9. Peggy waited by the phone for the interviewer said she would call today.

10. Are you going to buy the shoes or do you want to wait until they go on sale?

11. The toddler built a sandcastle but the waves washed it away.

12. Bob gobbled down the two hamburgers and then he ate three orders of french fries.

13. Angela was on a diet yet she still managed to eat the strawberry shortcake.

14. The minister preached a good sermon but several people still fell asleep.

15. James sent in his reservation for he planned on attending the banquet.

16. The applicant was not prepared for the word processing test nor could she verify her speed.

17. The young girl enjoyed her first plane ride and thanked the flight attendant and pilot.

18. William bought a ticket but did not attend the concert.

19. Catherine wanted to be a basketball player and she practiced her shooting every day.

20. My friend was angry for the hairstylist had cut her hair too short.

CHECK YOUR ANSWERS ON PAGE 488.

EXERCISE 11-C: COMMAS WITH INTRODUCTORY WORDS AND EXPRESSIONS

Insert any necessary commas in the following sentences.

1. Yes I'll give your papers back on Monday.

2. Ms. Johansson can you help me with this problem?

3. In the early morning before dawn Rich went fishing.

4. If you arrive after the play begins you must wait until intermission to be seated.

5. No I am not working overtime tonight.

6. Since you will be the first to arrive would you please set up the chairs for the meeting.

7. Mr. Bryant could you get a temporary worker for me for next Friday?

8. Before leaving for work I did the laundry and washed the dishes.

9. After the meeting ended the coffee and cake arrived.

10. Since going to his reunion Jerry has renewed old acquaintances.

11. Before going outside the children were given the playground rules.

12. Well I am not sure if I can go with you this weekend.

13. When I attended business school I learned to use Excel.

14. Underneath the chair by the door Mickey found his missing glasses.

15. Oh I can't believe it's Monday already.

16. Arriving late for work Paula rushed up the steps.

17. Mr. Olivas when is our final exam?

18. When Suzie came in the door everyone shouted at her.

19. After the girls shopped for hours at the mall they went to the movies.

20. Even though Curtis had a lot of work to do he still took time to play ball with his son.

CHECK YOUR ANSWERS ON PAGE 489.

EXERCISE 11-D: COMMAS WITH NONESSENTIAL EXPRESSIONS

Insert the missing commas in the following sentences.

1. My son who likes to surf is a good swimmer. (I have one son.)
2. Dr. Harvey who is the president of the college will speak at the graduation ceremony.
3. My college roommate Toni Heiser is a successful entrepreneur.
4. Our reference book *Guide to Business Careers* is available on Amazon.
5. All residents young or old are invited to the film screening.
6. The lottery winner who is my brother-in-law will spend his earnings wisely.
7. This violin which I've had for years was passed down to me by my grandfather.
8. The city manager Mr. Ortiz will meet with the area civic leagues.
9. Our math textbook *Understanding Business Mathematics* explains how to round off decimals.
10. Leave an answer either yes or no on my voice mail about attending the seminar next week.
11. The mayor who is also a dentist was re-elected last fall.
12. The Phillies my favorite baseball team have won sixteen games in a row in Philadelphia.
13. Planning for your retirement a necessity for sure can never begin too soon.
14. My childhood friend a middle school classmate is visiting us next week.
15. Because of your patience with children a trait I admire I know you'll be a good child care worker.
16. To run a marathon 26-plus miles a year's training is recommended.
17. Employees are encouraged to use their vacation leave a minimum of two weeks per year to achieve a work/life balance.
18. Our French teacher who is also my aunt grew up outside of Paris.
19. The publisher Mr. Breeden urged me to write a book about my life.
20. The new president of the college a great guy is an alumni of our biggest football rival.

CHECK YOUR ANSWERS ON PAGE 489.

EXERCISE 11-E: COMMAS WITH QUOTATIONS

If the sentences are correct, write **C** in the blank. If a comma is needed, insert it.

_____   1. "Can you come to work early on Friday?" asked Mrs. Lincoln.

_____   2. "You may go home early" his supervisor said, "if all your work is done."

_____   3. My mentor always told me "A positive attitude will take you far in your career."

_____ 4. "Please" the professor said, "use specific examples to prove your answers."

_____ 5. Frank shouted "Watch out!" and snatched the child from the oncoming car's path.

_____ 6. His friends yelled "Surprise!" when Al came into the restaurant.

_____ 7. "Are you exempt from taking the final exam?" asked Mrs. Franklin.

_____ 8 Greg kept answering every question with "I don't know."

_____ 9. The supervisor instructed "Everyone must complete the questionnaire in fifteen minutes."

_____ 10. "All the students clapped after my speech!" Anna exclaimed.

_____ 11. Instead of saying he would take the job, the applicant just said "Maybe."

_____ 12. "Thanks for tutoring me in Spanish, Mrs. Edgars" said Timothy.

_____ 13. Lana's friends yelled "Good-bye" as her bus pulled out of the station.

_____ 14. "Who will drive the carpool van next week?" asked Mr. Lewis.

_____ 15. "Since the bank is closing," the manager explained "you must make an appointment for tomorrow."

_____ 16. "Can you believe this gorgeous view!" Melissa shouted.

_____ 17. Marvin asked "When will the word processing seminar begin?"

_____ 18. When Lester finished his speech, the audience yelled "Hurray!"

_____ 19. The student exclaimed "Wow, I got a 99 on the test!"

_____ 20. When his father gave him the keys to the new car, John could only say "Wow!"

CHECK YOUR ANSWERS ON PAGE 489.

EXERCISE 11-F: COMMAS WITH NAMES, DATES, AND PLACES

Insert the missing commas in the following sentences.

1. Jared Olansky moved to Lansing Michigan after graduation.

2. The children's museum in Washington DC has a new exhibition on safety.

3. The exchange student from Madrid Spain will live with the Kennedys.

4. Both his parents graduated on June 12 1995 from Penn State University.

5. My dentist James Kail DDS has just opened his own practice.

6. The commencement address on June 14 2013 was televised nationally.

7. My dad always says that San Francisco California is the most beautiful city in America.

8. Have you visited Disneyland in Anaheim California or Disney World in Orlando Florida?

9. James Little PhD spoke to our psychology class.

10. His birthday September 6 1990 is the same date as his uncle's birthday.

11. Did your brother live in Portsmouth New Hampshire or in Portsmouth Virginia?

12. John McGuire MD received his graduate degree from the University of Virginia.

13. On September 29 2008 the stock market suffered a severe loss in trading.

14. Will the yearly conference be in Tampa Florida or Charleston South Carolina?

15. Classes first began on Thursday September 5 1981 at this college.

16. On November 15 2010 John's father retired after thirty years with the company.

17. Both John P. Smith PhD and William R. Smith MD paid for a world cruise for their parents.

18. Our plane leaves from Pittsburgh Pennsylvania and we transfer in Denver, Colorado.

19. The conference will begin on Monday October 5 and end on Wednesday October 12.

20. Muriel Freeman MD will be the guest lecturer at the Pavillion in Newport Rhode Island.

CHECK YOUR ANSWERS ON PAGE 490.

CHAPTER 12

Punctuation: The Semicolon, Colon, and Other Marks

EXERCISE 12-A: THE SEMICOLON AND COLON

Insert semicolons, colons, and commas where needed in the following sentences.

1. Doctor Hobley who was our mayor will speak at the meeting he is an excellent presenter.

2. Sabrina ran toward the bus then she suddenly dropped all her packages.

3. Three players got base hits still the team could not score any runs.

4. Angela works two different jobs also she volunteers for the literacy council.

5. The owners sold a large amount of stock thus they could afford the new office space.

6. Mr. Barrows has suggested the following summer office hours 8 a.m. instead of 9 a.m. Monday–Thursday 8 a.m. to 2 p.m. on Fridays.

7. Your radio publicity schedule will be in the following cities Cambridge Massachusetts Portsmouth New Hampshire and Augusta Maine.

8. Joanna wanted a raise however she was afraid to ask her supervisor.

9. It is Mr. Bell's birthday his colleagues are planning a surprise party.

10. A heavy rainstorm is predicted for Friday therefore we are rescheduling the family day picnic.

11. Two of the panelists started arguing thus the moderator had to intervene to continue the discussion.

12. Avis is an excellent student she studies hard.

13. Consider this idea change the date to Monday July 5 canceling the event is not an option.

14. The organization is low on funds consequently we will not be buying a table at the fundraiser.

15. Please revise the following parts of the report the executive summary which is too long the charts which need to be verified and the statements I highlighted in yellow.

CHECK YOUR ANSWERS ON PAGE 490.

EXERCISE 12-B: THE COLON

Insert a colon where it is needed in the following sentences. Write **C** in the blank in front of any sentences that do not require a colon.

_____ 1. Sunrise will be at 545 a.m. tomorrow morning.

_____ 2. Karen's goals were the following graduation, career, and marriage.

_____ 3. We can schedule the banquet on February 8, February 15, or March 1.

_____ 4. Jonathan received double-time for working three holidays Thanksgiving, Christmas, and New Year's Day.

_____ 5. Benjamin Franklin wrote, "A penny saved is a penny earned."

_____ 6. Three interviewees were called back for second interviews Betty Mandez, Avis Bartlett, and Dan Baker.

_____ 7. At 1130, the teacher ended the lesson and assigned the following read pages 35–60, answer the questions at the end of the chapter, and write a paper.

_____ 8. Be sure to attend our Grand Opening on the following dates April 7, 8, and 10.

_____ 9. Registration will begin at 8 p.m., and the seminar will start at 9:30.

_____ 10. The door was clearly marked "DO NOT ENTER."

CHECK YOUR ANSWERS ON PAGE 491.

CHAPTER 13 | *Punctuation: The Fine Points*

EXERCISE 13-A: QUOTATION MARKS

Put the quotation marks where they are needed in the following sentences.

Example: When she completed her exams, Madrika exclaimed, "Hurray!"

1. Many students confuse accept with except.
2. Say I can instead of I can't.
3. Thank you, Mr. Lockner, Ryan said sincerely.
4. Look for the Silver Lining is the name of an old song.
5. Charlie yelled, We're lost!
6. The spell checker did not catch the word eligible when you meant to write illegible.
7. The article Money Management in this morning's paper gave me some good ideas.
8. A tradition in live theater is to tell the actor to break a leg, which means do well.
9. Mitch asked, Are you working overtime tonight?
10. Our most popular refrigerator magnet reads, Don't Feed Me!
11. The poem Still I Rise by Maya Angelou is a good one to recite.
12. April wondered, Should I ask for a raise?
13. Never use irregardless in your writing (or speaking): it's a non-standard word form.
14. The umpire yelled, Play ball!
15. Surfers going out to catch a wave during a hurricane are playing a dangerous game.

CHECK YOUR ANSWERS ON PAGE 491.

EXERCISE 13-B: THE HYPHEN

Place a hyphen in the compound words listed wherever it is needed.

1. The restaurant was located in a hard to find location.
2. We can offer the applicant a part time position until a full time one opens up.
3. We will auction off a high priced antique at tonight's charity event.
4. After ninety nine percent of the vote was counted, the networks announced the winner.
5. Every summer our catalog features a mid July white sale with deeply discounted prices.
6. Very young children can be taught the quality of self control.
7. The therapist recommended yoga and eight hours sleep for the stressed out executive.

8. The cubicle walls must be ordered in six foot sections that are interchangeable.
9. Please forward a copy of the most up to date report.
10. The CEO has a reputation as a kind hearted individual.
11. Older workers are advised to steer away from high risk investments.
12. The cost of a first class flight is prohibitive for most business travelers.
13. Larry's self taught language skills helped him land a high level job.
14. The battle worn staff members were given the day off after a 24 hour shift.
15. We provide the latest stock quotes to our clients, which is a no fee service.

CHECK YOUR ANSWERS ON PAGE 491.

EXERCISE 13-C: THE APOSTROPHE

Add an apostrophe ('), 's, or s where it is needed in the following sentences. Write **C** after any sentences that do not need to be changed.

1. Please place a flyer on Mr. Hernandez windshield.
2. The childrens choir will perform at the holiday festival.
3. The accident occurred when the childs skateboard was left on the landing.
4. Please type the boss memo concerning the new policy on company automobiles.
5. The two secretaries desks are too close together.
6. Someones briefcase was left in the conference room.
7. James computer crashed this afternoon.
8. Its so cold this morning that my teeth are chattering.
9. We expect sales of ladies handbags to increase over the holidays.
10. We are watching the competing companies new products very carefully.
11. Both authors opinions are given equal weight in the blog post I am writing.
12. Susan was determined to get all As in college.
13. John cant go to the office tomorrow.
14. The customers favorite dish comes from my mother-in-laws recipe.
15. The bank is willing to waive three months interest on the loan.
16. Are you planning to attend the Joneses party?
17. A lot of work gets done in the teachers lounge.
18. Someone going to have to wait until tomorrow for an appointment.
19. Early rock music was played in the 50s and 60s era.
20. If you are willing to advance me two weeks pay, I would be very appreciative.

CHECK YOUR ANSWERS ON PAGE 492.

EXERCISE 13-D: PARENTHESES, BRACKETS, AND DASHES

Add parentheses, dashes, or brackets where needed in the following sentences.

1. John my sister's first husband is coming for dinner.
2. The company party is Saturday I can't wait!
3. The dress costs $149 not $159.
4. Please make a donation we need your help now.
5. The mayor's statement said, "Due storm *sic* conditions, we are unable to predict when city services will return to normal."
6. Happiness it's yours for the asking.
7. Our source for the blog entry on cancer treatment (see Healthblog.com, April 12, 2013 note: I am not sure of this date) was Dr. Anita Denard of Harvard University.
8. Our new air purifier rated number one by *Consumer Reports* was on sale last week.
9. The new office tower more than 60 floors is on schedule for completion by 2015.
10. The new board members Dr. Duzeck and Ms. Swenson will meet with the press this afternoon.
11. The pageant judges entrants on style, grace, beauty, and intelligence not necessarily in that order, and the winner had them all!
12. Zelika Horton she was the winner praised her parents for their love and devotion.
13. I went to the office on Saturday from 8 a.m. to noon to complete the reports for Monday.
14. The June cover photo our first full wedding issue will be shot in Central Park's Sheep Meadow.
15. Refer to the 2013 Annual Report pp. 5–6 for the charts on our sales performance.

CHECK YOUR ANSWERS ON PAGE 492.

CHAPTER 14 — *Polished Writing Style*

EXERCISE 14-A: PRONOUN REFERENCE

Cross out the vague pronoun and replace it with more specific wording. Edit and change verb forms if necessary.

Example: ~~They~~ The management require~~s~~ customers to wear shoes and shirts.

1. Ms. Meyers trained Ellen on the new computer program, and she did a good job.
2. They say our taxes were overpaid.
3. Tiffany told her mother that they were allowed to go.

4. Helen saw Patricia talking to her daughter. (Helen's daughter)

5. Mark met Frank while he was in college. (both were in college)

6. They say you must bring a textbook, notebook paper, and a folder to class.

7. Leslie's mother is a successful woman, and I'm sure she'll be a success too.

8. Tim was a track star in high school; it was a sport he loved.

9. You are not allowed to smoke in the theater.

10. Lance's father is a carpenter, and he will be able to build them the way you want.

CHECK YOUR ANSWERS ON PAGE 493.

EXERCISE 14-B: SENTENCE VARIETY

Part 1. Rewrite the following sentences using the methods discussed in this chapter to connect ideas.

1. Teenagers are very fashion conscious. Their taste is often dictated by the choices of their peer group. _____
   _____

2. Consumers have the last word with retailers. If they buy the latest fashion, retailers profit and stores continue to stock the item. _____
   _____
   _____

3. Some people dress fashionably because they want attention. Other people dress fashionably because they are natural trendsetters. _____
   _____
   _____

4. For most businesspeople, dressing well is important. The reason is simple. It makes a good impression on their colleagues and clients. _____
   _____
   _____

5. Make a good first impression. Greet your clients by name. Welcome them with a friendly smile and a handshake. _____
   _____
   _____

6. He finished dinner. Afterwards, he returned to work. _____
   _____

7. You might go on a trip to China. Do not give your hosts expensive gifts. They might be embarrassed. They might not accept them. _____
   _____
   _____

8. Someone in China might invite you to dinner. You will get rice. Hold the rice bowl next to your mouth. _____
   _____

9. Chinese meals consist of a variety of foods. Your host will offer you several dishes. Eat from every plate to show good manners. _____
_____

10. It isn't necessary to know every custom. Building rapport with your host is easier, however, when you know something about the culture.
_____
_____

Part 2. Insert a transitional word in the blank to complete the following sentences.

11. Ron worked hard to get good grades; _____, he reviewed his class notes every night.

12. Mrs. Williams expected the best from her students; _____, they were always prepared.

13. The instructor handed out the course outline; _____, she explained every assignment.

14. Rose did not hear the alarm; _____, she was late for English class.

15. Twenty-five percent of the class received an "A"; _____, all the students passed the test.

16. Please sign in if you are late; _____, you will be marked absent.

17. The printer broke at 9 a.m.; _____, the teacher had the test ready for class.

18. Each student needs to rent a locker in the Student Union Building; _____, he or she must purchase a new lock.

19. The graduation ceremony is Saturday night; _____, the practice will be Thursday morning.

20. The director introduced the speaker; _____, he gave a summary of the speaker's qualifications.

CHECK YOUR ANSWERS ON PAGE 493.

EXERCISE 14-C: MISPLACED WORDS AND PARALLEL PARTS

Part 1. Underline the misplaced words in the following sentences.

Example: Thelma played a hymn in church <u>by Mozart</u>.

1. Keep watch for any sign of intruders with a keen eye.

2. The plumbers replaced the waterlines with plastic pipes that were leaking.

3. The ice cream was gobbled down by the guests with the chocolate swirls.

4. The show dog was chosen by the judge with the furry tail.

5. Take care that you do not give instructions to the temps if they are from the old manual.

Part 2: If the following sentences need parallel parts, write **NP**; if the sentence is correct, write **C** in the blank.

Example: Susan has red hair, fair skin, and is heavily built. **NP**

_____ 6. My uncle is a chef and an ambulance driver.

_____ 7. Bob would rather travel by train, by bus, and driving is his third preference.

_____ 8. When identifying people by occupation, take care to use gender-neutral language, make sure their job titles are correct, and avoiding misspelled names is equally important.

_____ 9. The crowd was noisy and the music played loudly.

_____ 10. The third baseman ran to first, slid into second, and scored the winning run.

ANSWERS ARE ON PAGE 494.

EXERCISE 14-D: ACTIVE AND PASSIVE VERBS

If the following sentences are examples of active style, write **A**; if the sentence is passive style, write **P** in the blank.

Example: Jonah typed the letter. **A**

_____ 1. The supervisor announced the new work schedule.

_____ 2. The compositions were corrected by the teacher.

_____ 3. The farmer collected antique tractors.

_____ 4. The man's name was mispronounced by all the speakers.

_____ 5. John threw the softball to his daughter.

_____ 6. The staff flew to Denver for the convention.

_____ 7. Her luggage was lost by the airline.

_____ 8. Richard wallpapered the bathroom.

_____ 9. The airline lost Bernadette's suitcase.

_____ 10. The telephone was answered by the department manager.

_____ 11. The cafeteria is serving your favorite dessert.

_____ 12. Too many "you knows" were used throughout the speech.

_____ 13. You should mail those contracts to the new address.

_____ 14. Last year the electric company increased the rates of its residential customers.

_____ 15. The radiologist read the patient's X-ray.

_____ 16. Several mistakes were found by the editors.

_____ 17. The reporter presented the top news story.

_____ 18. Mr. Bell coaches his son's Little League team.

_____ 19. "The Star Spangled Banner" was sung by the audience

_____ 20. The people of Scotland are called *Scots,* not *Scotch.*

CHECK YOUR ANSWERS ON PAGE 494.

EXERCISE 14-E: IDENTIFYING DANGLERS

Underline the dangler in the following sentences. If the sentence does not have a dangler, write **C** in the blank.

Example: <u>While walking through the park</u>, the wind blew my hat into the bushes.

_____ 1. His mother gave John, who received good grades, tickets to a rock concert.

_____ 2. When I finished browsing through the store, the clerk rang up my purchases.

_____ 3. Having received good grades, his mother gave John tickets to a rock concert.

_____ 4. While Janice was jogging around the block, her new shoes hurt her feet.

_____ 5. Being on the discount table, Ms. Jefferies saved $10 on the new gloves.

_____ 6. Ms. Jefferies saved $10 on the new gloves that were on the discount table.

_____ 7. Feeling as though she might faint, Debbie asked her colleague to take her to the hospital.

_____ 8. Feeling as though labor had begun, her husband took Debbie to the hospital.

_____ 9. Jogging quickly around the block, her new shoes hurt her feet.

_____ 10. Before going home, this account must be audited.

_____ 11. After browsing through the store, the clerk rang up my purchases.

_____ 12. In spite of having a crack, the customer purchased the antique vase for $1000.

_____ 13. Before you go home, this account must be audited.

_____ 14. Having forgotten the client's name, the phone call was made to the wrong person.

_____ 15. Facing the windows, the manager asked to have the artwork re-hung.

CHECK YOUR ANSWERS ON PAGE 494.

CHAPTER 15

Capitalization, Abbreviations, and Numbers

Use your reference manual as a resource when doing these exercises.

EXERCISE 15-A: CAPITALIZATION

Underline any errors in capitalization.

1. Independence day is my favorite holiday in the Summer.

2. Jonathan Branch graduated from Pershing high school in 1969.

3. When planning for retirement, most people are still counting on medicare and social security benefits.

4. a. Best Regards,

    b. Dee Mannix, PhD

5. A new, affordable housing development is being built east of city hall.

6. Our Spanish club is planning an outing in the spring.

7. Rosa's new job is on the west coast.

8. The exhibit of french masters is on display at the downtown art museum.

9. Jonah is the new manager of the southwest region.

10. The novel *Gone With The Wind* is one of my favorites.

11. a. Eco-friendly Industries

    b. 105 Main street

    c. Cheyenne, WY 90209

12. My boss advised me, "apply for the promotion and don't worry about your loyalty to me."

13. Drive South on FDR drive to wall street, a historic district at the tip of manhattan.

14. We invited a Peruvian Professor who teaches a course called ancient civilizations to join our discussion at the Conference.

15. Please do not call earlier than 6 a.m. Pacific Standard time.

16. The bar association is planning its annual Holiday reception for December 15.

17. The Sears Tower Building in Downtown Chicago is still one of the most popular tourist spots in the City.

18. Our term papers are due to the Professor no later than november 30.

19. Please call the congressman's office and ask for a copy of congressman Rutherford's speech at the monthly chamber of commerce breakfast.

20. Sincerely Yours,
    Julius Cortez

CHECK YOUR ANSWERS ON PAGE 495.

EXERCISE 15-B: ABBREVIATIONS

Underline either the correct form of the abbreviation or full word shown in parentheses.

1. We are opening a branch office on the (SE/southeast) side of town.

2. We are located on (Rte./Route) 12, just west of Main (St./Street).

3. I intend to visit three (U.S./US) national monuments on my vacation.

4. Articles for the (January/Jan.) newsletter must be submitted no later than the 30th of the month.

5. This Letter of (Agrmnt./Agreement) specifies that all parties must agree to the amendments.

6. On the way to downtown (LA, Los Angeles) we got stuck in traffic on the (freeway/fwy.).

7. Please send your reply to (Ms./Miss) Jennifer Holt, (HR/Human Resources) (Dept./Department).

8. (Cpt./Captain) Pauletta Lorenzo is the first female to hold the position in that precinct.

9. The (Federal Emergency Management Agency (FEMA)/FEMA) worked with our state's first responders to assist victims of the flood.

10. My (MBA/M.B.A.) advisor was (Dr. Khalil Ahmed, PhD/Dr. Kahlil Ahmed).

11. His son is named (Sidney Blumenthal, Jr./Sidney Blumenthal Jr.).

12. Refer to the chart on (p. 10/page 10) for statistics on male mortality rates in Europe.

13. Send the payment to (Alexis Tasheka, D.D.S./Alexis Tasheka, DDS) by next week if possible.

14. Our grand opening reception was scheduled for (Fri./Friday), (Oct./October) 3, but the (bldg./building) is not yet ready for occupancy.

15. Please send a messenger to the Empire State (Bldg./Building) to pick up the package.

16. We would like to have additional refreshments for the guests, (eg., e.g.,) hot hors d'oeuvres and a vegetable platter.

17. I would highly recommend our tax consultant, Charles Lightner, (C.P.A., CPA), if you have not already hired someone.

18. (Rev./Reverend) Derek Russell has agreed to deliver the invocation at the luncheon.

19. Our (Customer Management Center (CMC)/CMC) is looking for candidates who have experience in customer service.

20. Your appointment is scheduled for Thursday at (10 am/10 a.m.)

CHECK YOUR ANSWERS ON PAGE 495.

EXERCISE 15-C: NUMBERS

Underline the correct form of the number, abbreviation, or symbol shown in parentheses.

1. (June 1, June 1st) is the anniversary of my (5th/fifth) year with the company.

2. (One-third, 1/3) of our profits is derived from the sale of technology products.

3. Please send me new figures for the chart on (page 5, page five) of the report.

4. The sale price will be available until the (31, 31st) of October.

5. My fee for consulting services is ($50/$50.00/fifty dollars) per hour.

6. (65, Sixty-five) is the age at which you will be eligible for Medicare.

7. The meeting will begin promptly at (2 p.m./two o'clock) in Conference Room 14-B.

8. We are adding (three, 3) 2-story annexes onto our warehouse.

9. My plan is to achieve a net worth of ($1 million dollars, $1 million) by the age of 30.

10. (Ten percent/10 percent/10%) of the survey respondents would use the new product.

11. My Google shares increased (15 percent, 15%) in the last quarter.

12. Your proposal for the engineering contract must be submitted within (thirty, 30) days from the date of this letter.

13. The illustration in (Figure 2, Figure two) shows two similar concepts for the new building.

14. I lost (50 cents, 50¢) in the vending machine; may I please have a refund.

15. The gallery opening gala is (5 p.m. to 8 p.m., 5 to 8 p.m.), and the exhibit will be on view through (June 30/June 30th).

16. Each payday I deposit ($50/$50.00/50 dollars) directly into my savings account.

17. Since the (fourth/4th) quarter of last year, sales have increased (2%/2 percent) each month.

18. We are inviting (150, one hundred-fifty) guests to the fundraising dinner.

19. Please add to the job description that (2 yrs/2 years/two years) of experience is required for the job.

20. I am hoping to pay less than (one thousand dollars/$1,000/$1000.00) for a new laptop.

CHECK YOUR ANSWERS ON PAGE 496.

Appendix D: Answers

Chapter Self-check Exercises

This appendix contains answers to the self-check activities in each chapter. Use the score card to record your number of correct answers for each exercise. The Worksheet exercises are divided into lettered sections according to the different topics covered in each chapter. Your scores for each section will help you see where you need to review chapter concepts or complete more practice exercises. Consult with your instructor to determine the amount and type of extra practice you need.

PRETEST, POSTTEST, AND WORKSHEET SCORE CARD

CHAPTER 1 References and Resources	CHAPTER 2 The Parts of Speech	CHAPTER 3 Sentence Fundamentals	CHAPTER 4 Nouns: Forming Plurals	CHAPTER 5 Nouns: Forming Possessives
Pretest _____ of 10	Pretest _____ of 10	Pretest _____ of 10	Pretest _____ of 10	Pretest _____ of 10
Worksheet 1.1 A _____ of 10 B _____ of 15	Worksheet 2.1 A–B _____ of 10	Worksheet 3.1 A–B _____ of 20	Worksheet 4.1 A _____ of 20 B–C _____ of 15 D _____ 10	Worksheet 5.1 A _____ of 5 B _____ of 20
Worksheet 1.2 A–B ____ of 15	Worksheet 2.2 A–D ____ of 25	Worksheet 3.2 A–B _____ of 15	Worksheet 4.2 A–B _____ of 25	Worksheet 5.2 _____ of 20
Worksheet 1.3 A–C _____ of 15	Worksheet 2.3 _____ of 15	Worksheet 3.3 _____ of 20	Worksheet 4.3 A _____ of 10 B _____ of 15	Worksheet 5.3 A _____ of 15 B _____ of 15 C _____ of 1
Posttest _____ of 10	Posttest _____ of 10	Posttest _____ of 10	Posttest _____ of 10	Posttest _____ of 10
CHAPTER 6 Pronouns: Types and Their Uses	CHAPTER 7 Pronouns: Agreement and Writing Principles	CHAPTER 8 Verbs: Types, Tenses, and Forms	CHAPTER 9 Subject-Verb Agreement	CHAPTER 10 Adjectives and Adverbs
Pretest _____ of 10	Pretest _____ of 10	Pretest _____ of 10	Pretest _____ of 10	Pretest _____ of 10
Worksheet 6.1 A _____ of 25 B _____ of 5 C _____ of 8 D _____ of 5	Worksheet 7.1 A _____ of 10 B _____ of 5	Worksheet 8.1 A _____ of 20 B _____ of 10	Worksheet 9.1 A _____ of 10 B _____ of 20	Worksheet 10.1 A _____ of 15 B _____ of 10 C _____ of 10
Worksheet 6.2 A _____ of 5 B _____ of 20 C _____ of 5 D _____ of 5	Worksheet 7.2 A _____ of 6 B _____ of 15	Worksheet 8.2 A _____ of 20 B–C _____ of 20	Worksheet 9.2 _____ of 35	Worksheet 10.2 A–D _____ of 25 E _____ of 25
Worksheet 6.3 _____ of 25	Worksheet 7.3 A–B _____ of 20	Worksheet 8.3 _____ of 15	Worksheet 9.3 _____ of 20	Worksheet 10.3 A _____ of 5 B _____ of 10 C _____ of 10
Posttest _____ of 10	Posttest _____ of 10	Posttest _____ of 10	Posttest _____ of 10	Posttest _____ of 10

CHAPTER 11 Punctuation: The Comma	CHAPTER 12 Punctuation: The Semicolon, Colon, and Other Marks	CHAPTER 13 Punctuation: The Fine Points	CHAPTER 14 Polished Writing Style	CHAPTER 15 Capitalization, Abbreviations, and Numbers
Pretest _____ of 10	Pretest _____ of 10	Pretest _____ of 10	Pretest _____ of 10	Pretest _____ of 10
Worksheet 11.1 _____ of 25	Worksheet 12.1 _____ of 20	Worksheet 13.1 _____ of 15	Worksheet 14.1 A–C _____ of 15 D _____ of 10	Worksheet 15.1 _____ of 20
Worksheet 11.2 A _____ of 20 B _____ of 25	Worksheet 12.2 _____ of 10	Worksheet 13.2 A–C _____ of 25	Worksheet 14.2 A–B _____ of 10 C–D _____ of 20	Worksheet 15.2 _____ of 20
Worksheet 11.3 A–B _____ of 15	Worksheet 12.3 _____ of 15	Worksheet 13.3 _____ of 15	Worksheet 14.3 A _____ of 20 B _____ of 25 C _____ of 5	Worksheet 15.3 _____ of 20
Posttest _____ of 10	Posttest _____ of 10	Posttest _____ of 10	Posttest _____ of 10	Posttest _____ of 10

UNIT 1	Mastering the Art of Good Writing—Chapters 1–3

CHAPTER 1	References and Resources

PRETEST

1. unabridged
2. abridged
3. Standard English
4. archaic
5. copyright page
6. lexicographers
7. thesaurus
8. syllable
9. parts of speech
10. synonyms, antonyms, homonyms

WORKSHEET 1.1

A.

1. T
2. F
3. T
4. F
5. T
6. F
7. T
8. F
9. T
10. T

B.

1. noun; a social blunder
2. three
3. first
4. third

5. second
6. verb
7. second
8. maybe
9. Answers will vary, depending on the dictionary used.
10. first
11. Answers will vary: before or after
12. catalogue
13. catalog
14. noun and verb
15. hip-hop

WORKSHEET 1.2

A.

1. The word is Standard English, and there are no special restrictions for its use.
2. The second spelling shown is less acceptable for general use.
3. twin·kling
4. pair or pairs
5. True
6. at the bottom of each page or every other page and/or in the front matter
7. in the front matter
8. addenda, Latin
9. homonym
10. Madrid

B.

11. a. b
    b. c
    c. a
    d. c
    e. c
12. The following words should be circled:
    pronounciation (pronunciation), seperate (separate),
    congradulate (congratulate), persue (pursue)
13. a. sub·tle – accent on *sub*
    b. ra·tio·nale – accent on *nale*
    c. in·fra·struc·ture – accent on *in*
14. Answers will vary. Examples:
    a. matchless, unsurpassed
    b. unbelievable, implausible
    c. unpleasant, objectionable

15. a. accommodations
    b. indispensable
    c. judgment
    d. consensus
    e. acknowledgment

WORKSHEET 1.3

A. Answers will vary. Examples:

1. excellent, exceptional, gratifying
2. careless, foolhardy, rash
3. experience, expertise
4. displeased, annoyed, offended
5. irresponsible, not intelligent, not smart

B.

6. a. block
   b. modified-block
   c. simplified
7. memorandum
8. body
9. a. Securities and Exchange Commission
   b. Chief Executive Officer
10. formal and informal

C.

11. Almost 5,000 people attended the Alliance for Survival rally.
12. Can you list 50 ways to make $5 million?
13. The prime interest rate went to 15 percent (or 15%) today.
14. The judge said the US Supreme Court decision was favorable to my company.
15. The annual report listed the Midwest as the most profitable area of the country.

POSTTEST

1. ridiculous, occasion
2. a. Answers will vary (poor, careless)
   b. Answers will vary (incorrect, regrettable)
3. North Atlantic Treaty Organization
4. False
5. Ordinary conversation or writing; informal language
6. 1908

7. Chloe Anthony Wofford
8. miniature, tiny, minute (pronounced my·NOOT)
9. second
10. nationwide (adverb) and nation-wide (adjective)

| CHAPTER 2 | *The Parts of Speech* |

PRETEST

1. verb
2. adjective
3. pronoun
4. interjection
5. conjunction
6. preposition
7. adverb
8. noun
9. proper nouns
10. common nouns

WORKSHEET 2.1

A. The following words should be circled:

1. smile, situation
2. correspondence, United States, Asia, South America, Europe, Africa
3. career, people, cultures, individuals
4. slang, coworkers, English, language
5. neighborhood, classroom, workplace, United States, Canada, Great Britain, parts, world

B.

6. It
7. He
8. Who
9. She, her
10. They, her, him

WORKSHEET 2.2

A. The following words should be circled and underlined:

1. is
2. seems
3. am, are
4. were
5. think are
6. sounds
7. appears, being

B. The following words should be circled:

8. do work, have met
9. has read
10. are reading
11. has chosen
12. will be going
13. will have been working
14. might have noticed
15. does sign

C. Answers may vary.

16. need, have

17. spend

18. are asking

19. is

20. recruit

D. Answers may vary.

21. into

22. By

23. Through

24. Over

25. across

WORKSHEET 2.3

1. interviewers, applicants, competence, skills, emphasis, enthusiasm, ambition, flexibility

2. Underlined: He, it, it, she, it, she, she, She, who, her

   Circled: wrote, proofread, received, looked, read, invited, has, helped

3. is, appears, sounds, is, has, believe, seems, has, is

4. a. Circled: does, has

   Underlined: does enjoy, has stayed

   b. Circled: has

   Underlined: has met

   c. Circled: has, has

   Underlined: has left, has completed

   d. Circled: have

   Underlined: have concluded

5. a. Circled: no, new, a huge new

   Underlined: idea, carpeting, desk

   b. Circled: smart, important

   Underlined: You, ethics

6. Answers may vary.

   a. yesterday, today, immediately

   b. well, poorly, quickly

   c. carefully, recklessly, fast

   d. correctly, accurately, slowly, quickly

   e. always

7. a. and

   b. but

   c. or

   d. nor

   e. for

   f. yet

   g. so

8. Answers should include six of the following:
   a. after, although, as
   b. because, before, even though
   c. if, when, since
   d. so that, than
   e. unless, until
   f. which, while

9. a. Circled: with, in, to, for
      Underlined: you, jet, conference, achievers
   b. Circled: under, in
      Underlined: name, folder
   c. Circled: into, by, at
      Underlined: city, bus, restaurant
   d. Circled: of, from
      Underlined: city, window

10. a. Circled: at, into
       Underlined: at the return address, into the trash
    b. Circled: in, of, toward
       Underlined: in the workplace, of kindness and consideration, toward other employees and customers
    c. Circled: on, of, on
       Underlined: on the behavior, of people, on their lifestyles
    d. Circled: between
       Underlined: between a dream and a goal
    e. Circled: from, to
       Underlined: from your office, to my home
    f. Circled: at, for
       Underlined: at producing spot announcements, for their customers

11. a. adjective
    b. verb
    c. adjective
    d. noun

12. a. noun
    b. noun
    c. verb
    d. adjective

13. Answers will vary; examples are provided.
    a. Omar is reading a report from the president.
    b. Reading should be a lifelong habit.
    c. I lost a pair of new reading glasses.

14. Answers will vary; examples are provided.
    a. Let's plant roses and gardenias this year.
    b. In our Seattle plant we hire many environmentalists.

15. a. surely
    b. really

POSTTEST

1. noun
2. verb
3. adverb
4. preposition
5. adjective

6. verb
7. and, but, or, nor, for, so, yet
8. dependent
9. pronoun
10. pronouns

CHAPTER 3

Sentence Fundamentals

PRETEST

1. subject, verb, be a complete thought
2. nouns and pronouns
3. verb
4. person and number
5. clause
6. independent
7. dependent
8. sentence fragment
9. run-on sentence
10. comma splice

WORKSHEET 3.1

A.

	Subjects	Verbs
1.	director	could have filmed
2.	You	must be
3.	winner	sees
4.	loser	sees
5.	books	were put
6.	you/you	earn/learn
7.	members	have
8.	visitors	arrived
9.	(You)	give
10.	Professor Friede	found

B.

11. I   She couldn't arrange the reports in chronological order.

12. D   ~~because~~ Many organizations have similar problems with employees.

13. D   ~~although~~ An information technology professional needs excellent communication skills.

14. I In the workplace you may converse with many people.
15. D ~~since~~ They have limited English skills.
16. I Don't laugh at someone's pronunciation or grammar errors.
17. D ~~when~~ The trucker arrived with the shipment.
18. I It's better than I thought.
19. D ~~although~~ She prefers driving to flying.
20. D ~~after~~ You've learned a few phrases in other languages.

WORKSHEET 3.2

A. Conjunctions are in bold. Your answers may vary.

1. The future is that time when you'll wish you had done what you're not doing now, **although** you cannot undo the past.
2. He places big orders with us **since** his sales rep gives him a special discount.
3. The plant was operating on a 24-hour basis **because** management refused to adopt a three-shift schedule.
4. Professor Bailey explained that studying business communication at Wright Business School is enjoyable, **although** the new student wouldn't believe it.
5. Vanessa said we need the latest dictionary for Chapter 3 **because** language changes constantly.

B.

6. I wonder whether he uses voice recognition software.
7. The report is good, but where is the appendix?
8. Would you please send these items by overnight mail to us.
9. A winner says he fell. A loser says somebody pushed him.
10. Management makes important policies and decisions; we just carry them out.
11. Do you know what a subprime mortgage is?
12. Would Thursday be more convenient for you?
13. Take advantage of this deal today!
14. Would you please fax this report before you go to lunch.
15. I heard you got a new job. That's wonderful!

WORKSHEET 3.3

1. C A workaholic is a person who is addicted to work.
2. C He knows the definition of *workaholic*, <u>even though</u> he is not a person who is addicted to work.
3. R The highest achievers are passionately committed to their work; they are not workaholics.
4. C <u>Although</u> the highest achievers are passionately committed to their work, they are not workaholics.
5. C The highest achievers are passionately committed to their work, <u>although</u> they are not workaholics.

6. CS High achievers take more short vacations than the average person. They often get new ideas for their work during these vacations.

7. R Studies show that taking time off to relax results in a more productive workforce, yet many employers often have to remind their employees to use their earned vacation leave.

8. C Workaholics work long hours <u>because</u> they fear losing the job or not impressing the boss favorably.

9. C <u>Because</u> high achievers feel a strong sense of commitment to their work, they work long hours.

10. C High achievers define skills needed for their career and set out to get them.

11. CS Observations about high achievers are from Charles Garfield's book *Peak Performers*. Mr. Garfield studied hundreds of top achievers.

12. C Always leave a job on good terms, for you may need a reference in the future.

13. R During an interview, don't forget to ask *your* questions; also, remember to thank the interviewer for the appointment.

14. R Listen attentively during an interview, and make eye contact with the interviewer.

15. C Human Resources directors are skilled at asking questions that cannot be answered by a simple "yes" or "no."

16. C The winters are long and cold in Indianapolis, but this gives IVY Tech students more time to study.

17. CS "Love competence in the performance of your tasks; begin now." —Lao Tzu

18. C A rolling stone gathers no moss, yet it does get a certain smoothness from its rolling.

19. R "Mix a little foolishness with your serious plans. It is lovely to be silly at the right moment."—Horace (Roman poet and philosopher)

20. C Turn left at the corner of Boston Boulevard and Woodward Avenue, which is not a violation of traffic rules during most of the day.

POSTTEST

1. CS quickly, yet
2. CS errors, so
3. R floor, but
4. CS once, so
5. R conference, or

6. CS client, but
7. C
8. C
9. R office, but
10. CS planning, but

UNIT 2	Knowing Your Subject—Chapters 4–7

CHAPTER 4	*Nouns: Forming Plurals*

PRETEST

1. cabinets
2. allies
3. injuries
4. resources
5. facilities
6. tattoos
7. dominos, dominoes
8. accessories
9. altos
10. potatoes

WORKSHEET 4.1

A.

1. itineraries
2. portfolios
3. ferries
4. moneys or monies
5. wolves
6. zeros or zeroes
7. pianos
8. authorities
9. heroes
10. melodies
11. knives
12. tariffs
13. proxies
14. surveys
15. plaintiffs
16. wives
17. chiefs
18. cargoes, cargos
19. attorneys
20. mementos, mementoes

B.

1. corps
2. economics
3. deer (occasionally deers)
4. Georges
5. series
6. Chinese
7. Joneses
8. aircraft
9. fish (or fishes)
10. stepchildren

C.

11. P	12. S/P	13. S	14. S/P	15. S

D.

1. have	3. are	5. are	7. is	9. is
2. is	4. were	6. are	8. was	10. were

WORKSHEET 4.2

A.

1. formulas, formulae
2. alumni
3. bases
4. censuses
5. criteria, criterions
6. axes
7. parentheses
8. crocuses, croci
9. appendixes, appendices
10. concertos, concerti
11. indexes, indices
12. analyses
13. media, mediums
14. diagnoses
15. bureaus, bureaux

B.

16. S
17. P
18. S
19. P/S
20. P
21. P
22. medium
23. criteria
24. parenthesis
25. alumni

WORKSHEET 4.3

A.

Singular	Plural
1. follow-up	follow-ups
2. textbook	textbooks
3. trade-in	trade-ins
4. editor in chief	editors in chief
5. runner-up	runners-up
6. spaceflight	spaceflights
7. headhunter	headhunters
8. minor league	minor leagues
9. chief of staff	chiefs of staff
10. volleyball	volleyballs

B.

1. businesspeople/businesspersons
2. plaintiff
3. software
4. premises
5. editors in chief
6. cargo
7. corps
8. portfolio
9. proxy
10. proceeds
11. itinerary
12. memento
13. notaries public
14. chassis
15. write-offs

POSTTEST

1. d	3. c	5. b	7. c	9. c
2. b	4. c	6. b	8. d	10. c

CHAPTER 5

Nouns: Forming Possessives

PRETEST

1. boss's/what's/workers
2. city's
3. brother-in-law's
4. Men's/boy's
5. Mr. James's

6. Ms. Perkins'
7. Knox's/representatives'
8. *Whistler's*/world's
9. students'/world's
10. C

COMMUNICATIONS CONNECTION

1. c	6. s	11. a	16. g	21. v
2. f	7. b	12. i	17. l	22. p
3. k	8. q	13. h	18. n	23. t
4. j	9. y	14. d	19. r	24. m
5. x	10. o	15. e	20. w	25. u

WORKSHEET 5.1

A.

1. Mr. Smith's, Ms. Perkins', City's, week's
2. son-in-law's, son's
3. brother's, Martinezes
4. Women's, women's, men's
5. daughter-in-law

B.

1. C
2. editor's <u>stories</u>
3. C
4. brother-in-law's <u>manager</u>
5. C
6. attorneys' <u>offices</u>
7. South Dakota's <u>resources</u>
8. Men's, women's <u>clothes</u>
9. Ms. Lopez's <u>orders</u>

10. industry's <u>directors</u>
11. crew's <u>strength</u>
12. California's <u>gold mines</u>, <u>orange groves</u>
13. nation's <u>wine</u> and <u>raisins</u>
14. world's <u>toy manufacturers</u>
15. Men's <u>College</u>
16. C
17. Tom's <u>book</u>
18. hours' <u>work</u>
19. Penney's <u>success</u>
20. Barbie's <u>fame</u>, Mattel's <u>success</u>

WORKSHEET 5.2

Singular Possessive	Plural	Plural Possessive
1. representative's	representatives	representatives'
2. week's	weeks	weeks'
3. witness's	witnesses	witnesses'
4. James's	Jameses	Jameses'
5. country's	countries	countries'
6. man's	men	men's
7. Asian's	Asians	Asians'
8. wife's	wives	wives'
9. father-in-law's	fathers-in-law	fathers-in-law's
10. congresswoman's	congresswomen	congresswomen's
11. Jones's	Joneses	Joneses'
12. family's	families	families'
13. Webster's	Websters	Websters'
14. hour's	hours	hours'
15. Wolf's	Wolfs	Wolfs'
16. wolf's	wolves	wolves'
17. organization's	organizations	organizations'
18. boss's	bosses	bosses'
19. woman's	women	women's
20. child's	children	children's

WORKSHEET 5.3

A.

1. C
2. years'
3. person's
4. Men's, fashions, women's
5. minute's
6. Rokers', days
7. ladies'
8. Jones's
9. Brunswick's, years
10. Jenkins'

11. coaches', players'
12. Keat's
13. Mr. Hendrix's
14. brothers' films
15. guests' names

B. Answers are examples.

1. George's books are overdue at the library.
2. Mr. Adams' wife is my dermatologist.
3. A week's vacation is insufficient for a grand tour of Europe.
4. The Adamses' home is near Mr. Adams' office.
5. My sisters' store is on Fifth Avenue.
6. A restaurant server's name is not "Honey" or "Hey You."
7. We tried to solve the members' problems.
8. The salespeople's commissions are computed daily.
9. After two years' work, the plans for the subway were canceled.
10. My mother-in-law's studio is in Paris.
11. Charlton Heston quoted Moses' words.
12. Dallas's (or Dallas') streets are safe.
13. Please give me the auditor's report.
14. Ten minutes' notice is not enough.
15. Supervisors' expense accounts are audited.

C. Remove all apostrophes from this sentence.

POSTTEST

1. dean's
2. C
3. Mother's
4. Yesterday's, today's
5. company's
6. sisters-in-law's
7. city's
8. Jones's
9. Division's, CEO's
10. agencies'

CHAPTER 6

Pronouns: Types and Their Uses

PRETEST

1. D	3. A	5. A	7. A	9. A
2. A	4. A	6. D	8. B	10. B

COMMUNICATIONS CONNECTION

1. e	6. n	11. j	16. y	21. b
2. o	7. h	12. x	17. u	22. k
3. f	8. g	13. c	18. a	23. r
4. d	9. l	14. s	19. m	24. q
5. i	10. w	15. t	20. p	25. v

WORKSHEET 6.1

A.

1. she and I	8. her	15. He and I	22. him
2. me	9. we	16. me	23. me
3. They	10. he	17. he	24. they
4. We	11. me	18. We	25. me
5. I	12. me	19. her	
6. us	13. them	20. me	
7. me	14. him	21. he	

B.

1. I, subjective
2. him, objective
3. I, subjective

4. her, objective
5. Who, subjective

C.

Subject	Object of Verb
1. I	you
2. He	her
3. She	him
4. Who	them

Subject	Object of Preposition
5. I	him
6. We	it
7. He	her
8. They	whom

D.

1. does	3. does	5. can
2. he loves	4. you know	

WORKSHEET 6.2

A.

1. its/it's	3. Yours	5. you're/your
2. C	4. You're	

B.   The crossed out word is shown in parentheses.

1. C	6. C
2. themselves (theirselves)	7. I (me)
3. he (him)	8. C
4. he (himself)	9. themselves (themself)
5. me (myself)	10. you (yourself)

11. I (myself)
12. C
13. C
14. C
15. C

16. themselves (theirself)
17. C
18. himself (hisself)
19. myself (me)
20. C

C.

1. No one
2. Every one
3. C

4. someone
5. any one

D. Answers are examples.

1. no one, everyone
2. someone
3. himself

4. anything, someone/somebody
5. myself

WORKSHEET 6.3

1. whoever
2. that
3. who
4. who
5. Whom
6. Which
7. Whom
8. Whom
9. that

10. Whoever
11. whomever
12. that
13. that
14. whom
15. who
16. who
17. Which
18. that

19. whom
20. whom
21. who
22. which
23. who
24. whomever
25. that

POSTTEST

1. me
2. The applicants must stand in line for hours.
3. No one, I
4. she
5. they
6. yours, hers
7. Who
8. who
9. he, I, whoever
10. it's, whoever

CHAPTER 7 — Pronouns: Agreement and Writing Principles

PRETEST

1. its
2. his or her
3. his or her
4. his or her
5. his or her

6. their
7. his or her
8. their
9. voted
10. their

WORKSHEET 7.1

A.

	Best	Incorrect			Best	Incorrect
1.	c	b		6.	c	a
2.	a	d		7.	d	a
3.	b	d		8.	c	b
4.	b	c		9.	a	d
5.	d	b		10.	d	b

B. **Answers are examples.**

1. The company encourages employees to use direct deposit for their paychecks.
2. Edward took his car to the mechanic and told him he thought it needed a tune-up.
3. Some department stores open at midnight on Black Friday.
4. The Human Resources Department is interviewing as many qualified candidates as possible to identify at least five outstanding new employees.
5. As teachers and students prepared for the standardized tests, the teachers reassured the students and tried to calm their nerves.

WORKSHEET 7.2

A. **Answers are examples.**

1. group
2. class
3. jury
4. team
5. staff
6. committee

B.

1. plural
2. singular
3. its
4. it is
5. its
6. its
7. its
8. its

9. its
10. its
11. the janitorial service
12. trash shouldn't be thrown
13. the ideas
14. a
15. his or her

WORKSHEET 7.3

A.

1. its
2. Everyone, his or her
3. its
4. its
5. No one, I
6. his or her
7. their
8. their
9. their
10. the manager's
11. their
12. its
13. their
14. his or her
15. their

B. Answers are examples.

16. Members of this department [or All department members] should be sure their nouns and pronouns agree in number in their written communications.

17. All the mechanics finished their work quickly. *or* Each mechanic finished the work quickly.

18. Every child in the class needs a book. *or* All the children in the class need their own book.

19. All applicants should write their name in the blank. *or* Each applicant should write his or her name in the blank.

20. No one was willing to take responsibility for his or her part in the disaster.

POSTTEST

Answers are in boldface.

1. The chairperson asked the board members to cast **their** vote on the proposal.
2. C
3. Every speaker is expected to create his **or her** own presentation for the meeting.
4. Every person in the group needs **a** laptop.
5. Each participant should sign **his or her** name on the attendance sheet.
6. Every department must develop **its** budget based on historical spending.
7. C
8. The company moved **its** new operation to a downtown location.
9. Every member of the jury has cast **his or her** vote on the verdict.
10. The top ten salespeople will be able to take **their** chosen guest on an all expenses paid vacation.

UNIT 3	Mastering Verbs and Modifiers—Chapters 8–10

CHAPTER 8	*Verbs: Types, Tenses, and Forms*

PRETEST

The circled word is shown first; the second word is the correct answer.

1. talks/talk
2. was/is
3. keep/keeps
4. been/has been
5. hung/hanged

6. C
7. ran/run
8. C
9. C
10. was/were

WORKSHEET 8.1

A.

1. works
2. needs
3. moved
4. are sailing
5. waxed
6. are
7. looks

8. climbed
9. will find
10. want
11. wants
12. wanted
13. will want
14. influences

15. selected
16. will consider
17. is considering
18. stay
19. watched
20. discussed

B.

1. is	3. need	5. is	7. flow	9. is
2. is	4. are	6. are	8. knows	10. being

WORKSHEET 8.2

A.

1. broken/worn; cross out *broke* and *wore*
2. began (or had just begun)/rang; cross out *begun* and *rung*
3. chooses (or *chose*); cross out *choose*
4. chosen (or delete *had*); cross out *chose*
5. does/stands; cross out *do* and *stand*
6. risen; cross out *rose* (or delete *had*)
7. eaten; cross out *ate* (or delete *have*)
8. saw/did; cross out *seen* and *done* (or insert *had/have*)
9. flown; cross out *flew* (or delete *had*)
10. quit; cross out *quitted*
11. run/broken; cross out *ran* and *broke* (or delete both *hads*)

12. worn; cross out *wore* (or delete *had*)

13. given; cross out *gave* (or delete *had*)

14. saw/spoken; cross out *seen* and *spoke* (or delete *had*)

15. taken; cross out *took* (or delete *had*)

16. wear or wore; cross out wears

17. saw (or has/had seen); cross out *seen*

18. doesn't; cross out *don't*

19. swung; cross out *swinged*

20. gave; cross out *give*

B.

Present Participle (*ing* ending)	Simple Past (no helping verb)	Past Participle (requires helping verb)
1. being	was	been
2. biting	bit	bitten
3. blowing	blew	blown
4. coming	came	come
5. costing	cost	cost
6. falling	fell	fallen
7. forgetting	forgot	forgotten
8. freezing	froze	frozen
9. hiding	hid	hidden
10. leading	led	led
11. paying	paid	paid
12. shaking	shook	shaken
13. sinking	sank	sunk or sunken
14. singing	sang	sung
15. throwing	threw	thrown

C.

16. beaten/winning

17. paid

18. broken/hidden

19. hung/forgotten

20. written

WORKSHEET 8.3

Answers are examples.

1. She begins her job at the tennis club at 8 a.m.

2. Professor Jagel gives tough exams.

3. Mr. Davidson approves everything before we send it out.

4. Our horse is running very fast.

5. The sun is rising now.

6. My mechanic is fixing the brakes on my car.

7. My team won the sales contest.

8. The soloist sang the opening and closing numbers on the program.
9. After that I quit the choir.
10. The host had hidden the door prize before the guests began to arrive.
11. Alice had paid the bill before the guests arrived for the party.
12. The reservations had been made months before we were planning to leave.
13. New office furniture has cost the company a great deal of money this quarter.
14. Your order has shipped and will arrive by 10:30 a.m. tomorrow.
15. Several artists have produced drawings for the contest.

POSTTEST

1. live	3. chosen	5. were	7. were	9. does
2. were	4. employs	6. did	8. broken	10. sank

CHAPTER 9 — Subject-Verb Agreement

PRETEST

1. writes	3. arrive	5. was	7. is	9. records
2. want	4. is	6. does	8. cries	10. speak

WORKSHEET 9.1

A.

Subject	Verb (helping and main verb)
1. you (understood)	finish, leave
2. Everyone	was discharged
3. Lewis, Martin	told, sang
4. we	should tell
5. reason	seems
6. Nobody	likes
7. book, DVD	fit
8. Something	has arrived
9. phenomenon	wasn't detected
10. All	were taken

B.

Subject	Verb
1. you	Do enjoy
2. financial analysts	are doing
3. she	Will get
4. Clothing	should be

5. you (understood)	ask
appearance	sends
message	will benefit
6. women	should limit
7. diner	puts
he, she	cuts
8. knife	remains
9. Career advancement	is
who	get
10. work	turns
11. Playing Monopoly	is
12. sales	have risen
13. Grover Cleveland	said
women	do want
14. Everyone	is working
15. Google	made
16. assistant	is, will help
17. you	would like
18. turnover	is
19. poverty, riches	are
20. grammar, spelling	are

WORKSHEET 9.2

1. were to was	19. don't to doesn't
2. seem to seems	20. was to were
3. was to were	21. is to are
4. C	22. are to is
5. were to was	23. have to has
6. C	24. greets to greet
7. C	25. have to has
8. are to is	26. pack to packs
9. are to is	27. C
10. have to has	28. come to comes
11. is to are	29. leaves to leave
12. rides to ride	30. do to does
13. C	31. don't to doesn't
14. C	32. work to works
15. C	33. are to is
16. have to has	34. goes to go
17. has to have	35. have to has
18. are to is	

WORKSHEET 9.3

1. was to were
2. C
3. was to were
4. C
5. was to were
6. C
7. was to were
8. were to was/weren't to wasn't
9. was to were
10. was to were/it to they
11. takes to take
12. C
13. have to has/their to its
14. need to needs
15. was to were
16. was to were
17. favor to favors
18. C
19. are to is/ their to its
20. work to works

POSTTEST

1. deserves
2. is
3. have
4. is
5. have
6. marks
7. does
8. insists
9. was
10. has

CHAPTER 10 — Adjectives and Adverbs

PRETEST

1. type to types
2. an $11/an NAACP
3. nowhere to anywhere
4. more to most
5. best to better
6. quieter to more quietly
7. badly to bad
8. good to well
9. really
10. poorest to most poorly

A/AN PRETEST

1. an addition
2. a carrot
3. an egg
4. an apple
5. a giant
6. an honor
7. a heater
8. an even number
9. a hand
10. a one-day sale
11. a manager
12. an onion
13. an owl
14. an uncle
15. an Englishman
16. an heir
17. an island
18. a European
19. an IBM office
20. a CIA report
21. a UN member
22. a 2 percent tax
23. an X-ray
24. an unknown admirer

WORKSHEET 10.1

A.

1. a, an	6. An, an	11. An, a
2. A, an, an	7. A, a, a	12. an, an
3. an, a, an	8. *A*, an	13. An, an
4. a, an	9. an, an	14. an, a
5. A, an	10. a, a, an	15. A, a, an

B.

1. those kind to that kind
2. Them to Those or These
3. type to types
4. sort to sorts
5. delete *a*
6. delete *here*
7. kind to kinds
8. them to these or those
9. kind to kinds
10. delete *an*

C.

1. never to rarely or hardly ever
2. nothing to anything
3. none to any
4. no to any
5. C
6. nothing to anything
7. nowhere to anywhere
8. can't to can
9. C
10. couldn't to could

WORKSHEET 10.2

A.

1. wisest	2. wiser	3. better	4. best	5. longest

B.

6. delete most	10. best to better	13. brightest to brighter
7. the worst to worse	11. more heavy to heavier	
8. C		14. delete more
9. older to oldest	12. recenter to more recent	15. biggest to bigger

C.

Comparative	Superlative
16. more	most
17. worse	worst
18. littler or less	littlest or least
19. more	most
20. better	best

D.

21. Smoothly
22. beautiful
23. awfully
24. quickly
25. loudly

E.

1. badly to bad
2. clear to clearly, correct to correctly
3. sadly to sad
4. careful to carefully
5. legible to legibly
6. C
7. deep to deeply
8. fair to fairly
9. efficient to efficiently
10. graceful to gracefully
11. badly to bad
12. C
13. sweetly to sweet
14. quiet to quietly
15. quieter to more quietly
16. smoother to more smoothly
17. satisfactory to satisfactorily
18. more calm to calmer
19. C
20. more louder to louder
21. worser to worse
22. quieter to more quietly
23. capablest to capable
24. concise to concisely
25. oldest to older

WORKSHEET 10.3

A.

1. well
2. well
3. well
4. well
5. bad

B.

1. successful individuals
2. a special offer
3. an exclusive resort hotel
4. the beautiful Pacific
5. the crystal blue waters
6. the white sand beaches
7. exquisite guest villas
8. Mediterranean decor
9. luxurious jacuzzis
10. this paradise

C. Answers will vary. Several possible answers are listed.

1. away, there
2. more, less
3. rarely, seldom, never
4. really, always, never
5. elegantly, tastefully
6. extremely, very, such
7. most
8. not, very, sometimes
9. usually, often
10. much, even

POSTTEST

1. less	3. can	5. quietly	7. newest	9. most poorly
2. easier	4. faster	6. won't do any more	8. bad	10. the, well

UNIT 4 — Perfecting Sentence Punctuation— Chapters 11–13

CHAPTER 11 — *The Comma*

PRETEST

1. proficiency, and
2. C
3. firms, copyright
4. employment, which continues to grow rapidly in many industries, has
5. social service, and/demand," according
6. In fact, construction
7. Las Vegas, Nevada, company
8. month, or
9. years, we
10. C

WORKSHEET 11.1

1. C
2. unique, exciting
3. sports, but
4. came, what you wanted, and
5. paid, famous
6. work, and
7. small, elegant
8. bright, enthusiastic
9. Fort Worth, Dallas, and Austin.
10. C
11. profitable, highly
12. bonus, a million-dollar salary, and
13. C
14. Boston, and
15. work, and
16. C
17. workplace, but
18. sorority, and
19. morning, but
20. assistant, in October a data entry clerk, and
21. C
22. C
23. year, prices/down, and
24. brother, not
25. C

WORKSHEET 11.2

A.

1. month, at
2. C
3. train, you
4. meeting, he
5. C
6. directions, he
7. Hank, please
8. it, Eddie
9. Inn, we
10. C
11. attractive, modern dining room, which seats 250, you
12. know, real
13. *igloo, kayak, moccasin, skunk,* and *persimmon.*
14. C
15. speaker, indicate
16. C
17. salesperson, he
18. No, he
19. C
20. C

B.

1. stockholders, often members of the same family, and
2. C
3. C
4. C
5. C
6. C
7. Internet, the
8. will, of course, be
9. costs, as you probably know, are
10. administrator, Gloria Rojas, telephoned
11. office, which is in Room 103, is
12. Office, which is on the third floor, is
13. Simon, the auditor, found
14. C
15. C
16. C
17. worth, which
18. C
19. booklet, which gives complete information, for

20. C
21. idea, it has been said, comes
22. attending, "Career Networking in Cyberspace," begins
23. C
24. service, which was working fine yesterday, suddenly
25. C

WORKSHEET 11.3

A.

1. March 2, 2014, we
2. C
3. Long Beach, New York, nightclub
4. Friday, January 4
5. shop, and
6. Little Rock, Arkansas, was
7. Albuquerque, New Mexico, store
8. Edinburgh, Scotland, on
9. C
10. Marietta, Georgia, is

B. Answers are examples.

11. Jeff told the students, "Use last names in the workplace unless you're sure first names are appropriate."
12. "I emailed the price list two weeks ago," said Ms. Kato.
13. The instructor said, "The more public speaking you do, the more comfortable you will become," and then gave each student a chance to practice.
14. "It is important to look at your audience," he said, "and that means direct eye contact."
15. "I'm shocked!" shouted Jeff.

POSTTEST

1. Monday, March 6
2. lunch, do
3. oral, written, and nonverbal
4. C
5. C
6. Charles Darwin said, "A... life."
7. C
8. arrived, telephone
9. jobs, tax revenues, and
10. "In Dayton, Ohio, we have two factories that are about to close," the

CHAPTER 12

The Semicolon, Colon, and Other Marks

PRETEST

Use proofreading marks to correct semicolon and colon errors in these sentences.

1. accident; therefore, he
2. UPS: 100 reams
3. money (a great deal of money) by
4. could; nevertheless, it
5. hard—believe me—to
6. 30 years; therefore, he
7. now [*sic*] to
8. utensils: salad
9. class: plain
10. hours (from 9 to noon) will

WORKSHEET 12.1

1. more; now
2. high, your
3. money; they are, however, always
4. C
5. Dominic Anton, the transportation chief, was upset by the criticism; thus
6. Banks, he explained, pay depositors interest on their savings accounts, but
7. raise; that is, each
8. C
9. City Council; the
10. limited, keep
11. course; nevertheless, he
12. jobs; also
13. you; every
14. event; that is, they will arrange for the loction, the food, and
15. Louise Fuller, president; Sandra Hall, vice president; and Gina Hecht, treasurer
16. stock; therefore, they
17. about; for example, he
18. C
19. understand; it
20. applicants, his computer skills are good; however, we

WORKSHEET 12.2

1. chairs: two
2. weeks: candy, ice cream
3. life: getting
4. life: it
5. cities: Winston-Salem, Atlanta, Newark, and Pittsburgh
6. shoplifting: place
7. specials: ground beef, whole chickens, and sirloin steak
8. established: booths
9. about: A
10. duty: protecting

WORKSHEET 12.3

Answers may vary with use of dashes and parentheses depending on your interpretation.

1. The new board members—Dr. Duzeck and Ms. Swenson— will meet with the press this afternoon.
2. Charmaine Dillard—the scholarship recipient—has agreed to join our mentoring program.
3. The officers of this corporation (the president, the vice president, the treasurer, and the secretary) are all graduates of the same university.
4. The decimal equivalents (see Figure 4, page 80) will help you with the percentages.
5. Harbor Office Supply Company (I'll check the address) has ordered three photocopiers.
6. *Roget's Thesaurus*—treasury of synonyms, antonyms, parallel words, and related words—was first published in 1852 by Peter Mark Roget (look up the pronunciation of Roget).
7. The 7-11 chain—which featured spoon straws for Slurpees, plastic straws for sodas, and reusable straws for car cups—added straws that change color as a drink changes temperature.
8. Experience, intelligence, and personal skills are required on the job (if only more job candidates had them all).
9. C
10. She has all the attributes (strong sales, good contacts, product knowledge) of a top performer but no interest in getting promoted.
11. We must see him at once—not tomorrow.
12. Your bonus payment of $2500 (minus tax deductions) will be deposited directly to your account.
13. Roosevelt Island was described as "New York City's ideal place to live—a crime-free, auto-free, dog-free new [*sic*] island in the East River."
14. The report states that "the majority of new jobs created in America today—the second decade of the 21st Century—are in small companies" (with fewer than one hundred employees).
15. The three branches of the United States government (the executive, the legislative, and the judicial) derive their authority from the Constitution.

POSTTEST

1. today, though we don't realize it; for example, saying
2. cold—freezing is more accurate—when
3. dollars; for example, the
4. (www.pictureyou.com/weddings).
5. Springfield, Massachusetts; Urbana, Illinois; and Galveston, Texas
6. ab [*sic*] machine"; it
7. discount: 8 percent
8. desk; also
9. note: each
10. system, only one person—the president—can

CHAPTER 13   *Punctuation: The Fine Points*

PRETEST

1. "You're fired!"
2. Men's, it's.
3. "ineligible" or "illegible" (quotation marks or underline to indicate italics)
4. 1990s, technology-related
5. "The Stubborn Little Mark," <u>San Francisco Chronicle</u>.
6. never-ending
7. "oversleeps," and we'll
8. Shakespeare's, <u>King Richard III</u> , it's
9. You're, aren't
10. Let's, 20th-century

WORKSHEET 13.1

1. He shouted, "Your house is on fire!"
2. Why did FDR state, "The only thing to fear is fear itself"?
3. Alonzo whispered, "Are you sure you have the right data?"
4. "Are you positive the numbers are correct?" he whispered again.
5. Do you know whether Jessica said, "Reserve a rental car"?
6. If you use words like "ain't" and "theirselves," in some places, you will be considered uneducated.
7. My classmate said, "Are you aware that many professionals use sloppy language all the time?"
8. What does the phrase "negotiable instrument" mean?
9. He texted us as follows: "We depart from O'Hare on American Flight 23 at 8 a.m. and arrive at Kennedy at 10:30 p.m."

10. Was Mr. Higgins the character in <u>My Fair Lady</u> who said, "Results are what count"?
11. "We need more tacos for the company party!" Jim yelled.
12. "This shipment," the manager said, "will arrive in time for your January sale."
13. "Are you all right?" asked Ann. "Yes," groaned her dad, as he lifted the unabridged version of the <u>Oxford English Dictionary</u>.
14. Bach's "Suite No. 2 in B Minor" is first on the program at the concert.
15. University of South Carolina Professor Benjamin Franklin is tired of people asking him, "Why aren't you out flying your kite?"

WORKSHEET 13.2

A.

1. brother-in-law
2. C
3. semisweet
4. up-to-date notebook
5. third-generation heir
6. de-escalate
7. ex-boyfriend
8. rediscover
9. pre-established
10. C

B.

11. back-to-school, Windows-based
12. C
13. part-time, never-to-be-forgotten
14. seven-foot-tall, problem-solving
15. state-of-the-art, built-in, self-cleaning
16. C
17. self-esteem
18. mid-August
19. C
20. month-long

C.

21. cata/log	deter/mined	effect/tive
22. func/tion	be/lieve	hori/zontal
23. wouldn't	thou/sands	punctu/ation
24. aligned	impos/sible	inter/rupt
25. syl/lables	stopped	guess/work

WORKSHEET 13.3

1. couldn't, o'clock
2. i's, t's, you'd
3. C
4. C
5. 2011
6. Don't
7. C
8. it's, yds, lbs
9. '90s, workers
10. C
11. e's
12. Won't
13. A's
14. 2000s
15. Couldn't

POSTTEST

1. As the result of yesterday's storm, most subscribers' lines lost power, making even high-capacity services unable to take care of their customers.
2. Make Jake aware of his problem by saying to him, "Ask a friend for a frank opinion of whether you use double negatives all the time."
3. Albert Schweitzer said the following: "Ethics is the maintaining of life at the highest point of development."
4. "There is never a time in life when learning should stop," said the luncheon speaker.
5. Please deliver the following papers to my hotel room: the <u>Daily News</u>, the <u>New York Post</u>, and <u>The New York Times</u>.
6. The CEO wrote: "We are able to spread the cost over only the first- and second-quarter earnings, not the whole year."
7. Until you learn to use the word "misappropriation" correctly, choose a simpler word.
8. Please take Ms. Ellison's place; she won't be able to join us.
9. Don't accept just anyone's opinion of this 36-page report—it's too important!
10. The instructor wants a report on "Chapter 2: The Psychology of Fashion" from the textbook <u>Fashion Accessories</u>.

UNIT 5	Writing for Career Success—Chapters 14–15

CHAPTER 14	*Polished Writing Style*

PRETEST

Your answers may vary.

1. Review the sentence faults explained in Chapter 10.
2. Use words that identify people by what they do; then you can avoid sexist language.
3. After working hard on the report, he went home.

4. When they spoke, Angela forgot to invite her sister to the party.
5. Sarah worked in the sales department of the new company during her summer vacation.
6. Janet ate the huge bowl of ice cream, which was topped with chocolate syrup.
7. I turned on the computer.
8. The rookie delivered the best speech.
9. We won the prize.
10. The critics gave the film their highest praise.

ANSWERS TO PAGE 299

Dear Professor Cooper:

Thank you for the time and courtesy you extended to our representative Laura Mann at your college last month. She enjoyed her visit with you.

At Laura's request, we have sent you the new edition of *Mathematics for Business*. This was sent to you several weeks ago, and you should have it by now. We do hope you'll look it over. In addition, your name has been placed on our mailing list to receive an examination copy of *Business Math: Practical Applications*. A new edition of this book by Cleaves, Hobbs, and Dudenhef is expected off the press early next month.

We'll send your copy just as soon as it is available. If there is any way we can be of help to you, Professor Cooper, please let us know. Best wishes for a successful semester. We look forward to doing business with you in the future.

WORKSHEET 14.1

A. Answers may vary.

1. When you can do all the common things of life in an uncommon way, you will command the attention of the world.
2. Whenever an employee is asked to work overtime, that employee is entitled to compensation of one and one-half times the base hourly rate (Employee Handbook, page 25)
3. The manager was finishing the report while her boss was calling the CEO to explain why it was late.
4. Getting a learner's permit is a first step before a new driver can practice driving.

B.

5. Examples: however, therefore, for example, also, in fact, then
6. True
7. False
8. True

C. Corrections may vary.

9. C
10. He will complete the blueprints today; then he'll send them to the contractor.

11. High achievers do mental rehearsals; that is, they visualize themselves performing tasks successfully.

12. C

13. Your mind never sleeps; consequently, visualization is effective just before falling asleep. Your mind probably continues to work on the desired achievement as you sleep.

14. C

15. We find that some of the merchandise is damaged; therefore, we are going to return the entire order.

D. Answers may vary.

1. A college pennant and a Monet painting are on the wall of the student's room.

2. A house in need of painting sits far back among the trees.

3. Dennis and Mike spent all afternoon walking to the grocery store, bakery, and flower shop to prepare for a party.

4. An animal that appeared to be a hyena paced restlessly back and forth in the cage.

5. We realize travelers choose an airline based on the quality of its service, and we're sorry we let you down.

6. Enclosed is our check for $635.23 in payment of your May statement.

7. I missed the final examination because I had been out late the night before. Consequently, the instructor and the dean refused to change my F grade to "Incomplete" or "Withdrew."

8. For those of you who didn't know it, we have a nursery downstairs for small children.

9. Because Mr. Anderson is so busy, we don't recommend that Mr. Nguyen go to his office uninvited.

10. Despite our repeated reminders about nonpayment of your long overdue account, we have not received your check.

WORKSHEET 14.2

A.

1. We sat there in awed silence listening to his singing.

2. Ms. Griggs worked for CNN's Headline News Department during her vacation.

3. Genevieve Astor died at the age of 96 in the home in which she had been born.

4. The fire department brought the fire under control before much damage was done.

5. The car with the uneven paint job was returned by the customer.

B.

6. With the new software we hope to improve response time, reduce input errors, and identify system problems more readily.

7. Typing accurately can be more important than typing fast.

8. Linda is a full-time securities analyst, and her husband is a part-time insurance agent.

9. We would appreciate learning your views on how to introduce change, control quality, and motivate employees.

10. Ophthalmologists and optometrists may examine eyes and may also issue prescriptions for glasses and contact lenses.

C and D. Your answers may vary.

1. M   Oranges, which are not mentioned in your report, are a valuable source of vitamins.

2. M   Sitting by the fireplace with his dog, the English teacher was reading Shakespeare.

3. P   He is interested in science, math, and reading.

4. M   Mr. Gorjus was frantically searching his office for the missing telephone number.

5. P   The woman suggested that we fill out the form and leave it with her.

6. P   Ad for a famous cosmetic: Lady Esther Dream Cream is recognized by leading dermatologists as highly effective in improving skin's texture and smoothness and for counteracting aging.

7. P   I believe that playing a good game of chess is a better accomplishment than playing a good game of bridge.

8. P   Writing business documents requires excellent grammar and punctuation.

9. P   Her hobbies are painting, going to concerts, and reading blogs on the Internet.

10. C

11. M   After dinner, the father sat down in an easy chair to tell his children about his childhood.

12. C

13. P   A major Norwegian industry is producing and transporting oil and gas from offshore petroleum deposits.

14. M   With a population under five million, Norway is heavily dependent on world trade conditions.

15. P   We would like to hear your ideas on how to motivate employees and introduce change.

16. C

17. P   That program has too much sex, violence, and bad language.

18. C

19. P   She believed him as she had faith in him.

20. M   The old man, smoking a cigar, sat on a bench next to his grandchild.

WORKSHEET 14.3

A.

1. P	7. A	14. P
2. A	8. A	15. P
3. P	9. A	16. A
4. A	10. P	17. P
5. A	11. A	18. P
6. P	12. P	19. A
	13. A	20. A

B.

1. D   Having typed just half the report,
2. D   On examining the goods,
3. D   Like many people living in Alaska,
4. D   Having recovered from his illness,
5. C
6. D   Before going to lunch,
7. D   before going to lunch.
8. D   Walking quickly down the aisle,
9. D   While doing the daily chores,
10. D   Handing me the $50,000 order,
11. D   Having produced a printout,
12. D   While riding the bike down the street,
13. D   Thinking about a bunch of new toys,
14. D   Upon landing in Dallas,
15. C
16. C
17. D   Being in dilapidated condition,
18. D   If invited to dinner at a British home,
19. C
20. C
21. C
22. D   After standing and repeating the pledge,
23. D   While walking home,
24. C
25. D   after being on vacation for two hours,

C.   Your answers may vary.

1. Because you are one of our most discriminating customers, we invite you to attend this private showing.
2. When he turned the corner, the new building was right in front of him.
3. While I was using the computer, the cursor became stuck in the middle of the screen.
4. Unlike many high-tech millionaires in the 1990s, she became financially successful through her talents in fine art and classical music.

5. Before he has dinner with the woman he met through Ultimate Encounters Online, he needs to improve his table manners.

POSTTEST

1. D-2	5. B-2	9. E-2
2. C-1	6. A	10. A
3. B-2	7. E-1	
4. C-2	8. D-1	

CHAPTER 15 — Capitalization, Abbreviations, and Numbers

PRETEST

Your proofreading marks should reflect the changes shown.

1. Our English professor met Reverend Perez in this city last fall.
2. The team is trying to raise at least $1,000 for new uniforms and equipment.
3. Did Senator Charles West from Pennsylvania give a speech in northern Maine?
4. To get to Monroe College, go north on Jerome Avenue until you reach Fordham Road.
5. Rashid Ali, PhD, is the head of the Arabic Studies Department at the university.
6. Please send me the brochures describing the East Coast tours of fall colors.
7. The trip to Denver, Colorado, is planned for the spring.
8. Data indicates that 20 percent of total profits are earned in the third quarter.
9. We are located at 1920 Tremont Avenue, Bronx, New York.
10. I am writing to confirm your appointment for next Friday at 2:30 p.m.

WORKSHEET 15.1

1. Chairman, United Airlines, Uganda, Veteran's Day
2. World War II, Fabulous Fifties
3. My
4. If, German
5. Although, BS, MA
6. "Dear Credit Manager"; "Sincerely."
7. The Atomic Age, Hiroshima
8. We, American Airlines, Israel, South Dakota
9. Winston Churchill, *Triumph and Tragedy*, World War II
10. The, Supreme Court

11. I, Chinese, September, Chinese Literature
12. The Atlantic Ocean, East Coast, United States
13. New
14. Lalitha, Hindu, India, MD
15. The, "Dear Customer," "Sincerely
16. sales manager
17. Apartments, City, monthly session
18. department, general manager, Departments, company
19. east, summer, City
20. Governor, Senate, Independent, general election

WORKSHEET 15.2

1. Massachusetts, master's
2. Department, week
3. bachelor's, New Jersey
4. department, New York
5. David Wallace III
6. Parkhurst Avenue, COO, building
7. Friday, Saturday, Boulevard, Suite, Florida
8. FAQs
9. Carol Quinones, MD, UCLA
10. page 5, number, GPA
11. Captain Loretta Barker, September
12. Edward Brown, PhD, Bill Brown III
13. minutes, 8:30 a.m.
14. IRS
15. Professor Robinson, New York City
16. VIPs
17. OSHA, pounds
18. CFO, ext. 0702
19. FAX, Monday
20. US Foreign Service

WORKSHEET 15.3

1. page 5
2. percent, third
3. 1
4. July 15, percent
5. 12
6. July 26
7. #3 and #4
8. Twenty-one, 16
9. two and a half
10. $20,000
11. five
12. One hundred twenty

13. 15 percent
14. 30
15. number 3
16. one-half

17. 8- by 10-foot
18. page 5
19. 1990s
20. 50, pounds

POSTTEST

1. $35, Friday, February 1
2. NAACP, civil rights
3. United States, 300 million
4. company, $250,000
5. 4 p.m., O'Hare Airport
6. 18626 Anglin, Michigan
7. 4 p.m., Room
8. Los Angeles, $25
9. four- or five-minute
10. Q&A

Appendix E: Answers

Word Power: Vocabulary and Spelling

CHAPTER 1 — Word Power Play 1

a. 18	h. 3	o. 2
b. 16	i. 10	p. 20
c. 17a	j. 6	q. 1
d. 8	k. 9	r. 15
e. 12	l. 11	s. 5
f. 4	m. 13	t. 19
g. 7	n. 14	u. 17b

CHAPTER 2 — Word Power Play 2

a. 26	h. 29	o. 32
b. 28	i. 39	p. 36
c. 33	j. 21	q. 30
d. 25	k. 22	r. 34
e. 35	l. 37	s. 31
f. 40	m. 24	t. 23
g. 38	n. 27	

CHAPTER 3 — Word Power Play 3

a. 51	h. 53	o. 57
b. 41	i. 56	p. 60
c. 59	j. 43	q. 58
d. 50	k. 55	r. 45
e. 48	l. 49	s. 46
f. 47	m. 54	t. 52
g. 42	n. 44	

CHAPTER 4 — Word Power Play 4

a. 75	h. 61	o. 69
b. 71	i. 64	p. 63
c. 67	j. 74	q. 70
d. 77	k. 62	r. 72
e. 68	l. 79	s. 66
f. 80	m. 65	t. 78
g. 76	n. 73	

CHAPTER 5 — Word Power Play 5

a. 84	h. 100	o. 96
b. 85	i. 97	p. 82
c. 98	j. 87	q. 86
d. 91	k. 93	r. 99
e. 89	l. 95	s. 90
f. 92	m. 81	t. 83
g. 94	n. 88	

CHAPTER 6 — Word Power Play 6

a. 111	h. 119	o. 118
b. 101	i. 102	p. 109
c. 106	j. 110	q. 115
d. 116	k. 114	r. 117
e. 108	l. 120	s. 104
f. 107	m. 103	t. 113
g. 112	n. 105	

CHAPTER 7 — Word Power Play 7

a. 137	h. 138	o. 134
b. 123	i. 129	p. 140
c. 139	j. 127	q. 121
d. 122	k. 132	r. 124
e. 131	l. 136	s. 135
f. 133	m. 130	t. 128
g. 125	n. 126	

CHAPTER 8	Word Power 1–7 Review

1. NYSE
2. APR, CD
3. annual report, balance sheet, fiscal
4. turnaround time, turnover, downtime
5. public offering, stock, stockholders
6. exchange rate, euro
7. deficit, outsourcing
8. partnership, financial adviser, start-up, business plans
9. webmaster, cybersecurity, hacker
10. board of directors, shareholders, beneficiaries, bull market
11. mortgage, foreclosures
12. overhead, liabilities, liquidate, assets
13. concierge, itinerary
14. certified check, damages
15. 401k, fringe benefits, beneficiary
16. Outplacement, liquidated
17. workaholic, radar screen
18. Antitrust legislation, monopoly, multinational corporations, diversification
19. retainer, slander, plaintiff, defendant
20. glass ceiling, networking

CHAPTER 9	Word Power Play 9

1. accept, except
2. add, ad
3. dying, dyeing
4. dissent
5. descent
6. bizarre, bazaar
7. coarse, course
8. site
9. cite
10. sight
11. counsel
12. Council
13. access, excess
14. affect
15. effect
16. capitol, capital
17. allot, a lot
18. principle, principal
19. elicit, illicit

CHAPTER 10	Word Power Play 10

1. imminent
2. eminent
3. regardless
4. eligible/illegible
5. devise/device
6. desert/dessert/desert
7. choose/chose
8. defer/differ
9. conscience/conscious
10. besides/beside
11. envelop/envelope
12. fiscal/physical
13. complimented/complemented
14. guise/guys
15. it's/its
16. minor/miner

CHAPTER 11	Word Power Play 11

1. personal
2. loose
3. than
4. thorough/through
5. suite/suit
6. whether/weather
7. suit
8. prosecute
9. that
10. whether/weather
11. proceeds
12. rye
13. We're
14. proceed
15. morale
16. personal/personnel
17. prospective
18. prerequisite
19. morale, moral
20. were/were
21. perspective
22. respectfully
23. quiet/quit/quite
24. We're
25. whether
26. thorough/through
27. persecuted
28. Morale
29. proceed
30. suite
31. lose
32. personal
33. We're
34. Then/than
35. that
36. reality

CHAPTER 12	Word Power Play 12

1. apprise/appraise
2. bloc/block
3. canvass/canvas
4. everyday/every day
5. foreword/forward
6. have/halve/half
7. key/quay
8. lesson/lessen
9. marquis/marquise/marquee
10. navel/naval
11. ode/owed
12. precede/proceed
13. rain/rein/reign
14. peak/pique/peek
15. sometime/some time
16. stationery/stationary
17. taught/taut
18. vise/vice
19. wary/wear
20. waive/wave

CHAPTER 13

Word Power Play 13

1. eager/anxious
2. disinterested/uninterested
3. enthusiastic/enthusiasm
4. Explicit/implicit
5. per annum/per diem
6. Flammable
7. nonflammable
8. further/farther
9. Indigenous/indigent
10. emigrate/immigrate
11. fewer/less
12. Implies/infers
13. take/bring
14. simple/simplistic
15. rsvp
16. proceed/proceeds
17. principal/principles
18. rise/raise
19. past/passed
20. rational/rationale

CHAPTER 14

Word Power 9–13 Review

1. allot
2. eminent/bibliography
3. chose/defer
4. illegible/eligible
5. We're/proceed/their/rain
6. owed/canvas/appraised
7. It's/principle/capitol/elicit
8. We're/thorough/suite
9. wry/perks/guise
10. led/miner/lead/canvas
11. Regardless/fiscal/conscience/fiscal
12. fiscal/allot/altar/capital
13. advice
14. through/thorough
15. uninterested/disinterested
16. percentage/percent
17. passed/past
18. principal/principles
19. proceed/proceeds
20. fewer/less

CHAPTER 15

Word Power Play 15

A.
1. 2
2. 4
3. 3
4. 3
5. 2

B.
6. s, es
7. s

8. s
9. b, e
10. h, e

C.
11. T
12. F
13. T
14. F
15. F

16. F
17. F
18. T
19. F
20. F
21. T
22. F
23. F
24. F
25. F

Appendix F: Answers

Supplementary Practice Exercises

EXERCISE 1-A: DICTIONARY PRACTICE

1. embryology—branch of biology dealing with embryos
2. geology—science that deals with history of the earth and its life, especially rocks
3. seismologist—scientist who deals with earthquakes and vibrations of the earth
4. therapeutic—of or relating to the treatment of disease or disorders by remedial agents or methods
5. oxymoron—an expression or concept that combines contradictory or incongruous words or elements
6. egocentric—concerned with the individual rather than society
7. neurosis—mental and emotional disorder that affects only part of the personality
8. agoraphobia—abnormal fear characterized especially by the avoidance of open or public spaces
9. anthropology—the science of human beings and their ancestors
10. demographics—statistical characteristics of human populations

EXERCISE 1-B: SPELLING

1. absence
2. C
3. analyze
4. attendance
5. Britain
6. cemetery
7. changeable
8. changing
9. coming
10. deferred
11. dining
12. excellence
13. existence
14. forty
15. C
16. grievous
17. C
18. loneliness
19. ninety
20. omitted

EXERCISE 1-C: DICTIONARY CODE

1. Sep|tem|ber 3
2. won|der|ful 3
3. mer|ri|ment 3
4. meth|od|ol|o|gy 5
5. to|tal|i|ty 4
6. motor: noun, verb, adjective

7. metal: noun, adjective
8. facility: noun
9. grandeur: noun
10. make: verb
11. maudlin/MAWD len
12. nuclear/NEW klee er
13. literature/LIT er *uh* chur
14. spastic/SPAS tik
15. bastion/BAS chuhn
16. fanatic—Latin
17. syllogism—Latin, Greek
18. phonetic—Greek
19. oration—Latin
20. milieu—French from Old French

EXERCISE 1-D: USING YOUR THESAURUS

Answers are examples.

1. bad odor
2. misled
3. unintelligent
4. decline
5. made up
6. less expensive
7. unattractive
8. immature
9. become angry
10. slay

EXERCISE 1-E: USING YOUR REFERENCE MANUAL

1. b	3. a	5. c	7. b	9. a
2. c	4. d	6. a	8. a	10. a

CHAPTER 2 — The Parts of Speech

EXERCISE 2-A: NOUNS

1. professor, students, assignment
2. commuters, miles, work, day
3. proposals, weeks
4. syllabi, information, subject
5. Tina, Rose, applications, loan
6. Will, stomach, class
7. errors, emails
8. instructor, schedule, midterms
9. Larry, textbooks, notebooks, papers, backpack
10. classroom, computers, printers

EXERCISE 2-B: PRONOUNS

1. She, anyone
2. Your, his
3. I, our
4. Who, him
5. Something, her
6. Everyone, her

7. He, nothing
8. You, your
9. Those, you, who, your
10. Whomever, you
11. Somebody, his, her
12. everyone, no one
13. I, mine, hers
14. We, ourselves, our
15. Everything

EXERCISE 2-C: VERBS

1. welcomed
2. will be attending
3. was
4. has handed
5. required
6. will be
7. were jumping
8. brightened
9. echoed
10. were looking

EXERCISE 2-D: ADJECTIVES

1. irritated, busy
2. tired, thirsty, cold
3. noisy, water, law
4. blue ballpoint, wooden
5. few
6. efficient, ten-page
7. magnificent, inner, office
8. Twenty-five, new
9. heavy, laser
10. grouchy, fresh, brewed
11. Several
12. elegant, new, firm
13. old, faded, torn
14. enough
15. no

EXERCISE 2-E: ADVERBS

1. finally
2. diligently
3. immediately
4. very
5. well
6. really
7. extremely
8. almost
9. appropriately
10. accurately
11. cheaply
12. never
13. hard
14. today
15. too

EXERCISE 2-F: CONJUNCTIONS AND PREPOSITIONS

Part 1

1. Although
2. when
3. until
4. so that
5. or
6. but
7. while
8. and, since
9. if
10. whenever

Part 2

11. on the desk	16. into the file cabinet
12. in the folder	17. across the street
13. through the clouds	18. except Luther, on the business trip
14. along the path	19. during the lecture
15. above the business	20. beneath the other papers

EXERCISE 2-G: IDENTIFYING THE PARTS OF SPEECH

1. N	5. V	9. A	13. V	17. A
2. A	6. N	10. A	14. A	18. V
3. V	7. N	11. V	15. N	19. A
4. A	8. V	12. N	16. N	20. V

CHAPTER 3 — Sentence Fundamentals

EXERCISE 3-A: COMPLETE SENTENCES AND FRAGMENTS

1. C	5. C	9. C	13. C	17. C
2. F	6. F	10. F	14. F	18. F
3. F	7. C	11. F	15. F	19. C
4. C	8. F	12. C	16. C	20. F

EXERCISE 3-B: COMMA SPLICES AND RUN-ONS

1. CS	5. R	9. CS	13. CS	17. C
2. C	6. CS	10. R	14. CS	18. CS
3. R	7. C	11. R	15. C	19. R
4. C	8. C	12. C	16. R	20. C

EXERCISE 3-C: DEPENDENT CLAUSES

1. After the workers finished the project
2. until the clouds moved in
3. Because the biscuits were hard
4. Since Susan left town
5. When salespeople are successful
6. Although we had a wet spring
7. even though they have no money
8. when he was president

9. Even though his supervisor gave clear directions
10. Since wrong answers will be subtracted from the total number of correct responses

EXERCISE 3-D: DEPENDENT AND INDEPENDENT CLAUSES

Your answers may vary.

1. Because John is an excellent student, he gets good grades.
2. The store has the highest sales in the district because the manager trains the employees very well.
3. Since the short story was very dramatic, the students in the English Composition class responded enthusiastically.
4. Although Sigmund Freud was a pioneer in the field of psychology, modern psychologists do not all agree with his theories.
5. Although political activist C. Delores Tucker attacked the moral standards of hip-hop music in the 1990s, the public had mixed views on the subject.
6. Bobby Flay, who is one of the Food Network's top stars, prepared six different pork belly dishes.
7. Because many people are confused about how to tabulate mileage reports, the Accounting Department will issue new expense forms this week.
8. American Indians were stereotyped in films of the 1940s and 1950s when very few sympathetic portrayals were presented.
9. We cannot issue paychecks on the 15th of this month because our checks are late coming from the home office.
10. Even though Bob and Art are undecided, they will need to make a bid on the house by the close of business tomorrow.

EXERCISE 3-E: SENTENCE TYPES AND PUNCTUATION

1. D	3. F	5. I	7. K	9. H
2. C	4. G	6. B	8. A	10. J

CHAPTER 4 — *Nouns: Forming Plurals*

EXERCISE 4-A: REGULAR NOUN PLURALS

1. babies	6. countries	11. vetoes	16. roofs
2. alloys	7. churches	12. echoes	17. shelves
3. daisies	8. taxes	13. radios	18. wives
4. plays	9. wishes	14. altos	19. chiefs
5. rallies	10. glasses	15. leaves	20. dwarfs

EXERCISE 4-B: IRREGULAR NOUN PLURALS

Part 1

1. theses
2. bacteria
3. analyses
4. stimuli
5. algae
6. sheep
7. hypotheses
8. curricula
9. memoranda
10. fungi
11. antennae
12. appendixes/appendices
13. syllabi/syllabuses
14. crises

Part 2

15. data—P, S
16. crisis—S
17. media—P
18. alumni—P
19. algae—P
20. bacteria—P, S

EXERCISE 4-C: SINGULAR AND PLURAL NOUNS

1. economics—S
2. statistics—S, P
3. news—S
4. goods—P
5. thanks—S
6. scissors—S
7. civics—S
8. measles—S
9. proceeds—P
10. mathematics—S

EXERCISE 4-D: PLURALS OF PROPER NOUNS

1. Bushes
2. Kellys
3. Joneses
4. Hartmans
5. Jameses
6. Rodriguezes
7. Chens
8. Williamses
9. Booths
10. Morganthaus

EXERCISE 4-E: PLURALS OF COMPOUND NOUNS

Part 1

1. get-togethers
2. post offices
3. runners-up
4. chiefs of police
5. sons-in-law
6. nurse's aides
7. photocopies
8. hand-me-downs
9. chairpersons
10. letters of recommendation

CHAPTER 5 — Nouns: Forming Possessives

EXERCISE 5-A: POSSESSIVE NOUNS

1. men's
2. company's
3. employee'/'s
4. accountants'
5. month's
6. year's
7. nurses'
8. woman's
9. applicant's/s'
10. students'

EXERCISE 5-B: SINGULAR AND PLURAL POSSESSIVES

1. S/child's
2. P/customers'
3. P/students'
4. P/judges'
5. S/afternoon's
6. P/factories'
7. P/secretaries'
8. P/months'
9. S/European's
10. P/children's
11. S/Virginia's
12. P/men's
13. S/P/Macy's
14. S/company's
15. P/accountants'
16. P/industries'
17. P/years'
18. S/woman's
19. S/employee's
20. P/waiters'

CHAPTER 6 — Pronouns: Types and Their Uses

EXERCISE 6-A: PERSONAL PRONOUNS

1. I
2. us
3. They
4. me
5. We
6. him
7. they
8. us
9. me
10. He
11. her
12. us
13. she
14. me
15. I
16. me
17. she
18. We
19. us
20. he

EXERCISE 6-B: PRONOUN USAGE

Part 1

1. he
2. she
3. themselves
4. he
5. me
6. he
7. I
8. himself
9. themselves
10. ourselves

Part 2

11. C	16. himself
12. I	17. C
13. he	18. he
14. C	19. C
15. themselves	20. I

EXERCISE 6-C: POSSESSIVE PRONOUNS

1. its	6. Who's	11. It's	16. whose
2. whose	7. everyone's	12. Who's	17. anyone's
3. your	8. They're	13. you're	18. their
4. No one's	9. mine	14. Somebody's	19. My
5. yours	10. ours	15. yours	20. its

EXERCISE 6-D: WHO/WHOM AND WHO/THAT

1. who	6. Whom	11. whom	16. Whoever
2. who	7. whom	12. who	17. who
3. that	8. who	13. who	18. Whomever
4. whomever	9. that	14. whom	19. who
5. who	10. Who	15. whom	20. whom

CHAPTER 7

Pronouns: Agreement and Writing Principles

EXERCISE 7-A: PRONOUN AGREEMENT

1. Every one	11. their
2. Someone, his or her	12. his or her
3. anybody	13. his or her
4. somebody	14. his or her
5. Any one	15. their
6. Everything	16. their
7. nobody, who	17. his or her
8. Everyone, that	18. his or her
9. Something	19. their
10. Anything	20. their

EXERCISE 7-B: PRONOUN AGREEMENT (ITS/THEIR)

1. its	3. its	5. its	7. their	9. their
2. its	4. its	6. their	8. its	10. its

CHAPTER 8 — Verbs: Types, Tenses, and Forms

EXERCISE 8-A: VERB TENSE

Part 1

1. looks	present	9. explained	past
2. will sing	future	10. will paint	future
3. provides	present	11. takes	present
4. misunderstood	past	12. needs	present
5. consulted	past	13. earned	past
6. will fly	future	14. appreciates	present
7. stays	present	15. will talk	future
8. were	past		

Part 2

16. taken	21. begun
17. eaten	22. worn
18. drank	23. taken
19. processes	24. rung
20. chose	25. drunk

EXERCISE 8-B: IRREGULAR VERBS

1. written	6. forgotten	11. taken
2. thrown	7. drawn	12. hidden
3. sang	8. forgotten	13. drawn
4. hidden	9. threw	14. broken
5. frozen	10. sung	15. withdrawn

EXERCISE 8-C: VERB FORMS

1. are going
2. was elected
3. will wait/waited
4. going
5. are required

6. will be going
7. will be speaking/spoke
8. is expected
9. are having/had
10. is making/makes/made
11. are being reviewed
12. will be repaired/was repaired
13. slept/have been sleeping/have slept
14. were chosen/chose
15. would like

CHAPTER 9   *Subject-Verb Agreement*

EXERCISE 9-A: SUBJECTS AND VERBS

Subject	Verb
1. sun	rose
2. wolves	howled
3. you	do have
4. cooking	is
5. (you)	answer
6. newspaper	is delivered
7. students	are
8. mother, son	were found
9. job placement director	sent
10. you	did buy
11. restaurant	is
12. sign-ups	will be held
13. word	spread
14. Mr. Overton	attended
15. manufacturer	recalled
16. boy, grandfather	strolled
17. courses	are taught
18. residents	were warned
19. Sidney	will learn
20. team	practiced

EXERCISE 9-B: SUBJECT-VERB AGREEMENT

1. calls	4. has	7. is	10. are	13. is
2. have	5. are	8. have	11. talks	14. were
3. run	6. loves	9. are	12. are	15. does

CHAPTER 10   *Adjectives and Adverbs*

EXERCISE 10-A: ARTICLES

1. a	5. a	9. an	13. an	17. a
2. a	6. a	10. a	14. an	18. a
3. an	7. an	11. a	15. a	19. an
4. an	8. an	12. an	16. an	20. a

EXERCISE 10-B: POINTING ADJECTIVES

1. kinds	4. types	7. That	10. those	13. types
2. this	5. These	8. types	11. kinds	14. kinds
3. those	6. type	9. kinds	12. This	15. That

EXERCISE 10-C: DOUBLE NEGATIVES

1. anything	6. any	11. can	16. can
2. any	7. anything	12. ever	17. any
3. can	8. anywhere	13. any	18. could
4. anywhere	9. any	14. any	19. ever
5. ever	10. ever	15. anywhere	20. any

EXERCISE 10-D: COMPARATIVE FORMS OF ADJECTIVES

1. nicest	6. worst	11. oldest
2. kinder	7. strongest	12. most unusual
3. harder	8. a unique	13. most beautiful
4. most successful	9. worse	14. most
5. friendliest	10. better	15. better

EXERCISE 10-E: ADJECTIVES AND ADVERBS

1. well	11. either good or well
2. good	12. well
3. very	13. surely
4. more smoothly	14. more quickly
5. more carefully	15. really
6. delicious	16. clearly
7. well	17. neatly
8. bad	18. good
9. slowly	19. sure
10. loudly	20. well

CHAPTER 11   *Punctuation: The Comma*

EXERCISE 11-A: COMMAS WITH A SERIES OF ITEMS OR ADJECTIVES

1. hot, humid
2. C
3. chocolate, chewy
4. two eggs, one stick of butter, and two cups of flour
5. bright, cheery
6. warm, gentle
7. hard, crunchy
8. intelligent, competent
9. ketchup, mustard, and relish
10. accurate, efficient
11. long, fierce
12. friendly, honest
13. run, jump, and dance
14. draft the letter, proofread it, and
15. daring, competent
16. ridiculous, comic
17. hot, salty
18. a rose, a $100 gift certificate, and a big smile
19. operating system, accounting procedures, and auditing process
20. skinned his knee, bruised his arm, and broke his front tooth

EXERCISE 11-B: COMMAS WITH CLAUSES

1. paper, and
2. cookies, and
3. class, but
4. quickly, yet
5. telephone, but
6. hard, and
7. study, but
8. meeting, nor
9. phone, for
10. shoes, or
11. sandcastle, but
12. hamburgers, and
13. diet, yet
14. sermon, but
15. reservation, for
16. test, nor
17. C
18. C
19. player, and
20. angry, for

EXERCISE 11-C: COMMAS WITH INTRODUCTORY WORDS AND EXPRESSIONS

1. Yes, I'll
2. Ms. Johansson, can
3. morning, before dawn, Rich
4. begins, you
5. No, I
6. arrive, would
7. Mr. Bryant, could
8. work, I
9. ended, the
10. reunion, Jerry
11. outside, the
12. Well, I
13. school, I
14. door, Mickey
15. Oh, I
16. work, Paula
17. Mr. Olivas, when
18. door, everyone
19. mall, they
20. do, he

EXERCISE 11-D: COMMAS WITH NONESSENTIAL EXPRESSIONS

1. My son, who likes to surf, is
2. Dr. Harvey, who is the president of the college, will
3. roommate, Toni Heiser, is
4. book, *Guide to Business Careers*, is
5. residents, young or old, are
6. winner, who is my brother-in-law, will
7. violin, which I've had for years, was
8. manager, Mr. Ortiz, will
9. textbook, *Understanding Business Mathematics*, explains
10. answer, either yes or no, on
11. mayor, who is also a dentist, was
12. Phillies, my favorite baseball team, have
13. retirement, a necessity for sure, can
14. friend, a middle school classmate, is
15. children, a trait I admire, I
16. marathon, 26-plus miles, a
17. leave, a minimum of two weeks per year, to
18. teacher, who is also my aunt, grew
19. publisher, Mr. Breeden, urged
20. college, a great guy, is

EXERCISE 11-E: COMMAS WITH QUOTATIONS

1. C
2. early,"
3. me,
4. "Please,"
5. Frank shouted,
6. C
7. C
8. C
9. instructed,
10. C

11. said,

12. Mrs. Edgars,"

13. C

14. C

15. explained,

16. C

17. asked,

18. C

19. exclaimed,

20. C

EXERCISE 11-F: COMMAS WITH NAMES, DATES, AND PLACES

1. Lansing, Michigan, after

2. Washington, DC, has

3. Madrid, Spain, will

4. June 12, 1995, from

5. dentist, James Kail, DDS,

6. June 14, 2013, was

7. San Francisco, California, is

8. Anaheim, California, or Disney World in Orlando, Florida

9. James Little, PhD, spoke

10. birthday, September 6, 1990, is

11. Portsmouth, New Hampshire, or in Portsmouth, Virginia

12. John McGuire, MD, received

13. September 29, 2008, the

14. Tampa, Florida, or Charleston, South Carolina

15. Thursday, September 5, 1981, at

16. November 15, 2010, John's

17. John P. Smith, PhD, and William R. Smith, MD, paid

18. Pittsburgh, Pennsylvania, and

19. Monday, October 5, and end on Wednesday, October 12

20. Muriel Freeman, MD, will/Newport, Rhode Island

CHAPTER 12   *Punctuation: The Semicolon, Colon, and Other Marks*

EXERCISE 12-A: THE SEMICOLON AND COLON

1. Doctor Hobley, who was our mayor, will speak at the meeting; he

2. bus; then

3. hits; still

4. jobs; also

5. stock; thus

6. hours: 8 a.m. instead of 9 a.m., Monday–Thursday; 8 a.m.

7. cities: Cambridge, Massachusetts; Portsmouth, New Hampshire; and Augusta, Maine

8. raise; however, she
9. birthday; his
10. Friday; therefore, we
11. arguing; thus
12. student; she
13. idea: change the date to Monday, July 5; canceling
14. on funds; consequently, we
15. report: the executive summary, which is too long; the charts, which need to be verified; and

EXERCISE 12-B: THE COLON

1. 5:45 a.m.
2. following: graduation
3. C
4. holidays: Thanksgiving
5. C
6. interviews: Betty
7. 11:30/following: read
8. dates: April 7
9. C
10. C

CHAPTER 13 — Punctuation: The Fine Points

EXERCISE 13-A: QUOTATION MARKS

1. "accept"/"except."
2. "I can"/"I can't."
3. "Thank you, Mr. Lockner,"
4. "Look for the Silver Lining,"
5. "We're lost!"
6. "eligible"/"illegible."
7. "Money Management"
8. "break a leg,"/ "do well."
9. asked, "Are you working overtime tonight?"
10. "Don't Feed Me!"
11. "Still I Rise"
12. "Should I ask for a raise?"
13. "irregardless"
14. "Play ball!"
15. "catch a wave"

EXERCISE 13-B: THE HYPHEN

1. hard-to-find
2. part-time/full-time
3. high-priced
4. ninety-nine
5. mid-July
6. self-control

7. stressed-out

8. six-foot

9. up-to-date

10. kind-hearted

11. high-risk

12. first-class

13. self-taught/high-level

14. battle-worn/24-hour

15. no-fee

EXERCISE 13-C: THE APOSTROPHE

1. Mr. Hernandez's

2. children's

3. child's

4. boss's

5. secretaries'

6. someone's

7. James's

8. It's

9. ladies'

10. companies'

11. authors'

12. A's

13. can't

14. customers'/'s mother-in-law's

15. months'

16. Joneses'

17. teachers'

18. Someone's

19. C

20. weeks'

EXERCISE 13-D: PARENTHESES, BRACKETS, AND DASHES

1. (my sister's first husband)

2. Saturday—I

3. (not $159).

4. donation—we

5. [*sic*]

6. Happiness—it's

7. [note: I am not sure of this date])

8. air purifier—rated number one by *Consumer Reports*—was

9. (more than 60 floors)

10. members—Dr. Duzeck and Ms. Swenson—will

11. (not necessarily in that order)

12. Zelika Horton—she was the winner—praised

13. (from 8 a.m. to noon)

14. photo—our first full wedding issue—will

15. (pp. 5–6)

| CHAPTER 14 | *Polishing Your Writing* |

EXERCISE 14-A: PRONOUN REFERENCE

Your answers may vary.

1. Ms. Meyers trained Ellen on the new computer program, and Ellen did a good job.
2. The IRS says our taxes were overpaid.
3. Tiffany told her mother that the students were allowed to go.
4. Helen saw her daughter talking to Patricia.
5. Mark met Frank while they were in college.
6. The professor says you must bring a textbook, notebook paper, and a folder to class.
7. Leslie's mother is a successful woman, and I'm sure Leslie will be a success too.
8. Tim was a track star in high school; sprinting was a sport he loved.
9. Customers are not allowed to smoke in the theater.
10. Lance's father is a carpenter, and he will be able to build the cabinets the way you want.

EXERCISE 14-B: SENTENCE VARIETY

Part 1 Your answers may vary.

1. Teenagers are very fashion-conscious, but their taste is often dictated by the choices of their peer group.
2. Consumers have the last word with retailers; that is, if they buy the latest fashion, retailers profit, and stores continue to stock the item.
3. Some people dress fashionably because they want attention; others are natural trendsetters.
4. For most businesspeople dressing well is important simply because it makes a good impression on their colleagues and clients.
5. Make a good first impression by greeting your clients by name and welcoming them with a friendly smile and a handshake.
6. He finished dinner and returned to work. *or* After finishing dinner, he returned to work.
7. If you go to China on a business trip, don't give your hosts expensive gifts; they might be embarrassed or even refuse to accept them.
8. When you dine in China, hold the rice bowl close to your mouth.
9. Your Chinese host will also offer a variety of foods; it is polite to sample every dish offered.
10. Although you don't have to know every custom, it is easier to build rapport with your host when you know something about the culture.

Part 2 Your answers may vary.

11. Ron worked hard to get good grades; <u>for example</u>, he reviewed his class notes every night.
12. Mrs. Williams expected the best from her students; <u>hence</u>, they were always prepared.

13. The instructor handed out the course outline; <u>subsequently</u>, she explained every assignment.

14. Rose did not hear the alarm; <u>consequently</u>, she was late for English class.

15. Twenty-five percent of the class received an "A"; <u>furthermore</u>, all the students passed the test.

16. Please sign in if you are late; <u>otherwise</u>, you will be marked absent.

17. The printer broke at 9 a.m.; <u>nevertheless</u>, the teacher had the test ready for class.

18. Each student needs to rent a locker in the Student Union Building; <u>in addition</u>, he or she must purchase a new lock.

19. The graduation ceremony is Saturday night; <u>in addition</u>, the practice will be Thursday morning.

20. The director introduced the speaker; <u>that is</u>, he gave a summary of the speaker's qualifications.

EXERCISE 14-C: MISPLACED WORDS AND PARALLEL PARTS

Part 1

1. with a keen eye
2. that were leaking
3. with the chocolate swirls
4. with the furry tail
5. if they are from the old manual

Part 2

6. C	7. NP	8. NP	9. C	10. C

EXERCISE 14-D: ACTIVE AND PASSIVE VERBS

1. A	5. A	9. A	13. A	17. A
2. P	6. A	10. P	14. A	18. A
3. A	7. P	11. A	15. A	19. P
4. P	8. A	12. P	16. P	20. P

EXERCISE 14-E: IDENTIFYING DANGLERS

1. C
2. C
3. Having received good grades
4. C
5. Being on the discount table
6. C
7. C

8. Feeling as though labor had begun
9. Jogging quickly around the block
10. Before going home
11. After browsing through the store
12. In spite of having a crack
13. C
14. Having forgotten the client's name
15. Facing the windows

| CHAPTER 15 | *Capitalization, Abbreviations, and Numbers* |

EXERCISE 15-A: CAPITALIZATION

1. day, Summer
2. high school
3. medicare, social security
4. Regards
5. city hall
6. club
7. west coast
8. french
9. southwest region
10. *With The*
11. street
12. apply
13. South, drive, wall street, manhattan
14. Professor, ancient civilizations, Conference
15. time
16. bar association, Holiday
17. building, Downtown, City
18. Professor, november
19. congressman, chamber, commerce
20. Yours

EXERCISE 15-B: ABBREVIATIONS

1. southeast
2. Route, Street
3. US
4. January
5. Agreement
6. Los Angeles, freeway

7. Ms., Human Resources, Department
8. Captain
9. FEMA
10. MBA, Dr. Kahlil Ahmed
11. Sidney Blumenthal Jr.
12. page 10
13. Alexis Tasheka, DDS
14. Friday, October, building
15. Building
16. e.g.
17. CPA
18. Reverend
19. Customer Management Center (CMC)
20. 10 a.m.

EXERCISE 15-C: NUMBERS

1. June 1, fifth
2. One-third
3. page 5
4. 31st
5. $50
6. Sixty-five
7. 2 p.m.
8. three
9. $1 million
10. Ten percent
11. 15 percent
12. 30
13. Figure 2
14. 50 cents
15. 5 to 8 p.m., June 30
16. $50
17. fourth, 2 percent
18. 150
19. two years
20. $1,000

Glossary

abbreviation—a shortened form of a word or proper name.

abridged dictionary—a dictionary that has around 100,000 entries, front matter, and back matter.

absolute adjective—adjectives that have no degree of comparison, such as *unique* or *perfect*.

accent mark (also called **diacritical mark**)—a dictionary symbol used to show the syllable of a word that receives the most force or emphasis when spoken.

acronym—an abbreviation made of up of an organization's initials that is pronounced as word.

action verb—a verb that expresses the action of the sentence.

active voice—placement of the subject and verb in a sentence that directly emphasizes that the subject performs the action. This construction is the opposite of passive voice, which places the emphasis on the subject as the receiver of the action.

adjective—one of the parts of speech; modifies (describes, limits, or explains) nouns and pronouns.

adverb—one of the parts of speech; modifies (describes, limits, or explains) verbs, adjectives, or other adverbs.

antecedent—the word or words a pronoun refers to.

antonyms—words with opposite meanings.

apostrophe—the punctuation mark used to show possession and to form contractions.

archaic—outdated; the word used by many dictionaries for outdated words or definitions.

article—the adjectives *a*, *and*, and *the*.

back matter—material at the end of a dictionary that provides additional information about language and usage.

being verbs (also called **state-of-being verbs** or **linking verbs**)—forms of the verb *to be*, verbs of the senses, and a few other verbs. Being verbs link the subject of the sentence to a word or words that identify or describe the subject.

block letter style—letter format in which all of the parts are aligned at the left margin.

body—one or more paragraphs that make up the main content of a communication.

chronological resume—a format for resumes that lists employers and work experience from the most recent to the earliest.

clause—a group of words in a sentence that has a subject and a verb; a clause may be either dependent or independent.

closing—the final paragraph that concludes and/or summarizes a communication.

collective noun—nouns that name groups of people, animals, or things.

colon—the punctuation mark that is a stronger pause than a semicolon; it is used to introduce or emphasize.

combination resume—a format for resumes that merges the chronological and functional styles.

comma splice—two or more independent clauses joined with a comma but without a coordinating conjunction.

command—a statement that tells someone what to do; *you* is understood as the subject.

common noun—a word that names a nonspecific noun and begins with a lowercase letter.

comparative degree adjective—the form of an adjective used to compare two nouns or pronouns.

complete sentence—See *sentence.*

complete subject—a noun or pronoun and its modifiers that are the subject of a sentence.

complex sentence—a sentence that has one independent clause and one or more dependent clauses.

compound adjective—an adjective requiring two or more words; punctuated with a hyphen when it precedes the noun being modified.

compound-complex sentence—a sentence that has at least two independent clauses and one or more dependent clauses.

compound noun—a noun made up of more than one word.

compound sentence—a sentence that has at least two independent clauses.

compound subject—a subject made up of two or more nouns and/or pronouns joined by a conjunction (*and, or, nor*).

compound word—two or more words that express one concept.

concise writing—writing that ensures that each word contributes to the purpose of the message.

conjunction—one of the parts of speech; connects words, phrases, and clauses; types of conjunctions are coordinating and subordinating.

consonant—all letters other than the vowels (*a, e, i, o, u*).

contraction—two words joined together and shortened by removing letters and replacing them with an apostrophe, for example, *can't* or *won't.*

coordinating conjunctions—the words *and, but, or, nor, for, yet,* and *so;* used to join parts of speech in a series (nouns, pronouns, adjectives, adverbs, and verbs) and clauses.

courteous request—a sentence that may sound like a question but does not call for a reply; should be punctuated with a period.

dangling verbal—a verb phrase that acts as a modifier, but does not modify anything logically in the sentence.

dash—punctuation mark used to enclose nonessential expressions for emphasis, where you would otherwise use commas.

degrees of comparison—positive, comparative, and superlative forms of adjectives used to compare one or more.

demonstrative pronoun—a pronoun that points to and identifies a noun or pronoun: *this*, *these*, *that*, and *those*.

dependent clause—a word group that has a subject and a verb but cannot stand alone. It depends on other parts of the sentence to give it meaning and should not be treated as a sentence.

dependent conjunction (also called **subordinating conjunction**)—a conjunction used to introduce a *dependent clause*—a word group that has a subject and a verb and cannot stand by itself as a sentence.

descriptive adjective—an adjective that describes; it changes form to show comparison.

direct address—addressing the person to whom you are writing by name in the body of a communication.

direct question—a sentence that asks a question and calls for a reply and should be punctuated with a question mark.

direct quotation—use of the exact words of a person; must be enclosed in quotation marks and the source must be acknowledged.

direct writing style—writing that directly states the action of the sentence and approaches the subject of a communication with direct language.

double negative—two negative words used to express one negative idea (a violation of good grammar).

elliptical question—a shortened form of a question that, although not a complete sentence, should be capitalized and punctuated at the end with a question mark.

emphatic forms of verbs—words used to add special emphasis to a verb. The emphatic form combines *do, does, did*, or *will or shall* with the verb's basic form.

entries—the definitions and information about the words in a dictionary.

essential phrase—a phrase that is essential to the meaning of a sentence.

etymology—the origin or historical development of words.

front matter—explanatory information at the front of a dictionary that provides information such as the pronunciation key unique to that particular dictionary.

functional resume—a format for resumes that lists the job applicant's qualifications without tagging them to specific employers.

future perfect tense—verb tense that shows that action will have been completed before a specific future time.

gender agreement—in pronoun usage, means that the pronoun used must agree in gender with its antecedent; for example, a female antecedent requires the use of a female pronoun.

gender bias—the use of only male gender pronouns—*his, he*, or *him* or words such as *salesman* and *firemen*—to refer to both males and females or people in general.

gerund—the *-ing* form of a verb that acts as a noun.

gobbledygook—speech or writing with needlessly long words, superfluous words, or complicated sentence structure.

guide words—(1) the words located at the top of each page in the dictionary that list the first and last words on the page; (2) the preprinted words at the top of email templates and memo forms—*Date, To, From, Subject.*

helping verb—a verb that may precede the main verb—either action or being—to express time (present, past, and future), possibility (maybe), or emphasis.

hyphen—the punctuation mark used to connect compound words and to divide words at the end of a line of printed text.

hyphenated word—a compound word that is spelled with a hyphen.

indefinite pronoun—a pronoun that refers to nonspecific people or things.

independent clause—a word group that has a subject and verb and can stand alone as a complete thought (a sentence) that makes sense.

indirect question—a statement that sounds like a question; it should be punctuated with a period.

indirect writing style—a way of writing that states action or approaches the topic indirectly in order to be tactful or de-emphasize parts of a message.

infinitive—the word *to* plus a verb, such as *to go.*

interjection—an exclamatory word or phrase used to express emotion or enthusiasm; should be punctuated with an exclamation point.

interoffice memo (also called **memorandum**)—a document used for communicating within an organization.

interrogative pronoun—a pronoun form used to ask a question—*who, whom, what, which,* and *whose.*

introductory expression—opening words that introduce the main point of a sentence; is always dependent (i.e., it is not a complete thought).

irregular verb—a verb that changes spelling when changing tense instead of following the pattern of regular verbs which add *s, ed,* and *ing.* Irregular verbs may change spelling for past, present, and future, or spelling may change for only one tense.

keywords—phrases, terms, industry jargon, names of technology applications, and skills required in a particular field.

letter style (also called **format**)—the layout of a letter on the page. Block and modified-block are the most commonly used styles in business.

lexicographers—the compilers of dictionaries.

memo (memorandum)—a document that contains an organization's logo and the guide words *To, From, Date, Subject* at the top; mainly used for communicating within an organization.

memo of transmittal—a document that accompanies materials sent within or outside of an organization; provides a record of the transaction.

misplaced modifier—a modifying word or phrase that is in the wrong part of the sentence and ends up describing the wrong word.

modified-block letter style—the format of a letter in which the date, closing, and signature are indented while the other parts are aligned at the left margin.

modifier—an adjective, adverb, or phrase that adds information about *which one, what kind,* or *how many.*

nonessential phrase—a phrase that is not essential to the meaning of a sentence, although it may add important information.

noun—one of the parts of speech; words that name people, places, and things.

object—a noun or pronoun that receives the action of a verb or a preposition.

objective case—a personal pronoun acting as the object of a verb or phrase.

opening—the introductory paragraph of a communication.

parallel construction—the expression of parallel ideas—that is, similar sentence elements—in the same grammatical form.

paraphrase—to express someone's stated or written words in your own words; should not be enclosed in quotation marks.

participle (verbal adjectives)—a word that sometimes looks like a verb, has tenses, and may have an object but functions as an adjective.

parts of speech—the system for organizing words into the following categories—*pronouns, verbs, adjectives, adverbs, prepositions, conjunctions,* and *interjections*—depending on how the words are used in a sentence.

passive voice—placement of the subject and verb in a sentence that emphasizes that the subject is the receiver of the action. This construction is the opposite of active voice, which places the emphasis on the subject as the doer of the action.

parentheses—punctuation mark used to set off nonessential words that the writer wishes to de-emphasize.

past, present, and future—verb tenses that indicate the time of action or state of being in a sentence.

past perfect tense—verb form that indicates that one past action occurred before another past action; it is used to indicate the more distant past.

perfect infinitive—a verbal that functions as an adjective, adverb or noun; it consists of the word *to* plus a helping verb and participle form, for example, *to have finished*.

perfect participle—a verb form that indicates completed action; uses the helping verb *having*, as in "Having helped the man across the street, the stranger proceeded on her way."

perfect tenses—past perfect, present perfect, and future perfect tenses of verbs; perfect tenses are formed by combining *have, has,* or *had* with a past participle.

permanent compounds—compound adjectives that always require a hyphen and are listed in the dictionary.

personal pronoun—a pronoun that refers to people and things, such as *I, you, me, he, she, it,* and *they*.

phrase—a group of words that may contain a subject or a verb but not both; can function as subjects, verbs, and modifiers in a sentence.

plagiarism—the unlawful use of copyrighted work; failure to identify the title and author of a source.

polite request—a sentence that requests action and should be punctuated with a period even though it is phrased as a question.

positive degree adjectives—form of an adjective that modifies (describes a noun or pronoun without making a comparison).

possessive case—a pronoun form that shows ownership.

possessive noun—form of a noun that shows the relationship between two nouns; the first shows *who* or *what possesses*; the second shows *who* or *what is possessed.*

predicate—a verb that describes the action or state of being of the subject of a sentence.

preferred usage— the preferred pronunciation when two pronunciations are in common use; it is shown first in the dictionary.

prefix—an addition to the beginning of a word to denote a particular meaning such as *pre*, *post*, *un*, and *de*.

preposition—one of the parts of speech; a word that links nouns or pronouns to other parts of a sentence to show a relationship.

prepositional phrase—a word group that begins with a preposition and ends with a noun or pronoun, which is called the object of the preposition.

present infinitive—a verbal that functions as an adjective, adverb, or noun; consists of *to* plus the basic present tense verb form, such as *to take.*

present participle—the *-ing* form of a verb.

present perfect tense—verb form that shows that action began in the past but was completed just before the present, is being completed in the present, or is continuing.

progressive tense—a verb form that combines a form of *to be* with the present participle of a verb to show that action is or was in progress.

pronoun–antecedent agreement—the agreement in number and gender of a pronoun and its antecedent.

pronoun case—the role a personal pronoun is performing in the sentence; a pronoun may be in the subjective, objective, or possessive case.

pronoun reference—the word to which a pronoun refers (known as the antecedent); must agree in number and gender.

proofreading marks—a universally used system of symbols for marking errors in printed copy.

proper noun—a word that names specific persons, places, and things and always begins with a capital letter.

redundant writing—the purposeless repetition of words or ideas.

reflexive pronoun—a pronoun that ends in *self/selves*, such as *yourself* and *themselves.*

regular verb—a verb that forms tenses by adding *s*, *ed*, or *ing* to the basic form.

relative pronoun—a pronoun that refers to a noun that names people and things elsewhere in the sentence to clarify *who*, *whom*, *which*, *that*, *whichever*, *whoever*, or *whatever* is being spoken about.

run-on sentence—two or more independent clauses that are not joined by a connecting word (a coordinating conjunction) or punctuation (e.g., a semicolon).

semicolon—the punctuation mark that is midway in "pausing value" between a comma and a period.

sentence—a group of words that has a subject and a verb and expresses a complete thought.

sentence fragment—a word group beginning with a capital letter and ending with an end-of-sentence punctuation mark but lacking the key elements of a sentence—a subject and a verb forming an independent clause that is a complete thought.

simple sentence—a sentence that has only one independent clause.

simple subject—a noun or pronoun without modifiers that is the subject of a sentence.

Standard English—the common language used in the workplace across all fields of endeavor.

statement—a sentence that should be punctuated with a period at the end.

subject—a noun or pronoun that tells who or what a sentence is about.

subjective case (also called **nominative case**)—the form of a personal pronoun acting as the subject of a sentence.

subject–verb agreement—agreement in person and number between the subject and verb of a sentence—a key element of writing correct sentences; if the subject is singular, use a singular verb; if the subject is plural, use the plural verb form.

superlative degree—the form of an adjective that compares three or more nouns or pronouns.

synonyms—words with similar meanings.

transitional words and expressions—words used to show the connection from one idea to another, such as *however*, *therefore*, *in fact*, *in addition*, and *consequently*.

unabridged dictionary—a comprehensive compilation of English language words with typically at least 250,000 entries.

variety (in sentences)—variation in the length and level of complexity of sentences; a technique that makes writing more engaging for the reader.

verb—one of the parts of speech; types are action, being, or helping verbs; every sentence has at least one verb, also called the *predicate* of the sentence.

verb mood—verb form that conveys the manner in which the writer wants the action in a sentence to be interpreted by the reader. The three verb moods are indicative, imperative, and subjunctive.

verb phrase—a verb preceded by one or more helping verbs creates a verb phrase.

verb tense—the form of verbs that expresses time of action or state of being in the past, present, and future.

verb voice—the construction of a sentence that makes the verb active or passive.

verbals—forms of verbs that are functioning as nouns, adjectives, or adverbs. These include gerunds, participles, and infinitives.

vowel—the letters *a, e, i, o, u.*

writing process—a series of steps that writers take to produce polished written communications.

Index